P9-ARJ-761

POLITICAL REFORM AND THE AMERICAN EXPERIMENT

POLITICAL REFORM
AND THE
AMERICAN
EXPERIMENT

WILLIAM J. CROTTY
Northwestern University

THOMAS Y. CROWELL COMPANY
New York   Established 1834

FERNALD LIBRARY
COLBY-SAWYER COLLEGE
NEW LONDON, N. H. 03257

JK
1971
C76

POLITICAL REFORM AND THE AMERICAN EXPERIMENT

Copyright © 1977 by Thomas Y. Crowell Company, Inc.

All rights reserved. Printed in the United States of America.
No part of this book may be used or reproduced in any manner whatsoever
without written permission except in the case of brief quotations
embodied in critical articles and reviews. For information address
Thomas Y. Crowell Company, Inc., 10 East 53rd Street, New York, N.Y. 10022.
Published simultaneously in Canada by Fitzhenry & Whiteside, Ltd., Toronto.

Library of Congress Cataloging in Publication Data

Crotty, William J
  Political reform and the American experiment.

  Includes bibliographical references and index.
  1. Elections—United States—Campaign funds.
2. Voters, Registration of—United States.
3. Voting—United States. 4. Political parties—
United States. I. Title.
JK1971.C76 1977   329'.00973   76-45422
ISBN 0-690-00869-4

Contents

III   THE REFORM OF POLITICAL INSTITUTIONS

7. Primaries and the Reform of Presidential Nominating Methods   193

Preface

A poet has written:

> "At thirty, man suspects himself a fool;
> Knows it at forty, and reforms his plan;
> At fifty chides his infamous delay,
> Pushes his prudent purpose of resolve;
> In all magnanimity of thought
> Resolves and re-resolves; then dies the same."
>
> (EDWARD YOUNG, *Night Thoughts, I*)

Perhaps a nation is something like man. It runs through various stages, and maybe it never does do much but resolve and re-resolve itself into eternity, or death. Change, of any kind, comes slowly and painfully. At this particular juncture, though, it might be worth reconsidering aspects of some of this country's political institutions. Small abuses, overlooked and tolerated, lead to other and larger problems. Occasionally, there can result something as pernicious as the recent perversions of governmental authority, political selection processes, and the communications media, through the punitive and extra-legal use of government agencies and great accumulations of private wealth and public power.

A political system's most prized asset is the faith of its people in the judiciousness (and, possibly, inevitability) of its operations. There is some truth to the old Latin admonition to "keep what you have; the known evil is best." Change to new forms and altered procedures can lead to mischief—a disruption of structures and public expectations that can, conversely, further discontent. Yet there are times when political changes of varying orders or magnitude are necessitated by the public outcry brought on by some form of flagrant abuse.

The American political system has proven extraordinarily resilient and serviceable. If anything, the electorate has tended to overappreciate its virtue and ignore or discount its weaknesses. When crises in confidence occur, they tend to occur over issues of enormous consequence: minor problems left untreated until they explode in the civil rights confrontations of the sixties; the fundamental questioning of a leadership's veracity and judgment in the execution of an unusually cruel (and worse, disastrous) war with no apparent relationship to the national interest;

and, more recently, the systematic exploitation of a chief executive's enormous powers to pursue (beyond reach of legislative, public, or media scrutiny) the basest of political ends. Under such conditions, reasoned change appears a necessity, if not to correct the abuses, then at least to provide a basis for renewed confidence in the operations of governing agencies. The usual intent is to advance moderate and reasonable proposals to amend the worst of the publicly recognized problems. Should these not work, or worse, never be implemented, then the seeds of more drastic change have been nurtured. The objective should always be to improve the functioning of political institutions in such a way as to make them more open to and representative of the democratic citizenry for which they presume to speak.

REFORM IN AMERICA

The reformist tradition is an old one in the United States. It can be traced back to the founding of the nation and the often stormy application of moral and religious judgments to political matters. The results have not always been happy. "Reforms" over the years have had a curious way of rewarding the "elect"; that is, further institutionalizing the political and economic power of "them that has." A certain status quo or status quo ante atmosphere has surrounded some (although not all) of these movements that have attempted to penalize those that wished they had—the newcomers, in some sense, to the politics of the day. A canard of the old machine bosses, and one heard often in today's politics, is that reformers are simply those on the outside who want in—those who wish to wrest power from "them that has" and adapt it to their own ends.

There is a large degree of truth underlying these contentions, although the process, and the forces motivating it, are more subtle. It would be difficult to argue with a turn-of-the-century, affluent, middle-class Progressive that the animus he directed toward the urban machine reflected moral and social judgments about what society (through government) should and should not do that reinforced his own cultural advantages. Or to argue that the machine, unquestionably corrupt and crassly abusive of democratic forms, actually performed a number of *unique* societal activities dealing with the acculturation and representation of social groups normally excluded from political processes that were of actual benefit to a vital democratic system. Such insights would come later—well after the machine was no longer a dominating force in urban society.

Another impulse of the continuing American experience with reform, and possibly an implicitly dangerous one (although extremely popular), is the never-ending desire to impose a sense of order and efficiency on processes that traditionally do not lend themselves to a clarity and economy of purpose (and, more significantly, given the overwhelming importance of the subject matter, perhaps should not). The values of order and measurable productivity more properly associated with business operations or, by definition, with good management techniques, are of limited applicability to the functions of a government. Political decision making in a democratic polity deals with the full range of a society's demands. It is not neat, precise, nor terribly logical. Politics serves, in short, many masters. In its own curious way, it determines policy objectives and redistributes economic and other resources; it provides the electorate with a control lever, however indirect, over its leadership and their actions; and it lays the guidelines for the reallocation of vital resources. The stakes being contested in such awards are enormously high. Who participates (and who does not), *how* they participate, and the degree to which they influence the outcomes are questions of immense consequence. These are the priorities that "reforms" of varying sorts attempt to address. To confuse matters even more, this (at least potentially) quasi-rational distributive process is overlain with emotional overtones of sizable intensity of at least equal importance to the final calculations. Politics is, in addition to everything else, an outlet for all nature of emotions ranging from the highest of concerns (good will, selflessness, justice) to the basest (greed, vindictiveness, even hate). The process is not easy to operate or understand. Those rewarded by its deliberations or comfortable with its actions will resist any attempt at change. The burden is on the prospective reformer to show a need for improvement and to convince a fair portion of the citizenry that his proposals will accomplish larger and more worthwhile ends while producing a minimum of undesirable side effects. Human nature and the inertia residing in the processes of government ensure that the battle, even under the best of conditions, will not be an easy one.

A few words on my own views ("biases" might be a more appropriate word). The book that follows is written from a somewhat more activist orientation than one would normally expect from a political scientist. The presentation makes no effort to be exhaustive or to disguise value judgments, as the reader will no doubt soon be aware. Fair warning! Secondly, my own views tend toward the pragmatic. I am impressed with what is workable, democratic in intent, realizable, and, within these limits, moderately reformist. I have never felt satisfied with the view embodied in the Italian maxim that "change breeds more mischief from its novelty than advantage from its utility." Translated, the argument heard repeatedly by my generation of political scientists ran something to the effect that processes should be left as they are, despite obvious inequities, because they "work." Governmental institutions are organic agencies developed to meet specified human and national needs. Some atrophy and require revitalization. Others should be terminated. And still others are waiting to be created to serve the ever-fluctuating demands of an evolving social order. As to what exists at any given point in time, the relevant questions are: Why does it perform in the manner it does? Who benefits and who loses? What can, or should (or should not) be done about it?

It should be noted in passing that the research on this book began well before the "Watergate" travail and the assorted series of gross abuses of political processes it uncovered. The conception of the book has changed little because of the national scandals, although an effort has been made to include illustrative materials (especially in Part II, "Money and Campaigns") from the revelations that have cascaded from the Ervin Committee, the House Judiciary Committee, the Special Prosecutor's Office, the various trials, the testimony, writings, and admissions of the principals in the cases, and the followups—principally by the media—into the virtually endless byways of official misrule. The examples that some of the Watergate materials have replaced in the text, in the section on campaign contributions, for example, seem horribly quaint (and even reassuring) in comparison. The rot uncovered places the problems analyzed in a newer and more unsettling perspective. The problems to be faced are deeper, more serious, and more urgent than anyone would have imagined just a few short years earlier.

The foregoing is not to argue that Watergate preceded the abuses explored in this book. This would not be quite accurate. The difficulties pinpointed herein were recognized in principle (if not all their implications fully appreciated) prior to the Watergate revelations. In part, the accumulation of these deficiencies helps create the climate conducive to the reckless disregard for democratic norms evidenced in the official misconduct uncovered, specifically (although not exclusively) in the Nixon Administration and those employed directly or indirectly on its behalf. The problems assessed are but one part of the conflux of forces contributing to the range of political abuses made public. They make, I would argue, a key contribution to the official arrogance that instigated the Watergate evil. In all, a small advantage may be that the public concern stimulated by the events of Watergate in all its guises may help create a national climate receptive to the intelligent and ordered change advocated in this book.

With these caveats in mind, we can turn more directly to what is to follow. The problems to be reviewed are presented first in a discussion of their ramifications. Then background information of relevance to an understanding of the issue is developed, and a number of potential alternative approaches to resolving some of the dimensions implicit in the question are presented. Many of the proposed solutions have already received a degree of legislative attention. Most, if not all, should be on the nation's political agenda in the forseeable future. The remedies proposed do not represent all-embracing schemes designed to institute a new political order. Thoreau, undoubtedly, would have dismissed them as a tinkering, a "hacking at the branches" of (in this case) governing patterns rather than a fully committed attack directed at the roots of the institutions themselves. In essence, this view is correct. Nonetheless, and given the contemporary scene, the solutions recommended (or something closely akin to them) are realistic. They would not unduly disrupt the familiar (although imperfect) old ways; they do provide reasonable alternatives to the objections raised against the more arbitrary and discriminatory aspects of the processes reviewed; and they should result in a more equitable and responsive governing system.

The problems chosen for attention include areas of fundamental concern to a continuing democracy. Voting and voter registration (the certification process that determines who should vote) raise questions as to who should hold the franchise, how difficult should it be to qualify to vote, who actually does vote (and, more significantly, who does not), and what can be done to open and "rationalize" a system overlain with hundreds of years of moral judgments and an incalculable series of administrative decisions and requirements of bewildering complexity?

The problems associated with political financing—because of Watergate—are much appreciated by an aroused and informed electorate (the only issue covered for which such a statement can be made, unfortunately). Yet the solutions proposed are about as numerous and complex as the inequities they are intended to resolve. What is the real nature of the problem? How can the difficulties associated with financial abuse *and* undue financial advantage be dealt with in a reasonably fair manner? What are the dangers of uncontrolled private funding of political activities (painfully obvious after the well-financed Watergate assault on democratic operations)? Less apparent, what problems could arise of equal threat to an open democratic system from public funding practices that must discriminate among potential recipients, or from excessive control of electioneering (for example, a potential disregard for democratic privileges as to confidentiality in disclosure provisions; and the institutionalization of two increasingly moribund and conceivably irrelevant political parties at a time of electoral ferment and possibly new and innovative electoral alignments)?

Finally, and as the last comments suggest, there is the question of the parties themselves. Are they representative of the major divisions within the American electorate or are they fossilized remnants of an age long passed? More to the point of the present inquiry, can they be made responsive to the needs of their intended constituencies? Can their operations and structures (both in presidential nominating procedures as well as in the less visible areas of party operations) be opened to democratic impulses from below? Can they be representative of their base within the electorate and still propose differing policy programs of substance and value? Can they be expected to exercise some type of check on public officials of their own as well as those of opposition parties in their exercise of power while in office? We can not answer all of these questions. We can begin to explore them and, more importantly, shed some light on the degree to which the parties themselves are aware of their problems and what they are doing to rectify them. There has been change in the area although its direction and impact are not totally clear.

The difficulties to be reviewed can not be taken lightly. The proposed solutions are not drastic, although in several cases they do call for some basic rethinking about national priorities and long-run political goals, a type of hard reassessment that has not come easily to the American people or their leaders.

I wish to express a debt of gratitude to a number of people. First of all there is Ramsey Clark, an individual with an impressive social conscience and an even more amazing capacity to act upon his concerns, who helped channel my own more abstracted commitments into a tangible form of expression. I had an unusually stimulating opportunity to serve as executive director of the Freedom To Vote Task Force chaired by Ramsey Clark. The vice-chairwoman of the Task Force, Mildred Robbins, honorary president of the National Council of Women, gave graciously of her time and effort to a project that contributed a new understanding and some workable solutions to a question of basic concern to a democratic society. I was awarded an American Political Science Association Fellowship which made my work with the Task Force and an in-residence stay with the Democratic National Committee possible. I wish to thank Dr. Evron Kirkpatrick, executive director of the American Political Science Association, and Earl Baker, Walter Beach, and Thomas Mann for their many kindnesses which made my fellowship not only a productive and unique educational experience but a pleasurable one as well. To the people at the Democratic National Committee for their continuous help and constant intellectual stimulation, I owe my thanks. A listing of all who aided in this manner would be too extensive, but the citing of a selected few will serve to indicate my gratitude: Lawrence F. O'Brien and former U.S. Senator Fred R. Harris, national chairmen during my tenure with the committee, William Welsh, its executive director, and Dr. Andrew J. Valuchek, Sheila Hixson, Monica Borkowski, Joseph Brady, Barbara Hight Kelly, and Fleurette LeBow, among many others, all contributed to my education and the ideas contained in this book in one way or another. Dr. William J. Cassella Jr., executive director of the National Municipal League, and Richard J. Carlson, then director of the League's Election Systems Project and currently with the Council of State Governments, provided assistance in a number of ways, particularly helpful in the section on voting and registration. Greg Gardner contributed extensively in the data gathering and organizing stage, and my colleague, Kenneth Janda, was a welcome source of expert counsel and good advice. To all, I am indebted.

POLITICAL REFORM
AND THE
AMERICAN
EXPERIMENT

I
REGISTRATION
AND VOTING

1
The Evolution
of the Franchise

America prides itself on its democratic institutions—and rightly so. Among these none is more sacred than the right to vote. On this point few would disagree. It is the one visible act by which the individual chooses one's leadership, endows it with power, expresses one's own views on the conduct of government, and holds those in public office accountable to the will of the populace. It is the most significant single act the citizen engages in. It symbolizes the nature of the democratic experiment.

The Supreme Court, that curious body destined to give a living interpretation to the handiwork of the Founding Fathers, has been explicit in its commendation of the right to vote. In *Wesberry* v. *Sanders,* the Court argued:

> No right is more precious in a free country than that of having a voice in the election of those who make the laws under which . . . we must live. *Other rights . . . are illusionary . . . if the right to vote is undermined.* (Italics added.)

In another of the reapportionment cases *(Reynolds* v. *Sims)*, the high court was equally explicit.

> The right of suffrage is a fundamental matter in a free and democratic society. Especially since the right to exercise the franchise in a free and unimpaired manner is *preservative of other basic civil and political rights.* (Italics added.)

This is heady rhetoric, but before succumbing to it, it would be wise to pause and ask what type of issue before the Court could spur such absolutist claims for the "right" to vote. The Constitution, for example, guarantees no such "right" (although it possibly may be inferred from the language of the document). It may also be advisable to dwell considerably longer on the acrimonious battles that were fought over the efforts to extend and guarantee the franchise, a fight not yet over.

The answer to the first point is easily given. The Supreme Court was considering the reapportionment of congressional and state legislative districts to correspond to population, an issue it had assiduously avoided for almost 200 years. To maintain that representative districts had to be equalized, the Court had to establish the importance of the vote and the inequity of any practice (malapportionment) that would dilute its impact. In fairness to the justices, it should be noted that their strong stand on behalf of the essential value of the vote was reflected in other cases. The right to the vote is "too precious and too fundamental" to be abridged by arbitrary or ill-advised legislative regulations the Court ruled in *Harper* v. *Virginia Board of Education* (1966). Such a view dominates, with occasional backtracking, through most of the Court's contemporary writings.

But in fairness, also, it should be pointed out that the Court (like the nation more generally) is often belated in its strong advocacy of an unfettered vote. The Virginia case involved the long-discredited poll tax, a device that should have been outlawed 70 years earlier if any real agreement in the nation existed as to the truly fundamental nature of the vote. And this brings up the second point. The road to universal suffrage has been a long one, bitterly contested at every point; and though immense strides have been taken in the last few decades, the journey is far from complete. It is a road worth retraveling.

THE EARLY TIMES

One device after another has been used to attempt to restrict the franchise to the well-bred, "deserving" citizens of the community (and, coincidentally, those who would already control the governing apparatus) in each electoral period of America's growth. The picture is not a pleasant one for a people brought up on the stirring words of the Declaration of Independence and the legendary democratic achievements of the Constitutional Congress or the Jeffersons, Jacksons, and Lincolns that play so prominent a part in the nation's mythology. Religion, sex, race, economic position, probity, forebears, all and more have been used to bar groups from the electorate, keeping them from exercising a full voice in community affairs and inferentially, at least, making them something less than their neighbors. In recounting the struggle to achieve full suffrage it is worth remembering, however, that the trend and emphasis, despite at times substantial setbacks, has been clearly in one direction: toward a full and equal electorate. The democratic rhetoric in this context has meaning. It set the goal. The struggle has been to reach the objective.

SUFFRAGE IN COLONIAL TIMES

The early colonists demonstrated an ingenuity, as would their descendants over the next 300 years, in devising tests of citizenship that managed to reward the "chosen" rather nicely[1]. The seventeenth and early eighteenth centuries were not noted for their egalitarianism. With little or nothing to serve as precedents, the early colonists experimented with identifying the bounds of the suffrage, thus determining who would exercise disproportionate influence in the colony's affairs. For many, the concept of shareholders in a company—and it is well to recall that much of the colonizing was foreseen as an economic investment by early sponsors—served as a model in defining the inclusiveness of public decision making. The early settlers also borrowed rather heavily from English experience without apparently giving the matters a great deal of thought. In certain colonies, as the settlements grew, refinements were usually introduced to open the franchise to a wider spectrum of the population, although on occasion the settlers managed to introduce restrictions more arbitrary than those found in Britain.

The Puritans' devotion to God, for example, managed to find its way into the Bay Colony's laws. Massachusetts, a state that has received little credit for its pioneering efforts in delimiting the electorate (introducing many devices later adopted with great success by the defeated southern states), barred from participation in community affairs those not of "sober and peaceful" countenance. By 1664, the colony was intent on going further. Each person applying for the right to vote was required to obtain from his pastor a certificate vouching for his personal character.

Religion, not surprisingly, played a big part in determining the role of potential citizens in the theocracies which governed many of the early settlements. Massachusetts, for example, was petitioned by its English overseers to loosen the regulations that confined the franchise only to members of a Christian church. The colonies, characteristically, obeyed such directives only when they chose to.

Religious prejudice continued in many colonies as a basis for circumscribing voting rights. Massachusetts explicitly excluded Quakers. Rhode Island, Maryland, New York, and South Carolina discriminated against Jews (a carry-over, initially at least, from British antecedents). Race was a disqualifying factor in many states. South Carolina and Georgia enfranchised only whites. Virginia and North Carolina enforced prohibitions against blacks, mulattoes, Indians, and, in North Carolina, "mustees" (the offspring of a white and a quadroon). The racial distinction is all too familiar. The effort to devise categories to exclude certain racial, ethnic, religious, or other types (as with North Carolina) is less well recognized, but it too was broadly practiced and a close reading of many state constitutions shows that it persisted with greater success up to the modern era. Age qualifications were less clear. Although 21 as the age of majority was taken over from England, the laws were often vague on this point and it was rare that anyone younger than that age voted.

Economic substantiality—another factor borrowed from English practice—ranked high on the list of achievements the colonists prized. Many colonies, following the lead of England, introduced the freehold concept. Property defined public worth and represented a good indicator of moral values. Property represented the bond that tied the individual to the best interests of the community, a linkage the Virginia House of Burgess drew attention to in 1670.

While the concept of the significance of property holding for the community was shared by the colonies, the standards as to what constituted a sufficient investment in the common good to invite participation in decision making varied. New Hampshire permitted only those with freeholds of more than 50 pounds to hold the franchise. Rhode Island stipulated 40 pounds or 40 shillings annual rental valuation. Other colonies chose to define the franchise in terms of the size rather than the explicit value of the land. Virginia permitted the owners of 25 acres of "improved" land (usually homesteaded parcels) or 100 acres of unsettled land to vote. North Carolina, Georgia, South Carolina, Maryland, Pennsylvania, and Delaware enfranchised those with 50 acres. Virginia and New York further allowed the holders of indefinite leases on land to participate in the electorate. In still further relaxations of the original standards, some colonies permitted a broader range of indicators of wealth—stock, guns, food, clothing and the like—to qualify a man to vote.

Even in the early years, such laws did not receive universal support. South Carolina, demonstrating a commitment to wider participation, allowed anyone to vote who resided in the colony for at least two years and paid a reasonable tax. Such a standard, eventually, served as the benchmark for the states that had resisted serious change up to the present (Mississippi, for example, in the late 1960s still maintained a two-year residency requirement).

Dissent in the larger urban areas of the day (New York and Philadelphia, in particular) focused attention on the fact that machinists and tradesmen, a large proportion of the population, were often excluded from the franchise. As time passed and this segment of the population grew, the discontent eventually found an effective outlet through an early interest group, the Committee of Mechanics. This organization, in some ways a modest forerunner of the political party, managed to mobilize support in 1774 behind a successful effort to void the freeholding requirement. The victory was short-lived, however. The very next year the provincial congress reinstituted the property qualification with a slight modification intended to appease the discontents (anyone with 40 shillings worth of personal property could also enter the electorate). A "Mechanic Association" established in 1770 in Philadelphia organized its supporters, and although it had no immediate impact on the colony's 50-acre or 50-pound qualification, the Quaker State upon independence took another step away from an elite and propertied electorate by enfranchising all who paid taxes.

THE AMERICAN REVOLUTION AND SUFFRAGE: A TRANSITIONAL PERIOD

It is arguable that a handful of colonies beset by problems of survival would have little time to pioneer in the development of new democratic forms of expression. Rather, the line of least resistance would be to adopt the practices of the

Old World in modified form and then proceed with the business of civilizing a new continent. If this line of contention can be carried a step further, the forces for independence that eventually culminated in the Revolution should have set off related impulses resulting in this case in a broadened and less restrictive electorate. The American Revolution would provide the dividing line between an elitist system and one closer to modern conceptions of democratic representation.

The American Revolution did many things, but a major and lasting shift in democratizing the electorate was not one of its immediate consequences (Figure 1.1). In actuality, the colonies—for all of their problems—had initiated efforts to broaden the franchise, unquestionably borrowing much from England. But from the beginning, there was a move—at times, halting and uncertain—to introduce new forms of democratic representation (the town meeting, for example, was one of the most conspicuously successful). The movement, which had begun in the early half of the seventeenth century, gained momentum from the revolutionary spirit. Some of the old forms were not to withstand the newer, more intensive scrutiny.

Perhaps the concept most imbedded in the colonial consciousness—second only to the more sectionalized controversy over racial animosity—was the belief that property constituted a person's true measure of worth. The debate began with the arrival of the first colonists and was to continue in a sometimes passionate exchange up through the first half of the nineteenth century. Porter, in an analysis of suffrage in the United States, has explained the colonial's definition of the right to vote as similar to that of a stockholder in a corporation. Property more than religion, character, nationality, beliefs, or residency constituted the truest single guide to the worthy citizen[2]. Those with the greatest financial stake in the community were deemed the best qualified to guide its deliberations.

It is not difficult to understand the hold of these ideas on the early controversy over the limits of the electorate. Locke, Montesquieu, and Blackstone were all quoted in defense of the economic principle of representation. "The true reason of requiring any qualifications with regard to property in voters," as the eminent jurist Blackstone put it, "is to exclude such persons as are in so mean a situation as to be deemed to have no will of their own." If the basic assumption as to the critical importance of property can be accepted, all manner of argument defending its prerogatives could be expected. And about every variation was entertained. At the Massachusetts Convention of 1820–1821, one of the turning points in the move to broaden the electorate, orators warned of the evils of an enlarged franchise, ironically using movements underway in England to illustrate their point. "All writers agree, that there are twenty persons in Great Britain, who have no property, to one that has. If the radicals should succeed in obtaining universal suffrage, they will overturn the whole kingdom, and turn those who have property out of their houses[3]." The concern with England rings hollow, but the very real fear that the economically well off would lose all expressed a fear harbored by many.

FIGURE 1.1
PROPERTY QUALIFICATIONS
IMMEDIATELY BEFORE AND AFTER
THE AMERICAN REVOLUTION

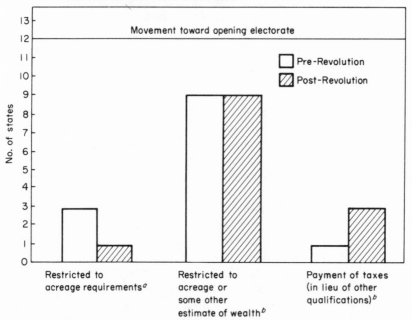

[a]North Carolina did have an acreage-only qualification for state Senate races. For the lower house and federal elections it had a tax provision, a move away from its prewar restrictions. Virginia is the only state in the postwar acreage-only category.

[b]For example, personal property worth 40 or 50 pounds or 40 shillings annual income.

SOURCE: Kirk H. Porter, *A History of Suffrage in the United States* (Chicago: University of Chicago Press, 1918), pp. 12–13. Copyright 1918, University of Chicago Press.

On a more positive note, property was thought to give a nation many, if not most, of its enduring qualities. The Massachusetts Convention heard the same delegate enlarge upon this theme. "Without the security of property, neither arts, nor manufactures, nor commerce, nor literature, nor science can exist. *It is the foundation upon which civilization rests.* There would be no security for life and liberty even, if property were not secure[4]." (Italics added.) The Supreme Court, even in its most enthusiastic embracing of the vote, could not match the reverence with which land and economic success were valued. Most importantly, the people making such arguments were the ones in power. Men of means, they would have to be persuaded to loosen their grip on the political structure of their day. The fight would not be easy.

The Revolution speeded up the process of change. Much of the thinking that underlay the Declaration of Independence and the conception of a constitution (and for that matter the political development of the early colonies) wrestled with such intangibles as divine law, natural rights, and a set of contractual obligations between ruler and ruled. No one doubted the significance of property, but many could argue with equal sincerity that the vote was a natural right of political man. The shades of opinion on this issue varied as much as those that equated property with political rectitude. Some argued for immediate universal suffrage with no qualifications. Others, more moderate in tone and more in line with the colonial experience, favored an expanded suffrage but would permit restrictions designed in the best interests of the state, the alternative eventually followed and still practiced. Still others talked vaguely of the evils of a misguided and misinformed electorate made worse by indiscriminate enlargement (another theme that persists today). This last group apparently would protect wage earners dependent on property owners for employment, income, and, at times, food and housing from political exploitation by their masters by totally excluding them from the vote. It is worth noting, and it forms a consistent strain in the efforts to enlarge the electorate, that the most preposterous and seemingly altruistic justifications come *after* the particular restriction has been enacted into law. The contention of the superior virtue of property qualifications in promoting the common good, for example, came after not before the measure was adopted. If you will, the "theory of democratic representation," intended to justify success of one faction or segment of the society, followed its victory. At this point, apparently, the explicit self-interest motives that propelled the restriction originally are too crass to explain what is difficult to justify in democratic terms.

THE CONSTITUTIONAL DEBATE

The Constitutional Convention implicitly recognized the importance of the vote. Perhaps it did accept it as a fundamental right, as the Supreme Court was later to contend, and possibly one too obvious to require elaborate explication. The Committee on Detail at the Constitutional Convention did consider at length several explicit requirements such as property holdings and militia service (the latter in effect another means of broadening the former, purely economic criteria) but in the final analysis recommended to the full convention that qualifications be the same as those for the lower house of the state legislature. All things considered, this move was probably as liberal a measure as could be gotten. The failure, however, to define the right to vote and to set limits on the types of restrictive qualifications to be placed on the franchise created problems that still exist today. It meant the Congress would have to return to the issue repeatedly over the years (the Fifteenth, Nineteenth, Twenty-third, Twenty-fourth, and Twenty-sixth Amendments especially), and in the interim other agencies (state constitutional conventions and legislatures at first, a reluctant Supreme Court later) would have to define the permissible limits of the franchise. The question was left open for future generations to resolve.

Gouverneur Morris, John Dickinson, and James Madison led the forces at the Philadelphia convention arguing for some type of economic discriminator in establishing the franchise. Benjamin Franklin and George Mason fought the property qualifications. Franklin sought a more representative democratic system and one that provided for those who had fought in the Revolution. Mason struck directly at the equation of wealth with good moral character and the alleged "irresponsibility" of a mass electorate (another strain that persists today). "Ought the merchant, the monied man, the parent of a number of children whose fortunes are to be pursued in their own country, to be viewed as suspicious characters, and unworthy to be trusted with the common rights of their fellow citizens[5]?" What, in short (although this was further than Mason would go), could justify an exclusionary franchise in the new nation?

The Constitutional Convention, as indicated, did a number of things. It gave the proponents of a more broad-minded approach to voting a national forum to argue their case. They did an effective job. No explicit restrictions of consequence were included in the Constitution. Unfortunately, on the other hand, a recognition of the inherent right to vote and any guarantee of its primacy as a prerequisite of a republic were also missing from the final document. An implied right to vote can be found in the Constitution.

The framers of the Constitution left it to the states to define the limits of the electorate in relation to the requirements set forth for selecting members of the lower, and more democratic, house of the state legislature. This was a concession to the democratic spirit of the age and the effectiveness of the proponents of a broadened franchise. It was possibly the most that could be expected given the tenor and practices of the time. It did serve to emphasize the move for a less restrictive vote. Its immediate consequence, however, was to shift the battle from the national level back to the constitutional conventions of the respective states.

THE SEEDS OF CHANGE

Social need, self-interest, and philosophic commitment all combined in uneven quantities at various junctures to influence the debate over the franchise. The honored freehold concept held sway in many states in the generation after the adoption of the Constitution. But change was on the way. The major cities, leading sources of discontent over suffrage limitations from the early colonial era up through the twentieth century, found many of the restrictions untenable. The largest cities—Boston, Philadelphia, New York, and Baltimore—with expanding populations and limited land found a vote based on a 50-acre holding increasingly impractical. Large segments of the electorate, including in some cases men of wealth, were excluded from politics. Discontent grew. The old battle cry that preceded the Revolution was revived concerning "no taxation without representation" and it proved a politically awkward one to resolve. In fact, it was unanswerable. Immediately after the Revolution, seven states liberalized their suffrage requirements to allow men with specified amounts of personal property to vote (Figure 1.2). Pennsylvania, a leader in this regard, required only that a person pay his tax in order to qualify to vote. In the first decade after independence, New Hampshire and Georgia introduced taxpaying qualifications in concert with moderate residency requirements. On entering the Union in 1791, Vermont went furthest of all, explicitly recognizing full manhood suffrage for all who resided in the state for a year and who were of "quiet and peaceable behavior." Kentucky (1792) and Indiana (1816) followed Vermont when they became part of the United States by requiring neither property nor payment of taxes as prerequisites to vote. Mississippi (which came into the Union in 1817) was the last state to place such restrictions on its electorate.

The progression toward a more inclusive electorate moved from landholding demands to more flexible property standards and finally to the even more representative taxpaying provisions. In all of this, however, it was implicitly understood that the franchise extended only to males of at least 21 years of age.

THE WESTWARD EXPANSION

The cities provided one impetus for change. The democratic arguments that justified the rebellion offered another. The effects of those ideals became increasingly apparent as the frontier areas, citadels of social equality, were settled and in time entered the Union. These newer states took the democratic rhetoric seriously and incorporated provisions protecting individual rights (including voting) into their state constitutions. The entrance of Tennessee and Ohio (as well as Kentucky and Indiana) posed new threats to the freehold concept. Ohio and Tennessee legislated negligible freehold requirements and Ohio allowed a taxpaying alternative or work on the state roads in lieu of the tax (one of the nation's first public works projects and an alternative qualification device other states were to use). Tennessee, never comfortable with the property requirement, eliminated it in the state convention of 1834.

The movement toward a broader electorate continued to gather force with the expansion of the nation. Jeffersonian principles were taken with increased seriousness. In addition, the social, economic, and political conditions of the frontier produced a leveling effect hostile to the elitist politics of Virginia, Massachusetts, and most of the earlier colonies.

THE STATE CONSTITUTIONAL
CONVENTIONS: 1800 TO 1850

Change was not confined to the frontier. The original states found the older restrictions increasingly untenable and difficult to justify. The need for more democratic government led to a rash of constitutional conventions in the first half

**FIGURE 1.2
THE DURATION OF
PROPERTY AND TAXPAYING
RESTRICTIONS IN THE FRANCHISE, 1776–1860**

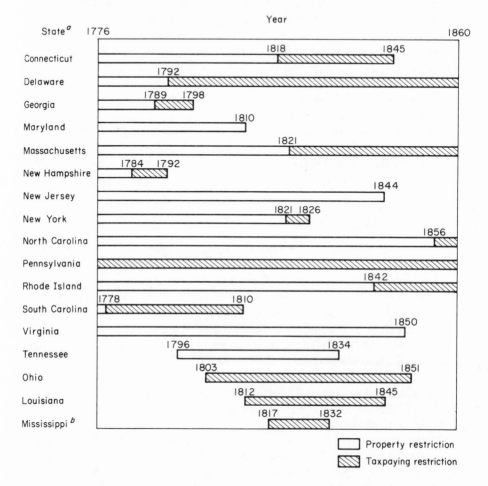

[a]Qualifications begin with date state entered the Union. Vermont (1791), Kentucky (1792), and Indiana (1816) came in without property or taxpaying restrictions and are not included in chart.

[b]Mississippi in 1817 was the last state to enter the Union with property or taxpaying qualifications.

SOURCE: Kirk H. Porter, *A History of Suffrage in the United States* (Chicago: University of Chicago Press, 1918), p. 110. Copyright 1918, University of Chicago Press.

of the nineteenth century. The battles fought in many of these gatherings were heated. The debate between the crusty elitist John Adams and the fiery Daniel Webster, assaulting the privileges of the landholders, is perhaps the most famous of those that ensued. Their arguments were repeated with equal vehemence, if less eloquence, in one state convention after another[6]. And the old privileges began to give way.

Again the motivations were practical as well as philosophic. The conservative Federalists in New Jersey, following the 1807 election, for example, led the fight for a franchise resting on a liberalized taxpaying regulation. Their concern centered less on expanding the electorate than in finding an alternative to the unhappy experience with attempting to apply regulations that barred from the franchise people with less than 50 pounds wealth, those under 21 years of age, and aliens. The laws in effect were unenforceable.

The New Jersey experience was not unique. An unequal application of the existing provisions plus a large element of fraud and applied self-interest led to modifications in other states as well. A legitimate confusion existed as to the types of property or leases that qualified a man to vote. Local election officials and sheriffs filled the void by interpreting the prevailing laws in the manner best suited to advance their own fortunes.

The widespread practice of "faggot" voting demonstrated how unworkable the regulations could be. The model was England. The idea was for a property owner to dictate the votes of a small army by distributing deeds to men who were otherwise disenfranchised. The landlord specified how the individual would vote and the deeds were returned to the original holders after the citizen had performed his duty.

The problems reached a crisis in New York. Predictably, Chancellor Kent led the forces of conservatism at the state constitutional convention of 1821. But he and the conservatives were to suffer a stunning defeat. The franchise was extended to state and county taxpayers, those who had served in the military, those who had labored on the highways (as a substitute form of taxpaying), and those who had resided within the state for at least three years. Blacks, additionally, were the sole target of a $250 property requirement. The changes did not suit the electorate, however. Five years later, the voters further expanded the franchise by suspending the tax qualifications through a referendum.

The weight of public opinion in the western states was overwhelmingly against any property limitations on the vote and by 1851 12 states had proceeded to the point of eliminating any taxpaying provision as a prerequisite to the vote. The contrast between the western states and those in the East was pronounced. The latter were older, more comfortable with the established ways, and more conservative and elitist. Change came slower and, in fact, widespread reform faltered over the taxpaying issues, the one the newer states found no difficulty in discarding.

THE FOREIGN INFLUX

Although a noticeable controversy existed from the earliest days of the Republic over property and wealth restrictions on suffrage, and progress was made in eliminating these, a number of other qualifications and their justifications were not thought through in great detail. Colonial and later state statutes and constitutions were extraordinarily vague about these other types of requirements. Possibly, they were assumed. If so, in the early years of the democratic experiment not everyone received the same message. Age and citizenship qualifications were usually left unspecified, although 21 was taken as the minimum age for voting. Sex, also, was assumed. Yet the prohibitions were not made universally explicit until the qualifications themselves became an issue. Women voted without incident in New Jersey during the state's early years, for example, until some drew attention to the unpublicized practice as an argument for women's suffrage. An upset legislature clarified the law to prohibit from exercising the franchise anyone but males of 21 years of age or more.

Residence requirements also became more popular and by 1800 most of the states had residency restrictions of from one to two years, a practice left virtually unchallenged until the present. Citizenship qualifications were a more troublesome issue. In a nation of immigrants, in a land that had been and continued to serve as a sanctuary for many and with an economy needing the influx of cheap labor, such a limitation could wreak great mischief. In fact, until the Louisiana Constitution of 1812, the issue was scarcely raised in state charters. The federal government was equally obtuse in its approach. The U.S. Constitution failed to provide an applicable definition until the Fourteenth Amendment, adopted in 1868. This elaboration of the Constitution in company with the Civil Rights Act of 1866 gave legal support to the common-law concept of *jus soli,* granting citizenship to all persons born within the limits and under the allegiance of the United States.

The generosity of the first immigrants was sorely tested by the new waves of immigration. The Federalists in Massachusetts took early exception to the Pennsylvania Constitution's permitting foreigners to vote after a two-year period of residency. Such provincialism was more the rule than the exception. The mood gave birth to the Naturalization Act of 1798, which proved indicative of things to come. The law was harsh. It required the registration of all aliens and a 14-year residency as a condition for naturalization. The statute was later changed and the residency period reduced, but the inhospitality evidenced toward alien voting persisted.

The waves of immigrants that began to engulf the eastern seaboard in the 1820s and 30s exacerbated the problem. The anger excited by the new immigrants, almost half of whom were Irish in 1820, fueled other prejudices. Nativist strains became apparent in the registration qualifications that began to be introduced, and this nativist mood later found expression in political movements and formed the basis for at least one political party. Nativist antipathy underlay several reform movements, including in part the (middle-class, Protestant) Progressive reaction against urban excesses and machine abuses in the years between 1890 and 1920. The issue was not to be effectively settled until the restrictions imposed on immigration after 1920 and the bringing into the national electorate of the urban ethnics through the presidential candidacy of Al Smith in 1928[7].

The Irish, the English, Scots, and Welsh, the Jews from Russia and Eastern Europe, the Germans and Swedes, and the Italians escaping from famine or religious or political persecution, all began to come into the country in great numbers. Most came in through New York City, and a large proportion of the Irish, Italians, English, and Jews who arrived never moved beyond the eastern population centers. An overwhelmingly rural and puritanical citizenry found little to admire in the noisy, allegedly immoral, and unaccomplished newcomers. The fact that the arrival of the immigrants paralleled and contributed to the emergence of the city as a powerful economic and political force reinforced the distaste in which the urban newcomers were held (Figure 1.3).

FIGURE 1.3
URBAN GROWTH, FOREIGN BORN,
AND IMMIGRATION[a] AS A PERCENTAGE OF
TOTAL POPULATION OF THE UNITED STATES, 1790–1950[b]

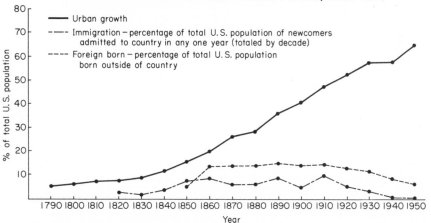

[a]Measured in 10-year totals (as percent of total U.S. population). For the years 1790 to 1820 U.S. Immigration and Naturalization Service estimates 250,000 persons entered the United States as immigrants (this is shown as total of 1820 population).

[b]Immigration figures available only for the period 1820 to 1950; foreign-born estimates available only for the period 1850 to 1950.

SOURCE: Total population, urban population, and foreign-born figures from U.S. Census, *Historical Statistics of the United States* (Washington, D.C.: U.S. Government Printing Office, 1957) and immigration totals from U.S. Immigration and Naturalization Service (as published in the *New York Times,* December 31, 1974, p. 26).

Distinguishing between newcomers and citizens in sorting out those entitled to the ballot proved difficult. The solution for the local politician, as usual, turned out to be simple enough. Immigrants were encouraged to vote by those with the most to gain, giving rise to the cries of corruption and mismanagement that have punctuated the interminable debate over civic probity.

By the late 1840s and the early 1850s, taxpaying clauses, the last vestige of a landed electorate, had begun to disappear from the majority of state constitutions. Full attention was now turned to the increasingly troublesome alien vote. Attitudes toward the immigrant varied markedly in the East and on the frontier. In the West, immigrants were welcomed and afforded early entry into the political system (see below). In the East, the situation was quite different. People of means had become increasingly angered by the aliens and by the immigrant Irish in particular, a group large in number and seeming to typify all that the native Americans abhorred. To make matters worse, these newcomers were hardly docile. The Irish were politically assertive; they did not have the great difficulty in adapting to democratic norms experienced by some other nationalities; they encountered no language barrier; and they demonstrated an early (and as it turned out lasting) proclivity for politics. As powerful ward and urban machines evolved in New York and Boston, the Irish and other ethnics were scorned as the ignorant handmaidens of a declining public morality. As a concept of politics as service to social and group needs began to develop, it was emphatically rejected by a nativist electorate that associated public service with religious commitment, valued honesty and frugality in government, and believed in a restricted public largesse and personal economic self-sufficiency.

The logical point of attack was on the residency requirements that kept the aliens off the voting rolls. State constitutional conventions during the first half of the nineteenth century witnessed repeated attempts to toughen the residency laws, most of which were defeated. The vehement nativist sentiment finally took a more avowedly political overtone, culminating in 1847 in the founding of the Native-American or "Know-Nothing" party (a name derived from the members' claim to know nothing of this secretive group's activities when questioned). The "Know-Nothings" were antiforeign, antiethnic (especially anti-Irish), and anti-Catholic. The party, with little notable success, attempted to restrict political participation to native Americans.

The Know-Nothings provided an emotional release for the more extreme elements of those who feared the foreign influx. A more subtle effort concentrated on tightening the naturalization laws to curtail immigration or, failing this, to remove such laws from the federal government and remand them to the jurisdiction of the states. If this could have been accomplished, it would then have been a simple matter to render the new groups politically impotent (through excessive residency qualifications and other devices) within the states in which they stirred the greatest antagonisms. This strategy also failed.

THE LITERACY TEST
AND THE IMMIGRANTS

The states, however, would not relent. They began to experiment with new forms that, if nothing else, demonstrated an active imagination. Many would later reappear in the 1890s in the successful efforts of the southern states to remove blacks from the voting rolls, and it is in this latter context that they received their greatest notoriety. The extent to which these devices were pioneered and discriminatorily applied in the same states that would later contest the motives as well as the practices of their southern neighbors has been unappreciated.

Some of the exclusionary devices were prosaic and would undoubtedly be familiar to someone who knew big-city politics or the politics of the rural (and antiblack) South[8]. Others were more sophisticated. The number of polling places was kept to a minimum and access to them was made difficult. In rural areas, few were willing to travel 30 or so miles at the end of a work day to cast a ballot. The problem was recognized early and, although it continued, many states moved to ameliorate it. As early as 1776 the Pennsylvania Constitution established election districts that corresponded generally to townships in an effort to enforce a dispersed and conveniently localized voting. New Jersey followed suit in 1797, and other states attempted similar tactics over the succeeding decades.

Another less subtle effort to dictate the vote involved what was called "stand-up" laws. Basically, this was a public vote cast, for example, by employees of a manufacturing firm in full view of town officials and the clergy. If these worthies did not agree with the ballot cast, they enjoyed the option of publicizing their discontent and demanding whatever punishment they felt appropriate. Many states prohibited such practices in their constitutions adopted immediately after independence. Others, such as Connecticut in 1817, relented only when the sensible electors increasingly refused to vote and the Jeffersonian Republicans effectively mobilized their opposition to the practices in effect.

Possibly the most pernicious of these early devices, as measured by impact and longevity (and one aimed exclusively at aliens), was the literacy test. The measure in its various forms has had a long and stormy history, moving from the cities of the East to the states of the South in the post–Civil War period. It survived repeated court tests in one form or another, including the historic *Williams* v. *Mississippi* (1898), which effectively gave the go-ahead to southern efforts to disenfranchise blacks. It was finally banned in the Voting Rights Act of 1965 (for jurisdictions to which the statute applied), and the Voting Rights Act of 1970 voided it throughout the United States.

A pure literacy test meant that a person had to demonstrate a capacity to read or write in order to vote. The argument in favor of such a standard was that these skills were the minimum requirements for an informed vote and an intelligent electorate—two holy grails that have been used over the years to justify a wide range of exclusionary devices. A modification of the basic measure, sometimes employed in addition to it, required a prospective voter to read and interpret to the satisfaction usually of the election official some part of the federal or state constitution or of a statute. When one realizes that a Supreme Court of nine learned jurists paid to devote their full energies to this task seldom agree on constitutional issues, one gains an inkling of how arbitrary such a test can be. Led by Connecticut and Massachusetts in the 1850s, a number of eastern states adopted the literacy test to control the ethnic vote (Table 1.1). A handful of western states enacted similar measures to exclude Orientals from the suffrage, and a large number of southern and border states found such standards to be extremely effective in disenfranchising blacks.

TABLE 1.1
STATES THAT ADOPTED
LITERACY TESTS AND DATES OF ADOPTION

State	Date of Adoption
Connecticut	1855
Massachusetts	1857
Wyoming	1889
Maine	1892
California	1894
Washington	1896
Delaware	1897
New Hampshire	1902
Arizona	1912
New York	1921
Oregon	1924
Mississippi	1890
South Carolina	1895
Louisiana	1898 & 1921
North Carolina	1900
Alabama	1901 & 1946
Virginia	1902
Georgia	1908
Oklahoma	1910

One of the problems with literacy tests was that they excluded ignorant whites as well as immigrants and blacks. In part, this hurdle could be surmounted by administering the tests through sympathetic registrars in the North or South who did their best to insure that those who were intended to vote actually did. Massachusetts went a step further. It excluded from the requirement anyone over 60 years of age (presumably a native American since the tests were intended to discriminate against newcomers) and anyone who had voted in previous elections, which when later copied and applied in the South came to be called a "grandfather clause." The Supreme Court eventually declared the grandfather clause as then applied in the South unconstitutional in two significant cases, thus beginning the tortuous process of reversing these limitations on the franchise (*Guinn* v. *United States,* 1915, and *Lane* v. *Wilson,* 1939).

The literacy test unquestionably is subject to capricious application. No matter how commendable the objective of an independently intelligent electorate may seem—and formal educational achievements may have only the most tenuous relationship to political wisdom—the tests were intended to discriminate; to prune from the electorate those whom the political authorities felt were undesirable (the Irish and Italians in the urban center of the East, blacks in the South) or who represented a threat to their continued political control. Nonetheless, if one can accept the assumption they are based upon, it is only fair to say that many states made an extended effort to apply the laws evenhandedly. New York and some other states excluded from the tests anyone who could produce a certificate of a sixth-grade education. Ethnics were the least likely, it might be added, to have such certification.

Whatever the intent and however beneficial the illusionary eventual goal may have seemed, the literacy tests developed in the Northeast were taken over by the southern states aound the turn of the century. These states suffered no illusions. They wished to restrict the vote, and with it political and economic power, to whites. Literacy tests proved a powerful and legally defensible addition to their arsenal of weapons[9].

THE IMMIGRANTS IN THE WEST

The hostility the immigrants found in the East contrasted sharply with the warmness of the reception accorded Germans, Poles, Swedes, and even the Irish and Italians in the Midwest, the Great Lakes states, and the Plains states. A number of far western states did exclude aliens explicitly, especially Orientals, from the franchise, but for the most part newcomers were welcomed to the sparsely populated frontier regions. Again, self-interest may well be the key. The settlers had preceded the immigrants by only a few years. They had no accumulations of wealth or bases of political power to protect. They needed good neighbors and security from attack. Land was plentiful, and the more land that could be placed under cultivation, the more everyone would benefit. An increase in numbers meant probable statehood and, once that was achieved, consistently larger congressional delegations.

Many frontier settlers believed that any arduous restrictions on the vote or any other fundamental rights would discourage newcomers. Aliens were allowed to vote with little or no challenge in Wisconsin, much to the discomfort of many easterners. Naturalization laws were confusing. Immigrants had to reside in the country for five years before becoming eligible for naturalization and had to declare their intent to undergo the process at least two years before citizenship. A number of states chose to ignore the law or to tie suffrage to the declaration of intent. Indiana, for example, allowed an alien to vote one year after declaring for naturalization, a process that allowed many to vote for up to four years before becoming naturalized citizens.

THE SUFFRAGETTES

The traditional idea of male supremacy dies hard. No truer indication of this can be found than in the long, hard fight to gain the vote for women. Politics was the male's domain. How far men were willing to go to keep it as such is difficult to understand in retrospect.

Women had voted statewide on occasion and in some areas, particularly the West, in local elections or on issues (school questions) considered of more concern to them. Historically, however, and dating all the way back to the first franchise requirements of 1430 in England, the electorate had been confined to males. The hold of custom proved difficult to break.

At least one commentator argues that the Seneca Falls Conference of 1848, which was to place the issue of female suffrage dramatically before the nation, was called to discuss women's rights and did not anticipate debating much less taking a stand on female voting. Once the issue was forced upon the meeting, it did not receive universal support. "It came like a bombshell upon the unprepared convention, and after a long series of discussions was passed by only a bare majority[10]." Nonetheless, once placed in the national agenda, it was not to recede from public discussion until the ratification of the Nineteenth Amendment in 1920.

The common law of the United States and England in the early years of the nineteenth century did much to implement the male's view of his own powers. According to law, the "husband and wife were one and that one [was] the husband." A married woman was effectively "dead in law." The husband exercised absolute control over the children and his wife's property. He could collect and spend all wages and, should the spirit move him, beat her, although "with a stick no bigger than a judge's thumb[11]." The husband *owned* the wife's person. Should she be injured in an industrial accident, he could sue for damages for loss of services. Should she rebel and run away, he could collect damages from whoever sheltered her. A spinster was hardly better off. She was dependent on her male relatives. "A girl was the absolute property of her father, or, if he was dead, of her brother or uncle, until she was married, when her husband exercised the same authority over her, often including the power of life and death[12]." These quotations are taken from admittedly propagandist literature—works published or written by the National-American Women Suffrage Association. Still, they begin to detail the legal and attitudinal problems emancipated women faced. They help explain the bias against the female vote and the interminable and at times silly pro and con arguments put forth.

The suffragettes liked to quote Rousseau's (an otherwise admirably innovative democrat) depiction of the role of women. It does help to define the mental set the suffragettes found so detestable. In *Émile* (1762), Rousseau wrote: "The education of women should always be relative to that of men. To please us, to be useful to us, to take care of us when grown, to make us love and esteem them, to educate us when young, to advise us, to console us, to render our lives easy and agreeable, these are the duties of women at all times and what they should be taught from infancy.[13]."

All was not quite this bleak. As indicated earlier, women did vote in some localities and in at least one state. On the frontier, women in many cases were considered the equal of men and the western states made the first significant progress in awarding the franchise to women in the last third of the nineteenth century, led by Wyoming, which granted full political equality to women in 1869. The first women's association was formed in 1833, although its intention was to fight slavery (and even then the concept of female public service was bitterly criticized by Massachusetts Congregationalists). The first women's national convention was held in 1837 and centered on the question of abolition. The antislavery movement, in fact, proved a training ground for a generation of female leaders (Lucretia Mott, Susan B. Anthony) who directed their energies to problems more specifically related to women (for example, redefining women's legal rights). All of this provided a backdrop for the bold step taken in the 1848 convention and opened a new chapter in women's fight for equality.

Success did not come quickly. Breakthroughs were made on occasion, but more often than not their efforts were met by failure and by ridicule. Kansas did permit women to vote in school board elections, the movement's most notable pre–Civil War success. The territory of Wyoming's 1869 grant of the suffrage was followed by Utah's in 1870 and Washington State's in 1883. All three efforts were invalidated by the federal courts or the Congress, but the territories persisted and in 1890 Wyoming entered the Union as the first state to give the full vote to women. Before 1900, Colorado, Idaho, and Utah followed suit and the rush had begun. Washington State, after having two previous efforts voided, voted for (and kept) female suffrage in 1910. California permitted women to vote in 1911; Arizona, Kansas, and Oregon in 1912; Illinois (in presidential elections only) in 1913; and Montana and Nevada in 1914. The East still resisted. Voters in Massachusetts, New York, New Jersey, and Pennsylvania rejected referenda on the issue in 1915. Still, the movement could not be denied. The platforms of the Democrats, Republicans, and Progressives all called for women's suffrage and in 1917 New York became the first eastern state to succumb to the tide. Three more states followed a year later (Michigan, South Dakota, and Oklahoma) and in 1919 a resolution to amend the federal Constitution (the Anthony Amendment) passed both houses of the Congress and was submitted to the states.

In fairness to the men, however, it should be pointed out that many of the public benefits that were supposed to follow the influx of female voters into the electorate never have materialized. The following "Plea for [an] Impartial Suffrage" indicates the qualities some of the more enthusiastic proponents expected to result from an enlightened suffrage:

> From the humblest specimen of female animals to the most intellectual lady, the law of peace and kindness reigns. The sex flies from noise and strife, as doves from vultures, or lambs from wolves. Hence the more female influence we have in enacting and administering laws, the more quiet and peace may we expect. Could their gentle influence permeate the entire mass of our discord—from the hearth-stone to the mansions of governors, presidents, kings, and emperors—far less blood and treasure were wasted in cruel wars. The masculine sex are ever ready to seize upon occasions for strife and combat, while Providence seems wisely and beneficently to have clothed the feminine part of his creation with powers of love and peace. These are much needed to soften and pacify the rash combativeness of the sterner sex[14].

Despite their inability to endow the electorate with the "quiet and peace" hoped for, women began voting nationwide in 1920 and have done so in increasing numbers ever since.

SUFFRAGE AND BLACKS

If there were moments of irrelevancy and possibly lightness in the effort to gain the vote for women, the fight for enfranchising blacks was deadly serious and relentlessly grim from the beginning. The primitive legal status of women provided some guidelines for the treatment of blacks. Historically, most of the legal fights to increase voter registration and enlarge the electorate have centered on black efforts to achieve the franchise. Constitutional, moral, economic, and cultural factors all entered into a controversy that was settled only by the Civil War. The compromise brought about by the election of 1876, however, quietly gave southern whites the opportunity to pursue ways of disenfranchising blacks and regaining political control. Physical violence, terrorism, and economic intimidation were all to play their part. But the real battle was to discover legally defensible means of excluding blacks from politics. The earlier successes of the eastern states in establishing strict registration qualifications were to eventually provide the ideal solution.

C. Vann Woodward has argued that the political impotence of blacks was not only a precondition for the reimposition of the prewar economic and social system, but that it also served to solidify whites and undermine the democratizing economic programs championed by the Populists. The rallying cry of the emerging order (as with that before 1860) was racial antagonism. Woodward contends:

> Having served as the national scapegoat in the reconciliation and reunion of North and South, the Negro was now pressed into service as a sectional scapegoat in the reconciliation of estranged white classes and the reunion of the Solid South. . . . The only formula powerful enough to accomplish that was the magical formula of white

supremacy, applied without stint and without any of the old conservative reservations of paternalism, without deference to any lingering resistance of Northern liberalism, or any fear of further check for a defunct Southern Populism.

The first step in applying the formula was the *total disfranchisement of the Negro* [15]. (Italics added.)

The pressures for accommodation were powerful in both North and South, and if the black was to bear the brunt of the new unity, so be it. The moral outrage that led into the Civil War appeared spent and the federal courts as well as the national government contented themselves with addressing troubles of a different order.

True to the history of such developments, many southerners accepted the disenfranchisement of blacks as a "reform," intended to prevent the political exploitation of an ignorant electorate[16]. An impressive roll call of devices was used to eliminate blacks from the electorate. Led by Mississippi, southern states activated stringent (but not unfamiliar) registration qualifications—property and-/or literacy restrictions as well as tests of statutory or constitutional interpretation (a form of the literacy standard). They then absolved whites of meeting the requirements through "grandfather" or "good character" clauses or more simply a differential application of the provisions. In addition to Mississippi's restrictions (1890), South Carolina (1895), Louisiana (1898), North Carolina (1900), Alabama (1901), Virginia (1902), Georgia (1908), and Oklahoma (1910) incorporated related measures into their state constitutions.

Florida, Tennessee, Arkansas, and Texas favored the poll tax (adopted also by the other seven states), which required a prospective voter to pay for the right to participate in both primaries and general elections (see Table 1.2 for the provisions of these acts in five states)[17]. Many found the fee, however nominal, excessive or unnecessary[18]. The official justification for the levy was that it served the best interests of sound government by helping to pay for the administration of the elections. Because it economically discriminated against poor whites in equal measure to blacks, the courts found it acceptable. States introduced variations, of course. In some, prospective voters had to pay all the back assessments they might have missed before qualifying for an election and in some they also had to present the receipt at the time of voting. Since the payment of the tax and the election might be months apart, a misplaced receipt meant no vote. Fortunately for whites, evidence of payment was normally demanded only of blacks.

The South also molded another "reform" to its peculiar ends. The direct primary had been a staple of the Progressive impulse. In the one-party South, the only election of consequence took place in the Democratic primary. Southern states not only introduced the primary (beginning with South Carolina in 1896) as the vehicle for determining party nominations but, on the dubious assumption that political parties were private organizations, officially barred blacks from participating.

TABLE 1.2
POLL TAX PROVISIONS
IN FIVE SOUTHERN STATES

State	Year Adopted	Liability	Exemptions[a]	Date Poll Tax Due
Alabama	Constitution of 1901	Every inhabitant over 21 and under 45 (not otherwise exempt)	1. All 45 and over[b] 2. Those permanently and totally disabled from following any substantially gainful occupation with reasonable regularity, whose taxable property does not exceed $500 3. Those who are blind or deaf 4. Those with honorable military service between Jan. 1, 1917, & Nov. 11, 1918; between Sept. 16, 1940, & Dec. 8, 1941; or at any time past, present, or future, when the U.S. was, is, or shall be engaged in hostilities whether or not as a result of a declared war with any foreign state 5. Members of State Guard during active membership and those who have served 21 yrs.	Payable only between Oct. 1 & Feb. 1
Arkansas	1908 constitutional amendment ratified by popular vote	Men over 21 and women over 21 desiring to vote	1. Women not desiring to vote 2. Any citizen while serving in U.S. armed forces 3. Those who become 21 after the time of assessing taxes next preceding an election	On or before Oct. 1

Approximate Period Due Before		Annual Rate	Cumulative Provision	Maximum State Charge (Not Including Penalties)	Optional Local Poll Tax (Additional to State Tax)
General Election	Primary				
9 months	3 months	$1.50	2 years preceding election	$3.00	None
1 month	10 months	$1.00	None	$1.00	None

TABLE 1.2 *(Continued)*

State	Year Adopted	Liability	Exemptions[a]	Date Poll Tax Due
Mississippi	Constitution of 1890	Every inhabitant over 21 and under 60 (not otherwise exempt)	1. All 60 and over[b] 2. Those who are deaf and dumb, blind, or maimed by loss of a hand or foot 3. Any member or veteran of the U.S. armed forces who, because of such membership, did not have an opportunity to pay	On or before Feb. 1
Texas	Constitution of 1902	Every inhabitant over 21 and under 60 (not otherwise exempt)	1. All 60 and over 2. Indians not taxed; those insane, blind, deaf, or dumb; those who have lost a hand or foot; those permanently disabled; and all disabled veterans of foreign wars with 40 percent or more disability 3. All members of state militia except for $1.00 tax for schools 4. Those who, at time of election, are, or within 18 months prior were, members of U.S. armed forces exempt for duration of war or within one year after close of the year in which the war is terminated 5. Those who become 21 after Jan. 1 and before the following election	Before Feb. 1

Approximate Period Due Before					Optional Local Poll Tax
General Election	Primary	Annual Rate	Cumulative Provision	Maximum State Charge (Not Including Penalties)	(Additional to State Tax)
9 months	18 months	$2.00	2 years preceding election	$4.00	$1.00, counties[c]
9 months	6 months	$1.50	None	$1.50	$0.25, counties $1.00, cities

TABLE 1.2 *(Continued)*

State	Year Adopted	Liability	Exemptions[a]	Date Poll Tax Due
Virginia	Constitution of 1902 (constitution of 1876 had capitation tax but abolished it in 1882)	Every inhabitant over 21 (not otherwise exempt)	1. Civil War veterans and their wives or widows 2. Those pensioned by the state for military services 3. Active members and recently discharged members of U.S. armed forces in time of war 4. Those who become 21 after Jan. 1 and before the following election	6 months before general election

[a] All of these states except Alabama had temporary exemptions applicable to the armed forces and veterans during and at the close of World War II.

[b] Except for the application of the cumulative requirement to those who have just reached the maximum age and are delinquent for the preceding year.

Approximate Period Due Before		Annual Rate	Cumulative Provision	Maximum State Charge (not including penalities)	Optional Local Poll Tax (additional to state tax)
General Election	Primary				
6 months	3 months	$1.50	3 years preceding election	$4.50	$1.00, counties, cities, towns[c]

[c]None actually levied as voting prerequisite.

SOURCE: Frederic D. Ogden, *The Poll Tax in the South* (University, Alabama: University of Alabama, 1958), pp. 33, 39–40, 46. Copyright © 1958 by The University of Alabama Press, used by permission.

That these measures were effective is beyond debate. The southern black electorate was expeditiously destroyed. The number of registered black voters in Louisiana in 1896 was 130,334. Eight years later, the total had dropped to 1342[19]. The number in 5 southern states (Louisiana, Mississippi, South Carolina, Texas, and Virginia) dropped by almost one-half (45 percent) in the period from 1884 to 1904. The pattern was to remain consistent. In the 1940 presidential election, voter turnout in the 11 states of the Old Confederacy ranged between 10 percent (South Carolina) and 43 percent (North Carolina) and averaged one-quarter (24.8 percent) of the adult electorate compared with an average turnout of three out of four (73.3 percent) of the voting age population in the other 37 states. The major reason for the poor performance can be illustrated by Louisiana, which kept explicit statistics on registration by race. The white voting age population totalled 890,361, of whom 701,659 were registered (78.8 percent). Of the 473,333 blacks, 886 (19/100 of 1 percent) had been enrolled. The turnout of the registered white electorate was poor (52.9 percent) compared with the enrolled populations in other states (California 86.4 percent, New York 90.4 percent, Pennsylvania 81.3 percent, Oregon 78.4 percent), but the response of the total voting age population was an anemic 27 percent (27.3 percent) (compared with an average of 71.5 percent for the four states mentioned)[20].

It was not until the voiding of the white primary in *Smith* v. *Allwright* (1944), the controlling decision in a welter of confused court verdicts; and the congressional Civil Rights Acts of 1957, 1960, 1964, and 1968; and, most significantly of all, the Voting Rights Acts of 1965 and 1970, that the discriminatory process was effectively reversed. To mark the changing mood, the Congress passed and the states enacted in 1964 a mostly symbolic manifestation of overkill, the Twenty-fourth Amendment outlawing the poll tax in federal elections.

VOTING RIGHTS AND THE COURTS

The federal courts have always played a dominant role in the determination of the limitations to be placed upon the American electorate. Their influence has not always been a happy one. The courts managed to interpret the constitutional amendments and the statutes growing out of the bloody Civil War so narrowly during the period from 1870 to, with few exceptions, World War II, that the impact of these measures in protecting black suffrage was negated[21]. In effect, the courts (and the federal government) served as a silent partner in the drive to disenfranchise blacks. More recently, the courts in their rulings on residency qualifications, poll tax applications, gerrymandering and malapportionment, electoral intimidation, voter harassment, and the more subtle forms of procedural disenfranchisement have proved a liberalizing force in the fight to assure every citizen the right to the franchise. It is also true that the Congress, in particular, has begun to give the courts and the nation the type of legislation and the explicit clarification of long-assumed rights needed to open the electorate. In this regard, the federal government (with some backtracking) has proven to be an increasingly aggressive proponent of an unfettered franchise.

Much of the progress that was made in the extension and protection of voting rights during the last century (especially before 1960) can be traced to Supreme Court applications of the principles embodied in the Fourteenth and Nineteenth Amendments, Section 24 (Title 18) of the U.S. Code, and with time, the various civil rights and voting rights acts passed by the Congress. The significant role the Court was destined to play became clear early. The Reconstructionists had attempted to guarantee the protection of blacks principally through three powerful constitutional amendments passed in the immediate aftermath of the Civil War: the Thirteenth (1869), Fourteenth (1868), and Fifteenth (1870). The first of these abolished slavery. The second, and by all odds the most important for future generations, contained long and involved sections that attempted to accomplish many things, including the punishment and political exile of the prewar southern white leadership. The most significant passage in the amendment provides that "no state shall abridge the privileges or immunities of citizens . . . nor . . . deprive any person of life, liberty, or property, without due process of law; nor deny to any person . . . the equal protection of the laws." The Fifteenth Amendment protected the right to vote from state restriction because of "race, color, or previous condition of servitude."

An aroused Congress attempted to supplement the amendments through the Enforcement Act of 1870. This statute prohibited the use of force, bribery, threats, or intimidation of voters; it declared the use of power over one's occupation or employment as a sanction on one's vote illegal; and it declared any one, two, or more conspirators who went "upon public highways or upon the premises of another" with intent to interfere with the other's constitutional liberties subject to criminal prosecution. Seemingly, the matter had been effectively settled.

The Supreme Court chose to take a highly restrictive view of the new amendments and statutes. In effect, it said any intimidation practiced by private individuals was beyond the federal government's power to influence. A major effort was underway at the time to keep blacks from the polls. A case *(U.S. v. Reese)* involving such actions made its way to the Court in 1876. The Court ruled that the Civil War amendments applied *only* to the states and their immediate agents. They did not restrict private individuals. Furthermore, the Fifteenth Amendment, as interpreted by the Court, did not confer the right to vote on anyone. It simply granted exemption from arbitrary discrimination on racial grounds. This one decision severely limited the application of the new amendments, a move that would take the patient work of generations of civil rights lawyers to reverse, and it subtly condoned or legitimized (without necessarily approving) the terrorism then being perpetrated upon southern blacks.

In a related controversy the same year *(U.S. v. Cruickshank)*, the judges were called upon to rule in a case indicting 100 people for the murder of 60 blacks in a politically motivated riot. The Court dismissed the indictments. Justice Bradley, speaking for his fellow justices, argued that congressional power to legislate the enforcement of voting rights did not extend "to the passage of laws for the suppression of ordinary crime [murder] within the States."

As a measure of how effective the justices proved in defusing the congressional acts, it took 92 years before the Court's interpretation was substantially reversed. This occurred in two 1966 cases, *U.S.* v. *Price* and *U.S.* v. *Guest.* Central to the successful prosecution of both cases were sections 241 and 242 (Title 18) of the U.S. Code. Section 241, known also as the "conspiracy law" (and embodying the substantive provisions of the Enforcement Act), made criminal the actions of two or more private individuals who willfully conspire to injure, oppress, threaten, or intimidate any citizen in the free exercise of any right guaranteed by the Constitution or the laws of the United States. Section 242 is targeted at the deprivation of constitutional and legal rights by state authorities acting under "the color of law." In the *Price* case, three civil rights workers in Philadelphia, Mississippi, were driven by the county sheriff to an isolated locale where they were murdered by 3 county sheriffs and 15 private citizens. The executions shocked the nation. When local authorities refused to act, the federal government moved in, investigated the case, and obtained convictions of the principals, not for murder but for obstructing the civil rights of another citizen (a lesser charge in line with the relevant federal legislation).

When the national government's action was challenged, the federal district court voided the convictions on the grounds that they did not fall under the mandate of the earlier law; specifically they did not constitute an action "under color of law" as required by Section 242. The Supreme Court reversed the decision. It ruled that it was sufficient that the 15 nonofficials willfully acted jointly with the agents of the state. The convictions stood.

In the *Guest* case, a black educator, Lemuel Penn, from Washington, D.C., was shot vigilante-style by night riders on a highway outside Athens, Georgia, while returning home from army reserve duty. The Court overturned the lower court and convicted the six defendants (none of whom were state agents), decreeing that Section 5 of the Fourteenth Amendment (the "enabling clause") empowers Congress to legislate prohibitions against conduct of any private citizens who employ violence to infringe upon Fourteenth Amendment rights. Equally significant was Justice Brennan's request that Congress specify what rights are to be guarded against private interference. This enumeration, an extremely significant one, was contained in the Civil Rights Act of 1968 and encompassed *the right to vote,* to participate in any program of the United States government or any activity receiving federal aid, to apply for and enjoy federal employment, to serve as a juror in federal court, to attend public schools, to participate in state and local governmental programs and employment, to union membership, to state jury service, to travel, and to use public accommodations.

The federal courts slowly and laboriously wrestled with the strategems employed to deny blacks the right to vote. The rulings in such cases as *Williams* v. *Mississippi* (1898), which established the constitutionality of devices such as the literacy requirement, were imbedded in law precedents that proved difficult to overcome. For generations, the courts favored nonintervention and shied away from an activist role in protecting voting rights. Yet the crudity and substantial discriminatory impact of the legal devices used against blacks in particular could not be totally ignored. Consequently, there emerged a series of confusing interpretations that allowed certain restrictions under specified conditions. The result was that each discriminatory practice had to be brought to the Court's attention and then fought out in repeated and interminable battles. As noted, it was not until 1944 that the "white primary" was effectively voided. Even then, South Carolina tried to argue that a Democratic primary was akin to an election in a private club and thus had the right to define its own membership (*Rice* v. *Elmore,* 1948). The Federal Appeals Court was unmoved. South Carolina Democrats then proceeded to allow blacks to vote in their primary if, incredible as it may seem, they swore an oath supporting racial segregation. The federal courts again voided the requirement and a sarcastic appeals court judge wondered why the state convention had simply not required an oath "that all parties [individuals] enrolling or voting should elect them in perpetuity and with satisfactory emoluments[22]." In 1960, Fayette County, Tennessee, was still struggling to find a way to reinstitutionalize the white primary. The legal resolution of this controversy finally appears to have put the matter to rest.

The poll tax and literacy test also endured long periods of controversy. The poll tax, ironically, constituted another "reform"—this time a quite legitimate one gone astray. It was introduced in New Hampshire after the Revolution (1784) to overcome restrictions that permitted only taxpayers in each of the states (with the notable exception of Vermont) to vote. This poll tax was levied at the polling place on all who met the other qualifications for the vote. Thus, it permitted them to participate in elections, although in concession to the evolving democratic commitment, it also was soon abandoned as too restrictive.

This bit of historical goodwill, of course, is long forgotten. The principal association of the poll tax is with the efforts of the southern states after 1864 to disenfranchise blacks. As Frederic Ogden repeatedly demonstrates, the poll tax was extraordinarily successful[23]. Still, it was not universally accepted. Legal challenges to its validity reached the Supreme Court in both 1937 *(Breedlove* v. *Shuttles)* and 1951 *(Butler* v. *Thompson).* In both cases, the challenges were denied. In *Breedlove,* the justices decreed Georgia's poll tax a legitimate fund-raising vehicle and one that did not violate on racial grounds the equal protection clause of the Fourteenth Amendment. In 1951, the Court said that Virginia's poll tax was not applied in a discriminatory manner.

The Twenty-fourth Amendment seemingly ended the practice in federal elections. To circumvent the new prohibition, Virginia amended its laws to allow the

FERNALD LIBRARY,
COLBY-SAWYER COLLEGE
NEW LONDON, N. H. 03257

substitution of a provision that required voters to file a certificate proving their residency *six months prior* to the federal election or be subjected to the tax. The Supreme Court struck it down. Finally, in *Harper* v. *Virginia Board of Elections* in 1966, Justice Douglas spoke for the Court when he declared that no "capricious or irrelevant factor" would be allowed to interfere with so fundamental a right as the vote, a stand more in line with the contemporary view of the Court. The poll tax was voided in local and state elections as a denial of "equal protection" under the Fourteenth Amendment[24].

Literacy tests, similar to the poll tax, do not on the face of it discriminate racially. Consequently, the courts upheld the device, although not all of its derivatives (the grandfather clause, favored treatment for those previously registered). In 1949 in *Davis* v. *Schnell,* the Court demonstrated a willingness to void the provision if reasonably conclusive evidence of a differential application could be shown. Ten years later, the Court reiterated that the test itself was not unconstitutional and if it could not be shown to have been administered in a discriminatory manner it would be upheld *(Lassiter* v. *Northampton Board of Elections).*

The most significant impetus for change was to come from the Congress. Basing their interpretation on Title I of the 1964 Civil Rights Act, the Supreme Court in 1965 struck down the sections of the Louisiana and Mississippi constitutions calling for the interpretation of various acts as a precondition of voting. The 1965 Voting Rights Act went further. It automatically disallowed any device used to limit the electorate in the five years preceding the statute's adoption. The legislation applied, in an ingenious "triggering clause," to any state or electoral subdivision in which 50 percent of the voting age population either was not registered or did not vote in the November 1964 presidential election[25]. The Civil Rights Commission could also appoint federal examiners to areas found by the federal courts to have shown evidence of violation of black voting rights. The Voting Rights Act, a drastic piece of legislation compared to its predecessors, was to prove immensely effective. When readopted in 1970 over the objections of the Nixon Administration, literacy tests were voided completely.

RESIDENCY REQUIREMENTS
AND VOTING

Provisions in state constitutions requiring an individual to have lived in a state or community for a period of time before qualifying to vote are longstanding. They go back to the colonial period and they have been relatively noncontroversial, bearing little relationship to the furor over the denial of voting rights to blacks that has captured most of the attention during the last 100 years. Yet as the nation became more mobile, residency standards became an imposing obstacle to a full and open electorate.

The state of Maryland argued, and the Supreme Court agreed (*Dryeding* v. *Devlin,* 1965), that the constitutionally permissible objectives of a residency law are to minimize voting fraud by excluding nonlegitimate residents of an electoral subdivision from participating in its elections, and to promote a more enlightened electorate through the involvement of people reasonably familiar with the problems and resources of a community. Neither the arguments nor the Court's acquiescence were new or unusual.

The Voting Rights Act of 1970 was exceptional in this regard, however. Section 202 of the act voided all state residency requirements for presidential elections, arguing that they did not relate to any compelling state interest associated with the conduct of the elections. This was to be the new standard in assessing residency qualifications. It did two things. It established a criterion that a state would have difficulty in meeting and it placed the burden of proof on the state not the litigant. A second part of the act prohibited a state from closing registration more than 30 days before the election, a provision upheld in *Oregon* v. *Mitchell* (1971)[26].

The act was destined to have a far-reaching impact. An assistant professor of law at Vanderbilt University brought action against the state of Tennessee in an effort to extend the provisions of the 1970 legislation to state and local elections (*Dunn* v. *Blumstein,* 1972). The argument was simple: the state of Tennessee had violated Blumstein's right to vote under the "equal protection clause" of the Fourteenth Amendment by durational residency requirements that were not intended to further "a compelling state interest." Significantly, the Supreme Court agreed[27].

Judged by a survey conducted in 1974 and previous efforts to test the Court's willingness to stand by landmark decisions, the issue is not dead. Still, compared with the results of an assessment of residency standards made in 1968[28], remarkable progress had been made in six short years (see below). The gains are also likely to be permanent. Unlike the literacy and poll tax provisions, there is little emotional undercurrent contained in the issue. Although there is an economic incentive for states to withhold citizenship status from short-term residents (reduced tuition at public universities, eligibility for welfare benefits), this problem can be handled by other means. Also, the federal courts and the Congress appear allied with the overwhelming majority sentiment for an accessible, minimally restricted vote.

THE CONTEMPORARY SCENE

A number of "nuisance" requirements qualifying entrance into the electorate remain. "Good character" provisions have served as a precondition for the vote since the time of the Puritans. Ohio in 1803 became the first state to prohibit idiots and the insane from voting. Forty-four states were to follow suit. Institutionalized persons and prison inmates, felons, or former convicts have been denied the vote (a curious form of social rehabilitation) in 47 states. Other states exclude paupers; those who refuse to take loyalty oaths; those who bet on elections or violate election laws; military personnel stationed in an area; those dishonorably discharged from military service; and such other exotic classifications as Indians "not taxed," "duelers," those of "bad moral character," and those engaging in "subversive activities." How many of these would stand serious court challenges is open to question. Provisions taken from the Idaho State Constitution indicate how far these prohibitions can go. Idaho, if its constitution is to be believed, eliminates from the franchise those who are not U.S. citizens; those who do not meet residency requirements; those under 18 years of age; those judged insane or placed under guardianship; those who commit a felony (unless their civil rights are restored, a rare occurrence); prostitutes; persons who frequent houses of ill fame; persons who lewdly cohabit; those in prison; those convicted of a criminal offense; bigamists; polygamists; those living in or encouraging others to live in "patriarchical, plural or celestial marriages"; those who teach state laws are not supreme; and those of Chinese or Mongolian descent.

Finally, the most subtle and least understood form of delimiting the electorate is through procedural requirements of varying degrees of complexity. Unlike qualifications such as "pauperism" that are easy to comprehend and can be argued up or down on their merits, procedural steps in enrolling voters attract little notice. They vary extensively from one state to the next and within states from one jurisdiction to another. They invoke highly specific and at times technical matters, and they are more resistant to sweeping court or national legislative remedy. For these reasons, they may represent the most arbitrarily pernicious form of contemporary devices for maintaining a restricted electorate. Yet paradoxically, as will be shown in Chapter 2, they may offer the greatest hope for significantly increasing voter turnout.

As with most reforms, these were also introduced with the best of intentions. Originally, when property qualifications were important, the presentation of a deed or some type of verification from the local assessor's office was sufficient to establish eligibility to vote. This system depended on the poll officer's knowing an individual or accepting his identification whatever it might be, and it was little changed until the flood of immigration, the expansion of the urban communities, and the growth of big-city machines created new abuses. Repeat voting, voting the "graveyards," clearing out skid row alleys and lodging houses, voting under assumed or false names, marching the patronage workers to the polls, and the like led reformers to seek some method of certified lists prior to the election to control abuses. This practice introduced the sometimes onerous physical certification process that most associate with registration.

Joseph Harris's classic work *Registration of Voters in the United States* (1929) [29] is concerned with this aspect of registration as is the reformist work of such organizations as the National Municipal League and the League of Women Voters[30]. The problem, unquestionably, is quite real. Harris reports that in Philadelphia, assessors controlled by the local political machines were charged with preparing the lists of qualified voters. Discrepancies between those listed as eligible to vote by these officials and those actually registered were considerable. One Philadelphia ward had, for example, 6879 names on the 1904 assessors' list yet with only 2824 persons registered in 1906, the nearest comparable date. For the city as a whole, using the same years, 385,036 names appeared on the lists while only 250,950 persons were registered two years later. Harris quotes sources to the effect that from 30,000 to 80,000 fraudulent votes were cast in Philadelphia elections. Chicago, an early advocate and long a leader in this form of excessive democratization, can illustrate the feelings such practices arouse. The *Chicago Tribune,* hardly an impartial observer, quaintly moralized on an early election.

> The main causes of *our* defeat are these: first, frauds of an enormous and most flagrant nature. . . . In the Sixth Ward there were almost as many illegal votes as legal votes polled. Both parties canvassed the ward thoroughly before election, and agreed that there were about seven hundred votes in the ward, and yet over twelve hundred were polled on election day. Can any sane man doubt that the most disgraceful frauds were perpetrated? . . . A wagon load of voters openly attempted to vote in four wards, and finally succeeded in voting by leaving their wagon at a corner and scattering themselves around.
>
> Early yesterday morning crowd after crowd of imported voters passed up Clark Street with their carpet bags in their hands, on their way to the depot, whence they took their departure for Joliet, Sycamore, and other places where they belong. They had accomplished their mission. They had received a dollar per head voted, and were satisfied[31]. (Italics added.)

In Chicago's and Philadelphia's defense, the same could be said of New York City, Boston, Baltimore, San Francisco, Louisville, and just about any city of consequence. The comfortable burghers of these urban areas occasionally stirred themselves to the point of officially investigating the election corruption and punishing the offenders. An inquiry into the outcome of a primary in one Chicago ward in 1926 showed that over 40 percent of the votes were fraudulent. Votes cast in the election were attributed to voters who were legally certified but who had not gone to the polls, to persons who gave a schoolhouse, a vacant lot, and an abandoned home as their place of residence, and to a dead man. Some house numbers given by voters did not exist when checked. A goodly number of electors gave no address, and a large number of people who had moved from the ward before the primary still managed to have a vote cast on their behalf by persons unknown[32]. A rash soul might contend that, although the proportion of fraudulent votes may have been larger in 1926, the practices uncovered remain substantially unchanged today in several Chicago wards.

This last point illustrates a problem the reformers apparently did not consider. Why would a local machine that efficiently controlled the election machinery be any less able in managing enrollment procedures, no matter how stringent, to its own satisfaction? One could argue that the causes of machine "democracy" and its attendant corruptions were social and economic and that a middle-class concern with a procedural restructuring of elections would do little to alleviate the root forces contributing to those corrupt practices. Fed by moral indignation, reformers nonetheless pushed on, introducing such "reforms" as periodic registration intended to cleanse the rolls of the unqualified at given (annual, biennial, quadrennial) intervals; personal registration in which citizens had to appear at an official enrolling station well in advance of an election and, usually, personally sign a statement, allowing for a verification of residency and a later comparison of signatures when they signed in at the polls; and official canvasses of neighborhoods to enroll prospective voters in their own homes, a practice that could be relied on more extensively. A number of municipalities introduced permanent registration systems designed to lessen the physical difficulty of enrolling, cut the city's expenditures, and enlarge the electorate. The citizens, in such cases, were continued on the rolls for as long as they voted and resided in the community. Depending on the locality, if they missed one or more elections, they then had to personally reestablish their right to certification. The burden was on the local government to keep the rolls free of fraudulent voters through occasional checks of those that had died or moved elsewhere.

Each of the procedural steps in certifying an individual's eligibility for the vote was, of course, open to abuse. Registration locations could be too few and undermanned. Hours could be inconvenient, beginning after most people had gone to work and closing before they had come home. The enrolling places could be underpublicized and registration periods could be kept to a minimum by law or held so far in advance of elections that few would have the motivation to vote. Texas developed possibly the most notorious abuse of this kind, closing registration in the January before the November election, a practice that much too belatedly (1971) was changed by the Texas legislature when suit was brought *(Beare* v. *Smith)* in the federal courts. In rural areas, registration offices could be located far from population centers, too far for a reasonable person to travel to perform such a ritualistic civil duty. Prospective registrants could be kept in long waiting lines and subjected to embarrassing questions in public about their qualifications. The enrolling places themselves could be difficult to find—the back room of the third floor of a school building—to discourage all but the most persevering[33]. The overriding American preoccupation, however, has been with preventing fraud, a view framed by the early attitudes toward immigrants and later the experiences with the urban machines.

Lincoln Steffens, "muckraking" reporter, author, and man of the world, makes the point rather nicely in the discussion contained in his *Autobiography* of the Rev. Dr. Charles H. Parkhurst, a minister and reform leader in New York City at the turn of the century. Speaking for himself and other reformers, Steffens says Parkhurst made "our vague sense of evil acutely definite by the simplest sort of moral revelation and reasoning[34]."

> Dr. Parkhurst's constructive ideas were as simple and moral as his charges, which he continued to deliver with force and effect. His analysis of his facts was that, since

only bad men would take bribes and since the Tammany police and political officers not only accepted but exacted them, our government was made bad because there were bad men in office. And the cure was to discharge the bad men and elect good men. That expressed our popular mind; our educated men know no better. . . . The problem was to find good men to nominate and elect[35].

The way to insure that "good" men once discovered were elected was to free election processes from corrupt practices, and a major tactic in the battle was to require severe registration procedures that would allow only bona fide electors to enroll.

The basically negative instincts of this approach as well as its handiwork—Steffens was to say the outcome of the reformers work was "merely destructive[36]"—contrasts sharply with that of Britain, Canada, and virtually every other democratic nation. Other nations are concerned with illegal voting and do an able job of controlling it. Although the tediously explicit American procedures undoubtedly have some effect on potential fraud, they also depress electoral turnout.

CONCLUSION

There are many ways of looking at the history of suffrage restrictions. For some, they were justified. For others, they indicated self-interest raised to the level of democratic theory. And for still others, they represented good intentions gone awry. Many were taken over from England with little thought given to their effect. Others were devised to meet specific problems and were defended as a means to produce an independent, better-informed, and qualitatively superior electorate. Once established, they became extraordinarily hard to dislodge as the long fights over black and female suffrage, the 18-year-old vote, and residency limitations repeatedly demonstrated.

Table 1.3 presents residency and other registration qualifications for two elections separated by more than 100 years. In 1860, voting restrictions had not developed to the extent they would in the period 1890 to 1920 with the Progressive movement in the North and the effort to disenfranchise blacks in the South. Prior to the election year of 1968, the civil rights movement began the process of eliminating the restrictions that have served to keep blacks from the electorate. What is impressive in assessing the qualifications on the vote listed is the relative lack of a broad movement to reduce the incremental restrictions introduced over the years. In fact, 1968 indicates a more systematic effort to cleanse from the electoral process those believed undesirable. Residence qualifications were more pervasive in the later election (this is, of course, before the second Voting Rights Act and *Dunn* v. *Blumstein*). Thirty-three states had some type of residency limitation and 21 had one of at least a year. In 1860, 7 had no state residency provision and 7 had one of less than a year. Three (Virginia, South Carolina, and Kentucky), however, had two-year requirements. The county durational resi-

TABLE 1.3
A COMPARISON OF 34
STATE REGISTRATION LIMITATIONS, 1860 and 1968[a]

| State | 1860 Qualifications | | | | | | | | |
| | Residency | | | | | | | | |
	State	County	Electoral District	Blacks[b]	Aliens	Mentally Incompetent	Paupers	Criminals	Other[c]
Alabama	1 year	3 months	—	X	X	—	—	X	X
Arkansas	6 months	—	—	X	X	—	—	—	—
California	6 months	1 month	—	X	X	X	X	X	X
Connecticut	—	6 months	—	X	X	—	—	—	—
Delaware	1 year	1 month	—	X	X	X	X	X	X
Florida	1 year	6 months	—	X	X	⁼	—	X	X
Georgia	—	6 months	—	X	X	—	—	—	—
Illinois	1 year	—	—	X	X	—	—	X	X
Indiana	—	—	—	X	—	—	—	X	X
Iowa	6 months	—	—	X	X	X	—	X	X
Kansas	6 months	1 month	—	X	—	X	X	X	X
Kentucky	2 years	1 month	60 days	X	X	—	—	—	—
Louisiana	1 year	6 months	—	X	—	—	—	—	—
Maine	—	3 months	—	—	X	—	X	—	X
Maryland	1 year	6 months	—	X	X	X	—	X	—
Massachusetts	1 year	6 months	—	—	X	X	X	—	—
Michigan	6 months	—	—	X	X	—	X	X	X
Minnesota	6 months	—	30 days	X	—	X	X	X	X
Mississippi	1 year	4 months	—	X	X	—	—	—	—
Missouri	1 year	3 months	—	X	X	—	—	—	X
New Hampshire	—	—	—	—	X	—	X	—	—
New Jersey	1 year	5 months	—	X	X	X	X	X	X
New York	1 year	4 months	—	—	X	—	X	X	X
North Carolina	—	1 year	—	X	X	—	—	—	—
Ohio	1 year	—	—	X	X	X	—	X	—
Oregon	6 months	—	—	X	—	X	X	X	X
Pennsylvania	1 year	—	10 days	X	X	—	—	—	—
Rhode Island	1 year	6 months	—	—	X	X	X	X	X
South Carolina	2 years	—	—	X	X	—	X	—	X
Tennessee	—	6 months	—	X	X	—	—	X	—
Texas	1 year	6 months	—	X	X	X	X	—	X
Vermont	1 year	—	—	—	X	—	—	—	—
Virginia	2 years	1 month	—	X	X	X	X	X	X
Wisconsin	1 year	—	—	X	—	X	—	X	X
TOTAL No. states with restriction (N=34)	27	21	3	28	28	14	15	19	20
%	79.4	61.7	8.8	82.3	82.3	41.1	44.1	55.8	58.8

NOTE: X = Group excluded by law from the vote
— = No restriction

[a] Exceptions to and exclusions from the various provisions by the states are not included.

[b] The Fifteenth Amendment banned any prohibition by race on the franchise and, therefore, this is not repeated for 1968.

[c] "Other" for 1860 includes military personnel and students only. Additional information was not immediately available.

[d] "Electoral District" for 1968 refers to city, town, precinct, or special district specifications.

[e] "Other" in 1968 includes such limitations as literacy tests, loyalty oaths, "good character" provisions, and a host of other prohibitions on who may not vote (those dishonorably discharged from military

1968 Qualifications							
	Residency						
State	County	Electoral District[d]	Aliens	Mentally Incompetent	Paupers	Criminals	Other[e]
1 year	6 months	3 months	X	X	—	X	X
1 year	6 months	1 month	X	X	—	X	—
1 year	90 days	54 days	X	X	—	X	X
—	—	6 months	X	X	—	X	X
1 year	90 days	30 days	X	X	X	X	X
1 year	6 months	—	X	X	—	X	X
1 year	6 months	—	X	X	—	X	X
1 year	90 days	30 days	X	X	—	X	—
6 months	60 days	30 days	X	X	—	X	—
6 months	60 days	10 days	X	X	—	X	—
6 months	—	30 days	X	X	—	X	X
1 year	6 months	60 days	X	X	—	X	—
1 year	6 months	3 months	X	X	—	—	X
6 months	—	3 months	X	X	—	—	X
1 year	6 months	6 months	X	X	—	X	X
1 year	—	6 months	X	X	X	X	X
6 months	—	—	X	—	—	X	—
6 months	—	30 days	X	X	—	X	—
1 year	1 year	6 months	X	X	—	X	X
1 year	60 days	10 days	X	X	X	X	X
6 months	—	6 months	X	—	X	X	X
6 months	40 days	—	X	X	—	X	X
3 months	3 months	—	X	X	—	X	X
1 year	—	30 days	X	X	—	X	X
1 year	40 days	40 days	X	X	—	X	X
6 months	—	—	X	X	—	X	X
90 days	—	60 days	X	—	—	—	X
1 year	—	6 months	X	X	X	X	X
1 year	6 months	3 months	X	X	X	X	X
1 year	3 months	—	X	—	—	X	—
1 year	6 months	—	X	X	X	X	X
1 year	—	90 days	X	—	—	—	X
1 year	6 months	30 days	X	X	X	X	X
6 months	—	10 days	X	X	—	X	X
33	21	26	34	29	8	30	26
97.0	61.7	76.4	100.0	85.2	23.5	88.2	76.4

service, those who have defrauded the government, duelers, those who wager on elections, Indians not taxed, etc.).

SOURCES: 1860 data adapted from Kirk H. Porter, *A History of Suffrage in the United States* (Chicago: University of Chicago Press, 1918), table III, p. 148; copyright 1918 by the University of Chicago Press; the 1968 information is from Freedom to Vote Task Force, *Registration and Voting in the States* (Washington, D.C.: Democratic National Committee, 1970), pp. 41–59. A comparison can also be made with the 1960 election by using the data contained in the President's Commission on Registration and Voting Participation, *Report on Registration and Voting Participation* (Washington, D.C.: Government Printing Office, 1963), p. 65.

dency demands are proportionately the same, although the restrictions are a little stricter in the latter period, and the number of states with some type of similar provision at the local level has jumped from less than 1 out of 10 to 3 out of 4. The consistency of the coverage in the residency laws is the major difference between the two points in time on this dimension. No state of the 34 examined permitted alien voting in 1968, and in all but one of the categories (the one relating to paupers), the more recent totals are higher. Apparently, enlightened thought had not been given to such matters. The impetus of the civil rights movement of the sixties is in the process of moving into other areas of a restricted vote and quite possibly—as the Voting Rights Act of 1970 and 1975 and several Supreme Court cases in the early to mid-1970s portend—a period of explosive change may be in the offing. If so, its coming is overdue.

Beyond the specific qualifications themselves, and less well understood by the public, is a completely independent second order of registration barrier: the *procedure* used to certify the eligibility of the prospective voters. This complex interrelationship of laws, people, and institutions may well constitute the most formidable barrier to an increased voter turnout at the present time.

Many, if not most, of the exclusionary devices employed to maintain a limited electorate are elitist. Rather than accommodating the greatest number of people in the quest for a truly democratic and representative electorate, they punish or eliminate from the franchise unwelcome groups or protect economic and political advantages. The objective should be the broadest electorate possible[37]. This goal deserves top priority. Next, and on a far different plane, the conducting of reasonably open and fraud-free election contests should be approached as an administrative problem amenable to reasonable solution without unduly penalizing prospective voters. Neither objective is necessarily exclusive of the other.

NOTES

1. Useful treatments of the colonial era are A. E. McKinley, *The Suffrage Franchise in the Thirteenth English Colonies in America* (Boston: Ginn, 1905), Kirk H. Porter, *A History of Suffrage in the United States* (Chicago: University of Chicago Press, 1918), and Chilton Williamson, *American Suffrage: From Property to Democracy 1760–1860* (Princeton, N.J.: Princeton University Press, 1960). The concise approach of the Porter analysis has proven especially helpful in the development of the chapter.
2. Porter, *History of Suffrage,* pp. 2–3.
3. Merrill D. Peterson, ed., *Democracy, Liberty and Property: The State Constitutional Conventions of the 1820s* (Indianapolis: Bobbs-Merrill, 1966), p. 77.
4. Ibid., p. 76.
5. Dudley O. McGovney, *The American Suffrage Medley* (Chicago: University of Chicago Press, 1949), p. 29.
6. Peterson, *Democracy, Liberty and Property.*
7. Among the many good discussions on immigrants and their problems are Oscar Handlin, *The Uprooted* (Boston: Little, Brown, 1951) and Nathan Glazer and Daniel

P. Moynihan, *Beyond the Melting Pot* (Cambridge: The M.I.T. Press, 1963). The Al Smith candidacy is treated in Handlin, *Al Smith and His America* (Boston: Little, Brown, 1958).

8. On contemporary Chicago election practices William J. Crotty, "Anatomy of a Challenge: The Chicago Delegation to the Democratic National Convention," in *Cases in American Politics,* ed. Robert L. Peabody (New York: Praeger, 1976) is helpful; on the South, see the report of the U.S. Commission on Civil Rights, *Political Participation* (Washington, D.C.: U.S. Government Printing Office, 1968).

9. See C. Vann Woodward, *The Strange Career of Jim Crow* (New York: Oxford University Press, 1957) for a readable introduction to the developments described.

10. Jessie J. Cassidy, *The Legal Status of Women* (New York: The National-American Women Suffrage Association, 1897), p. 109. This section also relies on Joanna Kay Bowers, *Women's Suffrage in America: Developments in Illinois,* mimeographed (Evanston: Northwestern University, 1973).

11. The National-American Women Suffrage Association, *Victory: How Women Won It* (New York: H. H. Wilson, 1940), p. 4.

12. Cassidy, *Legal Status of Women,* pp. 5–6.

13. Cassidy, *Legal Status of Women,* p. 5.

14. A Lawyer of Illinois, *A Plea for Impartial Suffrage* (Chicago: Western News Company, 1868), pp. 39–40.

15. Woodward, *Strange Career of Jim Crow,* pp. 65–66.

16. Ibid., p. 66.

17. An exhaustive study of the poll tax and its effects in the South can be found in Frederic C. Ogden, *The Poll Tax in the South* (University, Ala.: University of Alabama Press, 1958). The story of the introduction and effectiveness of the measures designed to curb black political activity and the blacks' struggle against these has been told in many places. A list of worthwhile readings on different aspects of the problems encountered would include Emil Olbrich, *The Development of Sentiment on Negro Suffrage to 1860* (Madison: University of Wisconsin Press, 1912); the report of the U.S. Commission on Civil Rights, *Political Participation;* Pat Walters and Reese Cleghorn, *Climbing Jacob's Ladder* (New York: Harcourt, Brace and World, 1967) on the civil rights movement in the South during the 1960s; Hanes Walton, Jr., *Black Politics* (Philadelphia: J. B. Lippincott, 1972); and the Report of the U.S. Senate Committee on the Judiciary, *Voting Rights: Hearings* (Washington, D.C.: U.S. Government Printing Office, 1969).

18. McGovney shows the amounts of money that can be involved. In Jefferson County (Birmingham), Alabama, the amount paid by prospective voters for a cumulative poll tax varied from $1.50 to $36.00. Not surprisingly, and despite provisions in some states for exemptions—those (whites) over 45 years of age in Alabama—only 12 percent of the electorate voted in a highly contested 1944 Democratic primary (and therefore determined election) for the U.S. Senate in the county. Of those who voted, 42 percent had been excluded from paying the tax. Mississippi enforced a poll tax of two dollars and allowed a county to add another one dollar. Since the tax was cumulative for two years, the right to vote could cost six dollars. McGovney, *American Suffrage Medley,* pp. 146–47.

19. Woodward, *Strange Career of Jim Crow,* p. 68. Ogden develops a significant amount of comparative data on the decline in turnout in his *Poll Tax in the South.* For an updated bibliography and a case study of the effects of repeat in one state, see Robert

H. Talbert, "Poll Tax Repeat in Texas: A Three Year Individual Performance Evaluation," *Journal of Politics* 36 (November 1974): 1050–56.

20. The statistics are taken from or based on information found in McGovney, *American Suffrage Medley,* pp. 66–67, 81–83.

21. Of particular help in this section on Court developments prior to 1970, is Richard Claude, *The Supreme Court and the Electoral Process* (Baltimore: Johns Hopkins Press, 1970). A fuller discussion of the significance of the cases and the legal trends can be found here. I wish to thank Greg Gardner for his help in developing the legal sections of this chapter in particular.

22. Ibid., p. 72.

23. The impact of the tax is a major theme in Ogden's study. See Ogden, *Poll Tax in the South,* pp. 111–77

24. Claude, *Supreme Court,* p. 81.

25. The report of the U.S. Senate Committee on the Judiciary, *Voting Rights,* p. 586.

26. Report of the Supreme Court of the United States, *State of Oregon* v. *John N. Mitchell, Attorney General of the United States,* decided December 21, 1970.

27. Report of the Supreme Court of the United States, *Dunn, Governor of Tennessee* et al. v. *Blumstein,* decided March 21, 1972. The "compelling state interest" doctrine applied here, in *Mitchell,* and more generally in the registration cases of the 1970s originated in *Kramer* v. *Union Free School District,* 395 U.S. 621 (1969). Succinctly put, it means that if a state grants the right to vote to some and not to others, the state must demonstrate that such exclusions promote a compelling state interest.

28. For 1968, the following reports can be compared with those for 1972: Freedom to Vote Task Force, *Registration and Voting in the States* (Washington, D.C.: Democratic National Committee, 1970), pp. 41–48, and Legislative Reference Service, *Election Laws of the Fifty States and the District of Columbia* (Washington, D.C.: Library of Congress, 1968). For 1972, see Office of Federal Elections, *Federal-State Election Law Survey* (Washington, D.C.: Government Accounting Office, 1973). Briefly, in 1972, 30 states had no durational residency requirement for voting in presidential elections, 16 plus the District of Columbia had 30-day restrictions, 3 (Massachusetts 31, Arizona 50, and Vermont 3 months) enforced more than the Supreme Court recommended, and 1, Arizona, had a requirement of only 10 days.

29. Joseph P. Harris, *Registration of Voters in the United States* (Washington, D.C.: The Brookings Institution, 1929). Harris's book contains an extensive early listing of the relevant literature.

30. Committee on Election Administration, *A Model Registration System* (New York: National Municipal League, 1927) and, more currently, National Municipal League, *A Model Election System* (New York: National Municipal League, 1973) and the League of Women Voters Education Fund, *Administrative Obstacles to Voting* (Washington, D.C.: League of Women Voters, 1972).

31. Cited in Harris, *Registration of Voters,* p. 82.

32. Harris, *Registration of Voters,* p. 357.

33. For examples and discussion of each of these, see the League of Women Voters Education Fund, *Obstacles to Voting,* Task Force on Elections, *Report of the Mayor's Task Force on Election Reform* (New York: Office of the Mayor, 1970), and U.S. Commission on Civil Rights, *Political Participation.*

34. Lincoln Steffens, *The Autobiography of Lincoln Steffens,* vol. 1 (New York: Harcourt, Brace & World, 1931), p. 247.

35. Ibid., pp. 249–50

36. Ibid., p. 249. Steffens did change his view from his early years on these matters and, as *Autobiography* makes clear, became involved in some unusual experiments to supplant the machine with constituent services provided by a cadre of enlightened businessmen, doctors, and the like. The approach was unrealistic but interesting.

37. The philosophic and practical advantages of an enlarged electorate are incisively presented in E. E. Schattschneider, *The Semi-Sovereign People* (New York: Holt, Rinehart and Winston, 1960). For a stress on the policy consequences and practical concerns of voting, see William C. Mitchell, *Why Vote?* (Chicago: Markham, 1971).

Voters

and Nonvoters:

Who Gets Left Out?

And Why?

If nonvoting fell randomly on the citizen population, low voting turnouts would be lamentable occurrences but of less significance to society. Unfortunately, they do not. Certain groups—those at the lowest end of the social order—contribute a disproportionate share of those unrepresented in political decision making through elections. The people most in need of an equitable political representation are precisely those least likely to receive it.

A misconception is that a modest level of election participation has always been characteristic of the United States. This is not quite correct. Participation of the eligible population—recognizing this was often defined in exclusionary terms—has varied considerably and frequently was commendably high. Participation has always related also to forms governing democratic involvement and the significance of the outcome. This point can be illustrated by reference to the Republic's earliest years. At the time of and immediately after the Constitution was adopted, the voting returns for 10 of the original states show that the turnout was meager; 4.9 percent for the period 1788 to 1791; 5.2 percent for 1792 to 1798; and 8.3 percent for 1799 to 1802[1]. These figures are taken to be illustrative for the earlier, preconstitutional years (as well as for the other states not represented) and to demonstrate the effect of suffrage restrictions on the vote. The gradual increase in participation during the decade of the 1790s reflects a growing concern with suffrage limitations and the coming of competitive parties.

The period 1824 to 1840 is usually designated as the beginning of mass democracy on a significant scale. The election of 1824 revolved around the selection of John Quincy Adams by the congressional caucus ("King Caucus" as it was called) over, most notably, the unpredictable Andrew Jackson, hero of the frontier and symbol of the emerging power of the common man. Jackson captured the nomination in his own right in 1828 and his campaign, much like Al Smith's 100 years later, brought to the polls in increasing numbers the working classes in the cities and the freeholders in the West. Jackson in turn attempted to democratize nominating procedures through the introduction of the national conventions. By 1840, the Harrison-Tyler election, the first of the "modern" campaigns, had introduced torchlight parades, candidate slogans and songs, ambitious personal campaign tours, and the banners, placards, and other hoopla that have come down to the age of television virtually unchanged. From 1840 to 1900, voter turnout hovered around 75 percent (Figure 2.1a). Allowance should be made for the crude methods of estimating election returns, the corruption evidenced in many local elections, the small electorate, and the deliberate (and successful) attempts to exclude from actual participation city workers, ethnics, and, with their entrance into the electorate, blacks. Even taking all of these factors into consideration, the level of involvement is impressive[2].

Involved registration procedures were introduced on a systematic basis nation-wide beginning in the 1890s. The South wished to neutralize blacks politically and to do so in a manner the courts would find legally defensible. Registration qualifications admirably fitted their needs. In the North, the problem was some-what different, but the solution was the same. Registration limitations had been employed since colonial days to restrict participation to only the most notewor-thy, usually defined in the conventional terms of economic success and good moral character. In the 1830s and 40s, with the decline of property considerations and the rise of immigration, many of the devices later employed with outstanding success in the South were introduced on an experimental basis. It was not until the blatant abuses of the second half of the nineteenth century that reform movements began to advocate a purifying of elections. One of the means to accomplish this goal was stringent registration procedures. The old restrictions about who could or could not vote were maintained, and the new laws insured that only those legally eligible actually voted. Unfortunately—and possibly it was not anticipated—the more demanding registration process discouraged even greater numbers of eligible voters from participating in elections.

By 1920 another element had been introduced: female suffrage. Whenever a new group enters the electorate, as with the 18- to 20-year-olds in 1972, its initial showing is poor. It takes time to become acclimated and to develop an interest in the procedures sufficient to discover and master the hurdles encountered in the voting process. As a consequence, the percentage of eligible persons voting, with the electorate about doubled in 1920, fell (as it was to decline in 1972, although less drastically) to just below 50 percent. The Smith campaign of 1928 is impor-tant in this regard. Most of the attention in the election has been given to Smith's political sponsorship and his religion. The real significance of the contest is both that Smith commanded a higher proportion of the vote than his two Democratic predecessors and that his campaign helped increase the turnout by over 7.5 million voters. The trend line for the period since 1920 (Figure 2.1b) shows a

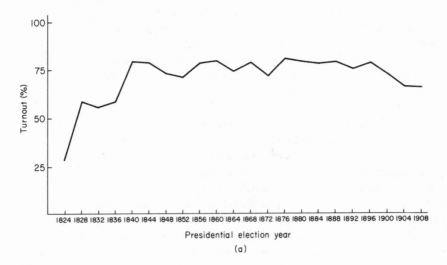

Presidential election year

(a)

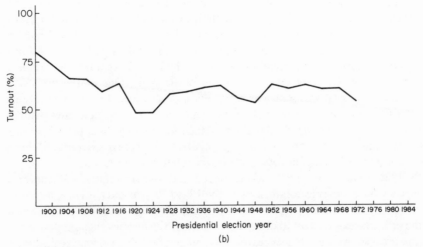

Presidential election year

(b)

SOURCE: Data for elections between 1824 and 1968 supplied by Walter Dean Burnham to Freedom To Vote Task Force and published in their report, *Registration and Voting in the United States* (Washington, D.C.: Democratic National Committee, 1970).

gradual, but respectable increase in the turnout from just below 50 percent in the first half of the twenties to slightly above 60 percent during the 1960s. Aberrations do occur, but they are averaged into the trend line. These include the 1944 election which took place at the height of World War II, and the unique Truman-Dewey campaign of 1948 and its depressing effect on participation. In 1972 a new factor—the 18-year-old vote—had been added, which lowered participation even further. It appears that voter participation will stabilize (allowing for unusual occurrences) at something in the vicinity of 55 to 60 percent. It is unlikely to ever exceed 65 percent of the eligible voting-age population under present conditions.

NONVOTING IN
THE PERIOD 1952 TO 1972

There is another way of looking at the matter. Percentiles deal with relative comparisons and they can be misleading. They do not take into account the size of the population. If the *numbers* of nonvoters are taken into consideration, the problem assumes a more ominous tone (Figure 2.2).

The year 1952 provides a nice point of departure. It marks the time when television began to be used as a principal form of communication, increasing candidate exposure and voter awareness and stimulating potentially higher turnouts. Figure 2.2 graphs the total electorate and the number of nonvoters for the six presidential elections being examined. Between the elections of 1952 and 1968, the ranks of the nonvoters increased by 6.5 million people. *Over 40 million* otherwise qualified voters were not going to the polls by the late sixties, in itself a small nation within a nation. It is difficult to comprehend in any meaningful fashion statistics of this magnitude. In the days of the billion-dollar budget and airplanes that cost as much as the operating budgets of universities, statistics of this order appear to be only part of the general inflationary cycle. Possibly, they can take meaning through specific illustrations.

In the 1968 Nixon-Humphrey contest, a popular vote of only 500,000 (8/10 of 1 percent of the major party vote, 6/10 of 1 percent of the total vote) separated the Republican and Democratic contenders. The number of nonvoters in this election could have reversed the winner's plurality 80 times over. John Kennedy's margin in 1960 was less than 1 vote a precinct, and the change of a few critical votes in key states could have reversed the outcome in a contest in which over 38 million persons of voting age did not participate and in which only 118,500 votes separated the two principals. It would be difficult to argue that the elections were not important. The 1960 Kennedy victory gave birth to the New Frontier–Great Society programs of the Kennedy-Johnson years, with notable achievements in domestic affairs and civil rights and, less commendably, in foreign affairs such as the Viet Nam War. The 1968 election laid the basis for the distasteful Watergate episode.

FIGURE 2.2
VOTING AGE POPULATION
AND THE NUMBER OF NONVOTERS
IN THE UNITED STATES, 1952–1972

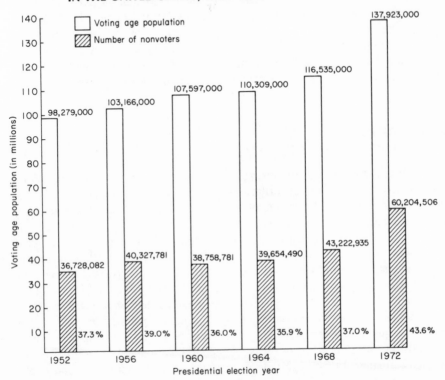

Less than 1 vote a precinct in Ohio (won by Truman by only 7107 votes) or California (won by only 17,865 votes) could have thrown the 1948 presidential election into the House of Representatives. The 1974 U.S. Senate race in New Hampshire was decided by 10 votes (with a Democratic victor) or 2 votes (the Republican the winner) depending on which "official" recount one chose to believe. The election was to be contested in the state and federal courts and in the Senate before its outcome would be decided by a second election 10 months after the first. For most of the period following the election, New Hampshire was represented in the Senate by an interim gubernatorial appointee. The examples of close elections being swung by a few votes (much less a thousand or a million) are innumerable. The lesson about the unpredictability of the outcome of crucial elections caused by increasing the electorate appears clear enough.

The election of 1972 was admittedly unusual. Many people reacted negatively to the candidates of the established parties and to politics in general, perhaps as a result of the turbulent sixties and the inability of the country to disentangle itself from an unpopular war. The Twenty-sixth Amendment added 21 million people to the eligibility pool. Nonetheless, an unprecedented 60 million people did not vote in 1972, a body of nonvoters three times the size of California or New York and greater than the total number of people living in such countries as France, West Germany, Italy, Egypt, Mexico, Canada, or the United Kingdom. In fact, this "nation" of nonvoters if independently constituted would rank as the world's eighth largest country.

Presidential elections excite the most interest. People are more aware of the candidates and usually of some issues in the campaign. As a consequence, presidential contests result in the highest turnout. A survey of 38 municipal and district elections in 1969 covering races that included, at a minimum, mayoral or aldermanic contests (and usually several others such as school boards, sheriffs, district attorneys, and judicial officials) showed a turnout ranging from a depressingly low 9 percent of the eligible voters to a high of almost 59 percent. The average turnout was 35 percent, one-third of the potential electorate and well below the participation rates for presidential contests[3].

Only 38 percent of the voting age population participated in the 1974 off-year election. Congressional elections consistently do less well than presidential contests in attracting voters (Figure 2.3), evidencing a 5 to 10 percent or more drop-off in votes when compared with concurrent presidential levels of participation. The turnout for off-year elections is even more depressed, running well below the participation figures for the presidential years. In 1974, the expanded

FIGURE 2.3
TURNOUT IN CONGRESSIONAL
ELECTIONS IN PRESIDENTIAL YEARS, 1920–1974

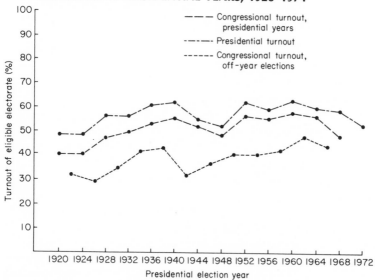

electorate and the gross disillusionment with politics occasioned by the Watergate episode undoubtedly influenced participation. But even a slight increase in the number of voters that year could have reversed a number of outcomes. The U.S. Senate race in North Dakota is but one illustration. Because of the closeness of the race, the North Dakota Senate contest was not decided until more than a month after the vote.

The same year, a Gallup poll attempted to ascertain why so many failed to exercise the franchise. Fifty percent of the nonvoters, twice the number who gave such reasons as "lack of interest" or "poor candidates," cited a failure to meet in some manner registration qualifications as the cause of their nonvoting. If the registration system could be simplified and the physical act of enrolling made less taxing, it is reasonable to believe that considerably more people could be included in the electorate—surely not an automatic 50 percent but possibly participation could be increased to something close to three out of four in presidential contests. Prospective voters should be free to concentrate on the choices offered them rather than bothering with or running afoul of the arcane provisions of localized enrolling processes[4].

There is not a great deal anyone can do to force a higher turnout or to command a more enlightened vote. It is possible, however, to reduce the formal barriers that have developed over the years that hinder and, in some cases, entirely prohibit more inclusive electoral participation. If qualifications remain as they are, there is no reason to believe that turnout will improve over the next several decades. Based on current population projections and a 60 percent turnout of the voting age population (possibly an ambitious assumption given the most recent elections), the forecast is not encouraging. The United States may have between 93 million nonvoters by 1980 and 122 million by the year 2000. Even in an age of statistical and every other type of overkill, these figures are striking.

NONVOTERS:
WHO ARE THEY?

A close examination of the U.S. Census reports on the 1972 election corroborates the findings of a large number of academic studies on political participation over the last quarter of a century[5]. The U.S. Census reports do not include military personnel in their surveys of nonvoting, a group known for its low levels of involvement (usually below 40 percent) and one that has to contend with local residency laws and the erratic system of absentee balloting[6]. The census also excludes all institutionalized populations (prisoners, patients in mental institutions, hospitals, and nursing homes) from their reports on voting. The census statistics, in addition, traditionally overrepresent voter participation for other reasons not under their immediate control (for example, people in the postelection period, attempting to comply with what they feel are socially acceptable standards of behavior, claim to have voted when they actually did not). Still, the *comparative* rates of turnout among different groups should reflect the proportionate levels of involvement and can be used to illustrate the tendencies.

The census results, as noted, reinforce the findings of numerous other studies: Socioeconomic factors are a major conditioner of voter participation[7]. The young, blacks, the least educated, the unemployed, blue collar workers, and some of the nationality groups (the newer ones and presumably those with the greatest cultural dislocations) are the people least likely to be part of the electorate. Table 2.1 presents these findings in detail. A Gallup poll of 1557 voting age adults in the mid-1970s attempted to establish why 62 percent of the electorate failed to take part in off-year elections. Forty-two percent of the nonvoters said they either did not register or, because of residency qualifications, could not register. Of the two next highest categories, 24 percent said they were discouraged by or not interested in politics and 13 percent volunteered that they did not like the choice of candidates. Although the reasons given by people about why they did not vote often elicit such ambiguous replies as "lack of political interest," these figures would indicate that those who do not vote are usually not registered. According to the Bureau of the Census, 62 percent of nonvoters are not registered. An intensive examination of registration practices and voter turnout in the 1960 presidential election in the nation's largest urban areas concluded that "registration requirements are a more effective deterrent to voting than anything that normally operates to deter citizens from voting once they have registered[8]." It may quite reasonably be assumed that disinterest in elections carries over to the more demanding act of registering.

If it truly is important that government policies and officeholders reflect the full range of community opinions for which they presume to speak, then it may be necessary for the government to assume a more aggressive role in simplifying the enrollment process. To achieve broader participation, the plethora of archaic registration qualifications must be codified and reduced to the minimum necessary for the conduct of orderly elections. Second, the government must insure that each individual experiences the minimal physical difficulty in enrolling to vote. Measures that accomplish these goals, especially the second, will be discussed in the following chapter. Some are already in effect in many states, although they receive little notice. Others may profitably be drawn from practices current in other democratic nations.

The extent to which generalizations remain true concerning the greater exclusion of the less well off from voting and enrolling is almost startling. The pattern is virtually flawless. Far fewer blacks than whites register or vote. The majority of Spanish-speaking people, who may face citizenship difficulties as well as language and cultural barriers, do not vote[9]. Between one-half and two-thirds of Mexican and "other" Latin groups are not registered and over 60 percent of both groups fail to vote. Puerto Ricans, who are U.S. citizens and should be familiar with democratic procedures, still number almost one-half (47 percent) of their group unenrolled and over one-half not voting. Forty percent of the unemployed

TABLE 2.1
SOCIOECONOMIC CHARACTERISTICS AND
NONREGISTRATION OF VOTERS, 1972 PRESIDENTIAL ELECTION[a]

Social Characteristic	% Not Voting	% Not Registered
Age		
18–20 years	51.7	41.9
21–24 years	49.3	40.5
25–29 years	42.2	33.9
30–34 years	38.1	28.8
35–44 years	33.7	25.2
45–54 years	29.1	20.7
55–64 years	29.3	19.8
65–74 years	31.9	21.5
75 years and over	44.4	29.3
Sex		
Male	35.9	26.9
Female	38.0	28.4
Race		
White	35.5	26.6
Black	47.9	34.5
Ethnic origin		
German	29.2	21.0
Italian	28.5	22.5
Irish	33.4	23.3
French	36.8	27.3
Polish	28.0	20.2
Russian	19.5	14.3
English, Scottish, Welsh	28.7	19.9
Spanish	62.5	55.6
(Mexican)	(62.5)	(54.0)
(Puerto Rican)	(55.4)	(47.3)
(Other Spanish)	(64.5)	(63.2)
Years in school		
Elementary:		
0–4	67.0	51.8
5–7	55.7	40.5
8	44.8	32.0
High school:		
1–3	48.0	37.0
4	34.6	26.0
College:		
1–3	25.1	18.3
4	17.7	12.9
5 or more	14.4	11.2

TABLE 2.1 *(Continued)*

Social Characteristic	% Not Voting	% Not Registered
Employment status		
Employed	34.0	25.7
Unemployed	50.1	41.3
Occupational grouping		
White collar workers	23.6	17.6
Blue collar workers	45.8	35.1
Service workers	41.4	31.8
Farm workers	36.4	24.0
Home ownership[b]		
Own home	16	NA[c]
Rent	44	NA

[a] These U.S. Census figures do not include military personnel or institutionalized populations.

[b] These totals are taken from the Gallup poll as reported in AVM Corporation, *The Tally Sheet* (Fall, 1971), p. 15.

[c] NA—Figures not available.

SOURCE: Bureau of the Census, Current Population Reports, Population Characteristics, *Voting and Registration in the Election of November 1972* (Washington, D.C.: U.S. Department of Commerce, October, 1973).

are not registered and 50 percent do not vote (compared with 26 percent and 34 percent, respectively, for those with jobs). A majority of the least educated (four or less years of formal education) are unenrolled and two-thirds do not exercise the franchise. Of those with four years of college, only 13 percent remain unregistered and only 18 percent fail to vote. White collar personnel register and vote on almost a 2 to 1 ratio over blue collar workers and on both counts do substantially better than service and farm workers. Figures added to the census tallies from a Gallup poll indicate that home owners are far more likely to enroll than those that rent. Sex appears to be unimportant, although age is not. Forty percent of the under 25 are not enrolled and one-half of this age category does not vote. The percentage decreases with each successive age classification until advanced age (65 and older) presents apparently insurmountable physical barriers to the use of the franchise. It is not until the 65 and older group that the incidence of nonvoting begins to approach the lower turnout figures for the 18- to 25-year-olds. Even for the older group, however, the relative numbers registered well exceed those for people at the other end of the age continuum.

PERSISTENCE IN
VOTING PATTERNS

Many of the social characteristics (excluding youth which is an independently serious problem) such as income, education, occupational status, race, and ethnic background complement and reinforce one another. Moreover, an inspection of the census figures for the presidential elections of 1964 and 1968, as well as 1972, on such variables as race, formal educational achievements, and age indicate a consistency in the types of people who vote or do not vote. There is, in short, a permanent "disenfranchised electorate"—a body of citizens badly underrepresented and relegated to a kind of permanent political limbo. The candidates, issues, and economic circumstances of a particular election do not account for the withdrawal of this group, which remains stable and persists through any given number of elections.

The off-year elections with their lower turnouts (see Figure 2.3 above) simply accentuate the trends already observed in presidential contests. The 13 percent that dropped out of the electorate in 1970 (compared with 1968) or the 18 percent in 1974 (compared with 1972) reemphasize the inequities among the groups represented. Again, the U.S. Census is helpful. Its report on the 1970 congressional election shows that twice as many high school graduates voted (66.3 percent) as those below this level of education (33.7 percent) and almost the same ratio prevailed among those employed (64.1 percent) compared with those outside of the civilian labor force (35.9 percent). The highest turnout was among the middle-aged and older voters (the 45 to 64 category), 64 percent of whom voted, and the lowest, a mirror image of the older group, was found among the young (the under 30 category), 65 percent of whom did not vote. Twenty-nine percent of those with family incomes over $15,000 failed to vote, a figure that climbs to 56 percent for those families earning less than $5000 annually. Blacks voted appreciably less than whites (44 percent to 56 percent respectively) despite the fact that blacks in large metropolitan areas increased their turnout from 1966 (the first year the census specifically reported on off-year registration and voting) to 1970 by 15 percentage points. The census concludes that voter turnout in the 1970 congressional elections was not atypical: "the voting patterns of various segments of the population maintain substantial similarity from one 'off-year' election to the next[10]."

The Bureau of the Census estimates that 78 percent of the electorate was consistent in its behavior (either continuing to vote or not to vote) in the 1968 and 1972 presidential elections. By its figures, three-quarters of the electorate voted in both elections and one-quarter in neither. Of the rather small 16 percent that voted in only one of the elections, 12 percent voted only in the first election. Forty-two people out of the 12% were unregistered (and therefore could not vote had they wanted to) and of these 8 percent were unable to register and another 6 percent could not meet residency tests. Fifteen percent (of the 42 percent unregistered) were "not interested" and the remaining 13 percent were distributed over categories too broad to interpret. Even among these few hardy souls, the familiar socioeconomic conditions, which correlate so well with both the unenrolled and the large classification of nonvoters, again are disproportionately associated with the dropouts from the one election to the next.

The groups at the lower end of the social scale are the least able to enter the political arena. Should they be included? More significantly, should a sustained effort be made to encourage their political participation? Most, presumably, would answer yes to such questions. If so, then what kinds of alternatives are available to help make voting a more inclusive and representative political act?

A MASS MEDIA,
MASS PARTICIPATION APPROACH

One answer, and the one repeatedly favored in American society, is to initiate some type of voluntary public relations program. This is largely a waste of effort, however; a superficial approach to a serious problem. It manages to avoid any prolonged investigation of the causes of nonparticipation and fails to provide fundamental correctives. Occasionally, under extraordinary circumstances, such an approach can succeed. Proponents are fond of pointing to one of the few notable successes of such a campaign. A civic rivalry between Wausau, Wisconsin, and Highland Park, Illinois, in 1956 resulted in the registering of 99 percent of the eligible voting age population. Whether a contest that mobilizes the full resources of two relatively small communities is representative of volunteerism is questionable. The long-range contribution of such a drive is also unclear. The example does serve to demonstrate, however, that the unenrolled can be registered.

More representative of the usual outcome is New York city's attempt in 1969 to encourage voter registration for a mayoral election through a newspaper, radio, and television campaign. Seventy thousand prospective voters were enrolled, a meager 3 percent of those unregistered. In all, only 35 percent of the eligible voting age population registered for the election.

The New York illustration represents the principal criticism of voluntary appeals. Despite often hard work and the good intentions of civic leaders, these campaigns produce minimal results. They may soothe the consciences of the sponsors and they do permit television and radio stations to carry innocuous public messages as mandated in their federally approved licenses, but the effect on the unregistered is negligible. Frequently, the civic appeals to vote come at the close of an enrollment period or even after registration has come to an end. For reasons to be discussed later, the campaigns do not reach the hard-core nonvoter and they make no effort to change the rules that could simplify and facilitate a wider registration. The advertisements are directed toward those most likely to participate anyway. They have no long-run effect of consequence.

Even if an individual public relations campaign produces results, the entire process has to be repeated for the next election. An effective voluntary program takes intricate planning, good organization, and a serious commitment by a large number of individuals. There should be little wonder that such a programmed approach arises only sporadically and is usually directed to selected audiences (labor union members, high SES districts by Republicans, low SES areas by Democrats). The turnover of voters between elections may be enormous. Murphy and Schneier make the point well: "No matter how thoroughly the job [registration] had been done before, it must be done again. Between 1972 and 1974, 8 million Americans turned 18. Almost 40 million eligible voters moved and must re-register. In every congressional district, there are . . . anywhere between 40,000 and 100,000 eligible voters who are not properly registered[11]."

PUBLIC INFORMATION CAMPAIGNS

George Bernard Shaw quotes Hegel to the effect that "we learn from history that we never learn from history." In another context it could be said that social science research has much to contribute to political understanding but is often ignored by those in a position to use it. At times, such ignorance may be all to the good; at other times, it is lamentable. Numerous well-documented studies have been done on why public information campaigns on civic issues (such as voting) tend to fail. The work is not new. In a summary of the research, Hyman and Sheatsley point out that these usually well-intentioned efforts do not take into account the psychological state or the relevant motivations of the audience they are presumably attempting to reach. Their study points out that there is a chronic group of "know-nothings" about whom there is something "*which makes them harder to reach, no matter what the level or nature of the information*[12]." Interested people acquire the most information. Those without interest screen it out. Add to this the fact that the campaigns on voting are periodic in nature, that they lack intense concentration on the target group of habitual nonvoters, and that they are general in content and tone, and at best one can expect them to reinforce those already most likely to vote (that is, those registered).

People seek information in accord with their prior attitudes. If there is no tradition of involvement in elections, spot announcements or newspaper editorials are not likely to attract the nonvoter's attention. Conversely, if such individuals could be made to vote, their receptivity might be heightened and they might then participate on a qualitatively higher plane (that is, with more information) and with greater frequency. In the words of Hyman and Sheatsley, "As people learn more, their interest increases, and as their interest increases, they are impelled to learn more[13]." The difficulty is in stimulating the initial interest. And to develop that interest so that it functions independently requires a restructuring of basic attitudes of long-standing duration. On its own, a public information campaign strategy is unlikely to do the job. In motivating people to vote, the attempt should be made not only to restructure an attitude but to change a behavior pattern. Such a demand is too much for a 30-second political commercial. And, of course, if the stimulus to act could be provided, individuals would still be faced with mastering a set of registration procedures foreign to their experience. In all, the highly publicized, public-spirited "get-out-the-vote" campaigns can expect limited results.

ADMINISTERING REGISTRATION LAWS

Recognizing the significance of registration in determining voter turnout and the increasing dissatisfaction with the haphazard maze of state and local qualifying procedures, the League of Women Voters (with funding from the Ford Foundation) conducted a study of registration laws and practices in 251 counties in the fall of 1971. The results were then compared with a sampling of practices in an additional 600 localities. The prime sample chosen encompassed the dwelling areas of 40 million people, one-fifth of the nation's population. No effort was made to select problem communities. On the contrary, the intent was to gain an accurate picture of registration and election practices in all manner of governmental situations. The results of the investigation are disquieting.

The league study *"documents the fact that the current system of registration and voting functions inefficiently for citizens throughout the United States.* [14]." (Italics in original.) Its report takes not of the reasons originally employed to justify registration systems and of the prospect in some areas of electoral fraud. It then adds: "It could be argued . . . that such abuses are a function of community mores and will exist in some communities no matter what election procedures are established. More noteworthy . . . is the fraud perpetuated on the American people by a system which excludes millions of eligible voters from the electoral process in the name of preventing a few dishonestly cast votes[15]."

The league then goes on to document its case in a manner not before attempted. State law usually requires registration offices to be clearly identified but does not say how. Fifty-two percent of the 300 places investigated were not clearly identified and 40 percent of the communities opened no additional registration offices even during peak periods. One-quarter of the places did not have convenient parking facilities and over one-half were not easily accessible by public transportation.

State law provides that registration lists be made available to the public but again does not specify in what manner. In over one-third of the cases, some type of official permission was needed to acquire the lists and over one-half of the localities charged for them. Three-quarters of the communities had no evening or Saturday registration and more than one-third provided for no additional hours during busy periods. Twenty-nine percent of the areas that legally authorized additional deputy registrars had none. Eighty-nine percent of the counties studied made available no voter information guide; over one-fourth required no training for poll workers; 30 percent in areas needing bilingual assistance provided none; one-half of the organizations securing voter lists and attempting to use them to enroll voters found the documents inaccurate and in one out of two cases the degree of error exceeded 10 percent; and 31 percent of the offices that permitted deputy registrars restricted the number and 10 percent even the amount of blank forms they would make available to prospective enrollers.

The league found that the county and local registrars do not use the statutory powers given them to reach and enroll citizens; that offices charged with administering election codes and overseeing registration count this as only one of many duties (and apparently one of less priority); and that state election officials "have little knowledge or control and exert practically no leadership over local election officials and the manner in which they administer the state election code[16]."

Local administrators apply in their own manner the standards within generally permissive state laws. "Long lines, short office hours, inaccessible registration and polling places, and registration periods remote from the date of election are common experiences to many Americans[17]." Furthermore, while representatives of voting rights groups see these as serious barriers to the franchise, election officials were, in the league's words, "generally insensitive to them[18]." Many election administrators "*illustrate an attitude . . . which tends to obstruct rather than encourage the efforts to expand the electorate*[19]." (Italics added.) These same public officials deny the need for change and many actively oppose it. This attitude persists despite the fact that league observers estimated that 3 out of every 100 people who actually showed up at a registration office left without enrolling because of time delays, mechanical breakdowns, and general administrative inefficiency. The wonder is not that there are so many people unregistered but "that so many citizens do vote."

Election laws are arbitrary and economically and socially discriminatory. The administration of these procedures is haphazard at best and at worst highly personalized and restrictive. Incremental changes directed at insensitive officials on the local level, such as those proposed in the 1963 report of the President's Commission on Registration and Voting Participation, are unlikely to improve matters[20]. One final statement from the League of Women Voter's telling report serves as an appropriate transition to an overview of procedures based less on negative assumptions and more successful in encouraging a fully representative electorate. The league concludes:

> Election officials seem to view the government as a passive participant in the electoral process with no responsibility for reaching out to citizens. They apparently believe that the initiative lies entirely with the citizen. . . . The issue clearly goes beyond the generally accepted explanation of voter apathy. Viewed from another perspective, the question arises that if the government can find a citizen to tax him or draft him into military service, is it not reasonable to assume that the government can find that same citizen to enroll him as an eligible voter and include him in the active electorate[21]?

AN EXPERIMENT
IN INCREASING PARTICIPATION:
THE VOTING RIGHTS ACTS

A belated concern with the effective disenfranchisement of blacks in the South began to surface in the 1950s. No southern state at this point had enfranchised as much as 40 percent of its voting age black population. The drive paralleled the broader problems encountered in the civil rights movement and resulted in some remarkable pieces of legislation. The most powerful manifestations of the new concern, the Voting Rights Act of 1965, the critical breakthrough in the struggle, demonstrates the effect on restrictive practices democratizing statutes can have when backed by a politically aware public opinion.

An innovative legislative era, which while losing the momentum of its success has yet to spend itself, began with the Civil Rights Act of 1957. This statute strengthened the role of the federal government in dealing with intimidation, threats, or coercion in abetting racial discrimination against voters in federal elections[22]. Justice Department attorneys were empowered to file suits for preventive relief to stop the discriminatory conduct of election officials. The act established a six-member Commission on Civil Rights as a fact-finding, quasi-judicial body to determine and draw to public attention the specific types of problems involved in the civil rights area. The attorney general, in addition, was authorized to appoint an assistant attorney general to head a civil rights division.

Three years later the Civil Rights Act of 1960 strengthened the hand of the Justice Department by declaring states to be legal entities and therefore subject to suits. This second act demanded that voter-turnout, registration, and poll tax documents must be preserved for 22 months and that they be sent to the attorney general upon request. More notable was the 1960 act's provision for the assignment of "voting referees" who could be appointed by the federal district courts to assume the duties of a registrar if it had been established to a court's satisfaction that the conduct of a given registrar had contributed to a consistent pattern of discrimination. If so, the court could also issue a consent decree to have the specific complainants listed on the registration rolls.

The 1964 Civil Rights Act, which followed Lyndon Johnson's assumption of the presidency, prevented local officials from applying criteria to some applicants that were not applied to others and outlawed the denial of registration for errors not relevant to the substantive qualifications. Another clause enabled those with proof of a sixth grade education to qualify under any literacy test a state might employ. The 1964 law attempted to expedite the adjudication of voting rights cases by allowing the attorney general to request the convening of a three-judge panel to hold a reasonably prompt hearing over any grievances. Delay proved to be the primary deterrent to the effective application of all three of the civil rights acts.

The legal principles supporting equality in voting were gradually hammered out, but the numbers of blacks exercising the franchise did not increase dramatically at first (Figure 2.4). The process continued to be painfully tedious despite the increasingly militant stance of the federal government. Several states did relatively well, North Carolina and Florida adding 23 and 19 percent respectively to their rolls to bring the total black voting population to about one-half (47 percent and 51 percent for each state) of those eligible. Virginia also increased black registration 19 percent but still counted only a little over one-third (38.3

FIGURE 2.4
PERCENTAGE OF BLACK
VOTING AGE POPULATION REGISTERED
IN NINE SOUTHERN STATES IN 1956, 1964, 1966, AND 1970

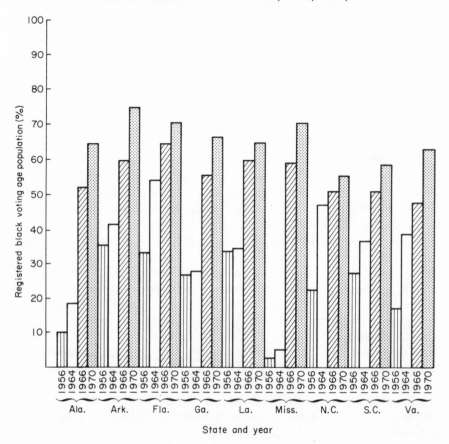

State and year

SOURCE: Data from U.S. Commission on Civil Rights.

percent) of the blacks as enrolled. Arkansas made only a 4 percent improvement in black registration; Alabama, 8 percent; South Carolina, 10 percent; Mississippi, 2 percent; and Georgia and Louisiana virtually none (4/10 and 6/10 of 1 percent respectively). The average increase for the nine states was, disappointingly, less than 9 percent, while the average number of blacks enrolled in the states remained low, one-third of the voting age population.

Then came the Voting Rights Act of 1965. The new legislation was a radical departure from its predecessors. The act stipulated that *no* test or device that had been administered unconstitutionally to deny or abridge voting rights could continue to be applied in *any* state or political subdivision thereof in which less than 50 percent (the "triggering clause") of the eligible voting age population had neither voted in the 1964 presidential election nor was registered to vote as of November 1, 1964. The suspension of registration limits was to run for five years. To avoid further stratagems to disenfranchise blacks, an all-too-familiar pattern in the 100-year-old fight over black voting rights, no state or subdivision so affected could implement any other test or device unless it could adequately establish before a three-judge panel of the U.S. District Court for the District of Columbia that such a test was not susceptible to abuse for the purpose of denying or abridging consitutionally protected voting rights. In addition, the Civil Service Commission could appoint (upon direction by the attorney general) examiners to those counties where local officials made impossible the registration of new voters. The examiners took over the responsibility of the local officials to enroll all applicants legally qualified to vote.

The act had an enormous impact. Literacy tests were eliminated in Alabama, Georgia, Louisiana, Mississippi, South Carolina, Virginia, and in 40 counties of North Carolina. Examiners were assigned originally to 41 counties in 1966 and over the next three years to 17 additional ones. In all but seven of these less than 10 percent of the black population had been registered in 1964. At least 62 other counties where less than one-tenth of the black population was registered did not receive examiners.

The Voting Rights Act of 1965 failed to establish specific numerical guidelines to determine when and where federal personnel should be substituted for local officials in enlisting prospective voters. The decision to assign examiners had to be in response to a "meritorious" complaint from at least 20 citizens. The application went to the attorney general's office, and if it was felt that the problem could not be resolved without outside intervention, federal enrollers would be dispatched to the county[23]. The procedure was novel and it was used with discretion, but it worked impressively in the states that received federal officials. The federal examiners enrolled 150,000 blacks (and 7000 whites) in the five deep southern states within the first three years of its enactment. Sixty-four percent of the increase in black enrollment was accounted for by federally sponsored officials (compared to less than 4 percent of the new white registrants). Still, and lest the new legislation be thought of as some form of reverse discrimination, three-quarters of the eligible white population was registered two years after the act was passed compared to 57 percent of the enrollable blacks—a marked improvement, nevertheless, for blacks over the pre-act period (Table 2.2). Mississippi and Alabama increased their black registrants to one-half (from 7 percent) and one-third (from 19 percent) of the enrollable population, respectively, and for all the states affected, black enrollees numbered more than one-half of the eligible population to a high of almost three out of four in Tennessee. By 1970, with the Voting Rights Act extended for another five-year period, white registration in the 11 southern states had risen to 83 percent and black registration to 66 percent.

TABLE 2.2
REGISTRATION IN 11 SOUTHERN STATES PRIOR TO AND AFTER ENACTMENT OF THE VOTING RIGHTS ACT OF 1965 (1967)

| State | Voting Age Population[a] | | % Registered | | | | % Change | |
	White	Black	Pre-Act White	Pre-Act Black	Post-Act White	Post-Act Black	White	Black
Alabama	1,353,122	481,220	69.2	19.3	89.6	57.6	+20.4	+32.3
Arkansas	848,393	192,629	65.5	40.4	72.4	62.8	+ 6.9	+22.8
Florida	2,617,438	470,261	74.8	51.2	81.4	63.6	+ 6.6	+12.4
Georgia	1,796,963	612,875	62.6	27.4	80.3	52.6	+17.7	+25.2
Louisiana	1,289,216	514,589	80.5	31.6	93.1	58.9	+12.6	+27.3
Mississippi	751,266	422,273	69.9	6.7	91.5	59.8	+21.6	+53.1
North Carolina	2,005,955	550,929	96.8	46.8	83.0	51.3	−13.8	+ 4.5
South Carolina	895,147	371,104	75.7	37.3	81.7	51.2	+ 6.0	+13.9
Tennessee	1,779,018	313,873	72.9	69.5	80.6	71.7	+ 7.7	+ 2.2
Texas	4,884,765	649,512	NA[b]	NA[b]	53.3	61.6	NA[b]	NA[b]
Virginia	1,876,167	436,718	61.6	38.3	63.4	55.6	+ 2.3	+17.3
	20,097,450	5,015,933	73.4[c]	35.5[c]	76.5	57.2	+ 8.8[c]	+21.1[c]

[a] Voting age population is for 1960.
[b] NA—Figures not available.
[c] The figure is for 10 states (Texas is excluded because of the absence of base data prior to the Voting Rights Act's passage).
SOURCE: U.S. Commission on Civil Rights, *Political Participation* (Washington, D.C.: U.S. Government Printing Office, 1968), table 1, pp. 222–23.

A comparison with the counties in the same states that did not receive federal officials provides a useful measure of the legislation's effectiveness (Table 2.3). Discriminatory qualifications in these counties also, of course, were suspended. The black population in the counties not monitored by federal officials (37 percent on the average) was considerably below that in the counties that received examiners (54 percent on the average) and the percentage of black registrants before enactment of the Voting Rights Act, not surprisingly, was almost three times that of the first group of counties, ranging between one-twentieth to over one-third of those eligible. In the post-act period, white enrollment figures, already high were to jump to over 80 percent in both categories of states (and in six instances exceeded 90 percent of the voting age population). The threat of an increasing black vote spurred a white registration effort. Black enrollments in the nonexaminer counties went up 26 percentage points, a noticeable improvement but one-half that found in the counties under direct federal supervision. Over one-half of the eligible blacks were enrolled in counties without national officials, a respectable showing, but as with the blacks in the first category, still significantly below the white totals.

The success of the Voting Rights Act of 1965 as an instrument to forge a more inclusive electorate cannot be denied. For the 11 southern states as a whole, the total proportion of whites enrolled changed little, stabilizing at about three out of four of those eligible. These figures, however, hide some decisive changes within individual states. An average increase of nine percentage points was recorded by 10 of the 11 states for which comparable information is available. Whites increased their enrollment between 13 and 21 percentage points in four deep southern states (Alabama, Georgia, Louisiana, and Mississippi), and in one state (North Carolina) the white registration actually dropped by over 13 points, apparently from an updating of inaccurate rolls.

Black registration increased by 21 percent with the most notable gains, as expected, in the deep southern states (see Table 2.2). Blacks in Mississippi, in the short period of three years, had become a significant part of the voting electorate for the first time since registration laws were permitted as a device to eliminate black electoral participation in the 1890s. The Mississippi case is dramatic testimony to the legislation's effectiveness. Despite three major civil rights bills in the preceding eight years, black enrollments had not changed appreciably. Less than 10 percent of the number of eligible blacks in Mississippi had been enrolled. The Civil Rights Commission reported in early 1968, however, that the proportion had risen to almost 60 percent and by 1970 when the Voting Rights Act of that year took effect (a modified version of its predecessor), two-thirds of the black population in Mississippi was registered[24]. It is not too much to say that the Voting Rights Act of 1965 made democratic participation for blacks in Mississippi and in numerous other places a reality. As a consequence, the politics of the South, and of the nation, was irretrievably changed.

TABLE 2.3
REGISTRATION IN COUNTIES IN FIVE DEEP SOUTHERN STATES
PRIOR TO AND AFTER ENACTMENT OF THE 1965 VOTING RIGHTS ACT

Registration in Counties That Received Federal Examiners

| State | Voting Age Population[a] | | % Registered | | | | % Change | |
| | White | Black | Pre-Act | | Post-Act | | White | Black |
			White	Black	White	Black		
Alabama	374,866	214,804	57.3	14.8	87.2	59.3	+29.9	+44.5
Georgia	9,022	9,581	85.1	10.3	100+(sic)	62.8	+14.9(+)	+52.5
Louisiana	183,012	94,621	70.4	9.4	79.3	53.5	+ 8.9	+44.1
Mississippi	284,469	136,739	83.7	8.1	90.8	70.9	+ 7.1	+62.8
South Carolina	12,344	13,105	100+(sic)	17.3	100+(sic)	71.6	0.0	+54.3
	863,713	468,850	67.2	11.3	83.4	61.4	15.2[b]	51.6

Registration in Counties That Did Not Receive Federal Examiners

| State | Voting Age Population[a] | | % Registered | | | | | |
| | White | Black | Pre-Act | | Post-Act | | % Change | |
			White	Black	White	Black	White	Black
Alabama	978,246	266,416	73.7	22.9	94.0	45.4	+20.3	+22.5
Georgia	1,787,941	603,294	62.5	27.6	80.2	52.5	+17.7	+24.9
Louisiana	1,106,204	419,968	82.0	37.1	95.4	60.2	+13.4	+23.1
Mississippi	466,797	285,534	76.7	4.5	93.5	50.3	+16.8	+45.8
South Carolina	882,803	357,999	75.4	38.1	81.2	50.5	+ 5.8	+12.4
	5,221,991	1,933,211	71.9	30.2	87.4	52.5	+14.8	+25.7

[a]Voting age population is for 1960. The sources for the various figures can be found in the U.S. Civil Rights Commission's *Political Participation* (Washington, D.C.: U.S. Government Printing Office, 1968), pp. 222–25.

[b]Average includes only those four states where change was possible.

SOURCE: U.S. Commission on Civil Rights, *Political Participation* (Washington, D.C.: U.S. Government Printing Office, 1965), tables 2 and 3, pp. 222–25.

THE POST-1970 PERIOD

The federal examiner program came to an abrupt end with the accession of a Republican to the presidency in 1969. In fact, and with good reason, it was feared that the 1965 act which was due to expire in 1970 would be left to die. The Nixon Administration did not favor its retention and, at a minimum, hoped to weaken its more forceful provisions. Congressional sentiment for continuing the legislation was strong, and after a period of public debate and legislative-executive branch negotiations, a series of acceptable compromises was struck. The power to include new registration qualifications in their laws was returned to the states. A state no longer had to seek the approval of a three-judge federal panel for changes in its procedures of administering elections, although these modifications still had to be submitted to the attorney general's office, which if so disposed could file suit to suspend its provision. The process could be a long one, which meant that the provision applied in the interim while the administration and then conceivably the courts debated its merits. Not surprisingly, the attorney general's office under John Mitchell did not seek to bring challenges. Still, blacks were voting in increasingly greater numbers in southern states where the emphasis was changing from a politics of racial exclusion in many areas to one in which candidates attempted to build cross-racial, often "populist" coalitions. Under such conditions, extensive backtracking on voter registration—which would have had to confront an increasingly aggressive Court stand against all such requirements—was unlikely.

Other parts of the 1970 act improved upon the 1965 legislation. All literacy tests were voided and the federal examiner program was extended to include *any state or electoral division* in which less than 50 percent of the voting age population was either unenrolled or did not participate in the 1968 or 1972 presidential elections (a strategy originally intended to anger northern representatives into voting against the bill). Actually, federal examiners were to be used in a locality only under the most extreme of provocations. Finally, a significant new step toward an open electorate was taken with the ban on all durational residency requirements that exceeded 30 days. The states were also prohibited from closing their enrollment period more than 30 days before the presidential election.

The major application of the new bill—at least the most publicized one—was to be in a northern city, New York. The registration totals for certain Puerto Rican and black sections of Brooklyn, the Bronx, and Manhattan were so low that the turnout in the 1972 election fell below 50 percent of the eligible voting age populations. Less than 35 percent of those eligible were registered in a band of electoral districts that ran across the north-central sections of Brooklyn where the black population was concentrated. Similarly low percentages were found in the Spanish-speaking neighborhoods of the South Bronx as well as Harlem and East Harlem. Virtually all of the areas having 90 percent or more white residents were found to have at least 65 percent of their voting age populations enrolled[25].

CONCLUSION

Just possibly a national system of equitable, minimal registration qualifications and, although this is more uncertain, an evolution toward a facilitative administrative process for enrolling those eligible to vote may be in prospect. A precedent at least has been set through the enactment and application of several remarkable pieces of legislation. These statutes, along with the increasingly sympathetic position of the federal courts, have had an enormous impact on voting patterns in various states and, almost of equal importance, on the thinking relating to an area which until recent years was of little public knowledge or concern. A climate receptive to fundamental change in the assumptions underlying enrollment processes as well as in the maze of procedures themselves may be in the offing. The question is—beyond the dramatic voting rights legislation authorizing direct intervention in cases of clear discrimination—what types of alternative systems provide the best opportunity for the maximum number of people to participate in elections with the minimum amount of difficulty? The innovations employed in many of the states and the systems currently operating in other democratic nations may provide some guidance. It is to these we now turn.

NOTES

1. George D. Luetscher, *Early Political Machinery in the United States* (New York: Da Capo, [1930] 1971), p. 25.
2. There is an increasing literature on the evolution of voter turnout and the factors that serve to increase or depress it. See Walter Dean Burnham, "Theory and Voting Research: Some Reflections on Converse's 'Change in the American Electorate,' " *American Political Science Review* 68 (September, 1974): 1002–23 and the "Comments" and "Rejoinder" by Philip E. Converse, Jerrold G. Rusk, and Burnham, pp. 1024–57 in the same journal; Burnham, "The Changing Shape of the American Political Universe," *American Political Science Review* 59 (March, 1965): 7–28; Burnham, *Critical Elections and the Mainsprings of American Politics* (New York: Norton, 1970); Converse, "Change in the American Electorate," in *The Human Meaning of Social Change,* eds. Angus Campbell and Philip E. Converse (New York: Russell Sage Foundation, 1972), pp. 263–337; Jesse F. Marquette, "Social Change and Political Mobilization in the United States: 1870–1960," *American Political Science Review* 68 (September, 1974): 1058–74; Jerrold G. Rusk, "The Effect of the Australian Ballot Reform on Split Ticket Voting: 1876–1908," *American Political Science Review* 64 (December, 1970): 1220–38; and Stanley Kelley, Jr., Richard E. Ayres, and William G. Bowen, "Registration and Voting: Putting First Things First," *American Political Science Review* 61 (June, 1967): 359–79.
3. Freedom To Vote Task Force, *That All May Vote* (Washington, D.C.: Democratic National Committee, 1970), app. VII.
4. On the effects of such provisions, see William G. Andrews, "American Voting Participation," *Western Political Quarterly* 19 (December, 1966): 639–52; Michael

W. Traugott, "The Electoral Context and Voter Turnout in the 1968 Election" (Paper prepared for delivery at the Annual Meeting of the Midwest Political Science Association, Chicago, Ill., May 3–5, 1973); Warren E. Miller, "Assessment of Significance of State Laws Governing Citizen Participation in Elections," (Washington, D.C.: A Report to the President's Commission on Registration and Voter Participation, 1963); W. Ross Yates, "The Function of Residence Requirements for Voting," *Western Political Quarterly* 15 (September, 1962): 469–88; and, of course, the periodic reports issued by the Bureau of the Census and the U.S. Commission on Civil Rights.

5. See Lester W. Milbrath, *Political Participation* (Chicago: Rand McNally, 1965); Don R. Bowen, *Political Behavior of the American Public* (Columbus, Ohio: Merrill, 1968); Sydney Verba and Norman H. Nie, *Participation in America* (New York: Harper & Row, 1972); and Angus Campbell, Philip E. Converse, Warren E. Miller, and Donald E. Stokes, *The American Voter* (New York: Wiley, 1960).

6. Aspects of the problem are discussed in U.S. Senate Committee on the Judiciary, *Voting Rights: Part I* (Washington, D.C.: U.S. Government Printing Office, 1965), p. 499.

7. This finding was emphasized in the earlier voting studies in particular. See Paul F. Lazarsfeld, Bernard Berelson, and Hazel Gaudet, *The People's Choice* (New York: Duell, Sloan and Pearce, 1944); and Berelson, Lazarsfeld, and William N. McPhee, *Voting* (Chicago: University of Chicago Press, 1954). Consult also the citations listed in note 5.

8. Kelley et al., "Registration and Voting," p. 362. Andrews, "American Voting Participation," has done the most thorough examination of the effects of registration qualifications and procedural barriers on the presidential vote (in 1960). He concludes that 14.85 million were legally excluded and another 8.6 million were illegally or indirectly excluded (those ill, traveling, in the military service, intimidated blacks, and those who did not vote because of religious preference). Allowing for a 1.5 million overlap in categories, this means that 21.95 million were excluded from the electorate in one way or another. When the total is reduced from the 107 million estimated voting age population, Andrews concludes that the 1960 voter turnout was in the vicinity of 83 percent, a figure obviously much higher than the 63 percent or so usually estimated to be the vote. If Andrews's figures can be reworked a little to eliminate nonrelevant cases, roughly 57 percent of the nonvoters can be attributed to poor registration or absentee voting procedures.

9. Marcellino Miyares, "Models of Political Participation of Hispanic Americans" (Ph.D. dissertation, Northwestern University, 1974).

10. Bureau of the Census, *Voting and Registration in the Election of November 1970* (Washington, D.C.: U.S. Government Printing Office, December, 1971), series P-20, no. 228, p. 5.

11. William T. Murphy, Jr., and Edward Shneier, *Vote Power* (Garden City, N.Y.: Doubleday Anchor, 1974), p. 107.

12. Herbert H. Hyman and Paul B. Sheatsley, "Some Reasons Why Information Campaigns Fail," in *Public Opinion and Propaganda*, eds. Daniel Katz, Dorwin Cartwright, Samuel Eldersveld, and Alfred McClung Lee (New York: Holt, Rinehart and Winston, 1954), p. 523 (pp. 522–31). This study does not deal specifically with voter information campaigns, but its conclusions should be applicable to these.

13. Ibid., p. 526.
14. League of Women Voters Education Fund, *Obstacles to Voting* (Washington, D.C.: The League of Women Voters, 1972), p. 4.
15. Ibid., p. 5.
16. Ibid., p. 8.
17. Ibid., p. 11.
18. Ibid.
19. Ibid., p. 15.
20. See *Report of the President's Commission on Registration and Voting Participation* (Washington, D.C.: U.S. Government Printing Office, November, 1963).
21. League of Women Voters Education Fund, *Obstacles to Voting,* p. 11. The immense documentation behind the report is both impressive and persuasive. The league's project (in conjunction with another conducted by the National Municipal League on broadly related questions concerning registration) is one of the largest and best executed concerning registration problems.
22. These provisions and their legal ramifications are discussed in detail in Richard Claude, *The Supreme Court and the Electoral Process* (Baltimore, Johns Hopkins Press, 1970), pp. 108–43.
23. U.S. Commission on Civil Rights, *Political Participation* (Washington, D.C.: U.S. Government Printing Office, May, 1968), pp. 212–13.
24. Voter Education Project, Southern Region Council, "Voter Registration in the South, Spring-Summer, 1970" (Atlanta: Southern Regional Council, August, 1970). For a look at Mississippi in the post-act period, see F. Glenn Abney, "Factors Related to Negro Voter Turnout in Mississippi," *Journal of Politics* 36 (November, 1974): pp. 1057–63.
25. See, for example, Steven R. Weisman, "NYC, Mississippi: Surprising Pair," *New York Times,* January 13, 1974, p. E–4.

3

Registration
Systems: Some
Alternative Ways

There are many variations of answer to what is essentially a core problem for a democratic country: how to identify members of the electorate and certify them to vote in such a manner that both a representatively broad electorate is achieved and the integrity of the electoral process is maintained. Each nation has addressed the problem in a different manner. From a distance, some of the *results* attract attention. Since the outcomes are impressive—at times, 90 percent or better of the eligible population voting—the procedures that lead to high rates of participation elsewhere are held up persuasively as potential models for adoption in the United States.

All is not necessarily what it seems, however. When the United States averaged turnouts of 75 to 90 percent in the nineteenth century, the qualified electorate in some cases was restricted to as little as one-tenth of the adult population, and in others widespread corruption helped contribute to inflated turnout figures.

Registration systems evolve within countries in response to national traditions. Some procedures developed in other countries are not compatible with American democratic values and in some instances may actually include dangerous practices. Other enrollment processes, conversely, may include welcome features, many (as will be shown) not entirely foreign to the American experience at the state and community levels. This chapter will review selected examples of registration practices in other nations and in several states and then focus attention on the most promising of these.

ENROLLING PROCEDURES
IN OTHER NATIONS

Voter turnout in other democracies regularly exceeds that of the United States by significant margins[1]. The National Municipal League in a report published in 1973 estimated average turnout for parliamentary elections during the post–World War II period in France and Great Britain to be 80 percent, West

Germany 86 percent, Austria 95 percent, and Canada 76 percent[2]. In a study published three years earlier, the participation figures for six other democratic nations during the period 1965 to 1969 ranged between a low of 75 percent (Ireland) to a high of just under 90 percent (89.3 percent for both Denmark and Sweden) with an average turnout of 85 percent[3].

Some argue that these nations with their more liberalized election procedures and proven records of success might present a model from which the United States could profit. It is true that a selective borrowing of some features (many of which are already developed on a more limited basis in a number of states) of other systems might benefit American turnout. It is also quite likely that other aspects of the systems (a mandatory vote with minor legal penalties for nonvoting; enrollment lists administered by police authorities) should be avoided as incompatible with a democratic system based on free will and individual discretion. The electoral practices current in any one nation reflect different territorial problems, statutory demands, party systems (the multiparty as against the two-party, for example), and national traditions. All unite to condition a given country's performance of its democratic functions. If an open mind can be combined with a degree of caution then a review of some enrollment practices should prove useful.

SWITZERLAND   For some, the Swiss epitomize a democratic citizenry. Their reputation is based largely on their propensity to place virtually all major issues before the voters in plebiscite form. A Swiss voter can thus go to the polls four to five times a year. Such a democratic emphasis has its cost. Consistent interest in elections and a high turnout are difficult to maintain. Participation rates vary (the vote is not compulsory in many cantons) between 40 and 50 percent on referenda-type issues and near 60 percent for elections to office (overall between 1945 and 1966 it averaged 51 percent). Polls are kept open weekends and voters can deposit ballots—sent to them through the mail along with election information—in any of a series of places on election day. Each canton has its own enrolling practices, although the similarities among them are strong. Zurich requires registration within eight days of moving to the area on penalty of a fine. "Citizenship" is defined in terms of locality so that new residents must have both their identity papers reissued by local authorities and wait two years before qualifying for the franchise. Foreigners must remain for 12 years before they are accepted as voters. Applications are checked against a file kept in a person's former place of residence to insure a respectable past record. The Swiss passion for order, similar to that of the Germans and other nationalities, results in a penchant for national registrations for assorted civic obligations, although in the case of voting, citizens have the right to check their records two weeks before an election. Few, of course, do.

ITALY   Italian politics are tempestuous with a high turnover rate among prime ministers and with frequent elections. The party system ranges from strongly communist to conservative Catholic with smatterings of monarchists and fascists. The central government is not considered strong or stable. In such a volatile climate, a registration system could prove to be a sensitive point in the struggle for electoral supremacy. Actually, enrolling practices are fairly simple and conscientiously executed by a committee elected by all members of the local governing council and presided over by the mayor (who has no vote in its proceedings). Electoral lists are permanent and are updated twice annually. Unlike American rolls, they contain personal information on an individual's social standing (marital status, educational degrees, profession) as well as certifying the person as a voter. Registration qualifications are minimal—citizenship, residency in the commune, and no evidence of criminal convictions or mental incapacity. All persons reaching the necessary age (18 now for most elections, 25 for senatorial elections) are automatically included in the electorate. Anyone excluded from the franchise must be notified personally by the mayor at least 10 days before an election and all registration documentation concerning individuals is readily available to the public. While voting is not mandatory, it is considered a civic trust and, not surprisingly given the enrollment procedures, turnout is high, averaging over 90 percent (92.1 percent) between 1946 and 1968.

WEST GERMANY The German Federal Republic automatically enrolls anyone who reaches the age of 21 who is both a resident and a citizen. However, should registrants move they are required under penalty of fine to inform in writing officials of the city they are leaving and those of the city to which they are transferring. Copies of this form, filled out in triplicate, are sent to the registration office, the election center, and the police. Citizens notified that they have been excluded from the election rolls can appeal.

AUSTRIA With a mean voter participation rate of 96 percent between 1951 and 1965, Austria stands at or very near the pinnacle of this aspect of democratic performance. The country's constitutional provisions on enrollment explain why. A 1929 amendment to the constitution (suspended by the turmoil of the 1930s and the German occupation from 1938 to 1945 but in effect after 1945) confers the vote on all citizens at least 19 years of age and mandates that only federal law can provide the exceptions to nonparticipation. Residents must file the appropriate forms with the local authorities. Their names are then placed on the election lists which are revised annually. A failure to report a change of address is punishable by fine or two weeks imprisonment.

FRANCE The French system has some attributes of the Italian. An administrative commission composed of the mayor, one delegate appointed by the prefect, and another by the municipal council revises the enrollment lists annually. Any appeals of its decisions go to a committee consisting of the original commission plus two additional municipal councilmen. All residents qualify for enrollment who are 21 years of age or who have lived in the commune for six months or who have been on a list to pay direct taxes for five years (even if they no longer reside in the district). France being France adds a few novel provisions. Anyone at least 18 years old who holds the Légion d'honneur, the Médaille Militaire, or the Croix de Guerre automatically qualifies for the vote.

SWEDEN   Ninety-nine percent of the Swedes are registered and again the highly centralized enrollment system is the key. A National Tax Board retains authority for population registration, taxation, and the conduct of elections. In turn, the country's 24 counties and the city of Stockholm keep computerized files on individuals which the government uses for, among other things, generating voting lists. Individuals who move (or immigrants) by law must notify authorities in their locality within 14 days or be subject to fine. The 25,000 parishes of the Lutheran State Church function as an adjunct of the state by registering and reporting to the government births, deaths, marriages, and population moves. The system·is so efficient that the centralized county files on individuals are updated *weekly* and, without difficulty, a person's file can be transferred expeditiously to a new jurisdiction. Lists are printed annually, although, except for special referenda or vacated seats, the Swedes vote every three years. Individuals can cast a ballot either at their normal polling place or at the post office. Special cards identifying voters as well as information on polling hours and the election are sent to all eligible citizens. In their quest for precision, Swedish authorities also send those ineligible to vote a prevention card that notifies them of their status and the reasons for it. Ill or disabled persons can vote through the equivalent of an American absentee ballot if two people will attest to their incapacity at the time their vote is cast.

GREAT BRITAIN   The British have had annual registration since 1872. The system, while under the general authority of the Home Office, is far more decentralized than the Swedish and allows for individual discretion in the means used to register potential voters. It also is quite successful; 93 percent of the eligible voting age population is believed enrolled. A town clerk who knows the area is appointed by the local governing council and has the responsibility for drawing up the voter lists. He insures that a registration form is delivered (by mail or in person) to every household. Those not returning the original form receive another through the mail or in a door-to-door canvass and a warning that failure to comply can result in a fine as well as disenfranchisement. The process begins in August or September. In October, the form clerk begins to prepare the revised list which is published by late November. A short period of a little over two weeks is allowed for formal appeals—if serious enough these are adjudicated through a hearing, although an unsatisfactory decision can be taken by an individual to the courts. The final, amended voter lists are published by mid-February, and the process begins again in late summer.

BELGIUM The registration system in Belgium (similar to that in Luxembourg, Liechtenstein, and other places) is noteworthy for the "obligatory" vote provisions found in its (at least in the case of Belgium) constitution and (again for Belgium) the social and legal pressures exerted to enforce participation. A list is made of those who do *not* vote in Belgium in the eight days after an election by the police superintendent under supervision of the justice of the peace. The reasons for not participating are submitted by individuals to the justice of the peace who in consultation with the police superintendent or the state's attorney can accept them or penalize the nonvoters by a reprimand or a minimal fine (one to three francs) for the first failure; a fine of between 3 and 10 francs for the second offense in a six-year period; the inclusion of the persons' names on a list to be posted outside the city hall for a third failure to vote in a 10-year period; and, should individuals neglect their public duty for an unexcused fourth time in a 15-year span, their names are again posted outside the city hall, they are removed from all enrollment lists, and they are denied the vote for 10 years, during which decade of ostracism they can not receive any appointment, promotion, or award of distinction from any government agency.

CANADA The Canadian system bears serious consideration[4]. Their enrollment practices are considerably more thorough than the American procedures and at least as fraud-free. The problems that election officials face are, if anything, more formidable than those of their American neighbors. A relatively small population in many areas is scattered over a vast geographical expanse. And the basic ideas in Canadian enrollment have been long used in a number of states and localities in the United States.

In Canada, a chief electoral officer responsible to the parliament is appointed to supervise elections. In turn, a "Returning Officer" is appointed to oversee the federal elections in each of the 264 parliamentary districts. Each parliamentary district (akin to congressional districts in the United States) is subdivided into polling districts with an average of 250 voters per district. The procedures in urban districts (those with greater than 5000 population) diverge from and are somewhat more elaborate than those followed in rural districts. Two "enumerators" are appointed for each polling district, one by each of the candidates who received the highest number of votes in the district's previous parliamentary election. The enumerators receive a modest base pay plus 11¢ for every name on the registration lists. In the seventh week before the election, the enumerators (acting as a team) begin a week's door-to-door canvass to register each eligible voter (basically those 18 years of age and holding Canadian citizenship). If no one is at home, the enumerators leave a card giving a telephone number where they can be reached and/or the date of their next canvass. In the sixth week, the enumerators present their lists to the returning officer, who compiles a complete enrollment for the district and by the fourth week has printed copies made available to the political parties and the voters. These forms also contain information about how challenges to the list will be heard or revisions in them can be made.

To make revisions, the returning officer takes a number of the small polling districts and regroups them into somewhat larger units (revisal districts) and then appoints two "revisal officers" who hear challenges in the second half of the third week prior to the voting (and, at times, at the beginning of the second week of the preelection period). The time and place of these revision hearings are publicized through the media and revising officials also go door-to-door to check the accuracy of the lists, to include any people arbitrarily omitted, or to protect against fraud. The "revising officials" then make whatever corrections or modifications that are justified and these are then added to the original enrollment lists. These changes are published and are available to polling officials on election day.

The procedures employed in rural districts are close to those used in the urban districts but a little less elaborate. There is only one enumerator and a county court judge serves as the revising officer in deciding the changes needed. Nine of the ten provinces (British Columbia is the exception) also employ the door-to-door canvass in their provincial elections, a system patterned after national enrollment procedures. Significantly, the voting lists are used for one election (to serve the purpose of identifying the eligible electorate and preventing fraud) and *are then destroyed.* The process begins again when a new election is to be held. There is *no* centralized national file made from the information obtained from the canvasses and stored in a computerized national bank, a practice that is offensive to many civil libertarians and one that is open to substantial abuse. The Canadian system is not as complex as this rendering might make it appear. Its chief weakness appears to be a failure to provide for absentee voting, a minor problem susceptible to easy correction.

Walter Dean Burnham, a political scientist and a prominent student of American voting behavior, speaks of "the enormous decentralization of election administration and ... the absence in many key areas of uniformity in electoral laws[5]." Burnham believes that "one of the striking peculiarities of American electoral laws [is] that they have so rarely been discussed in comparative terms, or that any alternative seems ever to have been seriously considered—either by scholars or by legislators—to the personal registration requirement[6]." This omission is all the more odd when two additional propositions are entertained. First, and again it is Burnham who speaks, that "all but one of the Western nations which conduct open elections provide in one form or another that bureaucratic instrumentalities of the state assume the legal and operational responsibility for compiling and updating electoral registers. The exception is the United States[7]." Second, that "one of the most important changes in political consciousness which has occurred in this generation is the widespread recognition that, in a Lockean political universe of atomic individuals who enjoy equality of opportunity, some individuals are far more equal than others[8]."

Burnham's observations are well taken. There is much to learn from enrolling practices in other nations, although, as this brief survey has shown, some that look attractive are incompatible with basic American freedoms. The lesson is to borrow what furthers a democratic concern with a representative electorate and to avoid those methods which while equally effective could lead to unfortunate consequences. A considerable amount of discretion is advisable in the aftermath of Watergate. Finally, some of the best features of the enrolling systems reviewed —and Canadian procedures rank high in this regard—are not as "foreign" as the unfamiliar titles might make them appear. Many states have developed similar approaches on their own with generally encouraging results.

PRACTICES IN THE STATES

Perhaps the most striking observation concerning voter turnout is the extraordinary divergence among the states in the levels of participation (Table 3.1). Some states enjoy very high levels of participation, others quite low. And the patterns observed in any one election tend to be consistent for the majority of the states over time. If one goes back to any specific national election in the last 40 years or so, the same groupings of states usually do extraordinarily well or very poorly. The states that fall at the lowest end of the continuum for the period 1952 to 1972 as shown in Table 3.1 require no extended discussion. They are without exception southern states with all the problems of electoral participation touched on earlier. Of greater interest are the states ranking highest in voter participation for the two decades.

TABLE 3.1
MEAN VOTER TURNOUT
FOR THE HIGHEST AND LOWEST DECILES
OF STATES FOR PRESIDENTIAL ELECTIONS, 1952–1972[a]

High Participation States		Low Participation States Ranked in Order of Poorest Performance	
State	% Turnout	State	% Turnout
Utah	77.2	Mississippi	33.5
Idaho	74.6	South Carolina	35.0
South Dakota	72.1	Alabama	35.8
New Hampshire	73.4	Georgia	36.15
Connecticut	73.25	Virginia	39.1
West Virginia	73.0	Texas	44.1
Minnesota	72.5	Arkansas	44.7
Iowa	72.4	Louisiana	44.8
North Dakota	72.1	Tennessee	48.2
Indiana	72.0	North Carolina	50.4
Delaware	71.8	Florida	50.45

[a] Turnout is based on eligible voting age population.

Undoubtedly, the socioeconomic conditions, two-party competitiveness, the quality of the candidates put forth by the parties, an area's sense of civic duty (apparently very strong, for example, among Mormons in Utah and Idaho), and a state's political traditions all serve to reinforce a belief in the importance of voting. Of some significance also are the electoral procedures that serve to facilitate or prohibit extensive participation. Many states have pioneered in the use of simplified voting practices, although their efforts have received little national attention.

South Carolina, for example, has a modernized system of centralizing voter enrollment through computerized lists[9]. The process is well managed and provides accurate, inexpensive registration lists to local officials as needed. Many other localities have systems that approach South Carolina's (or possibly even surpass it) in efficiency and workability. There are problems with using such an approach, however. The registers, much like commercial subscription lists, may be made available to political parties or candidates, which some voters feel infringes on their right to privacy[10]; in states with income taxes, they may be used to verify tax return information, a process many fear and consequently will go to lengths to avoid; they may invite government inspection and potential abuse (retribution against individuals enrolled in one party seeking government contracts or aid—it is hoped this would be rare but it is not beyond possibility); or they may be sold to commercial businesses seeking expanded mailing lists. The last possibility may be justified in an effort to recoup some of the costs of the registration system[11].

The state of Oregon admirably illustrates the willingness of the former frontier areas to experiment with new forms designed to expand democratic participation. As the nation stretched beyond the tradition-encrusted East from Tennessee, Kentucky, and Ohio in the early days through the Plains states to the Far West, a radical democratic spirit prevailed that has come down to the present day. Oregon ranks high in both simplified qualifications for registration (among the most lenient in the nation) and procedures for actually identifying and enrolling prospective voters—the latter possibly the more serious of contemporary problems. Although state election officials profess disappointment at their "poor" showing, over 80 percent of the eligible voting age population is registered and the turnout approaches 70 percent of the potential vote. The difficulty in Oregon, as elsewhere, is in enrolling those groups which chronically remain outside the electorate: 84 percent of those with annual incomes over $15,000 are registered compared to 53 percent of those with incomes below $3000. Oregon provides no exception to the pattern[12].

As the Oregon secretary of state told a congressional committee, his state believes that registration opportunities should be "easily accessible" and the format "simple." The state makes good its claims. It is one of only 16 states with a deputy registrar provision, a system whereby additional help is deputized to seek out new enrollees. Some of the short-term registrars are employees of the county clerk's office, the agency charged with administering the act. Most are volunteers from such groups as the AFL-CIO, League of Women Voters, both political parties, the junior chamber of commerce, and other civic-minded organizations. Overall, approximately 2000 deputy registrars are added for elections, and in one county for which the figures could be checked there was a registrar for approximately every 350 voters (high even by Canadian standards). These deputies enroll new voters in schools, supermarkets, fire stations, housing projects, mobile courts, department stores, county and state fairs, and "almost any place where there is a high volume of people traffic."

In terms of simplicity, application forms are "easy to fill out, with no excessively detailed or embarrassing questions to be supplied by the applicant[13]." Residency qualifications are minimal and county clerks' offices are open for registration daily, including Saturdays, immediately before the close of the enrollment period. A person who moves into the state on the Monday preceding the presidential election can vote the following day for president through accommodation procedures designed by the state. Finally, Oregon even mails a packet of information on the election to enrolled voters before election day.

Idaho is another state with some interesting approaches. Its methods for reaching potential registrants are commendable as attested by enrollment totals of 91 (1968) and 83 (1972) percent of the eligible voting age population and turnouts of 73 (1968) and 65 (1972) percent. The distinguishing characteristics of the enrollment process are simplicity, clarity of responsibility, decentralization, accessibility of registration opportunities, and the aggressive search for those who are unregistered. The responsibility for registration rests with the county clerk, who appoints an official registrar for every precinct in the county by March 1 of an election year. The county commissioner has the option of assigning additional deputy registrars to any precinct in which they appear needed and at least one registrar must be assigned to each unincorporated area and each village. The registrars are paid on a wage scale that is not to exceed 50¢ per new enrollee. Those designated registrars must post in a minimum of three public locations during March, the times and locations in which they will enroll voters. The registration period remains open in the precinct until 10 days before election day and at the county clerk's office until 2 days before the day. On the election eve, the office stays open until eight o'clock. New housing developments or mobile courts can seek the appointment of a registrar specifically for their areas. Those absent from a county have until the seventh day before an election to request enrollment. Quite obviously, enrollment is taken seriously and every attempt is made to make it as convenient and painless as possible for those who qualify.

The state of Washington has relatively strict eligibility qualifications for the franchise, but its attempts to reach electors demonstrate a degree of imagination. The state provides mobile registration units in some localities; during the last 15 days of the enrollment period additional offices on the precinct level are opened;

door-to-door canvasses by deputy registrars (paid 20¢ for each person enrolled) are encouraged; and in 1973 the legislature passed a law mandating the county auditors to appoint as deputy registrars political party precinct committee members if they so requested. It would appear in the best interests of the committee members to enlist as many of their own supporters as possible. The state's registration fluctuated between 83 and 90 percent and its participation rate between 71 and 62 percent for the 1972 and 1968 elections, respectively.

A case study on the effectiveness of door-to-door campaigns was launched in 1970 on Oahu, Hawaii's most populous island. Teams of registrars were appointed from Democrats, Republicans, and independents. Team captains received $2.50 an hour while the other six members were paid $1.60 an hour plus 25¢ for each valid applicant. The teams, working mostly evenings, went house-to-house in each district. In an off-year election, they managed to increase voter enrollment 50 percent over that of 1968. Of all methods, this type of canvass appears to be the most effective.

California is notable for the administrative flexibility of its system. As with most other things, California has a little bit of everything. The state's election code authorizes deputy registrars (paid 25¢ per affidavit), door-to-door canvassing, and mobile registration units with sound equipment that tour neighborhoods notifying citizens of the dates, times, and places for enrolling. Registration can be canceled for failure to vote in the previous election—an unnecessarily stiff penalty. But disqualified registrants have to be notified, and if they return an affidavit to the county clerk affirming that they still reside at the same location, their rights are automatically restored[14].

The enrolling procedures used by these states do not begin to exhaust the list of potential approaches to voter registration experimented with by varying jurisdictions. Nonetheless, and despite the forward-looking efforts of many electoral districts, the overall picture is negative. Since the states are primarily concerned with protecting the ballot from those unauthorized to use it, they all too often place cumbersome and unnecessary obstacles in the path of those who wish to vote—barriers that in truth have little to do with the exercise of the franchise. At least one state (North Dakota) has no registration procedures and manages to do rather nicely. Less well known, many midwestern states permit their electoral jurisdictions to enforce many, some, or no registration requirements or to rescind those they have. Four-fifths of the land area of Missouri, for example, is not subject to registration demands, although the principal urban areas are. Turnout in nonregistration areas averages, not surprisingly, 10 to 12 points above those with them. A 10-percentage-point difference existed between levels of participation in registration and nonregistration counties (excluding Philadelphia) in Pennsylvania during presidential elections in the 1930s. For the same category of elections in Ohio for the period 1948 to 1960, turnout averaged three percentage points more for counties with partial requirements and eight points more for those with no qualifications compared to those with a full set of restrictions. For 1960 alone, the mean difference between counties with a complete list of qualifications and those with none was 12 percentage points[15]. It is questionable how long the federal courts can tolerate such obvious inequities in the distribution of the franchise[16].

Many registration procedures were introduced by rurally dominated, nativist-oriented state legislatures to penalize urban areas. Until 1957, for example, New York's legislature required that in cities with populations over a certain size (a provision only New York City fulfilled) individuals register *personally* at enrolling stations and that they enroll prior to *each* election in order to maintain their eligibility. Undoubtedly, such restrictions had the desired effect of depressing participation. Today they appear mainly as holdovers from long-forgotten political wars of the nineteenth century. And, in fact, as Oregon's secretary of state has argued, the present elaborate system may actually place a greater burden on the prospective rural voter[17]. Whatever the relative degree of inconvenience, the system is mostly a negative one.

Frustrated by overlapping, expensive, and inefficient attempts to register new voters in the 1970 election—including in Tucson "the existence of only one registration site, . . . insufficient voluntary registrars to register outlying populations including Indians on reservations, registration limited to working hours, partisan avoidance of certain groups, and misinformation which hindered student registration," problems familiar to most veterans of registration campaigns[18] —the youth registration coordinator of the Young Democrats established a national network of state representatives (not confined to youth) in 1971 to examine what went wrong. These new entrants to the registration field "found an incredible catalogue of administrative and legal obstacles to registration[19]." The results of their survey appear in Table 3.2.

A quaintness, as well as an arbitrariness characterizes this cataloging of deficiencies. The registrar of Florida's fourth largest county refused to appoint a special registrar for mobile units because, so he is reported to have said, citizens should come to the courthouse to observe firsthand government in action. Montana allows two party appointments per precinct, but these two have full power to designate all supplemental help and no work can be done out of their presence. An inactive precinct registrar who refuses to abdicate can effectively nullify the entire process. More generally, 35 states did not offer mobile registration, 27 restricted or did not provide for the appointment of deputy registrars, 24 reported indifference or worse from election officials in registration efforts, another 13 experienced a politically biased administration of their trusts, and 17 of the 47 states for which data could be collected found the hours for registration too restrictive[20]. The message bears repeating: Present registration procedures are arbitrary, broadly discriminatory, and antiquated. The question is what can be done about them.

REMEDIAL ACTION

A little-noticed movement has been underway for a number of years to mend some of the more flagrant registration abuses. In large part, it is an outgrowth of the civil rights movement in the South and the awareness it produced of the effectiveness of the instrument of registration in depressing voter participation. Aware of the inequities of the enrolling system, President John Kennedy appointed a Commission on Registration and Voting Participation in 1963, chaired by the former director of the U.S. Bureau of the Census, Richard Scammon.

The commission's report had little impact. In part, the problem was a matter of timing. The commission delivered its recommendations to the White House on November 26, several days after Kennedy's assassination and at a time when the nation's attention focused on more immediate problems. Contributing to the problem was the nature of the proposals advanced and the conservative strategy adopted for their implementation. The commission did review such approaches as door-to-door canvassing, deputy registrars, and precinct and mobile registration. The majority of its recommendations, however, centered on piecemeal improvements in local practices—well-equipped polling places, longer hours, accessible registration centers, shorter durational residency requirements, better absentee voting provisions, the sanctity of election lists, and the abolition of poll tax and literacy requirements[21].

The report did not propose any legislation or offer a core model against which each state's laws could be measured. Rather, the commission chose an essentially advisory role, confining itself to urging the multiplicity of state and local interests to adopt the type of proposals it advocated. This was an extraordinarily difficult way to achieve anything of consequence. In fact, it is fair to say it precluded by its very indirectness substantial reform.

During the late sixties and early seventies, the move to modernize enrollment picked up momentum with the drive for the 18-year-old vote and the general effort (partially associated with the unfortunate Democratic National Convention of 1968) to open electoral processes. Groups such as Common Cause, the League of Women Voters, the National Municipal League, the National Urban League, the AFL-CIO, Frontlash, the Student Vote, and other youth-oriented and civic organizations became increasingly concerned with the problem and began to explore and marshal support for improvements of various kinds. This loose coalition reinforced by a heightened public awareness began to score some major successes: the passage of the 1970 Voting Rights Act; the 1971 enactment of the Twenty-sixth Amendment enfranchising 18-year-olds, although as many soon realized this was only the beginning of their difficulties; the introduction and eventual passage in the U.S. Senate (and years later in the House) of a postcard registration system; the creation of the short-lived Office of Federal Elections in

TABLE 3.2
OBSTACLES TO REGISTRATION
IN THE STATES

State	Lack of Deputies	Lack of Mobile Registration	Lack of Sufficient Number of Hours	Distance	Lack of Official Cooperation	Political Preference Shown	Funding
Alabama		X	X				X
Alaska				X			
Arizona	X		X			X	
Arkansas		X	X				X
California	X^a				X		
Colorado		X	X				
Connecticut	X^b	X	X		X		
Delaware	X	X	X		X	X	
District of Columbia	X				X		
Florida		X^c	X			X	
Georgia	X	X			X		
Hawaii^d							
Idaho^e	X	X					
Illinois		X				X	
Indiana		X				X	
Iowa	X	X	X		X		
Kansas		X			X	X	
Kentucky		X				X	
Louisiana					X		
Maine	X		X			X	
Maryland	X	X	X		X^f		
Massachusetts	X	X^g					X
Michigan	X^b	X					
Minnesota	X				X		
Mississippi	X	X	X	X	X^h		
Missouri		X					
Montana	X^a	X^a			X^f	X	
Nebraska	X^i	X^i	X^i		X	X	
Nevada	X^j	X					
New Hampshire	X^b	X					
New Jersey	X		X				
New Mexico							
New York	X^k	X^k					
North Carolina	X$^{a l}$	X$^{a m}$			X	X	X
North Dakota							
Ohio		X	X	X			
Oklahoma							
Oregon	X	X			X^e		
Pennsylvania						X	
Rhode Island	X	X			X		
South Carolina	X		X		X		
South Dakota	X	X			X		
Tennessee	X	X			X		
Texas					X^l		
Utah		X			X		
Vermont		X					X
Virginia	X	X	X		X		
Washington					X		
West Virginia		X			X		
Wisconsin		X	X	X		X	
Wyoming		X					
TOTAL	27	35	17	4	24	13	5

the General Accounting Office (its functions were later taken over by the newly created Federal Election Commission, as was the responsibility for administering the system of postcard registration) to monitor progress in the states and the Congress and to investigate and publicize varying types of basically mechanical refinements in election procedures; and the improvement in the administration of registration processes in a number of states[22].

The most notable change on the state level resulted from the Supreme Court decision of March 21, 1972 (*Dunn* v. *Blumstein*) that extended the ban on excessively long residency requirements in federal elections as contained in the Voting Rights Act of 1970 to other elections. The Supreme Court declared lengthy residency qualifications for voting in state and local elections unconstitutional and suggested (but did not demand) a 30-day period as the standard[23]. The impact of this one decision (supported by congressional legislation in the 1970 Voting Rights Act) has been enormous. Table 3.3 presents the residency requirements in effect in 1973. Even allowing for the labyrinth of exceptions and restrictive applications the differences between, for example, 1968, which operated under the old system (see Chapter 1), and 1972, when the states were forced to comply with an aggressive new mood on such matters, is remarkable. The differences serve as a reminder of what can be accomplished in a very short period of time if governmental bodies are forced to act.

For the 1968 presidential election, 33 states and the District of Columbia mandated that a person be a resident for one year before qualifying to vote; 15 demanded a six-months residency (although Connecticut applied the provisions in cities only); and only two, New YOrk and Pennsylvania, permitted a then

---

*a*Ease varies by county.

*b*Need cross-deputization to register persons living in one city and working in another. Expansion of hours often insufficient, as workers may be fatigued and go straight home.

*c*Lack of absentee registration.

*d*State ombudsmen help solve citizen problems.

*e*Difficulty in disseminating registration information.

*f*Misinformed registrars on student residence, age, tax exemptions by parents as requirement, etc.

*g*Primarily relating to college students.

*h*Particularly in registering blacks.

*i*In small counties.

*j*Volunteer registrars allowed, but obtaining volunteer time is insufficient.

*k*Varies by county; New York City excellent.

*l*Student residency definition still a problem.

*m*Either in state/local registration laws or in administrative implementation.

SOURCE: Subcommittee on Census and Statistics, Committee on Post Office and Civil Service, U.S. House of Representatives, *The Concept of National Voter Registration* (Washington, D.C.: U.S. Government Printing Office, 1972), pp. 401–2.

liberal 90-day period[24]. Thirty-five states legislated county residence restrictions of from one to six months. Four states, in addition to Connecticut, had city or town minimal residencies of six months, and two cities had limits of three months. By 1972, 31 states and the District of Columbia had no residency criteria (subject, however, to various qualifications), 16 applied the Supreme Court suggestion of a 30-day grace period, and one state (Kansas) required only 20 days (Table 3.3). Only 2 of the 50 exceeded the Court's rule-of-thumb and these (60 days in Florida, 45 in Michigan) are modest by previous standards.

TABLE 3.3
STATE RESIDENCY QUALIFICATIONS FOR VOTING, 1972

No Durational Residency Requirement	30-day Residency Requirement	Other
Alabama, Alaska, California, Colorado,[a] Connecticut, Delaware, District of Columbia,[b] Georgia,[c] Hawaii, Idaho, Illinois,[d] Indiana,[e] Iowa,[f] Louisiana, Maine,[g] Maryland, Massachusetts,[h] Minnesota, Nebraska,[i] Nevada, New Hampshire, New Jersey, North Carolina, Oklahoma, South Carolina, South Dakota,[j] Tennessee, Texas, Vermont, Virginia, West Virginia, Wisconsin[k]	Arizona,[l] Arkansas, Kentucky, Mississippi, Missouri, Montana, New Mexico, New York, North Dakota,[m] Ohio, Oregon, Pennsylvania, Rhode Island, Utah, Washington, Wyoming	Florida, 60 days; Kansas, 20 days; Michigan, 45 days

[a]None for presidential elections, 32 days for state. [b]30-day registration requirement. [c]14-day registration requirement for presidential elections, governor and lt. governor. [d]None for presidential elections, 30 for state. [e]None for presidential elections, 60 for state. [f]10-day registration requirement. [g]When voting resident moves to another community, must have 3-month residency; retains voting residency in former community. [h]20-day registration requirement for primary elections, 31-day for state. [i]Registration requirement, 2d Friday prior to elections. [j]15-day registration requirement. [k]None for presidential elections, 10 days for state. [l]50-day for state. [m]10-day for presidential elections.

SOURCE: State questionnaires submitted to *Information Please Almanac*, 1974 ed. (New York: Dan Golenpaul Associates, 1974), p. 82.

The diversity of forms and procedures created over the last three and one-half centuries sprang from a variety of causes and are not susceptible to easy cataloguing or quick clarification. Richard Smolka, an expert on the administration of elections, made the point well in testifying before a congressional committee.

> The United States' election system is incredibly complex. It is the most decentralized and internally diverse in the world. . . . There are now over 521,000 elected officials in this country. These officials are elected through voting procedures which are so varied as to be a monument to the imagination of man. Elections are con-

ducted every week of the year. In Los Angeles County . . . alone, sometimes sixty elections are going on at one time at different stages. Registration procedures for participating in local elections cover the entire range of processes known to the Western World[25].

Add to this that a voter qualified in one state or locality may not be under the same conditions in another or that, conversely, the same person could be registered and eligible to vote in several geographic locations in the same election. As Smolka notes, in many places "the local jurisdiction is quite free to develop its own rules and regulations based upon a local interpretation of national and state law[26]." There is little reason underlying the multiplicity of demands and the differences in application designed by each of the electoral jurisdictions.

As could be expected, there are about as many solutions advocated as there are problems encountered, all springing from the same fertile imaginations. With this in mind, one may consider the following proposals: the effort to standardize voting qualifications, the national commission concept, universal voter enrollment, postcard registration, and absentee balloting.

THE PROPOSALS

RESTRICTIONS   There is little rationale for allowing any more than the absolute minimum of qualifications: 18 years old, a 30-day residency period at most, and citizenship (possibly). There appears little justification for exclusions based on purifying the electorate. More profitably, the emphasis should be placed on obtaining the broadest, most inclusive and representative voter turnout physically possible. In its own indirect way, the nation is moving toward just such a resolution of the problems concerning qualifications. Congressman Abner Mikva, in an appearance supporting a bill he introduced to accomplish such an equitable standardization, put the matter as follows:

> I consider important . . . the removal of existing categorical disabilities. . . . No person should be denied the right to vote merely because of his economic status, or his failure to vote in previous elections, or his refusal to take a loyalty oath. Nor should persons found mentally ill or those convicted of crimes be disqualified, unless by specific judicial action which comports with due process. Our present procedures for adjudging people's mental competence, particularly in civil commitment proceedings, are shamefully unreliable. They are not adequate to protect the constitutional rights of those subjected to their application. As for persons convicted of crime, we have come to understand that depriving the criminal of fundamental rights and responsibilities is not likely to aid in rehabilitation [or, it might be added, deter them from crime]. There may be some cases, such as vote fraud, where deprivation of the right to vote is closely related to the crime and therefore is justifiable. In those limited cases, a court finding would be in order[27].

In all situations, the presumption should be in favor of the individual's right to cast a ballot.

A NATIONAL VOTING COMMISSION   There is no need for another national investigatory committee. There has been a surfeit of these, and enough basic data exists to appreciate fully how registration systems operate, whom they favor or penalize, how they have developed, *and* how they can be improved. A proposal often made in the reports of these committees, and one now pending in a number of bills before the Congress, calls for some type of national election commission composed of nonpartisan (or some combination of bipartisan or politically independent) commissioners appointed by the president for fixed terms with the advice and consent of the Congress. The national election commission would be supplied with adequate staff and funding and would report both to the Congress and the president, much along the lines of the U.S. Commission on Civil Rights.

Duties of such a national election commission would include establishing and supervising a congressionally legislated system for the enrollment of voters for federal elections; assisting and encouraging all qualified voters to register; executing continuing studies of state, federal, and local election procedures with an eye to improving them; providing advisory, educational, and informational services to state and local election officials as requested; attempting to "encourage and foster, to the maximum extent possible, state and local efforts to achieve full voter participation"; collecting and maintaining records on the results of all elections held within the United States and making these available to the public through publication in some form; cataloguing all the enrolling and broader election statutes and procedures in the country and making information on these available to any interested person upon request; assisting localities on request in resolving their election problems; recommending legislative, judicial, or administrative actions as the commission deems necessary to facilitate participation; reviewing complaints of election irregularities (fraud, exclusion of voters, arbitrary or discriminatory application of the prevailing rules, etc.); *training* federal election officials and providing training grants for state and local officers who wish to participate; encouraging, through staff assistance and funding experimentation by public agencies and private groups, means of reaching and enrolling new voters; conducting election analyses; providing educational information on elections to voters, schools, private groups, and the media; and (although this would undoubtedly frighten some) retaining power to hold public hearings and subpoena witnesses and documents as needed to carry out its duties.

The proposals for such a permanent national commission, concentrating specifically on the administration of elections, vary, although not greatly. The clearing-house function alone of such an agency would justify its existence. For the first time, the world's most technologically advanced nation would have available inclusive, accurate data on its election results.

The funding for a commission with extensive authority to enforce a universal voter enrollment concept was estimated in 1971 to cost $5 million in the three years between national contests and $50 million in presidential election years[28]. The first figure is equivalent to one-fourth of the cost of an F-14 aircraft and the second is less than that of two navy (DE-1052) destroyer escorts. Taking the larger figure to be applied to presidential years and allowing for inflation and an underassessment of costs, not unusual in government programs, doubling the funding would equal roughly the cost of three B-1 bombers or about two-thirds the money needed for one nuclear attack submarine. It is, of course, a matter of priorities. At present, when it comes to insuring a representatively inclusive electorate—and despite the overwhelming significance of the decisions to be made in such electoral contests—the federal government spends virtually nothing.

DOOR-TO-DOOR NATIONAL CANVASS (UNIVERSAL VOTER ENROLLMENT) The most powerful of the recommendations is for a full-fledged government-initiated assumption of the obligation to register its citizenry through a door-to-door national canvass. The plan is basically a simple one: a federally-funded national commission would supervise 435 registrars (one for each congressional district) in enrolling voters during a specified period preceding a primary or general election. The district registrars, who would be paid, would in turn command an army of volunteer deputies—much as in Oregon, Idaho, or other states—who would go door-to-door to enroll all prospective voters. The system is roughly analogous to that employed in Canada. The voter lists would be destroyed within 30 days of the election unless a challenge necessitated their preservation. Under no conditions would they be deposited in a central data bank, or used for anything other than identifying members of the electorate. Stiff criminal penalties for various types of abuse as well as appeal procedures to correct registration oversights are also included in the legislation to create such an enrollment system.

The principal arguments against such a plan are the following:

1. It represents a new departure for the United States, although not as severe a one as some might believe. The government would assume responsibility for a process until now left almost entirely to the individual.

2. The operation is subject to abuse, particularly if a national data bank idea is incorporated into the concept; if social security numbers are employed to identify voters in an effort to prevent fraud; or if national identity cards are issued, (as Senator Russell Long once proposed) at birth (or as some others would have it) on a person's 18th birthday. In the post-Watergate era, everyone should be sensitive to the types of abuse such schemes entail. The seeds of a police-state mentality are evident, regardless of how well-intentioned the ultimate objective against which the present quasi-chaotic situation would appear refreshing.

3. It would cost too much. The question here is one of relative values as to where public funds should be put. Cost estimates will not move supporters or proponents very much one way or the other. Nevertheless, the door-to-door campaign on Oahu referred to above cost $1.71 per application, a relatively high figure[29]. There are conditions peculiar to Hawaii such as the geographical dispersion of the population, the relatively high initial registration (which meant the relatively modest percentage of unenrolled would probably be the most difficult to locate), and the state's decision to pay all canvassers who participated in the program. The Canadian system cost 70¢ per capita for the last two elections (which transposed to the American electorate would be something under $100 million). Multnomah County (Portland), Oregon, with a registration location every 1.3 miles and 3.4 deputy enrollers per square mile, an approach similar to the house-to-house canvass, spent for all registration activities in the period 1972 to 1973 only 10¢ per voter. Portland employed unpaid volunteer registrars (an impressive 1360 in all), an approach endorsed by the enrollment plan. Smolka found that these unpaid, volunteer "registrars receive training and written instructions and make few administrative errors. ... Business and community agencies are much more willing to donate their time and services if there are many volunteers. ... This means that no single deputy, and therefore no single business or government agency, is overburdened[30]." In contrast, New York City, using the old ways with all their restrictions and cross-checks, was able to register only 250,000 voters at a cost of over $2 million in 1972 for a per capita expenditure of $8.41 per registrant. And the expense is reportedly higher in the off-years[31].

These are only some of the major provisions and principal objections to the house-to-house enrollment system. Under some of the legislation submitted, for example, the system would function only in electoral jurisdictions that failed to register 90 percent or more of their voting age population, a "triggering clause" similar to that which proved so successful in the Voting Rights Act of 1965. Some of the legislation tends to emphasize professional, bureaucratic action on a limited, spot basis in given elections. It often does not contain the strict requirement to dispose of voting lists once the election is over (in truth, no worse than the practices now in effect). Also, several versions of the legislation encourage states or congressional districts to reach the 90 percent level by awarding to those that do so financial booster grants of approximately $100,000 to cover the administrative costs of elections. States or electoral units that made outstanding improvements (15 percentage points or more) would also receive financial awards of the same magnitude.

There are two major problems with the financial incentive provisions. One is that some agency would have to devise means of insuring (and probably policing the arrangement as well) that the voting lists are pruned regularly, that they are free of fraud, and that they are not systematically padded to qualify for the federal funds. The second problem is more serious. The intent of the more aggressive plans is to reach those areas where officials are indifferent to election performance or where they directly (or indirectly, for example, by making registration locations difficult to reach or opening them only at selected times) discourage enrollment. There is nothing in the financial incentive provisions approach that would meet this problem, the most basic of considerations in experimenting with a modernized set of procedures.

Excerpts from a one-hour television debate and from the congressional hearings on the relative merits of the universal voter enrollment plan serve to illustrate the diversity of arguments that can be raised against such a system. It is claimed it would create a vast, new federal bureaucracy; registration would become compulsory (not true; the individual opts in or out at his discretion); it is a step toward an "obligatory" vote; the Voting Rights Acts went far enough; Democrats would benefit unduly; the states and communities should be left free to enact whatever changes they desire; the process is open to political abuse; enough organizations presently—youth groups, federated labor, civil rights associations, the League of Women Voters, the major political parties—are already engaged in enrollment efforts and no more are needed; an "irreducible" core of nonvoters exists (magnitude left unspecified; perhaps 35 to 40 percent of the eligible voting age population?) for whom nothing can be done; not everyone should vote (and some would add, if they did it would be unhealthy for the democracy); the enrollment bill "complicates what is at present a fairly simple process"[32]; patronage considerations would arise in hiring district coordinators; nonvoting can be a rational decision (true; and it can be caused by other factors); voting procedures are presently and should remain under the authority of the states in a federal system (although the congressional right to enact such legislation under the Voting Rights Acts and the Supreme Court decisions is not challenged); and so on. As with every "reform," individuals will have to answer each objection according to their own values. Some of the counterarguments are serious, others are frivolous. Some of the prospective abuses can be guarded against; others call for a weighing of priorities.

One person who has given some thought to this process and not unexpectedly has emerged as a strong champion of the universal enrollment concept is Ramsey Clark. Fittingly (if temporarily), he should be given the last word. When asked to comment on the reasons behind the opposition to the voter enrollment plan, the former attorney general replied:

> Those that wield political power today don't want to share it. They don't understand the frustrations of being utterly powerless in America. Politics is a source of power. And if we revitalize democracy in this country and share power with the people, create new constituencies for our representatives, . . . we'll see America flourish. We'll see our people included in this system. We'll see a commitment to the rule of law because they participate in its making[33].

POSTCARD REGISTRATION   A fall-back position for the supporters of universal enrollment has been the postcard registration system, an approach that in various forms has been used in many localities[34]. In itself, the idea is a good one. Many of the bills embodying this more innocuous form of federal stimulation of enrollment have the virtue of including almost all of the provisions not crucial to the explicit door-to-door individual canvass—a national election commission, federal subsidies to the states to provide incentive to upgrade their registration procedures, and efforts to rationalize and simplify voter qualifications.

The supporters of postcard registration in its various forms include those who support the universal enrollment idea and, for that matter, most forms of registration and election procedural reform. Among its provisions, the plan would empower the Internal Revenue Service to mail registration forms to all taxpayers and upon their return to issue a certificate that declares them enrolled and eligible to vote. The proposal was made (in 1971) before the continuing abuses of IRS authority in the Nixon Administration severely damaged this agency's credibility. The bill explicitly states that no national registry should be kept. The director of the IRS did not want his agency to assume such an obligation, however— particularly the seeking out and contacting of nontaxpayers as a means of stimulating enrollment[35]. For those who fail to file a tax statement, the process could be a frightening one. He estimated the first year start-up cost at almost $11 million —an estimate perhaps intentionally made high to discourage pursuit of the idea. In fact, the sending of forms along with tax statements should be inexpensive enough. If the completed forms were returned to the national election commission (and a cross-check of IRS and commission files was prohibited), this could serve as a supplemental device for encouraging enrollment.

Another aim of the plan would codify much of the federal legislative and court rulings on the subject of voting rights, explicitly, for example, voiding any statutes or practices that deny "the constitutional right to vote" and "free movement across State lines" (while not sacrificing any election rights) and guaranteeing the rights and protections of the Fourteenth Amendment (among others) that do not "bear a reasonable relationship to any compelling State interest." These bills would establish a single national registration form and explicitly state the grounds for disenfranchisement, outlawing such devices as standards of mental health and most kinds of criminal conduct. In one of its derivative forms, this type of plan grants funds to states and it distributes enrollment forms through the mail to prospective voters. Lists of voters could be maintained indefinitely, but the penalties for unauthorized use are severe.

The most common form of postal registration authorization would distribute registration forms through the mails for federal enrollment. The completed application would be returned to a national voter registration administration located in the Bureau of the Census, which would then prepare lists and distribute these to the local electoral units. The duties of the administration would be similar to those of the national voting commission, a concept which is retained in some versions of the bill. The intent of placing the agency in the Bureau of the Census would be to call upon this organization's reputation for nonpartisanship and experience in identifying and locating individuals as well as its success in maintaining the confidentiality of its files. A version of the independent commission idea would include the director of the census as chairman. The prohibitions against misuse of authority are again stringent[36].

At the time congressional hearings were held on the postcard registration concept, the director of the census preferred avoiding responsibility for such a fundamentally political activity. He estimated the cost of establishing the system at a minimum of $30 million ($15 to $20 million for postage and $5 to $10 million to process voters' addresses and related lists), although the calculations are crude and the long-run costs may or may not be on this order of expenditure (in a later hearing, a census official estimated the annual postage costs at $10 million[37]). The Post Office reported that it would charge at commercial rates from 11¢ (per airmail ounce) to an incredible $1.66 (for an absentee ballot sent special delivery or registered mail). Why a postcard could not be delivered and returned free of charge is not clear.

The most elaborate estimates prepared by the General Accounting Office (GAO) for a basically independent agency with newly equipped regional field offices (including the construction of buildings, personnel and training costs, furnishings, etc.) amount to $191 and $527 million depending on the volume of registrations (40 to 140 million). The start-up estimates include a three-year period specified by the GAO needed to put the system in operation and $72 million for computer purchasing alone. The ongoing costs initially (second through the fifth years) again would be dictated by the volume of enrollment (projected at 22 to 36 million) and the cost of updating records would be between $52 and $134 million[38]. At least initially, the registration cost per individual in the most expensive plan is placed at $3.75 (which may be too high an estimate given previous costs of similar but more localized operations)[39]. Once the system was operational, presumably, the costs would decrease. These figures are well above those projected—in far cruder form—for the door-to-door canvass. The GAO estimates demand respect as the work of a professional accounting agency. Its projections are based on a full-time agency with none of the volunteer elements of the first proposal.

Still one has to wonder. The Canadian system of paid door-to-door enumerators if transplanted to the United States and the American costs were equivalent were estimated at approximately $100 million. Presumably, a modest proposal for a mail registration system would come to something below this figure. For a country that spends virtually nothing from the federal treasury on enrollment— but enormous amounts of time and money in competing local level registration drives by community groups and public agencies—any specifically definable cost should not appear excessive for a key link in the chain of democratic accountability. Taking the most ambitious of the GAO estimates, it is in the range of the cost of one high school or the amount of money one Oregon county pays to support the military[40].

Objections to the proposals on postcard enrollment, beyond the greater elaboration of costs, are much the same as those directed toward universal voter enrollment. Many Republican legislators, for example, have opposed it, fearing the unenrolled will prove to be principally Democratic voters. Such opposition has slowed enactment. Senator Robert Dole of Kansas, when Republican National Chairman, did add a small dimension to the familiar arguments by contending that the proposed system would not increase turnout because registration difficulties were not the principal cause of nonvoting[41]. But resistance to the concept was not strong. It is difficult to arouse opposition to a mail registration approach already in effect in some form in 31 states in the 1972 election and used by the federal government under the 1970 Voting Rights Act to enable federal civilian personnel abroad to vote[42].

The arguments against postcard registration, while reasonable, were not taken very seriously and the main question appeared to be who had the most to gain politically. The proposed bills do provide an opportunity to experiment to find out how a federal registration system would work. It would seem that the need for some improvement at least has been clearly established. The plan in some form is likely to be enacted fairly soon. In fact, Senate bills to establish a postcard enrollment have been passed, and a less enthusiastic House is in the process of following suit. Once established, the impact of the legislation bears close watching. The new system, although modest, might with some form of state incentives push registration figures to a respectable three out of four members of the eligible electorate (compared, for example, to the 61 percent reported nationally in 1970).

ABSENTEE VOTING   A final difficulty in the area of registration and voting to which an emerging bipartisan coalition has begun to direct attention is the problem posed by absentee voting. Absentee voters—those unable to register or vote in person at their specified polling location—may be persons who are temporarily away from home or ill, military personnel, college students, or Americans residing abroad. The difficulties faced by each group have certain similarities.

Travelers and sick persons are the most common absentee voters, and the most has been done to assist these individuals. Military personnel who wish to vote must inform themselves of the often complex legal requirements for enrollment and the procedures to follow to qualify for absentee registration and to cast an absentee ballot. For those serving in the armed forces, generally young persons with fragile political ties, lack of motivation is probably as important as physical barriers in contributing to a low level of electoral participation. Also, the military has had a tradition of noninvolvement in politics—perhaps a good thing in a democratic nation—that has fostered a nonpartisanship among professional officers that has carried over into the enlisted ranks. In recent years, stimulated by the passage of the Federal Voting Assistance Act of 1955, an intensive drive has been undertaken to encourage members of the armed forces to enroll, inform them of the difficulties they will encounter, and assist them in their efforts. The Defense Department has offered its support to those wishing to liberalize and standardize absentee provisions.

The debate over students' rights arose out of the clamor for an 18-year-old vote and the problems youth groups, and specifically college students, encountered in trying to qualify to vote. These difficulties have received by all odds the greatest media attention (due largely to the demonstrations and turmoil of the late sixties), but the problems—while real enough—will probably be the most quickly resolved. As students have shown themselves to be at least as apathetic as the voting population generally and not as irresponsibile and volatile as predicted, local registrars (prodded by the courts) have worked out their own accommodations. Generally, the process has been one of slowly acclimating governmental procedures to dealing more effectively with the problems associated with an enlarged electorate.

The last group, overseas Americans (primarily businessmen living in foreign countries), has begun to mount a campaign to draw attention to its objectives. Of all the groups, it is the one most systematically discriminated against and the one that arouses the strongest (now that the shock of the student vote has subsided), if isolated, pockets of resistance. The movement began during the 1964 election and led to the formation of the Bipartisan Committee on Absentee Voting [Overseas], a coalition of Republicans and Democrats that speaks for about 1.5 million prospective voters[43].

The absentee registration and voting provisions of the states are extraordinarily complex. They can be interpreted in at least 33 states to effectively disenfranchise citizens living abroad. Absentee ballots are made available (if at all) "only after [prospective overseas] voters have filled out page after notarized page of forms regarding everything from taxes to occupation[44]."

Of all the absentee voter groups, the states are least sympathetic to overseas Americans. The reasons for the antipathy are not difficult to understand. Any absentee accommodations substantially increase the paper work on a case-by-case basis for the agency with authority in the matter. Many states also believe overseas voters receive a free ride particularly on state taxes and since they do not pay their fair share, they should not be entitled to vote (the Bipartisan Committee claims this is a problem in only 12 states)[45]. The size of the vote is also threatening to some. It is likely that the affluent, well-read business community abroad would enroll and vote in disproportionately higher numbers than other absentee groups (and would probably vote Republican). If so, this voting bloc could rival the electorates of roughly 15 states. It could, in short, have a pronounced impact on the outcome of federal elections in particular.

The federal courts have attempted to protect the voting rights of American residents in foreign countries, but their decisions are open to several interpretations and this recourse has generally not proven satisfactory[46]. Simplified federal procedures are needed that would allow businessmen and professional people "temporarily" living abroad (although many remain for years) to participate at least in federal elections. The leadership of the Republican party has strongly supported legislative changes that would facilitate the enfranchisement of these voters, and the Democrats have listed them among the groups to be included in its general efforts to expand the electorate. The Bipartisan Committee supports the universal enrollment idea (since registration is at the heart of their problem) as well as other legislation that would enhance their claim to a voice in elections. As a consequence, some notable gains have been made. The 1970 Voting Rights Act simplified absentee provisions, especially applicable to federal employees in foreign countries, and a bill that includes a provision to extend mail registration and voting privileges in federal elections to Americans residing abroad has now passed the Congress. It is likely that over time a greater rationality will be introduced into absentee voting provisions, a necessity in such a highly mobile society.

CONCLUSION

Registration procedures constitute a very real impediment to a representatively high voter turnout. There is little of a glamorous nature in sorting through the maze of qualifications, administrative procedures and their applications, and the special problems encountered by certain groups that depress participation. Practicing politicians have long recognized that registration systems are the subtlest (that is, least appreciated by the public) but most effective means for structuring an electorate to reflect the qualities or economic interests considered important.

Solutions to the contemporary difficulties will not be easy. There is a bias and inertia built into the present system that should not be underestimated. The proposals reviewed involve departures from previous practice in favor of innovative use of government agencies—a type of commitment many are unwilling to make until the need is inescapable. Federal change along the lines proposed in the door-to-door national canvass and, to a markedly lesser extent, postcard registration systems would result in an accommodation of state procedures and eventually a modernization of the machinery of electoral systems throughout the nation. There are costs involved in such displacements, however, and it is not the type of problem administrators welcome. Also, public support for such technically demanding legislation as the door-to-door national canvass and postcard registration plans is hard to generate on a broad basis.

Nonetheless, change, inevitably, will come. Perhaps the easiest approach, and an eminently sensible one, would be to abolish registration altogether (a position, incidentally, supported by the American Civil Liberties Union[47]) and permit enrollment on election day at the polling place. The idea is not as fantastic as it might appear. One state[48] and a number of localities already have such systems. Richard Scammon, the former chairman of President Kennedy's Commission on Registration and Voting Participation, has testified that registration qualifications could be abolished in one-third of the United States to no great effect[49]. Suspected fraudulent voters could always be challenged and investigated and the penalties for such a crime, if anything, could be made more severe. The proposal would be reasonable enough if joined with a simplified absentee provision and possibly a postcard enrollment system for those not able for varying reasons to appear at the polls. Short of such a total change, some explicitly new developments in the assumptions underlying voter registration and the approaches used to enroll prospective voters are badly needed.

NOTES

1. The information in these sections (excluding that on Canada) comes primarily from reports made available by the Election Systems Project of the National Municipal League and the research done by the Freedom To Vote Task Force, Ramsey Clark, chairman. I wish to thank Richard J. Carlson, project director, and William N. Cassella, Jr., executive director of the National Municipal League for their generosity. The data later in the chapter on the individual states are from the research of the Freedom To Vote Task Force unless otherwise indicated.

2. National Municipal League, *A Model Election System* (New York: National Municipal League, 1973), p. 2. Other materials of relevance from the National Municipal League include Richard J. Carlson, ed., *Issues of Electoral Reform* (New York: National Municipal League, 1973) and National Association of Secretaries of State, *Proceedings: National Conference on Election Administration* (New York: National Municipal League, 1973).

3. Freedom To Vote Task Force, *That All May Vote* (Washington, D.C.: Democratic National Committee, 1970), appendix VIII.

4. There is a wide variety of materials available on the Canadian system and these can be obtained from the appropriate government agency (Office of the Chief Electoral Officer, Ottawa). A good introduction to the system can be found in the description and documentation provided by the chief electoral officer to the Subcommittee on Census and Statistics of the House Committee on Post Office and Civil Service, contained in *The Concept of National Voter Registration* (Washington, D.C.: U.S. Government Printing Office, 1972), pp. 19–35.

5. Walter Dean Burnham, "Registration Statutes and Electoral Participation" (Report prepared for the Freedom To Vote Task Force, Washington, D.C., 1969), p. 6.

6. Ibid., p. 5.

7. Ibid., p. 1.

8. Ibid., p. 6.

9. South Carolina's Election Commission in Columbia has done an extensive number of analyses on the operation and efficiency of its system. For an overview, see O. Frank Thornton and James B. Ellisor, "Computerized Voter Registration in South Carolina," in *State Government* (Lexington, Ky.: Council of State Governments, Summer, 1969), pp. 190–93.

10. There is an impressive amount of materials on this question. See Committee on Government Operations, *Privacy and the National Data Bank Concept* (Washington, D.C.: U.S. Government Printing Office, August 2, 1968) and the bibliography in "A National Data Center for Registrants" (Report to the Freedom To Vote Task Force, Washington, D.C., n.d.).

11. On the costs of registration practices, see Richard G. Smolka, *The Costs of Administering American Elections* (New York: National Municipal League, 1973), pp. 47–62.

12. Committee on Post Office and Civil Service, U.S. Senate, *Hearings on Voter Registration* (Washington, D.C.: U.S. Government Printing Office, 1971), p. 153. See also by the same committee, *Hearings on Voter Registration* (Washington, D.C.: U.S. Government Printing Office, 1973).

13. Ibid. (1971).

14. On California, see Edmond Constantini and Willis D. Hawley, "Increasing Participation in California Elections: The Need for Electoral Reform," *Public Affairs Report* 10, no. 3 (June, 1969).

15. Burnham, "Registration Statutes," and Freedom To Vote Task Force, *Registration and Voting in the States* (Washington, D.C.: Democratic National Committee, 1970), p. 34.

16. See the reasoning of the federal courts as contained in *Oregon* v. *Mitchell* (1970), *Beare* v. *Smith,* (1972) and *Dunn* v. *Blumstein* (1972). In *Beare* v. *Smith,* the Texas legislature changed the registration statute in question before the case reached the Supreme Court.

17. Senate Committee, *Hearings on Voter Registration,* (1971), p. 155.

18. House Committee, *The Concept of National Voter Registration,* p. 399.

19. Ibid.

20. Ibid., pp. 399–408.

21. President's Commission on Registration and Voting Participation, *Report of the President's Commission on Registration and Voting Participation* (Washington, D.C.: U.S. Government Printing Office, November, 1963).

22. Office of Federal Elections, U.S. General Accounting Office, *A Study of State and Local Voter Registration Systems: Final Report* (Washington, D.C.: U.S. Government Printing Office, August, 1974). Also of importance in this regard is Office of Federal Elections, U.S. General Accounting Office, *Survey of Election Boards: Final Report* and *Survey of Election Boards: Data Base,* both published by the U.S. Government Printing Office, Washington, D.C., in May, 1974.

23. On March 19, 1973, the Supreme Court in two decisions permitted states (specifically, Arizona and Georgia) to impose residency qualifications of up to 50 days. The cases are *Marston* v. *Mandt* and *Burns* v. *Fortson.*

24. Freedom To Vote Task Force, *Registration and Voting in the States,* pp. 41–48.

25. Senate Committee, *Hearings on Voter Registration* (1971), p. 192.

26. Ibid.

27. Ibid., p. 141.

28. Ibid., pp. 95–112. The debate over costs is sprinkled throughout the two Senate reports and the inclusive House publication. See also Smolka, *Costs of Administering American Elections,* and the studies published by the Office of Federal Elections.
      The Federal Election Commission—created to oversee the federal funding of presidential elections—performs, to a limited extent, some clearinghouse functions

concerning electoral and, more specifically, registration procedures. It is also beginning (with a small budget) to fund studies of technical aspects of election administration.

29. See "Voter Registration Programs 1970," prepared by the Office of Lieutenant Governor, State of Hawaii, as reproduced in Senate Committee, *Hearings on Voter Registration* (1973), pp. 48–81.

30. Smolka, *Costs of Administering American Elections,* p. 55.

31. Ibid., p. 56.

32. This curious argument deserves specific reference: Professor Andrew Hacker in arguing against the proposition "Should the Federal Government Register Voters for Presidential Elections?" on "The Advocates," a Public Television Network presentation of KCET, Los Angeles, and WGBH, Boston, November 3, 1970 (Transcript, Los Angeles, 1970), p. 19.

33. Ibid., p. 24.

34. For example, Allegheny County (Pittsburgh), Pennsylvania, has employed a similar system with success. See Department of Elections, Allegheny County, "Allegheny County Blazes New Election Trails," mimeographed (Pittsburgh, July, 1967).

35. See the letter of October 20, 1971, from the Department of the Treasury to Senator Gale McGee, chairman, Committee on Post Office and Civil Service, in Senate Committee, *Hearings on Voter Registration* (1971), p. 27.

36. There are a number of variations on the central theme. The National Committee for an Effective Congress, for example, proposed a postcard registration system supplemented by mobile registrars or door-to-door canvassing in districts where the registration did not reach a minimum level (the organization recommended 65 or 70 percent, which is too low). Senate Committee, *Hearings on Voter Registration* (1971), p. 233.

37. House Committee, *The Concept of National Voter Registration,* p. 51.

38. Senate Committee, *Hearings on Voter Registration* (1971), pp. 95–112.

39. See Smolka, *Costs of Administering American Elections.*

40. These projections are based on those put forward by the cochairman of SANE, Seymour Melman in his book *The Permanent War Economy* (New York: Simon & Schuster, 1974). Readers can make their own comparisons from a simple reading of the local newspaper, for example, the $350 million spent by the CIA in an attempt to raise a 15-year-old Russian submarine from the floor of the Pacific.

41. Senate Committee, *Hearings on Voter Registration* (1971), p. 113. For an overview of the objections raised, see Senate Committee on Post Office and Civil Service, "Report Together with Minority Views" (Washington D.C.: U.S. Government Printing Office, 1971), pp. 20–26.

42. House Committee, *The Concept of National Voter Registration,* p. 439.

43. Ibid., pp. 479–80.

44. B. Drummond Ayres, Jr., "Democrats Abroad Seek Voting Law," *New York Times,* December 9, 1974, p. 45.

45. This is based on their interpretation of the applicability of state laws. House Committee, *The Concept of National Voter Registration,* p. 464. The complexities of the absentee laws are reviewed more extensively in the above work on pp. 323–98 and 460–80. On the tax issue, see the report prepared by the Congressional Relations

Service of the Library of Congress for Senator Barry Goldwater, reproduced in Senate Committee, *Hearings on Voter Registration* (1971), pp. 303–17.

46. See the testimony of Joseph L. Rauh, Jr., on behalf of the Bipartisan Committee in Senate Committee, *Hearings on Voter Registration* (1971), pp. 214–31.

47. Ibid., p. 256.

48. See Lloyd B. Omdahl, "Fraud-Free Elections Are Possible without Voter Registration—A Report on North Dakota's Experience," reproduced in Senate Committee, *Hearings on Voter Registration* (1971), pp. 202–10.

49. Ibid., p. 185.

II

MONEY

AND

CAMPAIGNS

4
The Mounting
Costs of Politics

The United States gained Abraham Lincoln for $100,000 in 1860. More than a century later in 1972, they retained Richard Nixon for something in excess of $65 million. The per capita cost by vote received soared from a nickel for Lincoln to over $1.38 for Nixon. Conversely, it cost Stephen Douglas $50,000 ($0.04 per vote) to lose in 1860 and George McGovern $23 million ($1.26 per vote) to duplicate the feat in 1972. As Will Rogers was fond of saying, "You have to be loaded just to get beat." Lincoln's budget would barely fund a competitive congressional race today.

By any standards, such figures as these represent a significant inflation of political costs. Quite obviously, political campaigns and the technology that accompanies them have changed dramatically in over 100 years. The campaign costs have risen sharply to meet the needs of the campaigner. The acceleration has been particularly marked in the years since 1948 and, not surprisingly, parallels the increasing reliance on television as a medium of political communication. This process can be illustrated by the period between the years 1912 (the first year of the presidential primary) and 1968 (the last of the pre-Watergate elections that marked a new era in campaign financing). Figure 4.1 presents costs in relation to consumer price index and votes cast.

From 1948 on there is a steep and unbroken upward spiral in campaign expenditures that still appears to be accelerating. No leveling off is indicated and the potential for campaign costs appears unlimited. If 1972 were added to the diagram, this trend would be dramatically reinforced. The financial outlays would roughly double those indicated for 1968.

The rise in cost since 1948 is *unrelated* in any significant way to the expansion in the size of the electorate or to general inflationary cycles in the economy, both of which climb modestly in comparison. While the funding of political campaigns has continued upwards at an alarming rate, it was only a prelude to the record expenditures of $425 million for all races in 1972 (Figure 4.2).

The remarkable growth in campaign costs for elections held during the two decades between 1952 and 1972 is clearly shown in Figure 4.2. The trend begins

FIGURE 4.1
INDEXES OF DIRECT CAMPAIGN EXPENDITURES
BY NATIONAL-LEVEL COMMITTEES, CONSUMER PRICES,
AND NUMBER OF VOTES CAST, 1912–1968

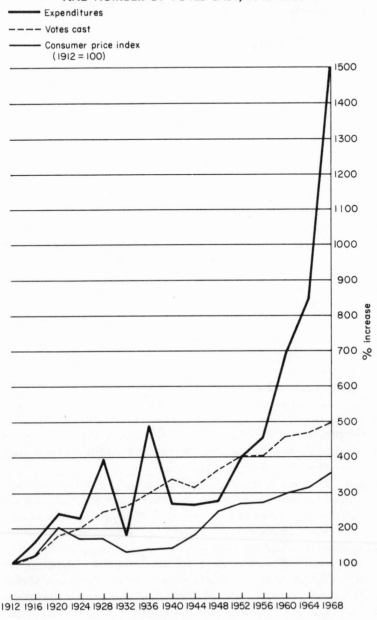

Presidential election year

SOURCE: Report of the Twentieth Century Fund Commission on Campaign Costs in the Electronic Era, *Voter's Time* (New York: The Twentieth Century Fund, 1969).

FIGURE 4.2
CAMPAIGN COSTS
ALL LEVELS OF ELECTION, 1952–1972

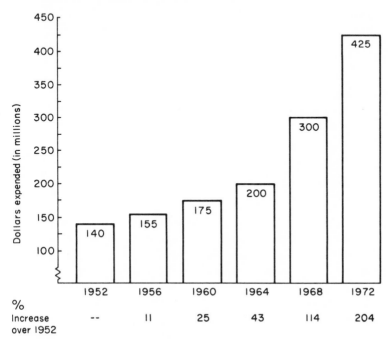

SOURCE: Data taken from Citizens' Research Foundation reports.

in the 1950s and then rises sharply in the sixties. The magnitude of expenses for 1968, $100 million above those of 1964, and for 1972, three times more than those of 1952, indicates the seriousness of the problem.

WHY THE SHARP INCREASE
IN CAMPAIGN COSTS?

This question is relatively easy to answer. The unbroken rise in campaign spending since 1952 coincides with an increased reliance on new technologies to reach the voter. By far the most expensive of these and the single greatest direct cause of the increase in campaign costs is television. In addition, there has been the introduction and widespread use of survey methods in assessing voter sentiments, the increasing reliance on professional public relations consultants in organizing and executing campaigns [1,] the substitution since 1948 of widespread airplane travel for the slower, less expensive reliance on the train, and the need, at the presidential level, to undergo prolonged prenomination fights with a particular emphasis on the expensive primary nominating systems. All of these cost money.

The 1968 presidential year with its competitive race for the party nominations and its relatively close final vote in the general election provides an example of the level of expenditure when neither party has an assured nominee. It also precedes the funding excesses associated with Watergate and thus is an adequately representative election year for analytic purposes.

Presidential prenomination campaigns require considerable funding. In the principal Democratic primary races, the expenditures of the two chief combatants, Senators Robert Kennedy and Eugene McCarthy, were as follows:

Primary State Expenditures (in dollars)

	Indiana	Nebraska	Oregon	California	South Dakota
Kennedy	750,000	150,000	394,000	2,400,000	100,000
McCarthy	700,000	160,000	400,000	1,000,000	30,000

The initial point is obvious: if Kennedy or McCarthy could have avoided these five primary encounters, which (with the exception of South Dakota) were to prove critically important to their respective nomination campaigns, they would have saved themselves, in monetary terms, $3.8 million and $2.3 million respectively. Kennedy and McCarthy each spent $9 million in the quest for their party's nomination. The Kennedy budget covers only the 85 days of his tragic effort. McCarthy's covers the period from the November preceding the election year. Candidates assured of the nomination have the luxury of investing their resources in the general election drive.

Precise figures are available for the ill-fated Kennedy venture. A total of $1.6 million was spent on the media, the exact allocation in each state depending on the extent of the competition encountered and the significance of winning (critical in California, for example, but not in Oregon). A healthy percentage of the individual state campaign budgets was invested in media promotions: 38 percent in Indiana, 45 percent in Nebraska; 26 percent in Oregon, 46 percent in California, and 35 percent in South Dakota.

Richard Nixon's well-executed prenomination campaign in 1968 cost $8.5 million. The campaign budget for five primary states alone, New Hampshire ($300,000), Wisconsin ($500,000), Indiana ($200,000), Nebraska ($100,000), and Oregon ($500,000)[2], came to more than $1.5 million. The Nixon campaign acknowledged spending $2.5 million on media advertising during this period. Even Nelson Rockefeller's abortive campaign to win the Republican presidential nomination, one of several he engaged in during the 1960s, cost an estimated $7 million, of which $3.5 million went into advertising.

The general election campaign expenditures of the two major candidates, Nixon and Hubert Humphrey, are difficult to compare directly because of the different accounting procedures used. Humphrey's costs, which were less than half of Nixon's, are easier to analyze because his staff allocated funds according to function. They are[3]:

Advertising	$6, 304, 000
Travel	875, 600
Personnel	759, 436
Communications	722, 700
Field expenses	578, 656
Contributions to state and local committees	380, 070
Polls and surveys	261, 521
Office expenses	250, 201
Miscellaneous	164, 205
Total	$10, 296, 389

The bulk of advertising expenditures went to television. The quarter-million dollars allocated for polling indicates one of the mandatory outlays of the modern campaign.

Nixon's expenditures, while far more elaborately detailed, list funds allocated for field offices, personal staffs, and such ambiguous items as "Key Issues Committee," "Truth Squad," "United Citizens," and so on. Two items are of comparative interest. A sum of $384,102 was spent on polling and the media advertising budget came to $11 million, 44 percent of the total campaign expenditures. Of this, $2 million was reserved for production costs while $6.3 million went directly into television air time[4].

Television, as indicated, is the principal villain. It makes available to the candidate a powerful instrument of persuasion with direct access to 99 percent of American homes. But it is an inordinately expensive tool and one employed increasingly as a substitute for good campaign organization at the grassroots level and the personal contact and the exhausting individual schedules that have marked so many presidential efforts. The amount of money that could be spent during campaigns in the medium is virtually unlimited. The period 1956 to 1968 provides a basis for analysis. Television and radio expenses amounted to $3.6 million for the 1952 presidential election year[5]. By 1956, the overall election investment in television had reached $6.6 million, an escalation process that would result in expenditures for television alone of $10 million in 1960, $17.5 million in 1964, and $27 million in 1968 (Table 4.1). By 1972, television air time in all elections (both primary and general) had reached $37.2 million[6].

The television cost increases not only parallel (and, of course, fuel) the general inflation in campaign expenditures, but there has been a selective focus in both the nature of the races increasingly dependent on television and in the manner in which the medium is being used. Delmer Dunn has calculated the amount of

TABLE 4.1
TOTAL CHARGES FOR POLITICAL BROADCASTS:
GENERAL ELECTIONS OF 1956, 1960, 1964, AND 1968

	1968 ($)	1964 ($)	1960 ($)	1956 ($)
Total charges	40,403,498	24,603,989	14,195,278	9,818,342
Republican	22,504,858	13,032,575	7,558,809	5,381,891
Democratic	15,447,989	11,012,626	6,204,986	4,120,712
Other	2,450,651	558,788	431,483	315,739
Television—Total	27,087,027	17,496,405	10,052,322	6,635,946
Network—Total	7,362,240	3,807,011	2,927,235	2,930,514
Republican	4,189,298	1,911,616	1,820,360	1,733,073
Democratic	2,500,517	1,895,395	1,106,875	1,197,441
Other	672,425	—	—	—
Stations—Total	19,724,787	13,689,394	7,125,087	3,705,432
Republican	10,993,574	7,519,494	3,610,933	2,004,090
Democratic	7,923,423	5,819,699	3,307,987	1,159,347
Other	807,790	350,201	206,167	151,995
Radio—Total	13,316,471	7,107,584	4,142,956	3,182,396
Network—Total	662,674	119,365	78,867	320,940
Republican	468,871	88,863	44,546	144,645
Democratic	177,803	30,502	34,321	176,295
Other	16,000	—	—	—
Stations—Total	12,653,797	6,988,219	4,064,089	2,861,456
Republican	6,853,115	3,512,602	2,082,970	1,500,083
Democratic	4,846,246	3,267,030	1,755,803	1,197,629
Other	954,436	208,587	225,316	163,744

SOURCE: Federal Communications Commission, *Survey of Political Broadcasting: Primary and General Election Campaigns of 1968* (Washington, D.C.: Federal Communications Commission, August, 1969), table 3.

media spending in presidential campaigns that can be accounted for simply through increased time costs for television usage between 1956 and 1968. He finds that only 22 percent of the additional expense in presidential races is caused by the increase in the cost of purchasing air time. Over three-quarters of the $11 million spent for presidential television air time is due to the more extensive use of the medium. In contrast, almost one-half (47 percent) of the increased television expenditures for all other offices are explainable in terms of cost changes related to buying the progressively more expensive television air time rather than by an expansion in the use of this communications outlet. The reliance on television as a campaign tool has increased disproportionately in presidential contests.

Finally, in this vein, candidates began to rely with far greater frequency on spot advertisements during the period examined, in place of various other types of political programming. By 1968, spot announcements on the networks had more than doubled to about one-half of all paid political advertising. In terms of placement with individual television statements by 1968, they had all but eliminated program formats in attempting to reach prospective voters. As politicians relied more heavily on this form of communication, its cost shot up 247 percent over the four elections, far outstripping any comparative increment in cost for newspaper or magazine advertising, radio commercials, or, for that matter, full program time on television (the last of which increased by a less heady 105 percent) [7].

Television spot commercials have been severely criticized as oversimplified, emotional appeals not worthy of influencing the type of decision a voter has to make. Presidential candidates, detergents, and a General Motors car are all indistinguishably presented to passive viewers in hopes they will respond positively to the appropriate cues. There is a good deal of merit to such arguments. Still, viewed from the perspective of the candidates or their campaign managers, television advertising is both an absolute necessity in campaigns the magnitude of a national presidential race and a good investment on a cost/benefit basis. While television expenditures were increasing markedly from 1952 onward, the number of families with television sets rose from 47 percent in 1953 to 90 percent in 1960 and 94 percent in 1964 before stabilizing at an incredible 99 percent of American households. No other vehicle offers a national candidate so direct, personal, and, in these terms, inexpensive a way to reach virtually the entire American electorate.

One further word on costs. Politics is expensive and the recent steep climb in campaign spending certainly indicates this fact of political life. But the expenditure of $65 million or more by one candidate in 1972 is unconscionable. Overspending of this magnitude cannot be justified and, as Watergate demonstrated, constitutes a direct threat to orderly elections. The 1968 election, consequently, provides a more responsible guideline. Even if the political spending of that campaign year is judged to be overly generous, the gross amount ($300 million for all elections) is only *slightly more than the advertising budget for one corporation,* Procter and Gamble, whose $270 million outlay led American business in 1968[8]. The election costs in 1968 amounted to 0.03 percent of the country's gross national product. The cost per voter came to $1.50, a relatively modest figure compared with other democratic nations. Herbert Alexander has put the matter well. "The $300,000,000 spent on all campaigns in 1968 was 0.1 percent of the $282,600,000,000 spent by governments at all levels in that year. Is 1/1000 of the cost of government 'too much' to select the people who will decide how tax money is to be spent, or who will run the government [9]?" Is any sum too large to fund adequately so important a link in the act of democratic governance? Economies are argued, strangely, for some of the least deserving areas.

More significant at this point is the question as to the equity of the distribution of political funding and the source of the money. If the money available is given in good faith and is distributed evenly among incumbents and challengers; liberals, moderates, and conservatives; Republicans, Democrats, and independents, then the magnitude of the costs—the chief target of many reform proposals—may be a diversionary issue. If, however, the political funds simply reinforce advantages already built into the electoral system, then the problem—in terms of the equalization of resources—demands attention.

PRESIDENTIAL CAMPAIGNS

Presidential elections have traditionally been the nation's most expensive. The first million-dollar campaign (using 1860 as the starting date) occurred in 1880 and although there are sharp variations (topped by Alf Landon's $8.9 million contest in 1936, a figure not to be surpassed until the Nixon and Kennedy race of 1960), the average expenditure in the 23 presidential campaigns between 1860 and as late as 1948 by a presidential candidate amounted to less than $4 million. In 1948, the combined expenditures of the principal contenders, Harry Truman and Thomas Dewey, fell below $5 million. By 1952, campaign costs were approaching $12 million, however, and the escalation had begun.

The period preceding 1952 then is one of relatively constant costs. Nonetheless, the trend figures hide some information that could be instructive. For example, Republican presidential candidates outspent their Democratic counterparts in more than three out of four contests on the average of $2.5 million to $1.5 million. Political scientists are fond of pointing out that money does not win elections; in itself, a truism. It does help, however. The only Democratic candidates to spend more than their Republican opponents—Grover Cleveland in his two victories, Woodrow Wilson in 1912, and Truman in 1948—did manage to win. On the whole, the candidate who spent more won in over 80 percent of the contests; prior to the realignment of 1932, the larger spender won in all but one of the 18 contests —Wilson's surprise victory over a factionally divided Republican party in the three-man race of 1912. Franklin Roosevelt alone accounts for two-thirds of the exceptions. In all, from 1860 through 1972, the larger spender won 75 percent of the time [10].

A few other patterns of note are apparent. For the 18 races between 1860 and 1972 when an incumbent president was seeking reelection, it could be assumed the man in office would have had greater access to funds—one of the many advantages of incumbency—and thus would be able to spend more in the campaign. This turned out to be true in over 60 percent of the cases. Almost two-thirds of the exceptions are accounted for by Democratic incumbents being outspent by Republican foes. The exceptions to this general rule are President Grover Cleveland, who lost in 1888 to Benjamin Harrison's more lavish campaign but came back four years later to outspend and defeat the incumbent Harrison; and Woodrow Wilson, who spent slightly more than the Republican incumbent Taft in 1912 but less than the combined totals for his two Republican opponents, Taft and Teddy Roosevelt running as a Bull Moose Progressive.

The magnitude of the difference in expenditures can be startling. The presidential election of 1896 was an extraordinarily important one, in the parlance of the political scientist a "critical" or "realigning" election (one of only three, 1860 and 1932 being the others). The Republican candidate, William McKinley, spent an extraordinary $3.4 million to save the country from the radicalism of his Democratic-Populist opponent William Jennings Bryan. The amount was twice as much as that spent for any previous election. Bryan could collect only 20 percent of this total. The discrepancy was increased four years later in a repeat performance by both candidates. Warren Harding outspent his Democratic rival by a ratio of 3.8 to 1 in a successful effort in 1920 to return control of the presidency to the Republican party, and both Herbert Hoover and Alfred Landon at the height of the Great Depression and amid a mass voter condemnation of Republican policies still managed to field more expensive campaigns than Franklin Roosevelt. Even Barry Goldwater in 1964, a candidate with little public support and virtually no chance of victory, outspent his Democratic rival, the incumbent Lyndon Johnson, by a ratio almost of 2 to 1.

In sum, there is a definite trend to expenditures in presidential campaigns. Republicans outspend Democrats with regularity and sometimes in critical contests by amounts that affect the ability of the candidates to push their message across to the voters. Like it or not, the heavy spenders usually won. Incumbents, those in a position to do something for their contributors, normally expended more than their rivals, and the costs of presidential campaigns—at least through 1972—increased at an extraordinary rate.

EXPENDITURES AT OTHER LEVELS

An examination of campaign costs over any extended period of time reveals the marked variety in levels of expenditures. These vary by candidate, by office sought, by state, and by election year, and the differences appear to defy rational explanation. For example, the candidates for governor in Massachusetts in the off-year election of 1962 spent approximately one-half million dollars each, while the U.S. Senate candidates of the two parties spent one-half that amount. The winning contender for attorney general spent almost as much as the Senate candidates while the secretary of state needed only $7000 and the state auditor $767 to retain their offices[11]. In the 1956 U.S. Senate campaigns, Thomas Kuchel (R.) spent $374,000 (compared to $182,000 for the Democratic candidate) in California to win his seat, while Democrat Frank Church captured his in Republican Idaho for $41,000, about $9000 less than his opponent's campaign cost. Republican-turned-independent-turned-Democrat Wayne Morse retained his Senate position in Oregon in a campaign costing less than $150,000—$75,000 below the expenditures of his nationally-known challenger. Everett Dirksen beat back the attempt to win his seat with $111,000—$30,000 below what his competitor spent. Senator Norris Cotton in New Hampshire needed only $8000 to win reelection. His challenger spent an incredibly low $350, the sign of a truly futile race. Senator John Sparkman (Ala.) spent $500 to insure his 1966 reelection, probably an extravagance given the seriousness of the opposition. Senator Richard Russell in neighboring Georgia during the same election year required no campaign financing at all; he was unopposed in both the primary and the general election. Edward Brooke, the Republican Senate winner in Massachusetts in 1966, recorded over $400,000 in campaign expenses. While some House candidates reported spending nothing that year in their elections (and others simply did not report) or a token $150 or so (Wilbur Mills, for example), some admitted to financing campaigns of over $50,000 in both highly competitive and, more strangely, one-party areas.

The 1970 gubernatorial elections found the usual discrepancies A Democrat beat the incumbent Republican governor in South Dakota for $21,000, less than half his opponent's budgeted costs. Another $20,000 won a Democrat the Nebraska governorship against an incumbent Republican whose outlays totaled far more. Victorious Democratic gubernatorial candidates in Ohio and Pennsylvania recorded expenses between $500,00 and $600,000. Both California Senate contestants admitted to budgeting almost one-half million dollars for their campaigns. The most expensive Senate seat that year, however, fell to New York. Heir to a plywood lumber fortune, Congressman Richard L. Ottinger, lost $641,151 in an unsuccessful bid for the Senate against Republican Charles E. Goodell ($569,443), the incumbent, and Conservative James L. Buckley ($516,472), the ultimate victor. To represent the fickleness of the whole process, consider the following. In 1970, former governor Carl Sanders spent $290,207 in the Georgia Democratic gubernatorial primary and lost. The primary campaign of the winner, Jimmy Carter, cost $170,000 and the general election another $100,000. George Wallace needed $396,000 to recapture the Democratic nomination for governor in Alabama in a race with the incumbent Democrat, Albert Brewer, whose campaign—as events were to show—had been financially supported by the Nixon Administration. Brewer spent $431,000 in a primary whose total cost came to over $800,000. On the other end of the financial scale, the Democratic challenger to U.S. Senator Hugh Scott in Pennsylvania could manage a campaign budget of only $25,374 (compared to Scott's $267,270) and yet lost the general election by only 0.6 percent of the total 3.6 million votes cast[12].

Among the high-water marks in political spending would be Ottinger's rumored $4 million campaign to win the 1970 primary and general election and

Senator John Tower's $2.5 million to hold his Texas seat two years later, the latter sum reportedly collected from the Republican national party and savings and loan associations whose activities were regulated by the Senate Banking Committee on which Tower served. Tower had no opponent in the primary and outspent his Democratic rival in the general election by more than a 4 to 1 ratio. Ronald Reagan needed an outlay of $3.5 million in 1970 to retain the governorship of California and, in what stands as the all-time known record for offices below the presidential level, Nelson Rockefeller spent an estimated $7.7 million in 1970 to win his fourth term as New York's governor[13]. Dwight Eisenhower (and each of his predecessors in both parties) spent less on his candidacy for the presidency only 18 years earlier.

Politics then is expensive. The costs do vary and traces of a pattern as to the factors influencing expenditures are often difficult to extract. Nonetheless, they exist. An in-depth look at the costs for political office in comparable races—the U.S. Senate and House races in 1972—helps to reveal the factors that relate to increased expenses.

THE SENATE AND HOUSE
CONTESTS IN 1972

The bill for the 1974 congressional elections, the most expensive in history to date, was $80 million, a quantum jump from the $10 to $18 million needed in the off-year congressional elections from 1954 to 1966, the $30 to $33 million spent on these races during the 1956 and 1960 presidential election years, and the $42.4 million expended for 1970.

Two recent and interrelated developments have made the systematic analysis of federal campaign contributions possible. The first was the adoption by the Congress of the Financial Disclosure Law of 1971. The second was the rise of citizen groups with the manpower, resources, and determination necessary to overcome the official obstructionism intended to make the disclosure laws inoperable. Prior to 1972, the Citizens' Research Foundation of Princeton, New Jersey, under the directorship of Dr. Herbert E. Alexander, was virtually alone in attempting to compile data on and assess the financial implications of politics. The CRF studies provide the basis for much of this presentation. It was not, however, until the well-financed, mass-based public interest groups arose that could mobilize citizen attention on the passage of decent legislation and then serve as a watchdog to insure full and impartial compliance with the new laws that the full dimensions of the level of expenditures in federal campaigns could be documented. Common Cause, of course, typifies the public interest groups referred to and it is primarily the information this group made available to the Congress— "the first comprehensive spending figures on congressional races ever made public"[14]—for its consideration of more far-reaching legislation that provides the materials for an analysis of the 1972 expenditures.

In presenting the results of its studies, Common Cause expressed its "grave doubts as to whether we presently have a competitive system of representation[15]." The basis for this dire reservation was the imbalance the group found in the financial resources available to incumbents and to challengers. Congressional incumbents in 1972 held a 2 to 1 edge in financing over their opponents. Of the money invested in congressional campaigns by special interests, two out of every three dollars went to incumbents. Further, less than one out of every three dollars came from small contributors (defined as those giving $100 or less). Money, of course, does not insure victory, but, as Common Cause argued, "it is essential to winning a closely contested race[16]."

The documentation supporting the conclusions is extensive. The total expenditure for both House and Senate races in 1972 came to $66.4 million, a figure that rises to $77 million when the expenditures of candidates who lost in the primary are added. Incumbents, regardless of party affiliation, had a relatively easy time in acquiring campaign funds and on the balance accumulated twice the totals of their challengers:

	Incumbents	Challengers
Democrats	$56, 364	$29, 656
Republicans	$60, 342	$32, 709

When incumbency was not a factor, the candidates of both parties averaged almost identical amounts of funding ($89,430 for Democrats, $88,375 for Republicans). Only 10 incumbent congressmen lost in the 1972 elections, and the challengers who won averaged expenditures of $125,000 compared to $86,000 for the officeholders they beat (Table 4.2). If a congressman chose not to run again, the candidates of the major parties seeking the incumbent's seat usually could find adequate, and relatively even, amounts of financing. If an incumbent sought reelection, his opponent was likely to receive little monetary support regardless of his party identification ($31,000 on the average).

Most House races are uncompetitive, won by 55 percent or more of the vote. In fact, 83 percent of the 1972 contests fall into this category (a figure which does *not* include those districts in which only one candidate ran). The mean expenditure for the winners in these elections came to $52,405, well above the $27,245 spent by the losers (Table 4.3). Funding discrepancies of this magnitude represent a subtle but nonetheless decisive advantage for those running on the majority party ticket or with the edge of incumbency. For example, a candidate in an election in which he won with two out of three votes cast presumably would require relatively little financing. The challenger, on the other hand, would need a comparatively large war chest to reduce the competitive factors working against him. In truth, the money available simply reinforces the ultimate winner's superiority. In such circumstances, the expenditure by the successful candidate is more than three times that of the loser.

TABLE 4.2
EXPENDITURES IN CONTESTS FOR THE U.S. HOUSE, INCUMBENTS AND NONINCUMBENTS, 1972

	Contributions ($)	Expenditures ($)
Major party candidates:		
Democratic	49,224	47,479
Republican	51,389	49,564
Races with no incumbent in primary or general election (52):		
Democrat	89,430	90,074
Republican	88,375	90,030
Winner	102,338	104,064
Loser	75,213	75,766
Races where incumbents were defeated by nonincumbents:		
In the general election (10):		
Incumbent	93,837	86,075
Winning challenger	123,450	125,521
In their party primary (7):		
Winning challenger[a]	132,411	141,153
Opponent in general election	59,167	59,379
Incumbents with major party challengers (318):		
Incumbent	58,359	50,873
Challenger	31,355	32,127
Democratic incumbent	56,364	50,009
Republican challenger	32,709	33,587
Republican incumbent	60,842	51,947
Democratic challenger	29,656	30,295
Incumbents with no major party opponents (52): Incumbent	24,984	17,372

[a] Totals cover primary and general election.

SOURCE: Common Cause data as reproduced in the report of the Committee on Rules and Administration, U.S. Senate, *Public Financing of Federal Elections* (Washington, D.C.: U.S. Government Printing Office, 1973), p. 105.

The highly competitive House races resulted in the greatest financial expenditures. Two races, one of which included Congressman Paul McCloskey, gadfly of the moderate-to-left Republican insurgent movement and a highly vocal critic of the Nixon Administration, resulted in expenditures of over one-half million dollars. As Table 4.3 shows, *both* winners and losers in the most competitive contests averaged costs in excess of $100,000. Will Rogers's comment at the beginning of this chapter merits remembering,

Expenditures in the 1972 U.S. Senate races were much the same. Table 4.4 presents illustrative information on 10 of the most expensive contests. As noted, the Tower race is something of a landmark, but it is worth observing that the cost per vote ($3.65) in this election, while exceedingly high, is *less* than that for both the winning incumbents, Percy ($4.12) and Baker ($3.70), in Illinois and Tennes-

TABLE 4.3
PARTY COMPETITION AND CAMPAIGN EXPENDITURES,
U.S. HOUSE ELECTIONS, 1972

Winning % (Range)	No. of Races in Category	Averages	
		Winner's Expenditure ($)	Loser's Expenditure ($)
70 to 90	97	38,729	7,479
65 to 70	66	42,212	16,060
60 to 65	91	55,065	30,483
55 to 60	60	73,616	54,600
Up to 55	66	107,378	101,166

NOTE: Unopposed candidate omitted.

SOURCE: Common Cause data as reproduced in the report of the committee on Rules and Administration, U.S. Senate, *Public Financing of Federal Elections* (Washington, D.C.: U.S. Government Printing Office, 1973), p. 104.

see, respectively. When all of the 33 contests for Senate seats that took place in 1972 are analyzed (data not shown in Table 4.4), 12 candidates *in toto* exceeded a 3 to 1 ratio in funds spent compared with their opponents. *All* 12 won and all but one were incumbents. Three—Hansen of Wyoming, Pearson of Kansas, and Hathaway of Maine (the only nonincumbent, a congressman who forfeited reelection to the House to run against Margaret Chase Smith)—outspent their rivals by enormous margins, 16 to 1, 16 to 1, and 14 to 1, respectively. To compound the imbalance, only the Hathaway-Smith contest was close. Both Hansen and Pearson won with over 70 percent of the vote. Both Republicans faced badly underfinanced opponents ($10,000 and $5000 campaign budgets, respectively) and both had a campaign surplus of over $90,000, not equal to Senator Edward Brooke's $304,000 (or Richard Nixon's $4.8 million in leftover 1972 campaign funds) but comfortable enough. In fact, if the financial resources *available* to the conservatives Hansen and Pearson are measured rather than the funds actually spent, possibly a better measure of competitive advantage, the disparity ratios reach a stunning 25 and 39 to 1.

The gap in expenditures between the candidates who succeeded (both office-holders) and their opponents in the highly competitive states of Michigan and Illinois suggests the electoral value of extensive funding. In one race, a few more dollars might have led to a different outcome. In the other, a heavy funding imbalance between the candidates prevented the challenger from ever positioning himself for a serious run for the office. Frank Kelley, the Democrat and loser in Michigan, while outspent by his opponent Senator Robert Griffin by a margin of 2.5 to 1, still came within a few percentage points of victory. The Illinois race is a curiosity. The Democratic challenger, a Daley organization follower who gave up a congressional seat to run, was poorly funded and captured only 38 percent

TABLE 4.4
THE 10 MOST EXPENSIVE
U.S. SENATE CONTESTS IN 1972

		Contributions		Expenditures	
	Vote Margin (%)	Total Contributions ($)	Contribution Ratio between Candidates ($)	Total Expenditures ($)	Expenditure Ratio between Candidates ($)
Texas:					
John Tower[a]	53.4	2,303,355	3.65	2,301,870	3.66
Barefoot Sanders	44.5	630,440	1.00	629,008	1.00
Michigan:					
Robert Griffin[a]	52.2	1,443,304	2.65	1,394,927	2.54
Frank Kelley	46.7	544,009	1.00	547,819	1.00
Illinois:					
Charles Percy[a]	61.4	1,399,374	4.12	1,408,822	4.20
Roman Pucinski	38.6	399,402	1.00	335,482	1.00
Alabama:					
John Sparkman[a]	63.9	703,342	.90	702,109	.92
Winton Blount	32.5	774,039	1.00	764,961	1.00
Kentucky:					
Walter Huddleston	51.0	653,412	1.09	653,590	1.09
Louie Nunn	47.6	611,013	1.00	603,649	1.00
Oklahoma:					
Dewey Bartlett	51.5	625,639	1.19	625,095	1.22
Ed Edmondson	47.9	525,900	1.00	512,058	1.00
North Carolina:					
Jesse Helms	54.1	659,895	1.33	654,246	1.39
N. Galifianakis	45.9	496,667	1.00	470,093	1.00
Tennessee:					
Howard Baker[a]	61.8	887,817	3.70	830,769	3.40
Ray Blanton	38.2	239,699	1.00	244,653	1.00
Louisana:					
Bennett Johnston	54.9	556,912	1.09	511,616	1.00
John McKeithen	23.2	394,510	1.00	394,510	1.00
Ben Toledano	19.0	118,906	1.00	116,347	1.00
Georgia:					
Sam Nunn	53.6	629,570	1.39	587,968	1.28
Fletcher Thompson	46.4	454,586	1.00	444,635	1.00

[a]Incumbent.

SOURCE: Common Cause data as reproduced in the report of the Committee on Rules and Administration, U.S. Senate, *Public Financing of Federal Elections* (Washington, D.C.: U.S. Government Printing Office, 1973), p. 102.

of the vote. The Percy campaign was a case study in financial overkill. Percy outspent his rival 4 to 1 and won handsomely. Yet the Percy campaign actually exceeded by a slight margin the lavish $1.4 million in campaign contributions it attracted.

The cost of increasing party competition is nicely illustrated by the data in Table 4.4. Eight of the ten most expensive Senate races occurred in previously one-party southern and border states. By the same token, however, and calling on figures not fully incorporated into the table, the least competitive races are noteworthy only for the lack of funding available to the losers. The winners who received more than 60 percent of the vote in the 11 contests also managed to outspend their opponents by $300,000 on the average ($476,567 to $165,848). The lone exception occurred in Alabama where Winton Blount, postmaster general in the original Nixon Cabinet, returned to challenge incumbent John Sparkman. Extremely well financed, Blount managed to spend more than Sparkman but captured less than one-third of the vote. The campaign costs of the Alabama Senate election—$500 total six years earlier—had risen in the Sparkman-Blount contest to $1.5 million.

The overall pattern is now familiar. Incumbent senators seeking reelection raised more than twice as much money ($525,809 to $243,070) as their challengers and the winning candidates spent twice as much as those who failed. Republicans, on the whole, raised more money, $16.3 million compared to $10.6 million for the Democrats, a factor reflecting in part the greater number of Republican officeholders attempting reelection. Four Republican senators (Tower, Griffin, Percy, and Baker) alone accounted for $6 million of the total Republican Senate campaign funds. With no incumbent in the race, Democrats on the average spent only slightly more than Republicans ($496,000 to $465,000). Furthermore, the nonincumbent races were not only more evenly financed, the voting results were also more competitive (a winner's margin of 53.5 percent compared to 58.8 percent for the more disproportionately funded contests).

The above data suggests the enormous problems posed by incumbency. Yet even the most enlightened of the proposed legislative solutions fail to deal adequately with the issue. California, in a progressive mood, passed a campaign reform act in 1975 that restricted an officeholder to 89 percent of the total expended by a challenger. The law is the first of its kind in the nation, but it scarcely begins to deal with the disparity between incumbent and challenger. Two economists at the University of Connecticut have estimated (Table 4.5) that if candidates' expenditures were limited by statute to $50,000, incumbents with 40 percent of the electorate in their district registered in their party could expect to receive 60 percent of the vote. In a district with voter registration evenly divided between the two parties, a challenger would have to spend something in the vicinity of 10 times the minimal amount needed by the incumbent to insure himself an equal chance for the seat [17].

TABLE 4.5
MAXIMUM LIKELIHOOD POINT ESTIMATE
OF CAMPAIGN EXPENDITURE NECESSARY TO GIVE CANDIDATE
AN EQUAL A PRIORI CHANCE OF ELECTION

Vote Registration in the Party of the Candidate (% of Total Registration)	Expenditures	
	Incumbent ($)	Challenger ($)
30	31,335.59	343,960.69
40	11,091.46	121,747.36
50	4,955.96	54,399.96
60	2,566.08	28,167.05
70	1,470.89	16,145.54

SOURCE: Study by W.F. Lott and P.D. Warner, III, Economics Department, University of Connecticut, as reproduced in the report of the Committee on Rules and Administration, U.S. Senate, *Public Financing of Federal Elections* (Washington, D.C.: U.S. Government Printing Office, 1973), p. 157.

There are inequities built into contests for public office. Unrestrained financing quite obviously exaggerates these, a conclusion that an examination of the nature of the contributors and the types of candidacies to which they contribute serves to reinforce.

SOURCES OF FUNDS: WHERE DOES THE MONEY COME FROM?

Watergate punctured many myths of American politics. One of the most persistent of these was the power of financing political campaigns through small donors. It has long been a dream of many political activists to be able to support serious presidential campaigns through small donors giving $10, $25, or $100. It was argued that candidates would then be free from the shackles of big industry and big labor and could act and vote in the best interests of the nation at large. A second aspect of the argument, and one more assumed than actually debated, was that adequate funding not tied to the need to forge a record accommodating to corporate support would allow a new breed of candidate to appear, one relatively free of old obligations and one that could speak to the issues of the day with decisiveness and imagination.

In fact, the effort to increase small contributions has met with some success. The Republican National Committee has long run a well-organized subscription program which brings in a sizable amount of funding and which it claims provides the major source for national level activities (exclusive of campaigning). Sustaining members with an average donation of $22 contributed 85 percent of the Republican National Committee's $4.5 million budget in 1973. Figures such as these led the Democrats in the post–1968 reassessment of party operations to make a heavy commitment to paying off its debt (then calculated at $9.3 million) and funding its annual National Committee budget (estimated at $1.5 million) through a professionally organized mail solicitation of prospective small donors. The effort has moved uncertainly at times, but in combination with an annual telethon intended to solicit new names and additional funds has begun to make a substantial contribution to the national party's budget.

As noted, such developments are impressive. Yet it is extremely doubtful whether small contributors have any more say over the leadership and operation of their national party organization than they did before. Both parties are still free to solicit large contributions, and without question they are far more sensitive to the person who gives $5000 than they are to the one who donates $15. Also, few influential donors consider it desirable to buy access to a national committee. Excluding the organizational activities associated with the national conventions, the national party staff does little more than service local party needs and function as a public relations arm to place the party's views before the electorate. For example, it is most unlikely that a person who wished to gain influence with the Nixon Administration would have done so by contributing to the Republican National Committee and then hoping to employ the committee's prestige to plead his case with the administration. The same holds true for Congress. Influence with a congressman over pending legislation is not gained by sending funds to the national committees. There are more direct ways.

The person who wishes to insure "access" ("buying access" is the euphemism usually offered to explain heavy political contributions) donates a substantial amount of money to a politician's campaign. The association is direct and immediate. The politician is grateful and the donor is guaranteed a sympathetic reception in Washington. This fact can be documented with devastating consistency, one further contribution of the Watergate abuses. The process is not necessarily illegal. Rather, this enforced mutual bond between giver and recipient is built into and has always been a fundamental part of the American political system. It is, nonetheless, just the sort of relationship those who originally supported small donor programs hoped to avoid. Until Barry Goldwater broke new ground in 1964, however, such an approach was difficult to organize and relatively expensive to execute. Nevertheless there have been some significant successes in recent years.

Many political issues appear to be of recent vintage until one finds that some of the same concerns have vexed politicians for generations. Stimulating a large number of modest contributions is one of those little-known, longstanding problems. Henry Clay in 1840 may have been the first to argue for such a plan. Clay proposed that the Whig party work through the Congregational church to raise one penny per week from each parishioner. The sum gathered would be adequate to the party's needs and would free it from dependence on a few large contributors[18]. Apparently, little more was heard of the idea. William Jennings

Bryan in 1896 and 1908 and Woodrow Wilson in 1912 attempted with limited success to finance their campaigns through small donations. The Democratic National Committee tried again in 1916 and the Republicans offered party memberships for $10 in a related move. The Democrats had hoped to attract 1 million contributors. They reached 20,000 and found that a campaign to seek a wide base of support in small denominations is expensive, costing about as much as the money brought into the party.

These experiences represented the accumulated wisdom in the field until Barry Goldwater's prenomination drive in 1964. On one of his earliest television broadcasts during the campaign, Goldwater set aside a few minutes at the end to ask for small contributions to finance his unorthodox drive for the presidency. The outcome proved surprising. Three hundred thousand persons contributed to the Goldwater campaign for the Republican nomination. Still, the results were dismissed as an artifact of Goldwater's appeal to fervent conservatives. Liberals, supposedly, could never hope to duplicate such a showing. Four years later, an equally atypical candidate of the Democratic party's left, Eugene McCarthy, attracted 150,000 small donors which helped to make the Minnesotan's challenge to the Johnson war policies a reality.

The election year of 1968 also witnessed the emergence of the Nelson Rockfeller of the small donors. George Wallace's campaign ("Send them a message!" and "There's not a dime's worth of difference between the Democrats and the Republicans") struck a responsive chord intensive enough for 750,000 individuals to contribute funds. This mark stands as the all-time record.

George McGovern in 1972 tried to duplicate Goldwater's and McCarthy's feats in the prenomination phase and Wallace's in the general election. Stressing small contributions of $25 or less and employing a young Alabama expert on direct mailing who had made his personal fortune from the technique, McGovern did very well. Six hundred forty thousand people contributed between $14 and $15 million to his campaign, a showing second only to Wallace. The funds McGovern brought in were roughly three times those secured by Goldwater. Encouraged by such results, state-level candidates began to adopt the same approach. Ramsey Clark ran for the U.S. Senate in New York in 1974 and 1976, refusing to accept contributions above a $100 level and still managed to run in 1974 a respectable, if not lavish campaign with a treasury of $900,000, against the popular incumbent, Jacob Javits.

Overall, the figures for the last two decades on the number of contributors and those giving in small amounts (liberally defined in the following as less than $500), both increasing, provides ground for optimism (see Table 4.6). The number of small donors has clearly increased. In the two most notable examples, small contributors accounted for $11.5 million of Goldwater's $16 million 1964 budget and $8.3 million of Wallace's roughly $9 to $10 million in expenditures in 1968. A staple of the 1972 McGovern candidacy in both the prenomination and general election phase was a wide base of small contributions.

TABLE 4.6
CONTRIBUTIONS TO PRESIDENTIAL CAMPAIGNS

Party	% of Contributions of $500 or Better					
	1952	1956	1960	1964	1968	1972
Democrats	63	43	59	69	61	40
Republicans	68	72	58	28	47	—
American Independent (Wallace)	—	—	—	—	6.8	—

Year	No. of People Contributing	
	Total	% of Adult Population
1952	3,000,000	4.0
1956	8,000,000	9.0
1960	10,000,000	10.5
1964	12,000,000	12.0
1968	8,700,000	8.0
1972	6,400,000	5.3

SOURCE: For the years 1952–1968, see: U.S. Senate Committee on Rules and Administration, 93rd Congress, *Public Financing of Federal Elections* (Washington, D.C.: U.S. Government Printing Office, 1973), p. 237.

A national Wallace campaign would have been impossible without the small contributions of a large number of people. The Wallace budget approaches Humphrey's $11.6 million expenditure, although the latter does not include, of course, significant outlays by organized labor on his behalf. Viewed historically, the Wallace effort was the most lavishly funded third-party drive ever recorded. Strom Thurmond's Dixiecrats in 1948 spent only $163,000 and Henry Wallace's third-party drive in the same year cost $1.1 million. Teddy Roosevelt's Bull Moose Progressives recorded expenditures of $665,420 in 1912 and the La Follette Progressives in 1924 budgeted only a modest $236,963 for their campaign. From such a perspective, Wallace's financial success is impressive[19].

The 1972 McGovern campaign better illustrates the strengths and liabilities of a small donor program within the major parties. McGovern was considerably better financed than his predecessor Hubert Humphrey in 1968 and, in fact, outspent Humphrey two to one. A lack of adequate financing effectively crippled the Humphrey campaign, forcing the presidential candidate to periodically break off touring to seek funds. The inadequate campaign budget also meant that, having to relinquish national television time he had reserved but could not pay for, Humphrey was unable to appeal directly to the American people on those occasions when he felt he had something of consequence to say. Even his critical Salt Lake City speech on Vietnam was broadcast nationally only at the last moment as the necessary funds became available. The Nixon campaign, of course, faced no such difficulty. It is conceivable that a formidably underwritten Humphrey effort might have provided the margin needed to turn a close election into a Nixon defeat.

McGovern, then, did not encounter problems of such magnitude. Equally important, he had some funds available early in the general election period when the commitments required by the media, airlines, telephone companies, and the like (under pressure from the Nixon Administration to enforce such provisions) had to be made. Still, small donor programs are slow and uncertain in yield. The drives alone have high start-up costs and in themselves can be expensive with costs ranging from an unusually low 7.5 percent of intake for a selectively developed, high-yield list to the more normal 60 percent of money received. They also require a fairly sophisticated collection operation throughout the life of the campaign as well as previously developed lists of potential contributors (obtained usually from other candidates or from sympathetic interest groups). McGovern did not exclude large contributions and in fact used these to finance and publicize his plea for a broad-based giving. Yet, despite the large investment of effort, McGovern was outspent on a three to one ratio and outfunded by an even larger margin. To this day, no one is quite sure exactly how much the Committee to Re-Elect the President [Nixon] and the White House had at its disposal. All agree, however, that the sum was substantial and well above anything McGovern could have hoped to duplicate.

Small donor campaigns are potentially valuable but limited in effect. They require a great deal of persistent cultivation of the prospective contributors. It is unlikely that they actually increase the control of grassroots supporters over candidates or their policies or over a national committee, as some have hoped they would. Yet an extensive number of small contributions are, despite the inherent difficulties, feasible and they can finance in large part nationwide campaigns. Furthermore, and most impressively, they allow a flexibility in leadership choice by permitting policy-oriented and factional candidates who could not hope to attract a significant amount of funding from conventional sources the opportunity to compete and to be heard. But, and this is significant, a campaign based on small donors can never hope to compete on an equal footing with one relying primarily on the traditional, large contributors. And, in fact, the highly publicized preoccupation with funding in small amounts may simply devert public attention from the real sources of financial power, the impact of whose contributions should not be underestimated.

TARGETING THE CONTRIBUTORS

A better understanding of the types of elections to which money flows and the nature of the "small" donors lends perspective to a more intensive examination of the larger contributors. Table 4.7 reviews the relative contributions of

TABLE 4.7
FUNDING SOURCES BY EXPENSE OF CONTEST, 1972, U.S. HOUSE CONTESTS

	Share of Funds Derived From	
Expenditure Level	Small Contributors and Party Committees (%)	Large Contributors and Interest Groups[a] (%)
0 to $30,000	57.9	27.1
$30,000 to $70,000	50.6	34.6
$70,000 to $120,000	46.7	36.5
$120,000 and above	39.1	40.4

[a] Large contributors defined to include all contributors of more than $1000. Figures include all funds provided by special interest committees.

SOURCE: Committee on Rules and Administration, U.S. Senate, *Public Financing of Federal Elections* (Washington, D.C.: U.S. Government Printing Office, 1973), p. 337.

large and small donors to the 1972 congressional elections in relation to the expense of the race. Small contributors (generously defined as those giving under $1000) and the funds provided by party committees are lumped together in the table. Still, the trend is clear. The less expensive the race, the heavier the dependence on small donors and party agencies for funding. As the cost of the campaign grows, the significance of the larger funder becomes increasingly obvious. Presumably, there is a relationship between the significance of the contest and the amounts expended in the campaign. It has already been established that highly competitive races (decided by 5 percent of the vote or less) are extraordinarily expensive as are "open" races (those with no incumbent seeking reelection). In addition, it has become clear that officeholders seeking reelection are well funded. Consequently, it is reasonable to assume that single contributors of large sums of money give disproportionately both to elections with incumbents and to those in which there is a good probability of capturing a seat. The less significant contests, those in which a challenger has little chance of victory, apparently are left to the friends and associates of the nominee to finance as best they can.

A review of Table 4.8 should dispel another illusion. Candidates of both political parties (as well as the national committees of the parties) are fond of picking out letters from widows who have dipped into their limited savings to contribute to a candidate or party they feel is crucial to the continued vitality of the nation. Undoubtedly, this happens and the publicized correspondence is often moving. Nonetheless, it represents the exception. Low-income people are the least likely (and the least able) to contribute to political campaigns. Yet a minimum of one-fifth of those earning $15,000 or more annually made political donations in 1972, and over one-third of those making $25,000 or more contributed to a political campaign. These figures are striking. The "small" contributions are

TABLE 4.8
PERCENTAGE OF INCOME CLASSES
CONTRIBUTING TO POLITICAL CAMPAIGNS

Income Group	1968 (%)	1972 (%)
0 to $4,999	3.0	3.7
$5,000 to $9,999	7.3	11.5
$10,000 to $14,999	8.4	11.5
$15,000 to $19,999	14.3	19.5
$20,000 to $24,999	13.3	23.4
$25,000 or more	30.6	36.8

SOURCE: Committee on Rules and Administration, U.S. Senate, *Public Financing of Federal Elections* (Washington, D.C.: U.S. Government Printing Office, 1973), p. 192.

coming disproportionately from the same individuals who are also represented through the allocations made by affluent professional and trade groups (see below) presumably seeking to protect their economic advantages. The number of small donors is increasing, but as a comparison of the years 1968 and 1972 (Table 4.8) indicates, it is increasing disproportionately for those at the higher end of the income scale. Small contributions come from those with the money to give and from those whose views are already well represented in governing circles. And the reliance on small contributors is significantly heavier in the less important races.

The picture becomes progressively bleaker when one begins to examine the names of the larger givers and the magnitude of their contributions.

THE MAJOR CONTRIBUTORS

Politics is a rich man's sport. The off-year election of 1970 can provide a starting point. This election was the last in which totally unregulated giving was to occur. Many of the gifts publicly (and legally) made in this year were to be prohibited by the campaign reform legislation in effect by 1972. The elections of that year also became targets for a new public scrutiny that made its own contribution to the pending legislative reforms.

There were, of course, laws in effect prior to 1972 that regulated campaign funding. It was illegal for any individual to contribute more than $5000 to any one national political organization or candidate. A person could donate funds to any number of local, state, or county political groups which in turn could relay the funds to national-level political groups or candidates. Individuals also could make financial gifts in the names of other members of their families—husbands, wives, children, grandchildren, cousins, and so on.

Business corporations and labor unions, the two most lucrative sources of political funding, also were regulated. Corporations could not contribute directly to campaigns, although its officials could. The aftermath of the campaigns in 1972 were to demonstrate exactly how freely this provision was interpreted. Professional and industry-wide interest groups also could donate funds. Although labor unions could not provide candidates directly with funds, their political action committees (COPE, for example) could solicit money from members and then allocate it among labor's political friends[20].

The laws, in short, were a fraud. They had been intentionally overloaded with loopholes and, beyond that, simply were not enforced. Senate and House candidates reported their expenditures (when and if they did report) to the secretary of the Senate and the clerk of the House, individuals who depended on them for their jobs. No criminal prosecutions were brought under the law in effect. Campaign regulations made large political contributions more cumbersome perhaps —for the conscientious—but little else. The election of 1970, as well as those of the sixties in general, clearly illustrate this point.

THE WEALTHY CANDIDATE

In the 1970 Senate elections, the National Committee for an Effective Congress reported that 11 senatorial candidates in the 7 largest states (more, that is, than, 3 out of 4) were millionaires: Lloyd Bentsen (D.) and George Bush (R.) of Texas, James L. Buckley (Cons.-R.) and Richard L. Ottinger (D.) of New York, Philip A. Hart (D.) and Lenore Romney (R.) of Michigan, Howard M. Metzenbaum (D.) and Robert Taft, Jr., (R.) of Ohio, Hugh Scott (R.) of Pennsylvania, Adlai E. Stevenson III (D.) of Illinois, and John V. Tunney (D.) of California[21].

The families of these candidates and their friends tend to be generous contributors to their campaigns. The Citizens Research Foundation compiled an analysis of such contributions, an incredibly tedious and painstaking task that took two years and resulted in the "most detailed study ever" of political contributions [22]. The results show that 28,600 people (all those who contributed $500 or more) donated a total of $45,658,000 to the 1970 elections. Of this group, 117 individuals or family groups made contributions of $25,000 or more and these 117 families alone accounted for $19 million (or 41 percent) of the sum collected. To carry the analysis one step further, 45 candidates or families contributed between $500,000 and $1 million to the off-year elections. How many $15 and $25 donations would it take to equal gifts of this magnitude?

At the top of any such list of supercontributors would have to be Nelson Rockefeller and the Rockefeller family. In 1970, when Rockefeller was governor of New York, his family gave "him the most money ever spent by an American to obtain and hold public office[23]." The total included family contributions of

$4.5 million in 1970, almost 60 percent of the governor's $7.7 million reported campaign budget. Through a laborious reading of state and federal campaign reports, the Citizens Research Foundation was able to identify donations of $77,500 from the governor himself and a total of $1.4 million from his brothers, John D. III, David, Laurance, and Winthrop and from his sister. His stepmother added $2.8 million more. Another $518,880 in campaign expenditures was paid out-of-pocket by the candidate and is not included in the family total. Incredible as it may seem, the governor's overall campaign expenditures in various races for governor and president between 1952 and 1970 reached an estimated $27 million. More than half of this amount came from family members[24].

U.S. Congressman Richard Ottinger received $3.9 million from his family in his unsuccessful race for the U.S. Senate, including approximately $2.7 million from his mother, $225,000 from his sister, and $161,000 from his wife. A wealthy businessman and contributor to Democratic causes over the years, Howard M. Metzenbaum received one-half million dollars in contributions to his unsuccessful 1970 Senate race from his wife and four daughters. Norton Simon, a millionaire food executive, and his wife contributed $1.8 million to his unsuccessful campaign against Senator George Murphy in the 1970 California Republican primary.

Other examples of personal and family contributions of $25,000 or more are:

Evelle J. Younger (R.), Los Angeles lawyer and former district attorney, who contributed $130,000 to his unsuccessful campaign for attorney general of the state;

Charles B. Yates (D.), New Jersey electronics manufacturer whose family contributions to his unsuccessful House contest amounted to $42,544;

Kevin H. White (D.), mayor of Boston, who contributed $46,428 to his unsuccessful campaign for governor;

Senator Lowell P. Weicker, Jr., (R.), whose family contributed $92,000 to his successful race for the U.S. Senate from Connecticut;

William D. Weeks (R.), Boston lawyer and former state senator, a son of Sinclair Weeks, former Secretary of Commerce, whose contributions to his own unsuccessful campaign for a U.S. House nomination amounted to $64,500;

Peter J. Sprague (R.), New York retail store executive and investor, who, along with his mother contributed a total of $240,425 to his unsuccessful campaign for the House;

Malcolm E. Smith (Cons.-R.), a New York radio station executive, whose wife contributed $183,000 to his unsuccessful House race;

Frederick H. Schultz (D.), former speaker of the Florida House, who contributed $309,000 to his own unsuccessful race for the U.S. Senate nomination;

Representative James H. Scheuer (D.), who, along with his family, contributed $126,440 to his reelection campaign;

Howard J. Samuels (D.), a self-made millionaire in plastic packaging and a public officeholder, who contributed $125,000 to his unsuccessful race for the New York gubernatorial nomination;

Jack M. Eckerd (R.), a drugstore chain and department store owner, who contributed $1.1 million to his unsuccessful primary race for the Florida gubernatorial nomination;

Alphonsus J. Donahue (D.), a Connecticut businessman, who contributed $669,700 to his unsuccessful race for the U.S. Senate nomination;

Wallace Barnes (R.), a Connecticut business executive and former state senator, who contributed $268,315 to his unsuccessful contest for the gubernatorial nomination;

Karen Burstein (D.), whose father, a New York lawyer, contributed $104,000 to her unsuccessful race for the U.S. House.

Personal wealth, of course, does not assure success in winning elections. It does place one, however, in a position to run for public office and it certainly does not hurt the campaign effort. Wealth, or access to it, while its role has always been considered important, may well play a far bigger part in defining the pool of eligible candidates for political office than has generally been realized.

Finally, taking a look at the expenditures in their party's 1970 primaries of eight of the richest candidates (five won, three lost, and seven of the eight were Democrats), the cost of the races for U.S. Senate and gubernatorial nominations ranged from $300,000 (a losing Democratic nominee in Alabama) to Norton Simon's $1.9 million bid in the California primary for U.S. Senate. The cost per vote received went from $0.98 (Bentsen in the Texas Senate primary) to $4.86 (Ottinger in the New York Senate primary). The average cost was $2.34. Representative James H. Scheuer, a wealthy New York Democrat, managed to spend $11.07 per vote in a primary in which less than 12,000 votes insured renomination [25].

The positioning advantages ready wealth allows a candidate are as well illustrated by these primary campaigns as by any other. Richard Ottinger's campaign budget in his successful try for the New York U.S. Senate nomination in 1970 amounted to $1.8 million, more than 90 percent of which was loaned by his mother. Ottinger, while an effective congressman, was unknown by two-thirds of the New York electorate. Employing expensive media consultants and television spot announcements, Ottinger won with 39 percent of the vote against three other candidates (and then lost the general election to another wealthy candidate, the Conservative-Republican nominee James Buckley). Undoubtedly, Ottinger's financial resources as heir to a plywood fortune accumulated by his father had more to do with his primary success than his liberal record in the Congress. Ottinger outspent his three rivals combined by more than a seven to one ratio.

New York has a law restricting primary spending to 10¢ per registered voter or a maximum in the primary of $350,000. The law, similar to its federal counterparts, is easily ignored by creating multiple committees to fund campaigns or by officially borrowing the needed funds. One of Ottinger's opponents, upstate congressman Richard D. McCarthy (reduced to gimmicks for media exposure such as skin diving in the polluted Hudson River to dramatize his record on water purfication) bitterly contended that the issue had become whether you "can buy a seat in the U.S. Senate [26]."

The charge may be unfair to Ottinger. The congressman defended himself by comparing his expenditures to John Lindsay's two campaigns for mayor or John Kennedy's 1960 campaign for president. He also could have mentioned the numerous campaigns of Nelson Rockefeller, those of several of the candidates in the New York Democratic gubernatorial primary of the same year, those of Ronald Reagan or Norton Simon in California, Milton Shapp in Pennsylvania, Lloyd Bentsen in Texas, Howard Metzenbaum in Ohio, or any of a host of others.

In 1974, Ottinger was eventually able to return to the Congress. This illustrates another aspect of the problem. Wealthy candidates not only have the freedom to run in the races they choose and to buy the television exposure they need to win, but should they lose they are able to return to compete again. Politicians without extensive family funds depend on a creditable showing to convince supporters of their legitimacy as vote getters. Should they fail in a key race, they may well be retired from public life permanently.

Howard Metzenbaum's personal fortune enabled him to overcome a gap in name recognition in a race with a popular opponent, former astronaut John Glenn (95 percent of Ohio voters knew Glenn, 10 percent recognized Metzenbaum's name) to win the 1970 Democratic Senate nomination. Metzenbaum lost the election but was chosen to fill a vacancy caused by the appointment of the incumbent (William B. Saxbe) as U.S. attorney general. In another bruising primary of 1974, the now incumbent Metzenbaum lost to Glenn, who went on to win the office in the general election [27].

Milton Shapp represents another of the many possible examples. Shapp spent $1.4 million in 1966 to win the Pennsylvania Democratic gubernatorial nomination. He lost the general election despite a campaign budget of $2.4 million. Four years later, he returned to spend $1.2 million, one-third of which went into television advertising in the last two weeks of the campaign, in a second successful bid for his party's nomination and then went on to become Pennsylvania's first Democratic governor in a dozen years.

Despite benefiting from the system, Shapp is a critic of its inequities. Another self-made millionaire, Howard Samuels of New York, contested twice on the state level and lost. Samuels' wealth unquestionably created the opportunities for him to seek elective office. Nonetheless, Samuels, a liberal as is Shapp, found the campaign funding practices he had used so successfully "disastrous." He proposed severe limits on campaign contributions and expenditures, strict postelection accounting measures, and equitable television exposure [28]. Needless to say, not all candidates with equal sources of family funding are so disposed.

THE CONTRIBUTIONS
OF THE VERY WEALTHY

Political campaigns depend on large contributors. Individuals with the resources to give usually do so, but they contribute disproportionately to one political party, the Republican. The presidential election of 1968 is a good example. The election took place prior to the systematic exploitation of the advantages of political office and the gross improprieties so evident four years later. The election was an open one, no incumbent stood for reelection, and the nominations in both parties were contested. The outcome, at least, was close and both parties rejected factional candidacies in favor of centrists (Humphrey and Nixon). To the extent one election can be representative of those occurring before Watergate, 1968 appears as close to the ideal as it is possible to find [29].

Working primarily from information supplied by the Citizens Research Foundation, Congressional Quarterly found that 46 of America's richest individuals contributed $1.5 million to the two major parties [30]. Of this sum, $1,377,313 went to the Republicans and a relatively meager $106,488 to the Democrats. The imbalance is so great as to obviate the need for any analysis. The names on this list of heavy Republican donors are, of course, readily familiar: the various members of the Rockefeller, Mellon, Ford, and du Pont families, John Hay Whitney, Bob Hope, Amory Haughton of Corning Glass, William L. McKnight of Minnesota Mining and Manufacturing, and so on. Among the wealthiest individuals in the country, the largest gift to the Democrats was $30,000 from the inventor of xeroxography.

The top ten funders in 1968 included (in first place) W. Clement Stone, the Chicago insurance tycoon and disciple of PMA (positive mental attitude) who claimed he gave $500,000 to Nixon in 1968 and $1 million to the Republicans in 1970, is listed as contributing $200,000, a probable minimum; Jack Dreyfus, Jr., long associated with mutal and investment funds, who gave $76,000 to the Republicans and $63,000 to the Democrats; J. Howard Pew of Sun Oil, $63,834 to the Republicans; Elmer H. Bobst of Warner-Lambert Pharmaceuticals, $63,-000 to the Republicans; and the wife of former convict John ("Jake the Barber") Factor, $100,000 to the Democrats.

The contributions of a liberally-oriented heir to a General Motors fortune, Stewart R. Mott represents one of the most complete statements on record of the scope of giving by one individual. Mott recounts that in 1968 he contributed $210,000 to Eugene McCarthy's presidential campaign and another $100,000 to Nelson Rockefeller's. Eight candidates for the U.S. Senate (George McGovern, Harold Hughes, J. W. Fulbright, etc.) received a total of $34,000 and another eight House candidates were allocated $8700. Adding to this the funds donated to political committees at various levels, Mott estimates he spent $365,000 in 1968 alone, about 7 percent of his total assets. Mott is unusual among well-off contributors in the targets of his largess (liberals), the considerable amount of his total fortune contributed in one year, and, more than anything else, his candor [31].

CORPORATE FUNDING

The difficulty in reviewing personal contributions is in separating individuals from their business identification. In some cases it is impossible. The tendencies in corporate funding follow a familar pattern. Corporate leaders normally contribute heavily to Republicans, although on occasion they will give to Democrats. As an example, Lyndon Johnson, the incumbent running against the unpredictable Goldwater, received a disproportionately large share of business contributions in 1964.

TABLE 4.9
BUSINESS COUNCIL DONATIONS
TO REPUBLICANS AND DEMOCRATS, 1956-1968

Year	Number Contributing[a]		Contributions		Average Gift	
	Republicans	Democrats	Republicans ($)	Democrats ($)	Republicans ($)	Democrats ($)
1968	67	5	280,913	83,000	4,193	16,600
1964	36	33	87,100	135,450	2,419	4,105
1960	73	7	241,060	35,140	3,302	5,020
1956	68	4	268,499	4,000	3,948	1,000
	244	49	877,572	257,590	3,597[b]	5,257[b]

[a]Number of Business Council executives included in total.
[b]Represents average contribution for the four election years.
SOURCE: Congressional Quarterly, *Dollar Politics: The Issue of Campaign Spending* (Washington, D.C.: Congressional Quarterly, 1971), pp. 34-5.

The executives who form the Business Council, a select, invitation-only group of top corporation leaders who advise on government policy, actually contributed more to the Democrats in 1964 than to the Republicans, the only exception in the four presidential elections from 1956 through 1968 (Table 4.9) [32]. Fifty percent of the total contributions to the Democrats in the four elections shown in the table is accounted for by this one year.

Corporations, as noted, are barred from directly contributing to political campaigns, although the executives of these companies, presumably acting on their own volition, are not. Congressional Quarterly surveyed the 1000 top executives of the nation's largest industrial corporations. Of these, 219 contributed a sum of $783,000 to the Republican party in 1968 and 26 a total of $132,000 to the Democratic party [33]. Among the corporations making the largest political contributions were: the Ford Motor Company, $87,100 to the Republicans, $53,000 to the Democrats; International Business Machines (IBM), $104,250 to the Republicans, $32,000 to the Democrats; General Motors, $114,000 to the Republicans and $1000 to the Democrats; and Gulf Oil, $73,800 to the Republicans and nothing to the Democrats [34].

A breakdown by occupation of the contributors of $10,000 or more in the 1968 presidential election illustrates corporate patterns of party preference (Table 4.10). The Republicans obviously do well, but the margin of funds they attract varies according to the occupational category of the contributor. Those identified with oil interests favored the Republicans by a 16 to 1 ratio. Similarly within the manufacturing category, those associated with the chemical and pharmaceutical industries contributed heavily to the Republican party ($256,817) and relatively little to the Democratic party ($34,000). Those in the clothing industry, however, made disproportionately larger donations to the Democrats ($106,000) than to the Republicans ($23,000). Within the professional category, those identified as authors, clergy, and educators gave $262,250 to the Democrats while contributing nothing to their opponents [35].

Herbert E. Alexander, the director of the Citizens Research Foundation, has aggregated the contributions of the officers, trustees, and directors of various trade and industry-wide professional groups to find that much the same tendencies persist. The Republican party does very well in contrast to the Democratic party. For example, the directors the American Petroleum Institute gave $429,366 to the Republicans and only $30,606 to the Democrats; the directors of the American Iron and Steel Institute, $25,000 to the Republicans and nothing to the Democrats; officials of the National Association of Manufacturers, $126,544 to the Republicans and $20,500 to the Democrats; and the officers and directors of the United States Chamber of Commerce and the National Association of Real Estate Boards, $40,000 and $26,500, respectively, to the Republicans and nothing to the Democrats. [36].

Problems develop as one delves below the industry trade associations, spokesmen for their varying memberships, to the specific corporations themselves. The difficulty (beyond acquiring the data) in assessing corporate leadership giving in any detail is the interchange between the leading industrial corporations and the top government contractors. Of the 25 largest corporations, 13 also appear on the list of the 25 most favored government contractors [37]. The motivation for giving can only be inferred at this stage, but it is worth taking a brief look in this pre-Watergate era at the political contributions of those who are known to have profited directly from government business.

TABLE 4.10
OCCUPATIONAL PURSUITS OF THOSE WHO CONTRIBUTED $10,000 OR MORE TO DEMOCRATS AND REPUBLICANS IN 1968[a]

Occupation	Contribution ($)	
	Republican	Democrat
Finance	796,286	907,686
Insurance	240,000	38,500
Professional	563,653	652,315
(lawyers, clergy, educators, physicians, etc.)		
Communications	112,400	132,838
Real estate	204,140	313,254
Natural resources	829,281	82,000
(mining)	(68,000)	(37,000)
(oil)	(739,485)	(45,000)
(timber)	(21,796)	—
Utilities	81,500	16,000
Transportation	141,700	28,500
Leasing	112,500	11,500
Food processing and distribution	111,200	77,250
Restaurant & hotel-motel	149,500	—
Wholesale & retail sales	61,596	118,750
(food, department stores, etc.)		
Manufacturing	1,151,827	652,322
Entertainment	127,511	154,096
Public officials	150,500	84,500
Philanthropy	2,135,804	619,750
(family & inherited wealth)		
Retired	130,000	138,500
Miscellaneous	272,316	115,100
Unidentified	186,446	147,700
TOTAL	7,658,160	4,290,561

[a]The data were compiled by the Citizens' Research Foundation. Of the individuals who contributed $10,000 or more, 94.3 percent are classifiable in the categories presented. The business identifications of some contributors could not be ascertained.

SOURCE: Herbert E. Alexander, *Financing the 1968 Election* (Lexington, Mass.: D.C. Heath and Company, 1971), pp. 325–29.

THE GOVERNMENT CONTRACTORS

"Politics is the art of putting people under obligation to you," according to Jake Arvey, long-time Chicago political boss of the pre-Daley era [38]. If so, the political parties have reason to be indebted. Not surprisingly, many of the same companies that contribute heavily to politics, regardless of how unselfish their motivation, manage to secure government contracts.

The data are incomplete due to the vagaries in reporting procedures and enforcement practices on the state and national levels. Nonetheless, with the help of materials developed by the Citizens' Research Foundation and reported by Congressional Quarterly, a fragmentary, but nonetheless impressive, picture of the donations by government contractors can be drawn [39]. The figures are taken from the political gifts made by the officials of the top 25 contracting businesses. The governmental agencies involved are the Department of Defense, the Atomic Energy Commission (AEC), and the National Aeronautics and Space Administration (NASA). These examples, of course, are only a fraction of the total number of companies contracting with these or other government agencies. They serve to illustrate the symbiotic relationship between political funding and success in government contracting.

The Republican party was heavily favored by donations from government contractors, receiving $1,054,852 to the Democrats' $180,550, roughly a ratio of six to one. Of the top 25 contractors with the Department of Defense, individuals associated with 24 of them directed 85 percent of their total $781,253 contributions to the Republican party. The 29 officers and directors of Litton Industries, whose president Roy Ash was destined to serve in the Nixon Administration, contributed $151,000 to the Republican party and nothing to the Democratic party. Litton ranked 14th in Defense Department contracting in 1968 and 9th in 1970. To use one company as an example, military contracts awarded Litton came to $465.7 million in 1968, $317.1 million in 1969, and $543.1 million in 1970. The 49 companies appearing on all three lists (Department of Defense, AEC, and NASA) that had made $1 million plus political contributions received military contracts amounting to in toto $19.1 million in 1968, $17.5 million in 1969, and $15 million in 1970 (Table 4.11). Obviously, a political contribution does not create the capabilities necessary to handle defense projects. Often, though, it does insure "access" and maybe even Arvey's sense of indebtedness.

Of the top 25 corporations on the list of those receiving military contracts, only Hughes Aircraft had no member associated with the firm making political contributions. Yet the Hughes empire and its money was to play a shadowy and poorly understood role in the Watergate affair to follow. Meanwhile, Hughes Aircraft

TABLE 4.11
VALUE OF CONTRACTS AWARDED

Agency	1968 (Millions of $)	1969 (Millions of $)	1970 (Millions of $)
Department of Defense	19.1	17.5	15.0
Atomic Energy Commission	1.2	1.2	1.3
National Aeronautics and Space Administration	2.9	2.5	2.2

SOURCE: Congressional Quarterly, *Dollar Politics* (Washington, D.C.: Congressional Quarterly, 1971), p. 38.

would move from 24th to 10th on the list in terms of the dollar value of the contracts awarded. The Hughes empire, as later events were to show, also was awarded a controversial $350 million contract in 1971 to recover a Soviet submarine from the floor of the Pacific.

The same pattern repeats itself in detailed examinations of the 25 leading contractors on the AEC and NASA lists. The value of the government contracts awarded by these agencies should not be underestimated. Political contributions may have nothing to do with the selection of government contractors. The sums involved are extraordinarily large and the public interest as well as the potential saving of tax dollars would be served if no grounds existed for speculation. Martin and Susan Tolchin ask in their study of political patronage: "How much of the $80 billion defense budget is actually used to protect the country?" In answer, they quote Mississippi Congressman Jaime Whitten: "I am convinced that defense is only one of the factors that enter into our determinations for defense spending. The others are pump priming, spreading the immediate benefits of defense spending, taking care of all services, giving military bases to include all sections. . . . We see the effects in public and Congressional insistence on continuing contracts, or operating military bases, although the need has expired [40]."

CONCLUSION

It is unlikely that 1970 or 1968 are atypical years for studying the pre-Watergate association between politics and money. More than likely, they represent the process as it worked up to the election of 1972. The difference in the latter instance is the extent to which improprieties were permitted and even encouraged on a scale not previously encountered. Watergate, however, was not an occurrence unrelated to all of the campaigns and funding practices that had preceded it. The seeds were sown early and the uncomfortable association between large sums of money and political preference has deep roots in American politics. Historians are fond of pointing to the outrages of the "age of boodle," the selling of public lands to the railroads, and the availability (for cash) of virtually anything within the elected politician's power to grant. The pickings would seem slim in comparison with the monetary gains to be obtained today through comparatively modest political investments. John Gardner of Common Cause has called the campaign gift "the modern all purpose equivalent of the old flat-footed bribe [41]." Those practices were tolerated—actually they represented something of a necessity in the parties efforts to campaign—and the controlling laws were feeble and unenforced. The monetary aspects of the Watergate abuses were almost predictable.

NOTES

1. These developments and their costs are discussed in Robert Agranoff, ed., *The New Style in Election Campaigns,* 2d ed. (Boston: Holbrook Press, 1976).

2. Nixon did not enter the California primary as a courtesy to favorite-son candidate Governor Ronald Reagan. The figures are taken from Herbert E. Alexander, *Financing the 1968 Election* (Lexington, Mass.: D.C. Heath and Company, 1971). This is the most thorough analysis available for any one election. See also Herbert E. Alexander, "Financing Parties in Campaigns in 1968," in *Political Parties and Political Behavior,* eds. William J. Crotty, Donald M. Freeman, and Douglas S. Gatlin (Boston: Allyn and Bacon, 1971), pp. 316–47, and on television costs more generally, Herbert E. Alexander, Stimson Bullitt, and Hyman H. Goldin, "The High Costs of TV Campaigns," *Television Quarterly,* 5, no. 1 (Winter, 1966): 47–65. For a broad perspective on campaign funding, particularly good on the elections of 1952 and 1956, consult Alexander Heard, *The Costs of Democracy* (Chapel Hill: The University of North Carolina Press, 1960). Funding in the 1964 election is assessed in Herbert E. Alexander, *Financing the 1964 Election* (Princeton, N.J.: Citizens' Research Foundation, 1966), and for 1972 in the same author's *Financing the 1972 Election* (Lexington, Mass.: D.C. Heath, 1976).

3. Alexander, "Financing Parties," p. 324.

4. Ibid., pp. 322–23, 338.

5. The figures are reworked from those presented in Alexander Heard, *The Costs of Democracy* abr. ed. (Garden City, N.Y.: Anchor Doubleday, 1962), pp. 346–47.

6. Fred W. Friendly, "Broadcast Industry and Campaign Financing," *Chicago Sun-Times,* May 19, 1973, p. 40. The article is excerpted from a speech to the American Society of Magazine Editors.

7. Delmer D. Dunn, *Financing Presidential Campaigns* (Washington, D.C.: The Brookings Institution, 1972), pp. 30–35. See also Thomas E. Patterson and Robert D. McClure, *Political Advertising: Voter Reaction to Televised Political Commercials* (Princeton, N.J.: Citizens Research Foundation, 1973).

8. Herbert E. Alexander, *Political Financing* (Minneapolis: Burgess, 1972), p. 38.

9. Ibid., pp. 38–39.

10. The totals for each campaign from 1860 to 1968 can be found in ibid., p. 6.

11. Kevin H. White, *Party Finance* (Medford, Mass.: The Lincoln Filene Center for Citizenship and Public Affairs, 1963), p. 9.

12. The figures for these years are taken from Congressional Quarterly, *Dollar Politics: The Issue of Campaign Spending* (Washington, D. C.: Congressional Quarterly, 1971) and from the relevant Congressional Quarterly reports for the years indicated. Studies that report on state and local funding practices include Herbert E. Alexander, *Money in Politics* (Washington, D.C.: Public Affairs Press, 1972, David W. Adamany, *Campaign Finance in America* (North Scituate, Mass.: Duxbury Press, 1972), and Adamany, *Financing Politics* (Madison: University of Wisconsin Press, 1969). A far-ranging series of comparative studies of political funding can be found in Arnold J. Heidenheimer, ed., *Comparative Political Finance* (Lexington, Mass.: D.C. Heath, 1970).

13. Ben A. Franklin, "Campaign Spending in '72 Hit Record $400 Million," *New York Times,* November 19, 1972, p. 1. The figures reported are taken from this article which is based on information supplied by the Citizens' Research Foundation. Common Cause places the Tower spending at $2.3 million, still very high.

14. Committee on Rules and Administration, U.S. Senate, *Public Financing of Federal Elections* (Washington, D.C.: U.S. Government Printing Office, 1973), p. 95. The

materials that follow are taken from the Common Cause report to the Congress and contained on pp. 92–111.

15. Ibid.
16. Ibid.
17. Ibid., p. 157.
18. Based on Alexander, *Political Financing,* pp. 32–34.
19. Alexander, *Financing the 1968 Election,* p. 87.
20. For discussion of political contributions by labor unions consult Heard, *Costs of Democracy,* and Alexander, *Money in Politics.* Federated labor was particularly effective in funding and executing a drive in 1968 to cut into George Wallace's support among working people. For an account of these efforts, see Alexander, *Financing the 1968 Election,* especially pp. 191–200, and Theodore H. White, *The Making of the President, 1968* (New York: Atheneum, 1969), p. 365.
21. These data are from Congressional Quarterly, *Dollar Politics,* pp. 28–31.
22. Reported in Ben A. Franklin, "Study of '70 Race Shows Vast Spending by Wealthy," and "Contributors of $25,000 or More to Campaigns in 1970," both in the *New York Times,* April 19, 1972, p. 28. The original lists are available from the Citizens' Research Foundation, 245 Nassau Street, Princeton, N.J.
23. Ibid.
24. Ibid.
25. Congressional Quarterly *Dollar Politics,* p. 30.
26. Ibid., pp. 28–29.
27. The spending figures are from Congressional Quarterly, *Dollar Politics.* The Internal Revenue Service brought charges against Metzenbaum in 1974 which he says were politically motivated and instigated by the Nixon Administration. The IRS contested an income tax deduction of $118,000 as invalid. The matter became a principal issue in the bitter primary fight. In April of 1975, well after the primary decision, of course, the IRS dropped the matter, effectively recognizing the validity of the original claim. Metzenbaum believed the Nixon Administration had intended to discredit a long-time Democratic contributor and party worker. Metzenbaum indicated he was considering another race for the Senate, this time a 1976 challenge to his old adversary, incumbent Republican Robert Taft, Jr. See "Tax Dispute Won by Metzenbaum," *New York Times* April 20, 1975, p. 16.
28. Congressional Quarterly, *Dollar Politics,* p. 31.
29. See Alexander, *Financing the 1968 Election,* for a thorough analysis of political funding during the election year.
30. See Congressional Quarterly *Dollar Politics,* pp. 32–40, and Alexander, *Financing the 1968 Election,* pp. 243–355.
31. Alexander, *Financing the 1968 Election,* p. 255.
32. Congressional Quarterly, *Dollar Politics,* pp. 34–35.
33. Ibid., p. 35.
34. The Congressional Quarterly figures represent the money given by persons associated with the corporations as ascertained from official federal and state records. Ibid.
35. Alexander, *Financing the 1968 Election,* pp. 325–29. The disparity between the political parties in attracting corporate funds, of course, is not new. See the reports by Louise Overacker on the elections of 1932, 1940, and 1944 and the treatment of

the Gore Committee *Report* (1957) and *Hearings* (1956) as contained in V. O. Key, Jr., *Politics, Parties, and Pressure Groups,* 4th ed. (New York: Thomas Y. Crowell, 1956), especially pp. 543–44. Heard, *Costs of Democracy,* is also valuable in this context. On the continuing financial indiscretions of Gulf Oil, see the *New York Times,* November 26, 1975, p. 1.

36. Alexander, *Financing the 1968 Election,* pp. 345–47.
37. Congressional Quarterly, *Dollar Politics,* p. 35.
38. Quoted in Martin and Susan Tolchin, *To the Victor . . .* (New York: Vintage, 1971), p. 3. For earlier examples of the practice of this "art", see Matthew Josephson, *The Politicos* (New York: Harcourt, Brace & World, 1938). Assessments of the effects of political corruption in a variety of settings include Arnold J. Heidenheimer, ed., *Political Corruption: Readings in Comparative Analysis* (New York: Holt, Rinehart and Winston, 1970), and James C. Scott, *Comparative Political Corruption* (Englewood Cliffs, N.J.: Prentice-Hall, 1972).
39. Taken from *Dollar Politics,* pp. 36–40.
40. Tolchin, *To the Victor . . .,* pp. 10–11.
41. Quoted in Friendly, "Broadcast Industry and Campaign Financing."

5
Watergate
and the Buying
of a Government

The now virtually forgotten first vice-president of the Nixon Administration, Spiro Agnew—one of the least qualified men in America to comment on the problem—characterized Watergate as "the misguided actions of a few zealots." His boss and president, Richard M. Nixon, speaking through his press secretary, labeled the affair a "third-rate burglary." Unfortunately, the "few zealots" Agnew mentioned worked out of the White House and commanded the full and awesome power of the federal government. Whatever the quality of the June 17, 1972, break-in to the Democratic National Committee, it was initiated, executed, and paid for by people in the White House and the Committee to Re-Elect the President, and was the most famous in a series of crimes that gives the presidential election of 1972 a very special notoriety.

The Watergate abuses taken together mark the most systematic, pervasive, *and* successful perversion of democratic electoral processes the United States has ever experienced. In this sense, the "Watergate election" was unique. In a deeper and far more disturbing way, Watergate was related to and a direct outgrowth of the shady deals, quid pro quo funding, and public hypocrisy that, in varying degrees, has characterized running for elective office in the United States. Those behind Watergate and the related assaults on American democratic forms went further, were better organized, and managed to have a more profound impact than any of their predecessors. And, perhaps only for the first time, Americans began to appreciate the role of big money in politics: where it comes from and what it can buy. The services of the federal government were available to those with the money to invest. And lest one feel an undue sympathy for the corporations, wealthy entrepreneurs, interest groups, and unions with the funds and inclination to give, sometimes legally, sometimes illegally, the rewards that accrued to them for their munificence more often than not were enormous.

THE MILIEU OF THE
POLITICAL DECISION MAKER

Perhaps the best place to begin is the trial of John Connally, acquitted of accepting a bribe to influence governmental policies favorable to the milk industry. Connally was accused of accepting bribes of $10,000 from an old friend and lobbyist for a dairymen's cooperative, Jake Jacobsen. Connally was found innocent of the charge in a federal court.

The bribery charge, although by far the most publicized aspect of the controversy, was perhaps of the least significance. What emerged from the trial, the various investigations into the charges, the playing of one of the famous Nixon tapes on the meeting that decided in favor of increased milk subsidies, and the comments of many involved in the episode is a large body of materials that attest to the manner in which some major political decisions are made—and paid for. This—and not the legal maneuverings over a relatively petty bribe—represents the bedrock scandal. The milk case constitutes, in short, as representative a case of what Ralph Nader has called "institutionalized bribery" as any of the dozens that might be called upon and one that has the virtue of being more fully documented than most.

"Big John" Connally had been a political protégé of former President Lyndon Johnson. He had served as governor of Texas and secretary of the Navy under John Kennedy, and he had been wounded in the fatal assassination attack on Kennedy in 1963. He was also a former college roommate of Robert Strauss, Democratic National Committee chairman and also a Texan, who testified as a character reference in the Connally trial and upon his acquittal hosted a party in Connally's honor. The former Texas governor had headed the "Democrats for Nixon" during the 1972 campaign, a halfway house for "fat cats" and other disillusioned Democrats that in the aftermath of Watergate was shown to have been financed by the Nixon Re-Election effort, contrary to the impressions it attempted to convey during the campaign. After this service, Connally converted from the Democratic party to the Republican party in 1973, on the grounds that the latter was more "responsive" to the people. Connally, who appeared to be a Nixon favorite, was soon appointed secretary of the Treasury and began a boisterous reign in the Nixon Cabinet.

Connally acted as one—and only one as it turned out—intermediary for the diarymen in attempting to have then President Richard Nixon personally reverse a ruling of his secretary of agriculture, Clifford Hardin. The secretary on March 12, 1971, had officially decided that for 1972 the government would offer 80 percent of parity rather than increase the level to the 90 percent the milk industry wanted. Perhaps Hardin had been naive. Possibly he did not know that the Associated Milk Producers, Inc., had hand-delivered $100,000 to the Nixon Administration *in August of 1969* in an elaborately staged meeting with Nixon's personal lawyer, Herbert W. Kalmbach. Perhaps he did not realize that a "courtesy meeting" between the president and the dairy leaders had been arranged by the White House after the president had been informed in writing that they had pledged $2 million to his 1972 reelection effort. Perhaps additionally he believed the White House rhetoric that proclaimed that "philosophically, the Nixon Administration had hoped to gradually move away from federal policies which provide massive subsidies." The subsidies, the administration implied, were simply one more gigantic boondoggle from the New Deal era that the conservative Nixon would end; unless, of course, he should be persuaded otherwise. Possibly also Secretary Hardin simply underestimated the persuasive powers of fellow cabinet member Connally.

The climactic meeting on the milk question took place on March 23, 1971. Present were the president, Connally, Hardin, Ehrlichman, George P. Schultz, the budget director, and three aides. A tape of this meeting, dominated by Connally, was made available to the Special Prosecutor's Office and was played at Connally's trial. The arguments in favor of the change in policy, that is, moving toward an appreciably higher support level, and the rationalizations in accepting it are worth noting.

Connally opened by telling Nixon that the dairymen "are organized; they're adamant; they're militant[1]." The lobbyists, he said, have a "legitimate cause." But the legitimacy of the argument seemed to focus on its political advantages. "They're amassing an enormous amount of money that they're going to put into political activities, very frankly," Connally reported (and, as matters turned out, Nixon knew only too well). The president should move to obligate the farmers to him, Connally urged. "I'm addressing myself to the narrow aspects, to the political aspects of it. I don't think there's a better organization in the United States. If you can get it, uh, you can get more help from, that, uh, will, uh, be more loyal to you.

"Uh, I'm not trying to talk about or discuss at any great length the, the economics of it, but as far as the politics are concerned, looking to 1972, uh, it appears very clear to me that you're going to have to move, uh, strong in the Midwest, you're going to have to be strong in rural America." The secretary of the Treasury contended that the Democrats in the Congress would enact the increase even if Nixon did not support it (which was probably correct, although the Congress would have had a very difficult time in overturning a Nixon veto had the president chosen to use this weapon). [As it turned out, the dairymen had contributed lavishly also to congressional campaigns (over $500,000 in 1969 and 1970) and, in a "hedging your bets" atmosphere, between $25,000 and $42,000 to the Humphrey campaign and a whopping (for the Democrats) $185,000 (38 percent of his total budget) to the presidential campaign of the influential chairman of the House Ways and Means Committee, Wilbur Mills.] Furthermore, Connally argued, the congressional Democrats would use their support for the new ceiling to hurt Nixon in midwestern farm states such as Missouri, Wisconsin, South Dakota, Oklahoma, Kentucky, and Iowa. "I wouldn't judge it on a moral basis," the Treasury secretary continued. "I judge it on the basis of the political aspects of it." That would appear clear enough.

The Nixon response is as instructive as the Connally presentation, which he had just entertained. "My political judgment is that Congress is going to pass it," the president replied. "I could not veto it . . . not because they're milk producers, but because they're farmers. . . . I think the best thing to do is to just relax and enjoy it." "All right," the president directed his aides, "make the best deal you can." With that, he ordered prices increased by 27¢ per hundred pounds. This decision cost the American taxpayer hundreds of millions of dollars.

The "deal," as noted, was for the dairy cooperatives to contribute $2 million to the Nixon Administration for various political uses. They gave generously but only one-quarter of the funds promised. The dairymen nonetheless did very well. For less than one-half million dollars (or even for $2 million, had they made good on their pledge), seemingly a staggering sum, they managed with the help of the nation's top decision makers to transfer from the taxpayer's pocket directly to their own about $1400 *for every dollar invested in the Nixon campaign.*

In a sense, the dairymen can not be faulted for playing the game the way others did. A letter from the president of one of the midwestern cooperatives to a supporter makes the argument explicitly.

> The facts of life are that the economic welfare of dairymen does depend a great deal on political action. If dairymen are to receive their fair share of the governmental pie that we all pay for, we must have friends in government. I have become increasingly aware that the soft and sincere voice of the dairy farmer is no match for the jingle of hard currencies put in the campaign funds of the politicians by the vegetable fat interests, labor, oil, steel, airlines and others.
>
> We dairymen as a body can be a dominant group. On March 23, 1971, along with nine other dairy farmers, I sat in the cabinet room of the White House, across the table from the President of the United States, and heard him compliment the dairymen on their marvelous work in consolidating and unifying our industry and our involvement in politics. He said, "You people are my friends, and I appreciate it." Two days later an order came from the U.S. Department of Agriculture increasing the support price of milk to 85% of parity, *which added from $500 million to $700 million* to dairy farmers' milk checks. We dairymen cannot afford to overlook this kind of benefit. Whether we like it or not, *this is the way the system works*[2]. (Italics added.)

Actually, the milk case is even sleazier than this brief recapitulation indicates. The access—directly to the Oval Office—began immediately after Richard Nixon was sworn in as president. As his vice-president, the official administration scourge of moral laxity in society, was in his office receiving payoffs for past services performed, the bonds between the milk producers and the White House were being sewn. Lobbyists for the three major dairy cooperatives involved in the episode had been in contact with John Mitchell, then Nixon's campaign manager, and Maurice Stans, his chief fundraiser, during the 1968 campaign. In 1969, the dairymen wanted favorable Justice Department action on a pending matter and an *active* identification of Nixon with their programs. The milk lobbyists were referred, possibly by then Attorney General Mitchell (the recollections differ), to Herbert Kalmbach. In a series of negotiations between March and August of 1969, supervised by the White House (and specifically by H. R. Haldeman, the president's chief of staff and alter ego), the dairymen agreed to contribute up to $250,000 in 1969 and to deliver $100,000 immediately if the administration agreed to (as recorded by Kalmbach when the money was turned over):

    (a) 90% price supports for dairy farmers;
    (b) President to address gathering in Kansas City, Mo. (A meeting of dairy farmers' cooperatives organized by Milk Producers, Inc. (open date));
    (c) Identification with the President—picture taking, etc[3].

The agreement was sealed with the transfer of the money. It appears that John Connally was not as persuasive as he may have seemed. The object of his attention had already made a commitment.

A number of events followed the initial payoff. President Nixon essentially made good on his word and met with dairy representatives in the White House (see the account above) and generally attempted to address their meetings and to associate himself with their objectives. He also, of course, decided on the higher parity. In turn, the money made from the initial contribution went to finance Anthony Ulascewicz's undercover work and it (along with other milk donations) was kept in a secret account in the White House (the "House Account") with Nixon's personal secretary, Rose Mary Woods, maintaining the list of contributors.

The White House, through the law firm of long-time Nixon advisor, Murray Chotiner (as well as through Charles Colson, Haldeman, and others), then dunned the dairy cooperatives for the rest of the promised money due for the 1972 campaign. Chotiner's firm, for example, constantly pressured the milk groups and even supplied them with the names of fictitious committees (25 committees at one writing, 24 more two weeks later) through which to channel the illicit funds.

Despite their constant bickering at the pressure, the dairy cooperatives did very nicely. The hundreds of millions of dollars in direct subsidies of public funds represented the most obvious gain. Additionally, however, an antitrust suit against one of the largest dairy cooperatives that had been brewing since the 1960s was rerouted and then derailed through the personal intervention of Attorney General Mitchell. And within two weeks of an explicitly written letter to President Nixon reminding him of the dairy contributions, import quotas on low-fat cheese, low-fat chocolate crumb, animal feed containing milk, and ice cream were personally revised by Nixon in a manner beneficial to the dairymen.

The contacts and mutual reinforcement between the White House and the dairy cooperatives are complex. Nonetheless, it is also well documented and the quid pro quo is starkly clear. Both groups gained direct monetary advantage from the relationship. The episode does serve to highlight the enormous influence money, through campaign contributions, can buy and to set the stage for and introduce the activities of a handful of corporations, labor unions, and interest groups (those caught in the act) engaged in the same game for much the same reasons.

THE MONEY HUSTLE

The dairy cooperatives were but one of the groups to contribute large sums to the Nixon Administration and to profit handsomely thereby. Far from it. The record is a sorry one. Although the scope of the corruption is too vast to be encompassed in one chapter, the dimensions of the problem can be shown and some representative cases explored.

At this point, the complete story is unlikely ever to emerge. Even though the financial and political interactions are not totally clear, they would include:

the "secret" bank accounts of Bebe Rebozo and his numerous business deals on behalf of or in concert with members of the Nixon family and their friends;

the persistent rumors of Hughes's complicity in various shadowy financing deals or contributions to Richard Nixon;

the contribution of International Telephone and Telegraph (ITT), the world's largest conglomerate, of from $100,000 to $400,000 to the Republican party and the expeditious dropping of two antitrust and one antimerger suit (resulting, in the latter case, in the largest corporate merger in American history; an arrangement agreed to by the government through the personal intervention of President Nixon and against the stubborn advice of the head of the Justice Department's Anti-Trust Division, who was moved into a federal judgeship);

the quiet contribution of from $600,000 to $700,000 by the trucking industry (with $25,000 systematically collected from the major trucking firms), facing a challenge to its traditionally paternalistic regulation of routes and rate schedules by a friendly Interstate Commerce Commission (in an effort to introduce more competition into the field);

the Nixon Administration's Price Commission's reversal of its decision to disallow an increase from 59¢ to 63¢ (compared to the 65¢ sought) in McDonald's hamburgers after Ray Kroc, the ebullient chairman of McDonald's board of directors, contributed $200,000 between May 31 (the date of the earlier decision) and September 8, 1972 (the date of the reversal), with another $55,000 of goodwill money following;

the contribution five days before the 1972 election of $100,000 (precipitously withdrawn from a New York bank in which the cochairman of Nixon's Finance Committee served as an officer) by the Seafarer's Union and the subsequent refusal of the Justice Department to prosecute a case against the union for illegal contributions to both parties in the 1968 campaign (the case was dismissed by a federal court for lack of a speedy trial);

the truly frightening implications of the Vesco scandal in which Robert Vesco's $200,000 contribution to the Nixon campaign (later returned to Vesco at his insistence) resulted in compromising the Securities and Exchange Commission's investigation into the allegedly illegal takeover of an international mutual fund (and its alleged looting of investor funds to the tune of $224 million) and led to the resignation of the chairman of the SEC (and his later probationary disbarment because of the incident by his home state bar in Nebraska), the trial and subsequent acquittal of two Nixon cabinet members, John Mitchell and Maurice Stans, for obstruction of justice, and the fleeing of Vesco to Costa Rica.

For other cases, the abuses are relatively well documented, resulting in convictions for many of the participants (although the sentencing could only be called symbolic). These incidents involved some of the best-known names in American industry, such as:

American Airlines. The airline made an illegal contribution from corporate funds of $55,000 to the Nixon campaign after personal solicitation by Herbert Kalmbach, who had asked for $100,000.

Braniff Airways. This airline donated $40,00 illegally from corporate funds to Maurice Stans for Nixon reelection efforts. Stans had asked for $100,000.

American Ship Building Company. This corporation made an illegal donation of $100,000 to the Committee to Re-Elect, under pressure from Kalmbach. The company had business pending before the government and won, in a settlement with the Justice Department, an agreement that (according to the Ervin Committee) gave "the company effective control of the grain shipping market on the Great Lakes[4]."

Gulf Oil. This oil processing giant made illegal corporate contributions of $100,000 to the Nixon campaign and $10,000 and $15,000, respectively, to the campaigns of Senator Henry Jackson and Congressman Wilbur Mills, both Democratic presidential aspirants.

3M (Minnesota Mining and Manufacturing Corporation). This company maintained a secret political fund since the 1950s. In 1972, it made illegal corporate contributions of $36,000 to the Nixon campaign and $1000 each to the campaigns of Senator Hubert Humphrey and Congressman Wilbur Mills.

Northrop Corporation. Two of this major defense contractor's officers (including Thomas V. Jones, the chief executive official) illegally contributed $150,000 in corporate funds to the Nixon campaign after being approached by Kalmbach, Stans, and Leonard Firestone, then chairman of the president's California Finance Committee and later one of the handful who served as a trustee for the ill-fated Nixon Foundation. (Firestone, a $100,000 contributor himself, also saw duty as the Nixon-appointed ambassador to Belgium.) Jones and the Northrop officials lied to the Ervin Committee, the Government Accounting Office, the FBI, and the grand jury in the investigations that followed of the sources of the funds before reversing their stand and pleading guilty in federal district court in 1974.

Phillips Petroleum. This oil corporation made illegal contributions of $100,000 from company funds to the Nixon reelection drive after solicitation by Stans, initially while he was still secretary of commerce in the Nixon Cabinet, and after proddings from other business executives and fundraising officers enlisted by the Nixon money raisers.

Goodyear Tire and Rubber Company. The executives of this corporation delivered $40,000 in corporate funds to Stans. Initially, they contributed $20,000 in cash, personally given to Stans who informed them that he felt $50,000 to be more appropriate. Within five days, an additional $20,000 in cash was turned over to the Nixon finance chairman.

Ashland Oil. This corporation made a $100,000 cash donation—via Geneva, Switzerland (as was the case with several other companies)—from corporate funds (after being personally asked by Stans) to the Committee to Re-Elect and purchased, in addition, a $10,000 advertisement in a brochure prepared for the Republican National Convention.

Criminal charges were brought against these companies, and they therefore rank among the more obvious examples of those attempting to buy entrée to government. They do not begin to exhaust, however, the number of corporations and special interest groups that invested huge sums in the Nixon campaign. In general, industries directly dependent on government favoritism gave the most generously (and, for the most part, secretly but legally) in support of the president's reelection. The defense and oil industries nicely illustrate the pattern. The nation's 100 largest defense contractors donated $5.4 million that can be accounted for to the Nixon campaign coffers, 60 percent of it contributed prior to April 7, when the new disclosure law took effect. Leading the list, officials of IBM gave $326,545; Tenneco, the country's sixth largest defense contractor, $307,286; Litton Industries, whose president served in the Nixon Administration, $226,187; RCA, $172,636; and American Motors, $159,577. Other names on the list (excluding oil companies, many of which did contract work on defense) include names readily familiar to the American public: Ford, DuPont, General Motors, General Dynamics, McDonnell Douglas, Flying Tiger Airlines, Goodyear, General Telephone, Hughes, Lockheed, Gulf & Western, Westinghouse, Motorola, ITT, General Electric, Sperry Rand, Xerox, Bendix, and Chrysler[5].

The data on oil industry contributions parallels that for defense contractors. Four hundred thirteen directors, officials, and principal stockholders of the oil corporations contributed $4,981,840 to the Nixon campaign. This sum does *not* include major contributions by individuals with vast oil and gas holdings but with other interests as well. For example, the Rockefellers gave between $1 and $5.25 million alone to the Nixon effort. The former board chairman of Midwest Oil and a director of Texas Pacific Oil both contributed over $100,000. None of these sums are counted in the totals attributed to the oil corporations.

Table 5.1 presents the 11 major donations by the oil companies. The "secret contributions" refer to those given prior to April 7. As an example, 96 percent of Gulf's monies—the oil corporation whose officials gave the most—was routed to the Nixon people during the period of no public disclosure. There was, in fact, a concerted move to raise as much of the campaign funds as possible on behalf of President Nixon before the new law became operative on the mistaken assumption that these contributions would never have to be accounted for. Three of the oil corporations on the list (Gulf, Phillips, and Ashland) eventually admitted illegally diverting a total of $300,000 in company funds to the president's reelection bid.

TABLE 5.1
OIL CORPORATION CONTRIBUTIONS
TO THE NIXON CAMPAIGN, 1972

Company	Total Contribution ($)	Secret Contribution ($)
1. Gulf Oil Co.	1,176,500	1,132,000
2. Amerada Hess Corp.	261,956	211,000
3. Getty Oil Co.	179,292	77,500
4. Standard Oil (Calif.)	166,000	102,000
5. Sun Oil Co.	157,798	60,000
6. Pan Ocean Oil Corp.	137,035	—
7. Phillips Petroleum Co.	137,000	100,000
8. Exxon	127,747	100,672
9. The Williams Companies	117,596	—
10. Shaheen Natural Resources	104,000	—
11. Ashland Oil, Inc.	103,500	100,000
TOTALS:	2,668,424	1,883,172

SOURCE: Report compiled by Congressman Les Aspin (D., Wisc.).

The consequences of such largesse should not be difficult to estimate. Congressman Les Aspin (D., Wisc.), who compiled the figures from reports chiefly made available by Common Cause, argued that commercial interests had "a stake in maintaining a bloated military budget" and that "many defense contracts were nothing more than political patronage," a point that appears increasingly obvious. Oil companies, of course, benefited from defense industry contracts. Additionally, Aspin contended, they had maneuvered Nixon (perhaps not unwillingly) into a position where he could not (or would not) deal effectively with the energy crisis. The oil corporations "have been the chief beneficiaries of the [energy] crisis, reaping huge windfall profits," declared the congressman, while the "entire burden of solving the energy crisis has been thrown on the consumer[6]." Allowing for political rhetoric, the nature of political funding in this country permits little optimism. It serves rather to limit the discretion and independence of the political leader. If the examples reviewed represent the norm or anything close to it, the most disturbing element in the entire chain of events is the extent to which private monetary gain appears to motivate so much of political decision making.

HOW THE MONEY WAS GIVEN

Swiss banks, dummy corporations, "laundering" through phony accounts, foreign corporations and unidentified legal and financial representatives in other countries, surreptitious money messengers, faked receipts for goods never delivered, payments for services not performed, false "bonuses" to company personnel (that went instead to campaign coffers), that and more became part of the American dialogue on campaign financing as a consequence of Watergate. The means of directing the funds to the Nixon campaign and, in the process, divorcing their parentage from the offending corporation taxed the imagination of some of the ablest business leaders in the nation. One of the simpler examples, yet one that can provide an inkling of the effort that went into such cover-ups and the lengths to which the corporations would go to disguise their illegal contributions, is provided by Braniff Airways[7].

The chairman of the board of Braniff personally made an unsolicited $10,000 cash contribution to Maurice Stans, who represented the Nixon people. Stans, being Stans, said that was nice but that he was thinking more along the lines of a $100,000 donation from Braniff. The board chairman said that he would see what could be done. Later, he decided an additional $40,000 would be appropriate. He then appointed a top-level committee comprised of company vice-presidents and a treasurer to devise a scheme for camouflaging an illegal gift of this magnitude. The committee, similar to many related ones in other corporations, devised an ingenious plan. The Braniff manager in Panama agreed to use a Panamanian company he personally owned as a conduit for the funds. Braniff then moved to issue a voucher as an advance to this Panamanian corporation (Camfab, as it was called) for "expenses and services." A check was sent to Camfab and then an accounts receivable item for $40,000 was listed in Braniff's books as due from Camfab. The president of the Panamanian corporation cashed the Braniff check in a Panamanian bank and then returned $40,000 in U.S. currency to Braniff (the "laundering" process) which was delivered to Stans (who, as usual, did not question the source of the money).

To complicate matters—and these dealings were intricate—as well as to validate the sum contributed, Braniff supplied their Panamanian representative and the president of Camfab with a "special ticket stock." As the Senate Watergate Committee recounted the arrangement:

> Tickets written upon this ticket stock were sold at the ticket counters only by the supervisor in the Braniff Panama office, generally for cash. If a customer wanted to pay by check, regular tickets were used. The receipts were not accounted for as ticket receipts, but were applied to the liquidation of the account receivable from the Panamanian entity. . . . Periodically, on his trips from Panama to the Dallas head office of Braniff, Fabresa [Braniff's Panama director] would take several thousand dollars in cash and deliver it to Braniff[8].

The fake ticket stock did not sell briskly enough to please Braniff's top echelon so their Panama representative then borrowed $13,000 ($27,000 in bogus tickets had been sold to that point) from a Panama bank and gave it to Braniff, thus closing the extraordinary account. The airline's representative then recouped the loan by continuing to sell the bogus ticket stock until it was depleted and his financial obligations had been met. The company, of course, paid no taxes on the sum raised supposedly through ticket sales, nor did it enter an accounting of the procedure in its annual report.

This mini-example—representative of the more intricate dealings on a larger scale by other corporations in their deceptive funding endeavors—takes one additional twist. Common Cause sued the Committee to Re-Elect in an effort (eventually successful) to force them to reveal the names of all donors who gave *prior* to the April 7 effective date for the new disclosure law. Stans told a Braniff official on one of the airline executive's personal visits in relaying the money that he would need a list of contributors who supposedly had donated the sum allocated for the campaign. Undaunted, Braniff delivered a list of nine individuals who reputedly made the donations, apparently without bothering to clear it with all of the people involved. When the Committee to Re-Elect was forced to hand over Braniff's list and its lawyer, Kenneth Wells Parkinson (later tried with Haldeman, Mitchell, Ehrlichman, and Mardian, and the only one of the group to be acquitted, in the most sensational of the Watergate trials) notified Braniff that the turnover was imminent, Braniff officials then contacted the individuals named and requested that they make personal contributions to the company to account for the unrecorded sale of tickets. The chairman of the board told the Ervin Committee that this was their real intention all along, although he admitted they did nothing until spurred to action by Parkinson's notification. When the personal checks arrived, they were credited to an unearned passenger transportation account and the matter seemed closed—except for one final incident. The company did plead guilty to breaking the law and it was fined $5000 and its board chairman an equally meager $1000.

The Braniff maneuvers begin to suggest the extraordinary duplicity involved in the unlawful fundings and the disingenuous lengths to which the corporations would go to disguise their activities. Once the inquiry into funding schemes began to gather momentum, the worldwide revelations of bribes, payoffs, bizarre intrigues, and shadowy interchanges between giant corporations and governments around the globe began to suggest that the American disclosures were part of an international business-politics ethic with broad, and previously unappreciated, ramifications.

WHY DID THE CORPORATIONS GIVE?

Possibly the answer to this question appears both obvious and, at this juncture, somewhat naive. Nonetheless, the corporations' explanations of their acts deserve consideration because the risks were potentially high and the corporations, it must be remembered, included many of America's most prestigious firms. The man who served as both chairman of the board and chief executive officer for Ashland Oil told why he and his company routed $100,000 in illegal contributions through an African subsidiary and a Swiss bank to the Nixon campaign.

> We were not seeking any particular privilege or benefit because we don't do any significant business with the Government. I think all we were attempting to do was to assure ourselves of a forum to be heard. Were we a larger factor in our respective industries, we could expect to have access to administrative officials in the executive branch of Government with ease, but being a relatively unknown corporation, despite our size [the 70th largest manufacturing concern in the United States], we felt we needed something that would be sort of a calling card, something that would let us in the door and make our point of view heard[9].

Many corporations were to echo the same argument. They were afraid not to give.

This may be true. But it is difficult to picture the business community as quite the naive prey that they chose to picture themselves as. Again, Ashland Oil can serve as the example. When asked if Ashland did not realize such contributions were illegal, the spokesman for the company replied that yes, they understood the law but felt it, like the statutes on Prohibition, was more honored in the breach than in practice. Ashland, with virtually all the other companies, admitted to similar previous experiences with both of the major political parties.

The manner of delivery of the funds was extraordinary. The donation was redirected through several countries and then given in cash personally to Stans, finance chairman for the president's campaign. Certainly, these actions did not constitute normal business procedures. Stans's attitude was also curious. According to the company executive who delivered the funds, Stans unceremoniously "dumped them in his desk drawer," a response more appropriate for a payoff than for any conventional transaction[10]. As for the size of the contribution, the company representative said, "The Republicans always cost you twice as much as the Democrats[11]." So much for the ethics, ground rules, and motivations for corporate giving.

It is a little difficult to credit the objective of establishing a vague (if costly) goodwill as the spur to an unlawful financial gift. Ashland, for example, claimed that their elaborately contrived donation "produced [no] distinctive benefit to Ashland Oil." Yet at least one government action on an import quota favored the company, and immediately after the contribution Ashland met with government officials on questions relating to obtaining greater supplies of crude oil. The same official who denied any business concessions from the government spurred by the Ashland gift took a somewhat different line in a letter to an apparently important stockholder. "There was a good business reason for making the contribution and, although illegal in nature, I am confident that it distinctly benefited the corporation and the stockholders[12]." The mood of the letter seems at variance with the official's testimony before the Senate Watergate Committee. When shown a copy of the earlier letter by the staff of the committee, the company's chief executive deftly retreated to generalities about the need for "access" to government officials. At a minimum, it seems clear that the handsome contribution buys such entrée.

American Airlines seemed to be in an unusually awkward position. The company realized from the size of the contribution requested, the solicitor (Kalmbach), and the indicated manner of delivery, that the entire operation was, at best, of questionable legality, a fact that American (unlike a number of other corporations) was willing to admit. In his testimony to the Senate Watergate Committee, the board chairman recounted that the amounts of money sought by Nixon's representatives were "so enormous that they drove people to do things they didn't want to do. I hated it. It was very much on my conscience[13]." In a similar vein, Ashland's board chairman also noted that Stans, in dunning him, had no reason to believe that he personally could afford $100,000.

If conscience was a factor and the violations of the law clear, why then did American Airlines comply? "There were two aspects: would you get something if you gave it [the contributions], or would you be prevented from getting something if you didn't give it[14]?" American Airlines had 20 matters pending before government agencies. The most important involved a proposed merger with Western Airlines. Incredibly, Kalmbach, who applied the pressure to American, was not only the president's personal lawyer, but he also represented United Airlines, American's principal competitor and then in the process of opposing them in the merger case before a government regulatory agency, an issue that would eventually go to President Richard Nixon for resolution (American lost).

Again the former chairman of the board of American:

> It is something like the old medieval maps that show a flat world and then what they called "terra incognito," with fierce animals lying around the fringes of this map. You just don't know what is going to happen to you if you get off it. I think sometimes, the fear of the unknown may be more terrifying than the fear of the known. I think this is a very large element in the picture.
>
> Most contributions from the business community are not volunteered to seek a competitive advantage, but are made in response to pressure for fear of the competi-

tive disadvantage that might result if they are not made. The process degrades both the donor and the donee[15].

As the implications of the corporate scandals grew, an unbelieving Congress and a befuddled public began to hear tales of multimillion dollar ITT intrigues (in collusion with the CIA) to undermine the government of a foreign nation (Chile); the accrediting of CIA agents as foreign representatives of American businesses (Ashland); the illicit distribution of bribes, kickbacks, political contributions, gifts, and so forth by American companies (Mobil, Northrop, Gulf, Exxon, Lockheed, ITT, United Brands, General Motors, etc.) to political parties, governments, and individuals in other countries and the defense of these as necessary to gain competitive advantage[16]. The stories that emerged were extraordinary by any accounting. Some took grotesque twists and others had their humorous elements. Exxon, for example, was accused of making payoffs to Italian political parties between 1963 and 1971 of from $27 to $49 million. When asked to justify the practice, a company spokesman said that it was simply attempting to preserve democracy. Later, it was revealed that $86,000 was directed to the Italian Communist party through, of all things, a communist front organization. Exxon declined any further comment. Perhaps a $2 billion Italian business justified the investment whatever the politics involved. The Communist party, in turn, was scandalized by the accusations of collusion with and support from an American capitalistic organization. The party denied the charges, arguing they would not sell out for a mere $86,000[17].

For those who believe confession good to the soul, or that public revelation has some type of inherent self-corrective powers, it is worth mentioning the case of Northrop, "a relatively small company in the aerospace industry" according to the *New York Times* but one with assets of more than $2 billion and one with a net income of $18.1 million in 1974[18]. The company increased its net income from the 1973 to the 1974 fiscal year by 56 percent. Its business consisted of supplying planes to the Defense Department (as called for, as an example, by its $5 billion contract in 1975 with the Navy for a lightweight aircraft) and to the military in 35 other nations. Two years after incidents related to funding abuses in the Watergate scandal had revealed a Northrop "slush fund" of $1.2 million for illegal payoffs and one year after the corporation, its president, and other officials pleaded guilty to making unlawful political contributions, the fund was revealed to be still in existence. Furthermore, for weeks after their court appearances and sentencing, Northrop officials continued to use corporate funds, channeled through a Parisian middleman (a onetime World War II hero decorated by President Truman), into payoffs of various sorts. The size of the slush fund itself was revealed to be $30 million between 1971 and 1973, a figure far in excess of anything previously known. And lastly, the information about the magnitude and duration of the political fund did not come from any actions initiated by the Justice Department, a regulatory commission, the Special Prosecutor's Office, or the Congress. Rather, the suit of an individual stockholder led to the subsequent, damning disclosures[19].

When the American Airlines representative was asked if he (and, by implication, all businessmen) felt politicians were all for sale, he replied that no, he didn't believe that for he had found "many offices in government where you can make a presentation on the basis of merit and be fairly treated[20]." Perhaps this is encouraging.

THE USE (AND ABUSE) OF GOVERNMENT AGENCIES

There are many examples of the Nixon Administration's perversions of governmental agencies as well as policies in the barter for political advantage. In effect, an attempt was made to mobilize the entire apparatus of the government to further Richard Nixon's bid for reelection, to reward his friends, and to punish his enemies. The actions were enormously successful. They also clearly violated the laws regulating campaign abuses and governmental favoritism, the oldest in this particular line of regulatory activity. The abuses of official power raised relatively little indignation in a public submerged in a sea of accusations and they received even less prosecutorial follow-up. The actions range from the "patronage" use (the Nixon Administration's own term) of the Department of Justice to the Internal Revenue Service's bullying of Nixon's opponents (the persistent auditing over a period of years of Democratic National Chairman Lawrence O'Brien's financial records is but one instance) to the corruption of the very concept of a politically independent civil service corps. The results are sad, involving (in cases that have been documented by the Senate Watergate Committee) activities relating to blacks, Spanish-speaking and other ethnic minorities; the elderly; the General Services Administration; regulatory agencies (including a crackdown on television licenses to media opponents of the Nixon Administration); the appointment of politically obligated federal officials; the Veterans Administration; HEW; HUD; OEO; ACTION; the Department of Labor; the Department of Agriculture; the Department of Commerce; and so on.

The types of official largesse to be used to promote directly Richard Nixon's reelection were outlined in a White House memo as follows:

THE BASIC TYPES OF PATRONAGE

1. *Jobs* (full-time, part-time, retainers, consultantships, etc.)
2. *Revenue*
Contracts (Federal Government as purchaser—GSA)
Grants (do-good programs—EDA, Model Cities, NSF research, etc.)
Subsidies (needy industries—airlines, etc.)
Bank Deposits (all Federal accounts)
Social Need Program (direct benefit to citizen, i.e., Social Security, welfare, etc.)
Public Works Projects
3. *Execution of Federal Law* (resides mainly in Department of Justice whose interpretive power touches every vested interest

4. *Information and Public Relations Capacity* (a professional (?) public relations office in each department and agency constitutes an enormous public information apparatus)

5. *Travel* (domestic transportation can be provided by law, foreign travel, international conferences, etc., are available)[21].

The White House's Personnel Office under the iron control of Fred V. Malek evaluated the direct political gain to the president from potential appointees to competitive federal positions. The applicant was graded on a scale as follows:

VALUE OF PLACEMENT TO THE PRESIDENT POLITICALLY

[ ]Highest Political Value (Must place)
[ ]High Political Value (Place if possible)
[ ]Moderate Political Value (Handle courteously)
[ ]Little Political Value (Handle routinely)[22].

The departments and agencies received such a report with an additional political commentary on each prospect and they were urged to take political considerations into account in making the appointment.

The "incumbency-responsiveness" program, as it was called in the public relations jargon of the White House, was not a paper warfare carried on by bureaucrats for their own amusement. People were rewarded on the basis of their political usefulness and others, who depended on merit, service, performance, and the like, were excluded. One instance, taken from an October 26, 1971 memo from White House political advisor Harry Dent to John Mitchell and H. R. Haldeman, should illustrate how serious the Nixon people were in using the full powers of incumbency to further the president politically. Dent mentioned that many government grants to blacks had been awarded to "large Democrat-oriented" groups (since most blacks are Democrats, this would appear normal). Dent recorded how he had been in touch with "some Southern black leaders about channeling money to groups whose loyalties lie elsewhere." Dent then added:

> I have also delayed the promotion of the southeastern OEO [Office of Economic Opportunity] man to the #3 spot in OEO *until he demonstrates proof-positive that he is rechanneling money from Democrats to RN* [Richard Nixon] *blacks*[23]. (Italics added.)

The incumbency-responsiveness program enjoyed an enormous scope. Only its outlines can be suggested, and one brief example (from the many available) will be presented to illustrate its operation. The case is typical of the maneuvering of government programs and funds to promote a fealty to Richard Nixon (and, in fact, the Dent memo just reviewed serves as an appropriate introduction to it). The name of at least one of the participants should be familiar, an indication of how high such a program can reach into the nongovernmental sectors of opinion leaders and the caliber of people who can be politically compromised.

THE INCUMBENCY-RESPONSIVENESS PROGRAM

The Ervin Committee defined the responsiveness program as "an organized endeavor 'to politicize' the executive branch to ensure that the Administration remained in power[24]." The significance of this effort—while apparently escaping the public and the special prosecutor—was starkly clear to the Congress. These abuses formed the basis for the Second Article of Impeachment voted by the House Judiciary Committee 28 to 10.

Concern with employing the federal government's enormous resources to best advantage in the 1972 presidential election began early. This much is certain and is reflected in the testimony of Haldeman, Erlichman, John Dean, Patrick Buchanan, Jeb Magruder, and a number of others. A January 1971 memo of Magruder's voiced the general feeling that "the Administration has not made effective political use of the resources of the Federal Government, the RNC [Republican National Committee], the White House, and outside groups and corporations. . . . In developing the structure for the campaign, proper use of these resources should be of primary concern at the outset of the planning[25]."

The "planning" went on from there. A May 12 White House memo from Dent's office reported on meetings between White House personnel and departmental representatives on the evolving program.

> A consensus emerged that the range of federal resources must be inventoried and analyzed with perhaps the federal grants area broken out for priority treatment because of the immediate benefits and some budget cycle timing considerations. Additionally, the matter of a delivery system which would put these resources at our disposal on a timely basis was considered to be imperative[26].

Malek's staff prepared a June 23 report for Haldeman.

> [The] President's direct control over awarding selected grants should be strengthened to ensure that political circumstances can be considered, if appropriate, in making awards.
>
> To ensure politically sensitive grant applications receive appropriate consideration, two basic steps must be carried out: (1) determine which grants are politically sensitive and (2) ensure these grants receive positive consideration from OMB [Office of Management and Budget] and the Departments[27].

A flurry of memoranda then followed laying down the guidelines for the program and the manner of its operation (including one stating that written communications were to be avoided for fear of exposure). Political circumstances would dictate "must" grants. In addition, government grants for localities where they would do the most good politically would be given expeditious processing. The loyalty of government employees to the Nixon reelection was to be cultivated, and key individuals within departments were to be identified to insure the approved programs were acted upon. These latter individuals "must have two prime qualities: . . . loyalty to the President and sufficient authority to ensure 'must' grants are approved and Departmental announcements of all grants conform to the guidelines discussed subsequently[28]." As the Senate Watergate Committee reported, "election considerations were to be taken into account in: the letting of government grants, contracts, and loans; the bringing and prosecution of legal and regulatory action; the making of Administration personnel decisions; the determination of the issues and programs to be stressed by the Administration; [and] the communicating of Administration activities to the voting public[29]."

Another memo of March 17, 1972, from Malek's staff to Haldeman spelled out the potentialities of the program.

> The Department of Commerce provides a good example. To date Gifford [an OMB official who cleared federal grant requests] has made some 35 requests. Most of these involved expediting the normal grant reviewing process and securing the release of information. Approximately a dozen of these requests resulted in favorable grant decisions *(which otherwise would not have been made)* involving roughly $1 million. Politically these actions have been most beneficial[30]. (Italics in Senate report.)

Nevertheless, the memo expressed some dissatisfaction, pointing out that $700 million in Department of Commerce funds in the current fiscal year and $700 million in the next remained to be "redirected" (their term) for political advantage. The memo continued that each department should *"systematically but discreetly seek out opportunities for improving services to target groups and geographic areas* and then ensure that appropriate action is taken[31]." (Italics in Senate report.)

The memo set the guidelines for the operation, for creating political priorities for programs, and for directing federal services to critical areas and groups. In addition to establishing clearance procedures and contact men, the memo concluded that the departments "must be given a clear understanding [that] the program [has] the President's full backing," although, and this point was made emphatically:

> the documents prepared [concerning the programs, grants, etc.] would not indicate White House involvement in any way. Also, oral and written communications concerning the program within the Department would be structured to give the impression that the program was initiated by the Department Head without the knowledge of the White House[32].

These same points, in different language, were made repeatedly. The tone of the communications was ominous (although Malek argued that the program was more benign than it sounded; he also contended that he never knew if the program had the president's "full backing").

A June 7, 1972, memo reported that the program was "on schedule." Malek informed Haldeman that he met with all but one of the department and agency heads to cover a number of aspects of the plan. Among other things, he "asked them to educate loyal appointees (including regional directors) concerning priorities and expectations, thus forming a political network in each Department[33]."

Some government agencies, to their credit, resisted, but it is disturbing how many fell in line and how little was heard about such systematic, large-scale policy abuses of impeachment magnitude until the election was well over and the mood of the country drastically changed by the revelations concerning its president. Malek, in fact, reported receiving "quite receptive" hearings from John Volpe, secretary of transportation, Peter Peterson, successor to Maurice Stans as secretary of commerce, and Earl Butz, secretary of agriculture.

Finally, Malek extended the operation one step further. Key party leaders and presidential representatives within the states were briefed in order "to encourage politically oriented requests for government action from these campaign officials[34]."

ONE CASE STUDY

The responsiveness program worked well and some made a handsome financial profit from it—awarded them in the form of government funds—for their electoral support of Richard Nixon. There are many quid pro quo illustrations of this relationship. One of the more controversial involved James Farmer, the prominent civil rights leader. A White House special assistant to the president and a campaign official met with Farmer on April 18, 1972, and reported back on their talk. According to this account, they discussed:

> 1. Farmer's willingness to work in support of the President. (It was agreed he might better serve at this time by maintaining a "non-partisan" posture.) . . .
> 2. His speaking engagements (he is to send a list of his engagements). We will seek to arrange media interviews in connection with his key appearances.
> 3. Farmer's interest in funding for his think tank proposal. He's seeking $200,000 seed money from HEW. (This should be moved on but should allow for a final Brown-Jones [the Nixon officials: Jones wrote the "Confidential Memorandum" on the meeting] check-off in order to re-inforce Farmer's involvement [35]. . . .

Ten days later another memo on the matter went to Malek and later was used to brief John Mitchell. Its message was clear enough. "Paul Jones [the Nixon campaign official] wants favorable action on an HEW grant for James Farmer that would enable Farmer to have time to speak in support of the reelection[36]."

Farmer received a grant of $150,000 from HEW. All involved in the award heatedly refused to admit it involved any impropriety. Still, on May 2, 1972, Malek wrote to Robert Finch, HEW secretary that he had several meetings with Farmer and as a consequence:

> 1. Farmer has been given a grant from OE [Office of Education] to fund his project here in Washington.
> 2. He will now be able to spend a major part of his time on the above project while also making time available to the re-election efforts.

TABLE 5.2
CONTRIBUTIONS OF AMBASSADORS
APPOINTED BY PRESIDENT NIXON

Name	Post	Confirmed	Pre.-Ap. 7 ($)	Post-Ap. 7 ($)	Total ($)
———	Ethiopia	5-1-71	—	—	—
Annenberg, Walter H.	Great Britain	3-13-69	250,000	4,000	254,000
———	El Salvador	2-8-74	—	—	—
Catto, Henry E.	El Salvador	9-29-71	25,000	—	25,000
———, Philip K.	Norway^a	5-1-69	—	500	500
Davis, Shelby	Switzerland	5-12-69	100,000	—	100,000
De Roulet, Vincent	Jamaica^a	9-17-69	100,000	3,500	103,500
Dudley, Guilford	Denmark	5-12-69	—	2,500	2,500
Eisenhower, John D.	Belgium^a	3-13-69	—	—	—
Farkas, Ruth N.	Luxembourg	3-26-73	—	300,000	300,000
Farland, Joseph S.	Iran^a	3-27-72	10,000	12,300	22,300
Ferguson, Clarence C.	Uganda^a	3-16-70	—	—	—
Firestone, Leonard K.	Belgium	4-10-74	100,000		
Franzheim, Kenneth	New Zealand	7-30-69	—	—	—
Gerard, Sumner	Jamaica	3-20-64	38,867	—	38,867
Gould, Kingdon	Netherlands	9-26-73	100,000		
Helms, Richard	Iran	2-8-73	—	—	—
Holland, Jerome H.	Sweden^a	2-16-70	—	—	—
Humes, John F.	Austria	9-24-69	100,000	500	100,500
———, John G.	South Africa	7-23-70	—	—	—
Hill, Robert C.	Argentina	12-19-73	—	750	750
Ingersall, Robert S.	Japan	2-25-72	3,000	—	3,000
Irwin, John N. III	France	2-1-73	50,000	500	50,500
Keating, Kenneth	Israel	6-15-73	—	3,000	3,000
Kinter, William R.	Thailand	9-26-73	—	—	—
———	Finland	3-26-73	—	29,500	29,500
Lodge, John D.	Argentina^a	5-23-69	—	200	200
Macomber, William B.	Turkey	3-26-73	—	500	500
Marshall, Anthony D.	Kenya	12-18-73	48,505	—	48,505
Meeker, Leonard	Romania^a	7-22-69	—	—	—
Melady, Thomas P.	Uganda^a	6-12-72	—	—	—
Middendorf, J. Wm.	Netherlands	6-12-67	—	2,000	2,000
Mitter, Lloyd I.	Trinidad & Tobago^a	12-19-73	—	25,000	25,000
Moore, John D. II	Ireland	4-18-69	—	10,442	10,442
Moynihan, Daniel P.	India		—	—	—
———, Robert G.	Morocco	9-19-73	—	—	—
Peterson, Val	Finland^a	5-1-69	—	—	—
———, Walter C.	Costa Rica^a	4-6-70	—	—	—
Pritzlaff, John C.	Malta^a	7-8-69	—	1,000	1,000
Rice, Walter I.	Australia^a	8-13-69	—	1,000	1,000
Rivera, Adm. Horacio	Spain	9-8-72	—	—	—
Rush, Kenneth	Germany^a	7-8-69	—	2,000	2,000
———, Fred J.	Denmark^a	1-3-71	—	—	—

TABLE 5.2 *(Continued)*

Name	Post	Confirmed	Pre.-Ap. 7 ($)	Post-Ap. 7 ($)	Total ($)
Sanchez, Philip V.	Honduras	5-17-73	—	—	—
Schmidt, Adolph	Canada	7-8-69	—	1,000	1,000
Scott, Stuart Nash	Portugal	12-18-73	—	—	—
Seldon, Armistead	New Zealand	2-27-74	—	—	—
Smith, Robert S.	Ivory Coast	2-8-74	—	—	—
Straus-Hupe, Robert	Sweden	4-25-74	—	1,000	1,000
Symington, J. Fife	Trinidad & Tobago	7-8-69	100,000	500	100,500
Vaughn, Jack Hood	Columbia	5-23-69	—	—	—
Volpe, John A.	Italy	2-1-73	—	2,000	2,000
Watson, Arthur K.	France[a]	4-6-70	300,000	3,000	303,000
		TOTALS	1,325,372	522,692	1,848,064

[a]No longer serving in post.
SOURCE: *The Senate Watergate Report* (New York: Dell, 1974), 2:65.

3. He has agreed to do speaking on our behalf and also to talk to key black leaders in an effort to gain their loyalties. I feel that Jim is in a position to make a major contribution to our effort and am confident that he will. At the same time we are going to try to maintain his involvement in a manner that is not overtly partisan and does not harm his credibility. Many thanks for getting this started and for putting me onto it[37].

HOW MUCH IS LUXEMBOURG?
THE SALE OF AMBASSADORSHIPS

One of the traditional means of selling opportunities in the federal service to raise campaign funds is to encourage large contributions through the promise, implicit or otherwise, of appointment as ambassador to a foreign nation. As is consistent with their emphasis throughout, the Nixon Administration exploited these opportunities more fully than any of their predecessors. Not everyone who gave excessively received appointments. W. Clement Stone, the mustachioed insurance tycoon from Chicago who reported contributing millions (some say as much as $5 million) to various Nixon campaigns and other Republican races, designated by the White House in the late sixties and early seventies, never did receive the appointment to the Court of St. James's he so ardently sought. Other wealthy donors were more fortunate. Table 5.2 lists the campaign contributions of the ambassadors appointed by Nixon. The total amount of the donations came to $1.8 million, with most of the sum (72 percent) being given prior to the April 7 disclosure deadline.

In all, about 30 percent of foreign envoy posts were awarded to noncareer personnel. The heaviest concentration of nonprofessional appointees was in West-

TABLE 5.3
THE CONTRIBUTIONS TO THE NIXON CAMPAIGN
OF AMBASSADORS TO PRINCIPAL EUROPEAN POSTS

Country	Ambassadors	Contribution ($)
Great Britain	Walter Annenberg	250,000
Switzerland	Shelby Davis	100,000
Luxembourg	Ruth Farkas	300,000
Belgium	Leonard Firestone	112,600
Netherlands	Kingdon Gould	100,900
Austria	John Humes	100,000
France	John Irwin	50,500
	Arthur Watson	300,000
Ireland	John Moore	10,442
	TOTAL	1,324,442

SOURCE: *The Senate Watergate Report* (New York: Dell, 1974), 2:66.

ern Europe which also happened to include the heaviest incidence of contributions of $100,000 or more among the ambassadors (Table 5.3). These posts, of course, are the most sought after, as Clement Stone's public campaign for appointment helps illustrate.

The ambassadorial posts in England and France have always represented top prizes. Senator Claiborne Pell (D., R.I.), commenting on the above listing, noted that appointments to the Benelux countries were also unusually expensive; the incumbents of these offices donated more than one-half million dollars to the Nixon Administration (see Table 5.3)[38]. Also popular—and with a curious history as an outpost for large campaign benefactors—were the Caribbean ambassadorships to Trinidad-Tobago. Two of the early Nixon appointees to these jobs, J. Fife Symington and Vincent de Roulet, gave $100,000 each to the Nixon campaign coffers. Both proved to be dissatisfied with their positions and through a process of direct and indirect negotiation (further campaign contributions to a secret Nixon fund for Republican senatorial candidates in 1970 and/or directly to the 1972 campaign) with Kalmbach and Stans, as well as Haldeman and Peter Flanagan of the White House staff, attempted to better their lots. Their efforts proved unsuccessful. They made the agreed-upon contributions but, according to Haldeman, they were "misinformed" about their prospects for landing in Lisbon or Madrid[39]. The replacements for Symington and de Roulet made sums of $38,867 and $25,000 available to the Nixon campaign, figures perhaps more in line with the prestige rankings of the posts in question.

Among the list of ambassadors making campaign donations is one—Ruth Farkas, ambassador to Luxembourg—whose situation provides as good an insight as any into the symbiotic relationship between campaign donations and highly visible foreign appointments.

THE FARKAS AFFAIR

Luxembourg has not been graced by American ambassadors of distinction. Among Mrs. Farkas's predecessors were Perle ("Call Me Madam") Mesta, prominent hostess of the Truman and Eisenhower years. Another American diplomatic representative, Wiley T. Buchanan, Jr., set a record for being the ambassador most absent from his post. Still, among such a sorry set of forerunners, Mrs. Ruth Farkas, the ambassador appointed by Richard Nixon in March of 1973, managed to establish something of a negative record on her own. In July of 1975, the *New York Times* quoted an American businessman living in Luxembourg to the effect that Ambassador Farkas had managed to keep "an invisible profile" in her new job and, the newspaper continued, diplomatic sources in the capital city of the Grand Duchy considered her a "lightweight[40]." How then did Mrs. Farkas ever become ambassador?

Mrs. Farkas's husband, George, founded the "Alexander's" department store chain in New York. He also contributed $300,000 (almost one dollar for every resident of Luxembourg) to Richard Nixon's campaign for the presidency in 1972 and some were unkind enough to suggest that this donation was explicitly given in return for the appointment. The tale is a bit odd.

Dr. Farkas (she holds a Ph.D. in sociology) admits that she and her husband donated the $300,000 to the Nixon reelection campaign, and all but $50,000 of it *after* the election. In fact, the bulk of the donations took place in December of 1972 and January and February of 1973. Mrs. Farkas's nomination was formally announced on February 27, although originally a notification (never made public) had been sent to the Senate Foreign Relations Committee on August 15 indicating the president's intention to nominate her as the next ambassador to Luxembourg. The Farkas money was delivered in $5000 checks to a plethora of Nixon finance committees and the number and size of the contributions, since these took place after the election, did not become known until her Senate confirmation hearings. The senator who presided over the committee sessions at which Mrs. Farkas appeared did refer to her nomination as "a little unusual," but in the best tradition of an independent legislative body her appointment was confirmed[41].

Dr. Farkas defended herself by saying that the pledge to contribute had been made in early 1972 and that she did not learn of the ambassadorial appointment until "August or a little before," and, in fact, she emphatically told the Senate Foreign Relations Committee the contribution "had absolutely nothing to do with whether I was getting an ambassadorship or not[42]." The substantial delay in delivering the funds resulted only from the need to liquidate stocks in an adverse market. Despite the awkwardness in securing the cash, the size of the contribution was in line, she said, with the couple's other donations. Why the Nixon campaign, which accumulated almost a $5 million campaign surplus, needed further funds after the election is unclear.

The denouement to the affair came during the summer of 1975 when it appeared that not everyone close to the story had been totally forthright. According to a "source close to the Farkases," the couple appeared before a Watergate grand jury and told a quite different tale. Allegedly in an effort to save herself from indictment and to put the blame elsewhere, Mrs. Farkas admitted her Senate testimony had not been true. She now charged that former New Hampshire congressman, Louis C. Wyman (then a claimant for the vacant Senate seat eventually to be settled by a new election), "seduced" and "tricked" her husband into the deal.

A few points are clear. Wyman did act as a middleman between the Farkases and Maurice Stans, representing the Nixon Administration. The dates and actual discussions that took place are subject to various interpretations (or memory lapses) by the principals—Stans, the Farkases, and Wyman, but again some points of convergence in the story do emerge. Apparently an ambassadorship was discussed in detail and the arrangement concerning cost made explicit. According to the Farkases' "source," George Farkas met with Wyman in Palm Beach and told him he wanted an ambassadorship for his wife, and in Luxembourg if possible. Wyman said it would cost $300,000 and allegedly Farkas replied "Done[43]!" After the appointment had been cleared through the State Department and with the government of Luxembourg, the Farkases began writing their checks to the various Nixon finance committees.

Wyman denied the story when it appeared and the Farkases had no comment. The former congressman did say, however, that if anything illegal had been done (and the selling of ambassadorships is unlawful) he was not culpable; "It wasn't my ambassadorship to sell, and I never saw any of the money[44]." Wyman added an observation that appears incontestable. Commenting on the relationship between big contributions and the awarding of ambassadorial plums, he commented, "You establish your eligibility" for a diplomatic post through a sizable donation[45]. He went on to make the point that no explicit guarantee of a job existed; the contribution simply put an individual into the running. When Herbert Kalmbach pleaded guilty to various charges related to his contribution to the Watergate scandal, he received an explicit, written statement of immunity from further prosecution relating to "contributions from persons seeking ambassadorial posts[46]." Based presumably on information supplied by Kalmbach, a source close to the investigation described the relationship between the campaign donations and appointments much as Wyman had. "What you were paying for was to have your name in the hopper. People were told they would only get it [the ambassadorial nomination] if they were 'qualified,' but they would only send the name over if he contributed[47]." At a minimum then, money bought the right to consideration. What effect such a primitive exploitation of personal wealth and governmental appointive power had on the quality of the United States representation abroad can only be guessed at but here again the Farkas case may be instructive. No one argued that Dr. Farkas had particularly distinguished herself in her diplomatic post, and the continual accusations and countercharges in the media did little to reinforce the image of a seasoned, highly trained, and career-oriented elite guiding America's foreign relations.

THE HUSTLERS

One aspect of the Nixon fund raising canvass has a particular fascination. Nixon's money hustle fell on the shoulders of two men principally, Herbert Kalmbach, a successful California lawyer and the president's personal legal representative, and Maurice Stans, the former secretary of commerce, who pleaded with the Senate Watergate Committee "to give me back my good name" (and who declared it restored and his integrity vindicated immediately after pleading guilty in a federal court to a series of campaign violations). Kalmbach was treated with a degree of deference by the Ervin Committee and, to his credit, it would have to be added that he (unlike Stans) appeared to cooperate fully with investigators.

Kalmbach began in 1970—under Haldeman's supervision—to canvass wealthy individuals for large campaign contributions. He was also placed in charge of the $1 million Nixon surplus from the 1968 campaign in January of 1969, a fund that included milk industry contributions and one that was used, through Kalmbach, to pay for the surreptitious activities of former New York policeman Anthony Ulascewicz and Donald ("Dirty Tricks") Segretti. This latter job he assumed at Stans's request. Stans took overall command of fund raising in both Nixon presidential campaigns. In addition to these two men, an industry by industry solicitation program was established under the directon of a third individual.

As with all aspects of the campaign, the money raising was handled diligently. Kalmbach toured the country asking industrialists to contribute to the upcoming Nixon campaign in line with standards he set—$25,000 for some, $50,000 for others, and $100,000 for the elite (if donors wanted to be known as "major contributors" they had to give more than the lowly $25,000). Kalmbach assured the potential contributors their gifts would be secret (and, in fact, over 80 percent of the money he raised came in before the April 7 deadline). He officially resigned from the Finance Committee to Re-Elect the President the day the new disclosure law took effect.

Kalmbach's hard-sell, yet sophisticated, approach and his listing of the cost of various "goodies" (implied or explicit) on his shopping list proved enormously successful. He gained pledges of $13.4 million and actually raised $10.6 million, as much of it as possible in hard cash. Kalmbach gained commitments for one-third of the total estimated Nixon campaign budget.

Maurice Stans, of course, was the acknowledged master of this aspect in campaign management. Bernstein and Woodward in their book *All the President's Men* depend on several sources to describe the Stans's appeal. Their sources assured them that Stans set up the whole, elaborate fund-raising operation, including the guarantees of anonymity to givers; the Mexican "laundering" operation in which all contributions in any form were taken to Mexico, deposited in a Mexico City bank by a person with no known ties to the Nixon campaign, converted to cash and returned to the president's campaign officials; and the establishment of a "tithe," a certain figure each individual or corporation should meet. Stans, similar to Kalmbach, did not request corporate funds or illegal contributions. They set limits for what they felt should be given (and these were unusually high) and then worked to sell the target group or individual to meet it. Where the money came from or how it was raised was of no concern.

Stans' technique was described by an impressed onlooker in Texas to the two reporters for the *Washington Post.*

> Maury came through here like a goddam train . . ., he was really ballin' the jack. He'd say to the Democrats, the big money who'd never gone for a Republican before, "You know we got this crazy man Ruckelshaus [at the time, head of the Environmental Protection Agency] back East who'd just as soon close your factory as let the smokestack belch. He's a hard man to control and he's not the only one like that in Washington. People need a place to go, to cut through the red tape when you've got a guy like that on the loose. Now, don't misunderstand me; we're not making any promises, all we can do is make ourselves accessible[48]*

According to the informant, however, the message was clear.

> Maury's a right high-type fellow; he would never actually threaten any of those guys. Then he'd do his Mexican hat dance, tell them there'd be no danger of the Democrats or their company competitors finding out about the contributing, it would all get lost in Mexico. . . . If a guy pleaded broke, Maury would get him to turn over stock in his company or some other stock. He was talking 10 percent, saying it was worth 10 percent of some big businessman's income to keep Richard Nixon in Washington and [to] be able to stay in touch[49].

Such tactics as these turned out to be most productive. Stans, Kalmbach, and the other fund raisers managed to raise the largest campaign kitty in the history of American politics.

CONCLUSION

The money-raising techniques employed by the Nixon lieutenants do not make for uplifting reading. They demonstrate the weakness of totally unregulated cash flows entering campaigns and show how the services and programs of government can be bartered for specified payoffs—if the government officials in authority have the will to do so. Seemingly, the public would be outraged by such a crass manipulation of public agencies and public monies. Any many were. Almost one year after Watergate, two-thirds of those interviewed in a Gallup poll

*Copyright 1974 by Carl Bernstein and Bob Woodward. Reprinted by permission of Simon & Schuster, Inc.

supported the public funding of campaigns, a jump in a few short months of seven percentage points[50]. The change in view took place mostly among Republicans disillusioned with what they had seen.

On a different level, one might reasonably expect those who had made contributions to be offended that their money—intended to help elect a president they believed in—had been put to such bizarre use. In September of 1973, the *Chicago Sun-Times* contacted individuals in the Chicago metropolitan area who had been revealed in recently published reports as secret contributors of large sums to the Nixon campaign[51]. The newspaper simply asked them if they would give again, knowing what they now did, to the Committee to Re-Elect the President. The majority of those contacted emphatically stated that they would repeat their donations: "I would still give it, on the basis that I am a supporter of the Republican Party" (official of a printing firm); "I made my contribution in good faith, and I think it's appropriate that such contributions be made. Would I contribute again? Yes, I would" (former president of the Milwaukee Road Railroad); "I believe I would contribute again. Despite Watergate, he's been a good President. Something went wrong, but I don't think he (Mr. Nixon) was to blame" (president of the Chicago and North Western Railroad); "I would definitely contribute again to Mr. Nixon's campaign if I were asked to do so. Definitely. I'm sorry it (Watergate) happened, but I'm a Republican—a Republican forever" (a philanthropist); "I would certainly do it again. The government has to run somehow, and I don't see how we can have a strong two-party system without voluntary contributions" (officer of an electrical motor company); and so on.

Has Watergate changed matters significantly? Obviously, the new funding laws (discussed in the next chapter) have drastically altered fund-raising procedures. Still, the mentality of the fund raisers and their general techniques may not have changed as much as some would like to believe. As the 1976 presidential campaign began to get underway, contributors (including Democrats) to the Nixon campaign of 1972 received mailgrams from David Packard, a former official in the Nixon Administration and the president of a firm highly successful in securing Defense Department contracts. Packard, newly installed as President Ford's finance chairman, asked the maximum donation possible ($1000) "as your vote of confidence in our President." Simultaneously, Vice-President Rockefeller circulated letters in envelopes marked "The Vice-President" asking for contributions of $25,000 (the maximum application in this case) to the Republican Senatorial Committee. The vice-president wrote: "I have asked the committee to separate answers to this letter from regular mail *so that I may have a complete report of the response to this personal request*[52]." (Italics added.) Why?

However, at least the goals of those who would serve in presidential campaigns may have taken on a new character. Howard Calloway, a conservative southerner and former Defense Department official in the Nixon Administration, told a home-state audience after being appointed as President Ford's 1976 campaign manager: "[While serving as secretary to the Army] I had an ambition not to get tarred by Watergate. In my new job I have another ambition: Not to go to jail[53]."

NOTES

1. The questions and accounts of the episode can be found in James M. Naughton, "Connally Payoff Alleged at Trial," *New York Times,* April 4, 1975, p. 4, "Connally Tape Calls Milk Price Political," *Chicago Daily News,* April 3, 1975, p. 9, Naughton, "U.S. Charges 'Footprints' of Payoff Lead to Connally," *New York Times,* April 3, 1975, p. 1, and John Hervers, "The Milk Case: A Lesson in the Politics of Pressure," *New York Times,* January 13, 1974. sect. 4, p. 1.
2. William A. Dobrovir, Joseph D. Gebhardt, Samuel J. Buffone, and Andra N. Oakes, *The Offenses of Richard M. Nixon: A Guide for the People of the United States of America* (New York: Quadrangle, 1973), p. 70.
3. *The Senate Watergate Report* (New York: Dell, 1974), 2:187. The incidents discussed can be found in the Report of the Senate Watergate Committee (hereafter referred to as *Report*). Both volumes 1 and 2 of the Ervin Committee's Report published by Dell in 1974.
4. *Report,* 2:13.
5. These materials are taken primarily from reports compiled by Congressman Les Aspin (D., Wisc.). See Austin Scott, "Oid Firms' Gifts Bind Nixon: Aspin," and "Defense Firms' Donations to Nixon Told," *Chicago Sun-Times,* December 10, 1973, p. 42, "Sirica Releases 2 Key Watergate Tapes to. . . ." *Chicago Daily News,* December 10, 1973, p. 2, and "Oil and Politics," "Parade Magazine," *Chicago Sun-Times,* February 17, 1974, p. 27. Consult also Congressional Quarterly, *Dollar Politics,* 2 vols. (Washington, D.C.: Congressional Quarterly, 1971, 1974).
6. See Aspin's comments in Scott, "Oil and Politics."
7. *Report,* 2:24–27.
8. Ibid., pp. 25–26.
9. Ibid., p. 22.
10. Ibid., p. 21.
11. "Oil Men Say They Used Subsidies," *New York Times,* November 15, 1973, p. 1.
12. *Report,* 2:23.
13. Eileen Shanahan, "Three More Corporations Tell of Illegal Gifts to Nixon Drive," *New York Times,* November 16, 1973, p. 26.
14. *Report,* 2:9.
15. Ibid., pp. 10–11.
16. For a brief overview, see "Overseas Bribes Make Things Work," *New York Times,* May 11, 1975, p. E-5.
17. "Exxon's Red Gift Called Indirect," *New York Times,* July 15, 1975, p. 43.
18. Eileen Shanahan, "S.E.C. Says Northrop Kept '$30 Million Secret Fund,'" *New York Times,* April 17, 1975, p. 1.
19. Ibid.
20. Shanahan, "Three More Corporations."
21. *Report,* 1:326. These abuses are detailed in the two volumes of the Watergate Committee's *Report* and, from evidence supplied principally by this committee, in the

House Judiciary Committee's impeachment proceedings directed against President Richard M. Nixon. Regarding these proceedings, see *The Impeachment Report* (New York: New American Library, 1974), pp. 155–242.

22. *Report,* 1:390.
23. Ibid., p. 326.
24. Ibid., p. 321.
25. Ibid., p. 323.
26. Ibid., p. 325.
27. Ibid., p. 327.
28. Ibid., p. 328.
29. Ibid., pp. 329–330.
30. Ibid., p. 330.
31. Ibid.
32. Ibid., p. 333.
33. Ibid., p. 343.
34. Ibid., pp. 344–345.
35. Ibid., pp. 376–378.
36. Ibid.
37. Ibid., pp. 377–378.
38. *Report,* 2:66.
39. Ibid., p. 73. The incidents are discussed on pp. 64–78.
40. Paul Kemezis, "Luxembourg Takes Stir Over Ambassador Farkas in Stride," *New York Times,* July 14, 1975, p. 4.
41. *New York Times,* March 14, 1973, p. 20.
42. Christopher Lydon, "Mrs. Farkas Said to Blame Wyman for Deal for Post," *New York Times,* July, 2, 1975, p. 12.
43. Ibid.
44. Ibid. See also Christopher Lydon, "Wyman Disputes Charge of Envoy," *New York Times,* July 3, 1975, p. 17, Lydon, "Mrs. Farkas Gave Most of Gift to Nixon Fund After Election," *New York Times,* March 14, 1973, p. 20, and Lydon, "What Was the Money For?" *New York Times,* March 18, 1973, sect. 4, p. 1.
45. Lydon, "Mrs. Farkas said to Blame Wyman."
46. "White House Refuses to Give Jaworski Data on Contributions by Envoy Choice," *New York Times,* March 17, 1973, p. 1.
47. Ibid.
48. Carl Bernstein and Bob Woodward, *All the President's Men* (New York: Simon and Schuster, 1974), p. 56.
49. Ibid.
50. As reported in George Gallup, "65% Support U.S. Funding of Campaigns," *Chicago Sun-Times,* September 30, 1973, p. 80.
51. Hugh Hough and Paul Malloy, "Would They Give Again to C.R.P.?" *Chicago Sun-Times,* September 30, 1973, p. 3.
52. Christopher Lydon, "Shriver Is Being Rebuffed by Kennedy Hands 'Waiting for Teddy,'" *New York Times,* July 22, 1975, p. 12.
53. *New York Times,* June 25, 1975, p. 66. Calloway later resigned his position while under fire for the alleged improper use of government authority to favor a ski resort in which he had financial interest.

6

Policing
Campaign
Financing

Three years after the Watergate break-in, a most unusual occurrence took place in a District of Columbia courtroom. A man who had pleaded guilty to a crime was sentenced to jail. He received two months in prison and an additional 10 months suspended sentence. The event was unique. The man happened to be a sitting congressman, George Hansen (R.) of Idaho. The crime he pleaded guilty to was not reporting funds (approximately $16,000) used in his primary and general election races as required by law (both charges are misdemeanors). As the judge logically observed in sentencing Hansen, "If the people who make the laws can't obey them, who can be expected to obey them[1]?"

The Capitol was shocked. One week later the congressman was back in the same federal district courtroom to plead for a reconsideration of his sentence. Among other points his lawyers raised in his defense was that other primary candidates could technically be guilty of the same crime (as well as, presumably, many if not most members of the Congress). This line of reasoning apparently had an appeal for the judge. The lawyer further argued that his client was not "evil," just "stupid." The congressman added, "Perhaps I was not careful. I apologize." The judge was moved. "I assumed when I sentenced him to jail he was evil," the judge said. "Now, I am not so sure. Stupid, surely." With that, the judge wrote into sentencing considerations a new set of criteria (besides, of course, breaking the law itself), fined the congressman $2000 and revoked his two-month prison term[2].

The incident nicely illustrates the impact of the campaign disclosure laws. The main effort in regulating campaign finances for almost one hundred years has been put into statutes of this nature. Their weaknesses are many. They are full of loopholes and therefore seldom regulate anything. Beyond this, they are usually ignored by those whom they presume to regulate, and they are not enforced by those charged with this responsibility. The only distinction the Hansen case can claim is that charges were brought[3]; the congressman chose not to contest them and pleaded guilty (apparently expecting an outcome similar to the final resolution); and the case actually went to court.

The history of the regulation of political financing is essentially one of a massive fraud perpetuated on the American public. The federal government as well as all but five of the states for a long period of time have had laws specifying various types of abuses. The laws are easily circumvented and few violators are punished. The laws are also basically negative. Political campaigns cost money and people who give particularly large sums expect something in return for their investment. Recognizing this fact, reformers have attempted normally to restrict (ineffectively as it turns out) the amount of money individuals can give and to outlaw other sources (corporations and labor unions primarily). This approach has an element of unreality to it. Until the 1970s, none of the federal statutes chose to deal with the problem of where alternative contributions to fund campaigns would be found. The pressure was therefore on politicians both to run in increasingly expensive contests and to fund these as best they could without being caught at doing something blatantly illegal. Money, for certain types of campaigns at least, was plentiful. As the practice evolved, a highly politicized Justice Department could be counted on to initiate no prosecutions. Regardless of which party held power, this unspoken agreement represented one of the quid pro quos of national politics. Furthermore, candidates for the U.S. Senate and House reported, in turn, to the secretary of the Senate and the clerk of the House. They could not have chosen more sympathetic overseers. The incumbents of both positions are dependent on the senators and congressmen for their jobs. As the years passed, their approach increasingly became one of protecting the national legislators from any scrutiny of their campaign finances by the media or the public. A vigorous enforcement of their legal responsibilities was inconceivable.

The hypocrisy of the prevailing ethos was illustrated by a minor-party candidate for Congress from Vermont in 1970. He publicly notified the clerk of the House that he would not comply with the law (the Federal Corrupt Practices Act of 1925) by filing a statement on his campaign expenditures and he further informed the Justice Department that he had violated the law. Nothing happened. In fact, the incident barely received any attention whatsoever[4].

THE HISTORY OF
FINANCIAL REGULATION

As with most problems in elective politics, the controversy over campaign funding and the efforts to deal with it effectively are about as old as the democratic experience itself. The first of the federal laws in 1867 was intended to protect government employees from one form of patronage, the kickback of contributions or of a specified percentage of an individual's salary to the party or candidate responsible for filling the position[5]. The assassination of President James Garfield by, as it was described in the press of the day, a disappointed office seeker, led to a push for civil service reform[6]. Combined with unexpectedly aggressive support from Garfield's successor, Chester A. Arthur, a machine product himself, the pressure for change led to the Civil Service Reform Act of 1883. This statute broadened the prohibition on soliciting government workers and expanded it to prevent federal employees from canvassing each other.

Charges of an excessive amount of funds from life insurance companies, banks, utilities, oil, and other corporate enterprises being funneled into the Republican presidential campaigns of William McKinley and Theodore Roosevelt at the turn of the century led Presidents Roosevelt and then Wilson to propose what was to become a staple of the Progressive movement, the federal funding of elections. A more hesitant Congress did prohibit banks and other business corporations in 1907 from making direct contributions to federal candidates. Three years later, Congress enacted the first disclosure law and in 1911 strengthened it and applied its provisions to primaries as well as general elections. The statute also limited the amounts that congressional candidates could spend in elections.

A 1921 Supreme Court decision, *U.S.* v. *Newberry,* limited the law's applicability, removing from federal jurisdiction any control over nominating practices. The case has received far more attention in the struggle for equitable black participation in primaries, especially in southern states, but it also served to defer federally enforced campaign disclosures until the 1970s[7].

The Federal Corrupt Practices Act of 1925 codified relevant statutes and required candidates for the House and Senate to disclose their receipts and expenditures. The law did not apply to presidential contests. Political committees operating in more than one state also came under the act's provisions and spending ceilings for House ($2500 to $5000) and Senate ($10,000 to $25,000) races were established. With slight modifications in 1944, 1947, and 1948, this act remained the basic federal legislation on the matter until the ambitious legislative enactments of the 1970s.

The Hatch Act passed in 1939 (and amended in 1940) placed a limit of $5000 on individual contributions to federal campaigns and a $3 million ceiling on the expenditures of political committees on behalf of federal candidates. The Hatch Act also further restricted federal employees from active political participation in campaigns. Government workers cannot manage political campaigns or engage in such activities as working at the polls or transporting voters on election day. And they cannot promise jobs or contracts to prospective supporters of political candidates. The act included penalties of a fine of $5000 and/or three years imprisonment. A few years later, the Smith-Connally Act of 1944 prohibited direct contributions by labor unions to political campaigns, a ban reiterated in the Taft-Hartley Act of 1947.

These pieces of legislation represented the total federal contribution to regulating political spending. This is not to suggest that a great deal was not written and intermittent attempts at reform did not receive a periodic emphasis. President John Kennedy established a Commission on Campaign Costs in 1961 to study the problem and to recommend solutions. Of more interest, in a bizarre twist of the legislative will, a bill (sponsored by Senator Russell Long of Louisiana and identified with him) to provide for a one dollar tax checkoff (two dollars for married couples) to go to a presidential election fund and to provide direct federal subsidies for these elections was passed by the Congress in 1966. The Long bill did not receive a thorough hearing in the Congress and contained funding provisions which grossly exaggerated the advantages of the two established parties (which in 1968, had the bill been operative, would have received $30 million apiece). A third party would have to receive 5 million votes to qualify for federal support. The subsidies could not exceed a party's expenditures or the amount of checkoff money available. The unexpectedness of the revolutionary new legislation as well as its seemingly discriminatory provisions appeared to shock the nation—or at least its media representatives—and the bill was repealed in May of 1967.

For three-quarters of the twentieth century, then, the Federal Corrupt Practices Act in its various modifications and the Hatch Act provided the nucleus of the federal controls over the funding of federal elections. The operative laws, of course, were ineffective in limiting the cost of elections or the sources and nature of the financial contributions. Despite occasional incidents, a generalized apathy over campaign funding reinforced the status quo. The hypocrisy of the approach and the disinterest of the Congress in improving it can be illustrated by one quaint, but highly publicized, controversy.

In 1956, an angered Senator Francis Case (R.) of South Dakota announced to the Senate that he had been offered a campaign contribution of $2500 by a lobbyist if he would support a specific piece of natural gas legislation. In truth, the Senator had already decided to vote in favor of the bill but when approached with the cash offer decided otherwise. Quite obviously, he was outraged. His Senate colleagues appeared to be equally incensed, and before long three congressional inquiries were underway. The Senate majority leader, Lyndon Johnson, and the minority leader, William Knowland, led 83 senators in cosponsoring a campaign reform act. The proposed legislation never came out of committee. Why? Herbert Alexander reports that the favorite explanation was that "with so many sponsors, the bill would have to be passed if it reached the [Senate] floor[8]." Nothing of consequence resulted from any of the congressional inquiries. The tale of the reported bribe became part of the political folklore and, resurrected periodically, it served over the years to remind observers of the perfidiousness of lobbyists and the basic integrity of the nation's elected representatives. The failure of the Congress to respond to the incident in any meaningful way or to even enforce laws on the books for decades received only passing attention.

THE 1970S AND THE BEGINNINGS
OF FUNDAMENTAL REFORM

The decade of the seventies witnessed a birth of legislation that marked a new departure in approaching the problems implicit in the cost of running for political office. First came the Revenue Act of 1971. The legislation, basically, had nothing to do with campaigns. It was a bill proposed by the Nixon Administration to stimulate the economy through a tax cut. Senate Democrats managed to attach a rider that in its final form accomplished something they had long sought. Individuals who gave to a campaign were allowed a tax credit of up to $25 for a $50 contribution (up to $50 for contributions of $100 on joint returns), a provision long sought by the Democrats whose strength lay with people who usually did not itemize their deductions. The bill also permitted a tax deduction of 50 percent of a political donation of up to $100 ($200 on joint returns), a move Republicans believed would appeal to their supporters.

Secondly, the bill contained a provision for a one dollar checkoff (two dollars on join returns) to be included on the income tax forms. The money would come from the federal taxes paid by the individual (it was not an additional levy) and would be used to subsidize federal elections (if such a subsidy were to be authorized). The Nixon Administration favored neither proposal. It did want the Revenue Act, a piece of priority legislation for the administration, and consequently agreed to the political financing items *if* the tax checkoff was not made operative until 1973, thus not affecting Nixon's last campaign. Even then, the deduction authorization was separated from the conventional IRS 1040 form and sunk within the instruction booklet. It took a threatened congressional inquiry and a court suit to force the administration to comply with the law and place the provision on the standard form. Not unexpectedly, only an estimated 3 to 6 percent of the taxpayers initially authorized money for the election fund. As it became simplified and its purpose better understood, the checkoff idea increased substantially in popularity.

The significance of the 1971 Revenue Act provision rested in the conscious effort to broaden the base of political financing and the initiation of the groundwork for an eventual federal program of election subsidies. The maneuvering that led to the tax credit/deduction and checkoff proposals was overshadowed by the political fencing surrounding a second, and more obvious, attempt to redirect the political financing of campaigns, the Political Broadcast Act of 1970. The bill passed the Congress but was vetoed by President Nixon on the paradoxical grounds (for an administration that used television as a whipping boy) that it discriminated against the broadcast media. "The problem with campaign spending," said President Nixon in his veto message, "is not radio and television; the problem is spending. This bill plugs only one hole in a sieve." In short, the legislation was not inclusive enough, a curious argument for an administration that opposed campaign reform and one destined to backfire on it.

The 1970 legislation would have limited the amount candidates could spend in general elections on radio and television to seven cents per vote cast for the office in the last election or $20,000, whichever was larger. The bill would also have fixed broadcast rates at the lowest unit charge the station offered to preferred commercial customers, that is, their biggest advertisers. The proposed legislation zeroed in effectively on one aspect of the problem. The Nixon message ended: "I am as opposed to big spending in campaigns as I am to big spending in government." The president, in effect, asked for a stronger and more comprehensive bill. Very few (including the administration) thought the Congress capable of moving along these lines. The 1970 Political Broadcast Act represented one of the most adventuresome pieces of legislation it had ever attempted[9].

Yet the Congress met the challenge. It passed (in January of 1972 to go into effect on April 7 of that year) what came to be called the Federal Election Campaign Act of 1971, a most extraordinary piece of legislation. The act abolished the ceiling on all campaign contributions (except for those by a candidate or his family). The immediate family of a contender or the candidate himself could only contribute a limit of $50,000 to a presidential race, $35,000 to a U.S. Senate contest, and $25,000 to a U.S. House campaign. A comprehensive system of disclosure was instituted. No contributions were allowed by one person in the name of another. Any committee that spent (or expected to spend) over $1000 on behalf of a federal candidate had to register with the government. Periodic reports were required (both at selected intervals prior to the election and then after it) of expenditures with full information on all donations received including the names and addresses of contributors and their corporate affiliations. All expenditures over $100 had to be accounted for and a continuing report made on campaign surpluses (if any) or the efforts to retire campaign debts. These requirements were the most stringent by far to be written into law and led to a fierce effort by the Nixon Administration, forced into signing it by political circumstances they helped create, to circumvent the provisions. In particular, the Nixon campaign team attempted to collect as many "anonymous" contributions as possible prior to the April 7 date on which the law formally went into effect.

A second part of the legislation took as its point of departure the vetoed 1970 Act. One of the Nixon Administration's arguments against the earlier bill had been that it did not include provisions regulating expenditures on such items as newspapers, magazines, billboards, and the like. This time the Congress stipulated a spending limit of 10¢ per voting age person in a jurisdiction for *all* campaign advertising (radio, television, newspapers, billboards, magazines, automated telephone systems, etc.). Further, no more than 60 percent of the total could be expended on radio and television. And broadcasters again were required to provide candidates with the lowest unit rate allowed favored advertisers.

Since it is difficult to disguise broadcast expenditures—these were already reported to the Federal Communications Commission by stations—the law had a fair chance of succeeding in one area of its principal concern. The disclosure provisions galvanized citizen groups and the media and provided the basis for the criminal convictions of a number of corporations and individuals who chose to ignore its restrictions.

It should be noted, however, that the law was not universally popular. Candidates in both parties were irked by its stringent disclosure regulations and almost simultaneously with its passage attempted to soften these. In particular, the number of reports, the detail required, and, most significantly, the corporate and professional affiliations of the givers came under attack. From 1972 through late 1974, coterminous with the worst of the Watergate revelations, congressional committees were meeting quietly in efforts to abort the new measures[10].

The reports filed by House and Senate candidates concerning expenditures are required by law to be made available to the public and the media upon demand. The respective House and Senate officials charged with executing this responsibility proved reluctant, as they had been traditionally, to make such information readily available. In fact, they actively obstructed the gathering of such information. Records can be duplicated at cost (an estimated 10¢ per page). An enraged congressman, Wayne Hays (D., Ohio), a foe of all such legislation and in effective control of the House clerk's office, upped the duplication cost from 10¢ to one dollar per page. With an estimated 1 million pages of forms to be filed by the various candidates, the cost quickly became excessive. Hays was unimpressed. "No one is interested in the reports, anyway, except the *New York Times,* the *Washington Post* and Common Cause—and they can afford to pay." The congressman did offer an alternative. "If they don't want to pay, let them write [the copies] out in longhand[11]." It took the threat of a court suit to demonstrate the seriousness of the media and public interest group lobbies in enforcing the law to bring the duplication costs back within the range of those intended.

Despite dilatory tactics and repeated efforts to weaken the 1971 disclosure law, the Congress took a historic step in the changeover from the chaotically-funded, free-spending election approach of the past to a programmed, more tightly controlled, and publicly subsidized *presidential* election system with the passage of the Federal Election Campaign Act (Amendments) of 1974 (effective January 1, 1975). For the first time in its history, and under immense pressure from the public, a more combative and self-assured press, and citizens' interest groups, the Congress agreed to pay the burden of the costs for the primary and general election of the nation's chief elective office. Significantly, the Congress did *not* include House and Senate campaigns within the bill's provisions. These offices, in effect, are still for sale and, as shown, incumbents have no funding problems. State executive and legislative races also remain open to gross financial manipulation, although there has been movement toward stricter disclosure provisions along the lines of the federal program in some states and, of greater significance, an enforcement of the relevant statutes[12].

The struggle for the presidential funding bill took two years of nip-and-tuck battling. Several times the Senate passed campaign funding measures only to have them die in Chairman Wayne Hays's House Administration Committee. More in line with the apparently dominant congressional thinking were the efforts to employ the presidential financing bill as a vehicle to render the earlier disclosure law impotent. Legislation was introduced to void the 1971 statute. Other 1972 modifications were considered by the relevant congressional committees that would have limited the reports to one 10 days prior to the election and one 30 days following it, obscure technical revisions but ones that Common Cause argued "would mean that from June 30 through the election for all practical purposes, it would be impossible to get that information, analyze it and get it out to the public before the election[13]."

The Senate Rules Committee actually reported to the floor a year after the Watergate break-in a measure that would require only a donor's name (no address or occupational listing) and would repeal, incredible as it may seem, the ban on direct contributions by business corporations (or labor unions) that held government contracts. And the Congress did manage, in an unpublicized move, to *reduce* the statute of limitations for illegal campaign acts from five to three years, an unhealthy sign that insures that a number of the funding offenses related to the 1972 election will not only never be prosecuted but more than likely will never be known.

It is important to remember—for those inclined to believe legislators work toward enlightened ends without public prodding—exactly when these actions took place. The Senate committee report, emasculating the disclosure law *because it had proven effective,* occurred at the height of the highly publicized Ervin Committee hearings; during a tumultuous series of White House firings, corrections, and redefinitions of events; and immediately after American Airlines' voluntary admission that it had illegally donated $55,000 of corporate funds to the Nixon campaign after being solicted by President Nixon's personal lawyer, Herbert W. Kalmbach. The American Airlines revelation was but the first of many concerning funding abuses by giant corporations[14].

In the end, the forces generated by Watergate and rekindled by the actions of the House Judiciary Committee and the Nixon resignation led Congress, which faced the prospect of an angry electorate in the 1974 midterm elections, to pass the historic legislation. Many problems remain, however. Should public concern lessen, the applicable statutes on funding undoubtedly will be weakened. The present laws contain many ambiguities concerning the types of events to be financed and controlled and the discretionary interpretation of various provisions could render some of these virtually inoperable. The Office of Federal Elections, established by the 1971 disclosure law in the General Accounting Office (GAO) to monitor presidential expenditures and commissioned to research election procedures with an eye toward improving them, was extremely cautious and uncertain in executing its new responsibilities. The 1974 funding act created a new election commission to assume these and other activities, much to the relief of the GAO, but the commission proved inordinately slow in hiring a staff, and both the White House and congressional leaders appeared reluctant to nominate their prospective appointees. It would appear that politicians at the nation's highest levels are responding hesitantly to public expectations of a new morality in campaign funding. The funding laws, even if successfully executed, apply only to presidential elections. They are but a first step in what promises to be a long road toward the reassertion of the voter's control over candidate selection processes.

Finally, an admittedly "odd coalition" of former senator and 1968 Democratic presidential contender Eugene McCarthy, Senator James L. Buckley of New York (Cons.-R.), and the New York Civil Liberties Union served notice of their intention to file suit in 1975 against the new campaign act. The group claimed that the law invidiously discriminates against third parties ("It is the same," said McCarthy, "as saying the country is going to have two established religions"[15]); that it violates constitutional guarantees of free expression by limiting arbitrarily the amounts of money individuals can contribute or candidates spend in their campaigns; and that it asserts a government presence in elections that could have unfortunate consequences. The principal grounds of the challenge are that the campaign law violates First Amendment guarantees of freedom of expression by "limiting political activities, circumscribing speech, institutionalizing advantages for incumbents, authorizing unprecedented Government surveillance over political association and establishing broad investigative powers of doubtful constitutionality[16]."

The issues joined are significant ones. The record of the Congress has not been an admirable one in equalizing the campaign opportunities essential to an adequate democratic performance. The pervasiveness of White House corruption of election practices in 1972 indicates that many of the fears voiced by McCarthy, Buckley, and the civil liberties association are grounded in reality. Nonetheless, the abuses engendered by uncontrolled money in politics suggest that governmentally funded elections and strictly enforced disclosure provisions are a necessity. Since it is reasonable to assume that the federal courts will consistently resist any fundamental challenges to the constitutionality of the funding laws, it will be up to the public, the media, and the small number of citizens' groups that are involved in such matters to insure that the statutes are impartially and effectively administered and that progressively more inclusive legislation is enacted on both the federal and state levels. The experience with these laws—including enforceable disclosure statutes—will be a virgin one for this nation. It is conceivable, however, that another well-intentioned reform could be perverted, making an already bad situation that much worse. And the next time systematic election atrocities occur, the nation may not be so fortunate.

As a concluding note of caution, it may be advisable to recall Jeb Magruder's remarks. Magruder, of course, as second in command of the Committee to Re-Elect the President, was one of the handful of top-level strategists in the Watergate mess. According to Magruder, had it not been for the Watergate embarrassments, the Nixon Administration would have become a "perpetual Presidency" by 1976. "We would have been in a position to elect whomever we wanted to elect. Once you learn to use the levers of power it becomes easy[17]."

It all sounds farfetched. But a rereading of the newspaper headlines for the relevant years of the Watergate era, the Ervin Committee hearings and reports, and the House Judiciary Committee's "Books of Evidence" indicate that no type of campaign excess is quite so unthinkable now as it once was.

CONTEMPORARY REGULATIONS OF POLITICAL FUNDING

The regulatory and presidential subsidy legislation enacted since 1970 has moved the traditional debate over policing expenditures in campaigns onto welcome new grounds. The questions no longer center on can it or should it be done but on how effective will enforcement be and to what extent should the present laws be broadened to include even more electoral contests. The more recent laws have also codified previous restrictions and they are complex. These statutes, which represent the *basis* for future developments, are presented in the following pages[18].

POLITICAL CONTRIBUTIONS FOR FEDERAL (PRESIDENT AND VICE-PRESIDENT, U.S. SENATE, AND HOUSE) CAMPAIGNS

Every candidate is required to have *one* official campaign committee (any unofficial committees working on his behalf have to identify themselves as such). The committee must have a treasurer who is directly responsible for all its financial transactions. He is required to maintain, for indefinite periods of time, records that include the name, date, and identification of every person making a contribution of $10 or more. For each individual who contributes $100 or more, the law requires a notation of their occupation and principal place of business. Receipts must be kept of all business transactions, and the particulars for every payment of $100 or over must be logged. The candidate's principal campaign committee must retain, in short, a complete record of all donations and expenditures during the campaign.

Every political committee that receives or expends (or expects to do so) money in excess of $1000 must register with the newly created Federal Election Commission. The registration protocol is extensive. The political committee must report the names and addresses of all its members, its areas of jurisdiction, its relationship (if any) to other organizations, the location of its accounts, the candidates it supports, the manner in which residual funds left over from a campaign will be handled, and, of course, its financing. When it disbands, it must also notify the Election Commission.

All political committees, including a candidate's, must report quarterly. They must also file a report 10 days prior to any election (complete as of the 15th day before the election) and 30 days after it. Any contribution of $1000 or more received after the 15th day and more than two days before the election must be reported within 48 hours. Political committees can, should the Federal Election Commission so desire, be forced to file statements on a monthly or even more frequent basis. The reports must contain *all* financial dealings of the committee or (as in the case of several committees) all made on behalf of a candidate. They would cover not only contributions and expenditures but cash on hand, money raised from dinners, rallies, the sale of items, and the like, all loans, and all other debts and obligations entered into by the committee. Any individual who makes political contributions or expenditures in excess of $100 or who distributes in any form material advocating the election or defeat of a candidate (excluding media representatives) is to be treated as a political committee and must also file the necessary statements.

The Congress, of course, provided some leeway in the matter for themselves. Any campaign services provided the members of Congress by their congressional campaign committees, the clerk of the House, the secretary of the Senate, the national committees of the two parties, or any, for example, photographic, radio, television, telephone, or, presumably, secretarial gratuities made available to them by virtue of their office for campaigns do not have to be reported. These are obviously the perquisites of the incumbents. They, of course, are not available (with the possible exception of national committee assistance) to challengers.

The Election Commission can waive the above requirements and, at its discretion, may not apply them to political committees that support state or local candidacies "primarily" or that do not operate in more than one state. The potential for a discretionary application of the laws and, hence, an abuse of their provisions may be implicit in this grant of power.

National and state parties that hold conventions to nominate presidential candidates (or, in the case of the state parties, to select delegates to the national convention) must file a complete financial statement within 60 days of the convention. If this provision is observed and if the Federal Election Commission specifies inclusive reports, this aspect of American politics will be open to public scrutiny for the first time. At present, these arrangements are secretive.

Candidates must designate one or more federal or state banks as the primary accounts and the depositories for all of their funds. Their political committees must pay all expenditures (excluding specified petty cash disbursements) by check. Expenditures of less than $100 need not be made by check, but a detailed record of these also must be kept. These aspects of the bill quite clearly are intended to avoid the monetary irregularities so prevalent in the Nixon campaign.

THE FEDERAL ELECTION COMMISSION

The committee established by the act to oversee its execution potentially can play a major role in controlling the funding activities of candidates and in leading the way over time to a more equitable deployment of campaign resources. Whether it actually will is in some doubt at present. The commission is composed of two members from each chamber of the Congress, one each selected by the majority and minority leader, and two chosen by the president. All are subject to confirmation by a majority vote of the House and Senate, an unlikely stumbling block regardless of the nature of the nominees. The party of the president (in toto four appointments) should control the balance of the commission. The clerk of the House and the secretary of the Senate are ex-officio members (without a vote). The members would serve six-year terms, although the tenure of the initial commissioners is staggered. Nothing, however, would bar their reappointment. The nominees would be paid in line with federal standards. The committee would meet monthly and provision has been made for staff assistance.

The powers of the Federal Election Commission are impressive. It has full authority to insure that the provisions of all of the laws regulating campaign practices are enforced. It is enjoined to investigate apparent violations "expeditiously" and, although it (quite correctly) can not punish transgressors (it reports these to the appropriate authorities), it does have subpoena power to force testimony from reluctant witnesses or demand the production of documents. The commission also is directed to initiate (if needed) civil actions and to seek injunctive relief in the local federal district court if it finds apparent violations of the law. Such cases take precedence over any others on the court docket. The committee is encouraged to provide broad policy leadership in the area of campaign financial regulation through the issuance of advisory opinions on the applicability of various campaign actions and through recommendations to the Congress for new legislation.

Special reports to encourage a broad appreciation of the process can be published on occasion, and the commission must make all records filed with it available to the public for review or duplication on request. It must maintain its file of the campaign records deposited with it for at least 10 years, *except* for House members where the period is reduced to five years (for no apparent reason). The commission then is a national clearinghouse for all manner of information on elections as well as, theoretically, a type of ombudsman acting in the public's interest. The commission also is charged with reporting to the president and the Congress by March 31 of each year.

Violations of the campaign law are subject to a $1000 penalty or one year imprisonment or both. Such a deterrent is not impressive, another weakness in the law. The fine is minimal and prison sentences, despite Congressman Hansen's close call, have been virtually unthinkable.

Finally, in the some-are-more-equal-than-others vein, all regulations apply to presidential candidates. Senate and House candidates, in an obvious move to allow themselves a degree of flexibility, would continue to report to the secretary and the clerk of their respective bodies, *not* the commission. These gentlemen would act as custodians of the required material, a job they have fulfilled with little distinction in the past. Things may not have changed as much as one would like to think.

A gratuitous addition, similar to those that creep into all laws, prohibits any funds from the 1964 Economic Opportunity Act or any employee of the Office of Economic Opportunity from engaging in any activity that affects election outcomes, such as the encouragement of voter registration. Overall, though, the commission is a major step forward. A conscientious approach to their duties by commission members could advance the understanding (as well as the regulation) of the role of money in elections significantly. The tools and the leadership vehicle for developing a rational approach to the problems in this particular area are now available.

SOLICITATION AND INTIMIDATION BY GOVERNMENT EMPLOYEES

The restrictions on government workers concerning solicitation and intimidation have direct relevance to the Watergate misuse of federal authority. Attempts to intimidate voters, of course, are prohibited. Also banned is the use of elective or administrative positions in the federal, state, or local government structures or in any departments or programs connected with these "for the purpose of interfering with, *or affecting,* the nomination or the election for any candidate" for federal office. (Italics added.) The questionable actions of many in the White House in 1971 and 1972 as well as those in the Justice Department, the FBI, the IRS, the CIA, the Department of Defense, HEW, and so on would appear to be a direct contradiction of this provision. Obviously, it is not taken seriously or enforced. Equally apparent, the penalties—$1000 or imprisonment for one year or both—are weak and by themselves unlikely to deter anyone.

A number of other provisions—and these have been part of the U.S. Code since at least 1940 and some date back to the turn of the century—relate to the exploitation of positions of authority evident in a number of the Watergate episodes (Chapters 4 and 5). In terms of criminal prosecutions, very little has been done. Nonetheless, the federal statutes on campaigning render liable to prosecution:

> 1. a candidate, [who] directly or indirectly promises or pledges the appointment, or the use of his influence or support for the appointment of any person to any public or private position or employment, for the purpose of securing support in his candidacy . . . ; and
> 2. [Anyone,] directly or indirectly, [who] promises any employment, position, compensation, contract, appointment, or other benefit, provided for or made

possible in whole or in part by any Act of Congress, or any special consideration in obtaining any such benefit, to any person as consideration, favor, or reward for any political activity or for the support of or opposition to any candidate or any political party in connection with any . . . election to political office.

There is more along these lines. These laws, as indicated, are not new. And they are explicit. Yet either they are unenforceable (the crimes alluded to cannot be proven in a courtroom) or a highly politicized Justice Department (a condition of national law enforcement not confined to the Nixon Administration) simply refuses to make the effort. Certainly, the penalties once again are minimal ($1000 maximum fine and/or one year imprisonment). Whatever the reasons these laws have fallen into disuse, they must be made enforceable, for they cover the very abuses that were central to the Watergate crisis. The official misconduct of the various governmental agencies, the milk fund controversy, ITT, the sale of ambassadorships, the discretionary appointment of political contributors to high-ranking Nixon Administration positions, the awarding of lucrative government defense and other contracts, the failure to prosecute antitrust cases and allegations of criminal misconduct by corporations, and the dismissal or sidetracking of punitive actions by regulatory agencies, all of these demand rethinking. The meager number of prosecutions to result from the prima facie evidence available concerning apparent official misconduct leads one to question the source of the difficulty. If the law is at fault, it can be improved. Of the very few prosecutions initiated, John Connally, former secretary of the Treasury in the Nixon Administration, was acquitted in a District of Columbia court of allegedly taking a bribe to influence support for the milk price increase and former Nixon Cabinet members John Mitchell and Maurice Stans were acquitted in a New York case of allegedly interfering in a regulatory agency disciplinary move against a heavy contributor to the Nixon campaign, fugitive financier Robert Vesco.

LIMITATIONS ON CAMPAIGN CONTRIBUTIONS AND EXPENDITURES

The restrictions placed on campaign contributions and expenditures relate directly to problems raised in Chapter 4. Candidates or candidates' immediate families (siblings, children, spouse, parents, and grandparents) may not contribute (or loan) in one year more than a total of $50,000 to their campaigns for president, $35,000 to their races for the U.S. Senate, or $25,000 to their contests for the U.S. House. No political committee, such as an interest group (excluding the candidate's main campaign committee), can donate more than $5000 in any one year to any contender for federal office. No individual can make political contributions in any one year in excess of $25,000 (the total for all donations regardless of the number of candidates or committees favored). Further, any money given through an intermediary or other conduit, a form of "laundering," is included in the sum, and the middleman must report the *original* source and the intended recipient of the funds. These additional provisions are a major improvement over previous requirements.

The limitations placed on campaign expenditures are also new and, with government funding of presidential contests and the independently strict disclosure laws, offer a realistic hope of enforcement.

Candidates are prohibited from spending in excess of:

a total $10 million in seeking the presidential nomination of their party and in any one state no more than twice the limit on contenders for the U.S. Senate nomination;

no more than $20 million in presidential elections (a drastic reduction in comparison with the Nixon expenditures and even less than McGovern spent in 1972);

8¢ times the voting age population or $100,000 in contending within a state for their party's U.S. Senate nomination;

12¢ multiplied by the voting age population or $150,000 in a U.S. Senate general election;

$70,000 by a candidate for nomination, or for election, to the U.S. House.

These figures are not only markedly different from earlier ones, they appear realistic. They also offer promise of providing a permanent base for future calculations. For example, the voting age population undoubtedly will continue to expand. The estimates of population growth for each state and congressional district are to be inserted at the relevant time by the secretary of commerce in the Federal Register, thus increasing the total sum of money that can be spent. Secondly, and in an innovative move, the total expenditures are tied to the Consumer Price Index. Beginning with the base year of 1976, the Bureau of Labor Statistics is directed to enter in the Federal Register the percentage difference between the price index for a 12-month period and that for the original year. Each of the limitations is then to be adjusted upward (or downward) by the percentage indicated.

The possible fine for violating these restrictions is higher ($25,000 and/or one year imprisonment), but still light given the enormous wealth of the organizations, political committees, and individuals the law intends to regulate.

National banks, business corporations, and labor unions are still prohibited from making any direct financial contributions to federal campaigns. The primary change in these provisions is the penalty clause. A corporation or union can be fined up to $25,000, not a serious deterrent. The Congress, however, did attempt to fix individual responsibility. Any corporation or labor official who consents to such an illegal contribution and anyone who accepts it can be fined the standard $1000 and/or one year in prison. Should the violation be willful (presumably a candidate or middleman might not realize the source of the funds, although under the disclosure laws this should not happen), the fine may go as high as $50,000 and the prison term can be as long as two years. These features of the law begin to fix the blame and make the consequences for the individual worthy of some thought.

Any contractor doing business with the government who "directly or indirectly makes any contribution of money or other things of value, or promises expressly or impliedly to make any such contribution, to any political party, committee, or candidate for public office or to any person for any political purpose or use" or who "knowingly solicits any such contribution from any such person for any such purpose" (presumably any future Kalmbachs) is liable to a fine of $25,000 and/or imprisonment for five years. It is still possible (as it always has been) in these particular cases, of course, for any segregated political fund to which people willingly contribute to be used for campaign contributions.

Foreign nationals, another, although quite limited, source of Nixon funds in 1972, can not contribute to political campaigns (the continuation of a ban long in effect). Any foreign national who does contribute or anyone who solicits or accepts such a donation could receive five years in jail and/or a fine of $25,000.

The Congress also moved to place a limit on other forms of financial abuse. No individual can contribute funds in the name of another or accept such contributions. Any elected official or administrative officer of the federal government who accepts honorariums in excess of $1000 (excluding travel and subsistence costs) or who earns more than $15,000 in such fees, a lesser known form of corporate and interest group supplementation of government salaries, can be fined between $1000 and $5000. In this respect, the Congress is making an effort to police itself (as well as, of course, executive branch officials involved in procurement or industry regulation).

Any person who makes a contribution in excess of $100 *in cash* is subject to a fine of $25,000 and/or one year in jail. And should candidates for federal office or their employees or agents fraudulently misrepresent themselves as speaking, writing, or acting for another candidate or political party on a mission intended to damage the other candidate or whoever participates or conspires to become involved in such a scheme is subject to a fine of $25,000 and/or one year in jail. Both provisions are direct outgrowths of Watergate. The limit on cash contributions, had it been observed, would have helped cripple the illegal aspects of the Nixon funding plans. Additionally, disbursements by check would have provided documentary evidence both for following the paths taken by the various contributions, never satisfactorily explained, and for making additional prosecutions. The second ban would have applied to the Segretti, Chapin, Colson, et al. "dirty tricks" operations intended to disrupt the various Democratic campaigns. The famed Muskie "Canuck letter" in New Hampshire and the vile personal accusations circulated by Segretti and his recruits in the Florida Democratic primary concerning Senators Hubert Humphrey and Henry Jackson would have fallen under this restriction. Moreover, anyone in the White House or the Committee to Re-Elect the President who had served as a party to the conspiracy would have been equally culpable.

TAX WRITE-OFFS

A tax credit of $25 ($50 for joint returns) or a tax deduction of $100 ($200 on joint returns) is allowed on income taxes for political contributions. Of greater interest, and less publicized, are the stricter rules pertaining to deductions for certain types of contributions made to political parties, bills left unpaid by the parties, or loans on which the party does not make good. It has been a common practice for airlines, telephone and and electric companies, automobile rental agencies, real estate agents, and the like to allow a candidate, a political party, or a campaign to run up a debt during a campaign period. After the election, the committee goes out of business or it or the party are too broke to pay its bills. The creditor then writes off the debt or settles for a fraction of its worth (as low as 10¢ on the dollar) and then tries, in many cases, to write the loss off on taxes as a standard business deduction. Such practices are now unlawful. Deductions are prohibited also for such things as advertising in a convention program (a lucrative source of income for the parties), dinners or programs that directly or indirectly benefit a party or a candidate, or such events as the costs involved in attending inaugural balls. In addition, in a shadowy area of tax obligations, a political organization (including a party, political committee, or funding group) is subject to taxes on the same basis as if it were a corporation, with the exception that contributions, membership dues, or proceeds from fund raising and entertainment events or campaign items sold to finance an election are exempt from consideration. Normal business (or profit-making) activities cannot be hidden under the tax-free veil of political fund raising. Finally, taxpayers can designate one dollar (two dollars on joint returns) of their taxes for the "Presidential Election Campaign Fund" by checking the appropriate box "either on the first page of the return or on the page bearing the taxpayer's signature."

THE PRESIDENTIAL
GENERAL ELECTION FUND

The Presidential General Election Fund is, of course, the most noteworthy departure from previous practice. To qualify for funding in the general election, a presidential candidate must be the nominee of a major party or must be the representative of a party with duly authorized presidential electors in 10 states. The candidate must register one principal campaign committee with the Federal Election Commission. Funds are to be paid through this committee for all duly authorized and reported expenses intended to further the election of the presidential candidate. Receipted information, of course, on all expenditures must be kept which is open to audit and examination by the commission. The payments are for the period from the candidate's nomination or from September 1 until 30 days after the date of the presidential election. Minor parties (controversially defined as those whose candidates received more than 5 percent but less than 25 percent of the votes cast "in the *preceding* presidential election") that qualify are funded for the same period as the major party with "the shortest expenditure report period" for the election.

Major party presidential nominees are automatically entitled in equal amounts to no more than the total sum specified in the campaign limits ($20 million). This is one provision McCarthy et al. believe helps to institutionalize the two-party system regardless of its relevancy. The candidates of minor parties that qualify may receive "an amount which bears the same ratio to the amount allowed ... for a major party as the number of popular votes received by the candidate for President of the minor party, as such candidate, in the preceding presidential election bears to the average number of popular votes received by the candidates for President of the major parties in the preceding election." In short, the vote/-cost ratio of the major parties is multiplied by the votes received by the minor party in the preceding presidential outcome. A "new" minor party, one that moves beyond the 5 percent standard for the first time in a presidential election, receives a financial subsidy in relation to its proportionate share of the vote in the election in question (and again calculated on the ratio of cost to votes cast for the major parties). Two things stand out in this formula. Both major party nominees receive their $20 million regardless of whether the previous election was competitive (for example, 1968, 1960) or a landslide (for example, 1972, 1964) and regardless of their percentage of the total vote. A minor party is confined to a payment based on its past performance (should it have received more than 5 percent of the votes cast) despite any improvement it might show in attracting new votes in the campaign being contested. A new minor party has an even more serious problem. It receives *no* funds from the federal treasury until *after* the election. Given the recent restrictions on the magnitude of contributions, it can expect an extremely difficult fund-raising problem and its efforts, in order to qualify eventually for a subsidy, must be geographically dispersed. These are the types of inequities that opponents fear and they offer the most fertile objective for court and legislative modification.

The Federal Election Commission must first certify the eligibility of the parties for federal money. The parties, in turn, must agree not to exceed in expenditures the legal totals found in the federal statutes. Further, the government will supply only the funds needed to replenish those expended (there is no automatic grant of $20 million; this represents only the highest possible amount that could be awarded). The sums provided, in addition, are expenses *less* contributions received. Should the tax checkoff system not provide the total amount of funds needed, the money available will be prorated among the eligible candidates.

The act further specifies that the federal treasury will pay the costs of national nominating conventions. The major parties would receive $2 million each for this event. The minor parties, under the same restrictions in the general election funding formula, would be permitted a figure considerably below that for the established parties. The parties that qualify can begin receiving payment as early as July of the year preceding the convention, actually a necessity given the preplanning and early commitments that have to be made to organize such a complex event.

The discretionary powers lodged with the Federal Election Commission in these matters can be enormous and could be subject to abuse. The Congress foresaw such a possibility and stipulated that any act, decision, or qualifying procedure entered into by the commission is subject to review by the U.S. Court of Appeals for the District of Columbia if any interested person petitions for such a hearing. In the application of other aspects of the legislation, the federal district court in the area in which the problem arises is given jurisdiction. The procedure appears to be a fair one.

Candidates cannot accept contributions that would force them over the campaign spending limits. Fraudulent records, of course, are prohibited and a failure to provide the commission with relevant documents as requested can lead to criminal prosecutions. The penalties for violating various sections of the funding statutes range from fines of $5000 to $10,000 (still not steep enough to deter abuses) and/or imprisonment for five years. And lastly, any kickbacks to or illegal contributions accepted by the national parties or presidential candidates or their political committees are not only subject to a $10,000 find and/or a five-year jail term, but the offending individual or group must repay the federal treasury an amount equal to 125 percent of the illegal kickback or payment. This type of punitive scale, employed in antitrust legislation, is promising. The penalty is tied to the unlawful sum in question. The more flagrant the violation, the more the offender risks and, if the disclosure aspects of the law are strictly monitored, the more he eventually will have to pay.

FUNDING OF PRESIDENTIAL NOMINATING RACES

Almost as noteworthy as the adoption of the government funding idea itself was the decision of the Congress to extend federal subsidies to presidential primaries (which, as defined in the statute, include nominating conventions and caucuses). The basic choice among a truly large range of policy advocates takes place in the primary. Some contend that this step is the single most important stage in the entire sequence of elective processes. In the general election, the choice is narrowed, for all practical purposes, to the two major contenders. In the primary, the range of choices—from liberal to centrist to conservative—can be staggering. Many also argue that unequal financial resources are much more effective in determining primary results than they are in effecting general election outcomes. The Congress, to their credit, accepted the view that the primary was a critical point in the elective process and consequently entitled to governmental underwriting.

The federal treasury will pay to qualified candidates seeking their party's presidential nominations an amount equal to the contributions received by the individuals beginning with the first day of the presidential election year. The matching funds will be only for all contributions of $250 or less (although contenders are not prohibited from seeking larger donations, these can not be included in the sum the government will equal). To be eligible for matching payments, a potential nominee must be seeking the nomination of a political party (major or minor), can not spend in excess of the limits stipulated (see the earlier discussion of restrictions on presidential nominating campaigns), and must raise contributions in excess of $5000 in *each of 20 states* (an effort to confine subsidies to only the more serious of the contenders). Only contributions of $250 or less will be counted towards the total needed ($5000) in each of the twenty states (the intention being to show the prospective nominee has wide support among a diverse number of party supporters).

The same types of judicial safeguards, criminal penalties (although the fines are a little stiffer, in the $5000 to $25,000 range, but still not heavy for campaign budgets of millions of dollars), reporting notices, auditing provisions, and the like relevant to the general election contests also apply to the presidential prenomination races.

These laws, despite some obvious deficiencies and several provisions that will be contested for years to come, represent signal improvements over the impotent, negative statutes that they replaced. The immediate problem, and it is a pressing one, is to insure that the new rules are enforced openly, impartially, and in the public's interest. The focus then has to be on their operation. If, for example, the tightened disclosure provisions are not severely enforced or should the Federal Election Commission display a cronyism and an inertia in operation, as past regulating agencies have in this area, and should it shrink from aggressively using the strong weapons placed at its disposal, not much progress will have been made. Even worse, and hopefully less likely, should the commission take to promoting the interests of one party to the detriment of another or should it favor major parties (a more likely occurrence) to the exclusion of minor parties, the whole experiment might well be doomed.

THE FUTURE

The recent innovations are an experiment, long overdue undoubtedly, but still only in the testing stage. To begin to equalize campaign opportunities and return effective control over elections to the general public, they have to succeed. This has to be the first item on any agenda.

Beyond this, the types of reforms needed are fairly obvious.

Government funding should be extended to all general elections and prenomination campaign activities (employing the federal policies as a guideline); the first step would be to extend these same provisions to U.S. House and Senate contests.

All funding records should be centralized in the Federal Election Commission, including those on congressional and senate races.

Abundant, *free* television and radio time for all levels of contest should be made available to candidates; it is often forgotten that the airwaves belong to the public[19].

Free photographic, radio, and television production services should be made available to *all candidates* for federal office (not just House and Senate incumbents as at present).

The Hatch Act provisions against "buying" contracts, official positions, and diplomatic posts should be enforced. A politically compliant Civil Service Commission and the abuse of governing agencies on a grand scale (and well beyond the scope of this report) make a mockery of the present laws[20].

The Freedom of Information Acts should be strengthened and used by the public and its representatives to acquire the information to insure that officials are living up to the spirit and letter of the law concerning government abstinence from political involvement.

The penalties for violating campaign legislation need to be strengthened. The maximum fines, in particular, should be increased and the idea of basing the penalty on the magnitude of the funding abuse (3 to 10 times the amount of the illegal contribution) represents a viable approach.

Offenses should be pursuable in civil rather than criminal proceedings, a type of judgment which is easier to acquire.

Political donations of any kind by any government contractors, corporations, trade groups, or labor unions should be prohibited (that is, the "segregated" political fund concept should be abolished).

Government contractors convicted of subsidizing a campaign or a candidate illegally should automatically forfeit all of their corporation's government orders.

Failure to comply with the disclosure law, the funding requirements, the limitations placed on contributions, and the "dirty tricks" prohibitions, as well as the other aspects of the campaign laws, should be made felonies (rather than the present misdemeanors) on the valid assumption that there is nothing more serious than the perversion of the elective process in a democratic system.

A special prosecutor's office should be permanently established, independent of the executive branch and the Congress, to oversee the fraud-free operations of the national government, to act as an ombudsman for the American people, and to insure that the campaign regulations are faithfully executed.

These proposals are not radical. Most are familiar. In fact, the Congress and the states (the latter have an even longer way to go in this regard) have begun to implement a number of the recommendations. The legislative development and the public awareness engendered during recent years are encouraging. They stand in dramatic contrast to the gross laxity evident on such issues for generations. If the country is serious about cleaning up the financial aspects of campaigns, the job could be done with dispatch. The basic problem is, as it has always been and as the incident that opened the chapter helps to illustrate, one of motivation.

NOTES

1. "Idaho's Rep. Hansen Ordered to Prison," *New York Times,* April 19, 1975, p. 14.

2. "Rep. Hansen's Prison Term Set Aside," *New York Times,* April 26, 1975, p. 42.

3. The point was made in the second court hearing that one of Hansen's opponents in the Republican primary (an incumbent also named Hansen) sat on the House committee that recommended to the Justice Department that it prosecute in the case. Ibid.

4. Congressional Quarterly, *Dollar Politics* (Washington, D.C.: Congressional Quarterly, 1971), p. 2. No candidate for the U.S. House or Senate was prosecuted under the act and only two senators immediately after its enactment in 1927 were prohibited from spending in excess of the act's limits.

5. This section is based, unless otherwise noted, on Herbert E. Alexander, *Money in Politics* (Washington, D.C.: Public Affairs Press, 1972), pp. 198–229 and Alexander, *Regulation of Political Finance* (Princeton, N.J.: Citizens Research Foundation, 1966). Earlier citations of relevant works can be found in *Money in Politics* in particular. See also Jasper B. Shannon, *Money and Politics* (New York: Random House, 1959), pp. 1–63 for a relevant discussion of earlier periods.

6. In truth, the assassin Charles Julius Guiteau was emotionally disturbed and probably psychotic. The political rationalization offered for the murder did channel public feeling into a constructive outlet, the adoption of civil service protections long on the reform agenda. See Murray Edelman and Rita James Simon, "Presidential Assassinations: Their Meaning and Impact on American Society," in *Assassinations and the Political Order,* ed. W. J. Crotty (New York: Harper & Row, 1971), pp. 455–88 and Charles E. Rosenberg, *The Trial of the Assassin Guiteau* (Chicago: University of Chicago Press, 1968).

7. The assumptions underlying *Newberry* were reversed in two complementary cases, *U.S.* v. *Classic* (1941) and *Smith* v. *Allwright* (1944).

8. Alexander, *Money in Politics,* p. 202.

9. For a discussion of the legislative history of the bill, see Robert L. Peabody, Jeffrey M. Berry, William G. Frasure, and Jerry Goldman, *To Enact a Law* (New York: Praeger, 1972) and, on this bill and other proposed reforms, Delmer D. Dunn, *Financing Presidential Campaigns* (Washington, D.C.: The Brookings Institution, 1972).

10. Seymour M. Hersh, "Hays Draft of Campaign Financing Is Said to Weaken 1971 Law," *New York Times,* March 25, 1974, p. 22, Hersh, "Senate Unit Votes to Ease Curbs on Election Funding," *New York Times,* July 8, 1973, p. 1, Jerome Watson, "Spending Limit a Vote Reform?" *Chicago Sun-Times,* February 21, 1974, p. 50, and "Campaign Spending Bill Gutting Seen," *Chicago Sun-Times,* June 5, 1972, p. 65.

11. Ben A. Franklin, "New Campaign Spending Rules Marred by Confusion," *New York Times,* May 1, 1972, p. 36. Congressman Hays was one of those delinquent in filing his campaign reports under the new law, a failure that was publicized by Common Cause and the media. A week after Hays was singled out, he decreed that the duplication cost per page would go from 10¢ to $1.00. Flora Lewis, "Campaign Funds to be Monitored," *Chicago Sun-Times,* May 9, 1972, p. 40.

12. For the effects in one state, New York, see Frank Lynn, "400 of State's Politicians Penalized on Fund Reports," *New York Times,* May 2, 1975, p. 2. The majority of one southern state legislature reportedly threatened to quit if a strict disclosure law was enacted.

13. "Campaign Spending Bill Gutting Seen." See also the other accounts cited in footnotes 10 and 11.

14. See, in particular, *The Senate Watergate Report*, 2 vols. (New York: Dell, 1974), 2:3–151.

15. "Buckley and McCarthy Joining to Fight Campaign Reform Act," *New York Times*, December 12, 1974, p. 33. See also Ben A. Franklin, "New Political-Fund Law Attacked on Two Fronts," *New York Times*, October 3, 1972, p. 32.

16. In addition to the articles cited in Note 15, see R. W. Apple, Jr., "New Voting Law Faces All-Out Legal Challenge," *New York Times*, May 19, 1975, p. 1. The Justice Department, in a Ford Administration never strongly supportive of the new law, was supposed to provide the chief defense in the legal attack. The department chose not to defend the law but rather to enter amicus curiae briefs on both sides of the issue. Robert Gruenberg, "Campaign Law 'Stall' Causes Gardner Howl," *Chicago Daily News*, May 24–25, 1975, p. 4.

17. See the commentary in Tom Wicker, "The C.I.A. and Its Critics," *New York Times*, February 23, 1975, p. E-13.

18. The laws are codified in Francis R. Valeo, Roger K. Haley, and Patrick T. Ortiz, *Federal Election Campaign Laws*, prepared for the Subcommittee on Privileges and Elections of the Committee on Rules and Administration, U.S. Senate (Washington, D.C.: U.S. Government Printing Office, 1975).

19. Section 315a of the Communications Act, the "equal time" provision, was continued by the new campaign regulation acts. The equal time concept is a well-intentioned effort to provide all candidates with equal television exposure (outside of news programming), but in practice it simply does not work. In effect, exclusive of the few exceptions like the 1960 Kennedy-Nixon debates and the 1972 debate among contenders in the New Hampshire Democratic primary, it discourages extensive, free television use by political candidates. Its repeal would be welcome as is the recent decision that allows debates among major party candidates if staged and sponsored by an independent agency and then covered by the media. This action allowed the scheduling of debates in 1976 by the League of Woman Voters between the Democratic (Carter) and Republican (Ford) nominees, which the television networks could cover as a legitimate news event. For a discussion of this problem and the role of television in campaigns more generally, see Delmer D. Dunn, *Financing Presidential Campaigns* and Commission on Campaign Costs in the Electronic Era, *Voter's Time* (New York: The Twentieth Century Fund, 1969).

20. See Ernest Holsendolph, "Job Favoritism Is Found in Study of U.S. Agencies," *New York Times*, May 7, 1975, p. 1 and *The Senate Watergate Report*, 2 vols. Two basically critical assessments of money and its effect on politics are David Nichols, *Financing Elections: The Politics of an American Ruling Class* (New York: New Viewpoints-Franklin Watts, 1974) and George Thayer, *Who Shakes the Money Tree?* (New York: Simon and Schuster, 1973).

III

THE REFORM
OF POLITICAL
INSTITUTIONS

7

Primaries
and the Reform
of Presidential
Nominating Methods

The primary system of nominations fits nicely into the hierarchy of values that underlie most reform attempts. This means of nominating candidates for public office was popularized as a vehicle for insuring a more democratic, open and representative electorate—goals underlying reforms of varying types from the expansion of the suffrage in the earliest days of the Republic to the more contemporary McGovern-Fraser improvements in delegate selection practices. The direct primary constituted a natural evolution in the continual expansion of political decision making to include greater public involvement.

The development of nominating procedures reflects the history of adaptation to change within the political environment. The national institutions are direct outgrowths of state and local methods that have proven successful. The state and local district agencies for candidate nominations arose from the desire to structure the electorate into opposing caucuses, a development recognizing the increasing salience of party factions. The old ways—the "self-nominating system" characterized by personalism and informalism—gave way in the decade of the 1790s, in particular, to the rudimentary experimentation with structures organized to electorally unite voters with commonly shared views as to the centralization (or decentralization) of federal authority, and as to the interests and groups governmental action should favor. The earliest of these efforts were closely associated with the Jeffersonian Republicans, the forerunners of today's Democrats and the first national political party. The move of the less organizationally conscious Federalists to counter their opponents by linking their national representatives to similarly mobilized grassroots support led to the inauguration of the party system. Both fledgling groups were attempting to systematize and coordinate participation in line with candidate and policy preference. This development, as with all "reforms" of political consequence, combined in uneven quantities necessity, a pragmatic idealism (that is, an emphasis on what worked), and a sophisticated calculation of political advantage.

The Jeffersonians exploited the new departure in political organization with far greater skill than their elitist adversaries. The embryonic party structure allowed the supporters of Jeffersonian principles to mobilize their forces to capture public office, their first priority. It also provided a form of representation, previously unavailable, for the party's base to assert itself in successively higher government councils. The use of the emerging party forms provided the Jeffersonians with an overwhelming superiority in political combat. The coalition of local committees that united behind Jefferson's presidential candidacy in 1800 dislodged the incumbent Federalists with impressive rapidity. With equal speed, the Federalist party was smashed and a one-party era introduced, giving way in the 1830s to a competitive two-party period and the cycle of one-party dominant and highly competitive sets of elections that have alternated since.

The rationale for the revolutionary new form of political expression was expressed in 1794. It is at least as relevant today as it was then.

> All governments are more or less combinations against the people; they are states of violence against individual liberty, originating from man's imperfections and vices, and as rulers have no more virtue than the ruled, the equilibrium between them can only be preserved by proper attentions and association; for the power of government can only be kept within the constitutional limits by the display of a power equal to itself, the collected sentiment of the people. Solitary opinions have little weight with men whose views are unfair, but the voice of many strikes them with awe[1].

These same impulses to more fully realize the promise of a democratic society that led to experimentation with party forms to better control public officials eventually dictated their improvement or their replacement. As the original institution became subject to abuse, newer and more democratizing procedures were introduced to correct the excesses and return the system to the assumptions underlying its original design. There is a degree of circularity (as well as progression) to the movements, especially noticeable from the early 1900s, when the creativity underlying the experimentation with innovative forms appears to have been exhausted. From this period on, the changes advocated have settled into a more predictable pattern—the imposition of tighter regulations on existing forms or the substitution for the device in effect by its logical alternative (the convention for the primary or vice versa).

Throughout it all, the often tacit assumptions as to the need for and the functioning of these agencies has remained much the same. The difficulty has been in the performance. In this respect, there has been a persistent tradition of dissatisfaction with the ability to hold public and party officials accountable. The problem has grown in severity as the nation expanded. The efforts continue until this day. The disillusionment that fueled the continual efforts to improve the operation of party mechanisms of leadership accountability appears far from spent. Presently, efforts are being directed toward the introduction of standardized tests intended to insure equal access to and influence by all party members, and the operation of nominating systems in line with their original objectives— the retention of the ultimate powers of control by the grassroots membership. Another reform cycle is underway. A limited amount of sentiment exists to scrap the familiar nominating procedures in favor of a national primary, a more radical (and potentially disruptive) departure from traditional practices than most appreciate.

This chapter will look at the development of nominating procedures with particular emphasis on the primary. The contemporary mix of convention, committee, and primary forms will be examined and the proposals for change—most relatively modest attempts to introduce a degree of rationality into a nightmarishly diverse and complex set of processes—will be evaluated.

THE HISTORY OF
NOMINATING PROCEDURES

The evolution of nominating systems parallels the development of political parties; it is the history of opening political decisions to control by the membership of the parties. The earliest means of offering a candidacy for elective office were remarkably simple. They should be familiar to anyone knowledgable about local politics in most communities. Recruitment in noncompetitive areas (for example, in most parts of the South until recent decades) would also exhibit the same characteristics. Almost anyone who wanted to could run, *theoretically.* To succeed, however, a candidate would have to command a bloc of supporters or lay claim to adequate financial or newspaper support to present their names and qualifications to a sufficient number of voters. Holding a person accountable for actions taken while in office or even raising an intelligent discussion of relevant issues provided extraordinarily difficult under such circumstances. The officeholder dealt with the electorate on a one-to-one basis. Personality, community status, personal visibility, good appearance, an easily identified name or family background, the backing of local notables—these were the qualities that took precedence. Candidates, if not self-starters, were put forward by a select group of supporters, usually men of affluence within the community. At present, such characteristics as these are largely associated with "nonpartisan" elections, another "reform" of the Progressive Era that similar to many of its contemporaries brought unforeseen consequences[2].

The entire system had an element of aristocratic indulgence that made electoral responsiveness and intelligent opposition frustratingly difficult to achieve. Edward McChesney Sait describes the process.

> Candidates were self-announced or, more usually, brought forward by a group of influential persons after some sort of "parlor caucus"; and even when mass-meetings were called for the purpose of making local nominations, they . . . probably did no more than ratify the proposals that were laid before them. The voters, themselves a very limited body according to our present democratic notions, accepted as a matter of course the leadership assumed by men of wealth and social prominence, the landed proprietors and members of the learned professions[3].

After deciding to enter a race, the candidate's road to election followed a generally predictable course. The new candidate would acquaint as many people as possible with his decision through circulars or newspaper announcements. The statement of a local office seeker in New Jersey in 1792 offers an illustration of the practice. "At the solicitation of a number of respectable friends, I am induced, with the greatest deference, to offer myself as a candidate for the office of sheriff[4]." Having overcome his natural hesitancy, and with the backing of "respectable friends," the candidate would then proceed with the more familiar campaign practices of meeting with individuals in person or in groups to solicit their vote —and always in a leisurely and gentlemanly manner.

The incumbent seeking reelection followed much the same path. His campaign would be punctuated by personal visits to old friends and supporters. Possibly, he might deliver an occasional speech or appear at public ceremonies at his discretion, one of the perquisites (then as now) of the officeholder. The entire process was loose, paternalistic, and informal. The communication to his constituents in 1789 of a Virginia state legislator seeking election to the first Federal Congress makes the point. After reviewing his qualifications, the legislator continues:

> I had fully intended to have paid my personal respects to you individually as well as collectively. But my duty in the Assembly, added to the short interval between its final adjournment and the election of members to Congress, together with the badness of the weather, and my own imposition, have unfortunately frustrated my intentions. Therefore it is that I am under the painful necessity of following those who address you by Public Letter; an example which, I confess to you, I am not very fond of imitating, though present circumstances may perhaps justify it[5].

Poor communications, great distances to be traveled, and the vagaries of the weather help explain the casual nominating practices. Of even greater importance was the lack of a precedent that offered a better example. The elitist democratic spirit of the time (and of later days as well) held that the unstructured system that existed was not only the most laudatory but the most democratic one conceivable. If the rule of the wellborn and a genteel anarchy in nominating practices constituted the preferred model of democratic behavior, then the point has merit.

As usual, the practices of the states varied. The southern states claimed the most open (in the sense of disorganized), and, consequently, the most chaotic system of nominations—a state of affairs that would come to characterize the nominating procedures in many of these states down to the present. Other areas scorned one of the few democratic components of the southern nominations, the candidates' personal presentation of himself and his qualifications to the electorate. Aristocratic New England handled the matter differently (in a manner that continued until the contemporary period and was particularly evident in the region's Republican parties). A restricted town meeting would be convened or a small group of community leaders would gather informally to discuss the office in question and the prospective individuals who might qualify and their virtues. In this manner, a nominee would be selected. One observer has written that "a man dare not solicit any office of the people; . . . he must wait till they are pleased to elect him; if he should ask their votes, he would not have one [6]."

It was not necessary that the meetings be broad-based or representative of the community at large. The respected citizens of the locality chose the candidate, who, in turn, could have few illusions as to where the community's (and his own) best interest lay. Since a candidate did not campaign, he did not promote any specific policies and he was not held directly accountable to the public for his actions once in office. In fact, it was considered improper even to answer in public any charges that might be directed against him. Elective office was a public trust to be conducted as such by men of obvious competence and esteem. Both New England and the South would be slow to respond to the demand to formalize procedures to insure broader and more accountable representation.

In the pre-party era, the alternatives that were available when disagreements over official policy occurred seemed equally destructive of democratic principles. An individual who objected to an action of the government could "call a promiscuous mob of people to decide on it by pressing resolutions without debate or . . . [he could set] about opposing government by secret intrigues, clubs, and cabals[7]." Even allowing for the bombast of the propagandist, should the indulgent practices of the South or the circumscribed ones of New England appear preferable to the more familiar campaign excesses of the present day, this complete lack of a realistic alternative to the existing system should invite a pause.

For increasing numbers of people, the old ways were not good enough. In the two decades after the Revolution, and in particular the years following the enactment of a strong federal Constitution, many began to feel that some form of structure was needed to bind voters into more effective political groupings and to relate policy concerns to candidates for public office. The divisions that emerged were inevitable and were not susceptible to the old patterns of resolution based on the good intentions of those who actively participated in the political process, a broadly based and virtually indivisible public interest, and a political foreordination that insured all would prosper. The naive faith of an earlier age was no longer able to cover over the fundamental cleavages in the society which were destined to find voice through new political forms. As Joseph Charles explains:

Each side, as the divisions grew wider, came to regard the other as traitors to the common cause of their earlier years. . . . How to administer machinery newly set up, what concrete meaning, in unforeseen contingencies, to give to words which no longer meant the same thing to all: these were the new problems which weakened old ties and sharpened earlier differences. . . .

Men who felt the future of republicanism depended upon the operation of a government based on a document so full of compromises as our Constitution were bound to divide on practical questions. . . . The fundamental issue of the 1790's was no other than the form of government and what type of society were to be produced in this country[8].

The major thrust in moving toward new forms of political expression came from the Middle Atlantic states (New York, Pennsylvania, New Jersey, Delaware, and Maryland), traditionally more suspicious of governmental authority and, at the time, receptive to the anti-Federalist mood. The party system evolved from this discontent. Within it, vehicles were needed to achieve representative and broadly consultative party nominations. The principal methods adopted to realize these ends were the caucus and the convention, political forms whose roots extended well back into the colonial period.

THE CAUCUS

The party caucus was a natural outgrowth of the Committees of Correspondence used to harness and then direct the revolutionary fervor. In New England, the name applied to any small group of political leaders that met to plan campaign tactics and to conduct political affairs. In most of the states, the term came to mean the legislative party members who gathered to nominate their party's candidates for governor and other state offices. The method was in use in Maryland in 1788 and, as party divisions increased, it became widely popular throughout the nation. The practice assumed its most famous exposition through the congressional caucuses from 1800 to 1824, which took over the function of nominating presidential candidates[9].

A certain logic underlay the arrangement. First, it did have historical roots and therefore a legitimacy bestowed by tradition. Second, it allowed the party's *elected* legislative representatives, a group presumably speaking for their electorate and holding its best interests as their main concern, to decide nominations. The congressional caucus could be assumed to know the state of national affairs and to be personally familiar with the respective strengths of the various contenders. Logistical problems rendered other forms of more direct involvement in nominations by large numbers of people difficult. The caucus was, in short, a practical solution to a sensitive problem and one that contained the necessary, if rudimentary, elements of representation[10].

Yet, the caucus system, whatever its merits, harbored structural weaknesses of considerable moment. It was removed from and (despite assumptions to the contrary) was not representative of party sentiments at the grassroots level. Those districts not electing members to a legislative forum were denied even an indirect say in nominations. The caucus was cliquish and contained elements of elitist representation. It resisted change, and distrusted mass democratic sentiments, shortcomings that eventually spelled its doom. In the words of Mosei Ostrogorski, the patrician Russian chronicler of party developments, the caucus was forced "to retire before the rising democratic tide[11]."

In actuality, caucus nominations had been under attack from the beginning. The Jeffersonian Republicans ridiculed the secretive Federalist caucus, the first of its kind nationally, employed to select the party's presidential ticket of 1800. The Republicans, however, managed to adapt the form to their own ends with little embarrassment. The Federalists, defeated in the election of 1800, came to distrust the instrument. In part, the demise of the Federalists can be traced to their antiorganizational bias: individualistic, elitist, and conservative, the party held suspect the evolving forms of democratic mass organization[12]. The caucus system, nonetheless, lingered on, well outliving its usefulness. The practice experienced its final trauma in the election of 1824, when the presidential candidacy of frontier hero and popular favorite, Andrew Jackson, was rejected in favor of the trustworthy William Crawford. The caucus nominee finished last in a four-man field in an election won by John Quincy Adams. Jackson, of course, went on to win the presidency on his own in 1828, breaking the monopolization of the office by the competing aristocracies of Virginia and Massachusetts. His election ushered in a vigorous era of democratic expansion and one of the promised reforms was the replacement of "King Caucus" with a more representative method of party expression, the national nominating convention.

THE CONVENTION SYSTEM

The first national convention was held by the Anti-Masonic party to nominate its candidates for president. A few months later the National Republicans (Democrats) adopted the idea and met for the first time in Baltimore to renominate Jackson. The forms adopted (from the credentials, platform, and other committees to the nominating regulations) and the general procedures introduced at this initial assembly proved remarkably durable. They established the basic structure which lasted for generations and, even at present, bears a striking resemblance to that still favored[13].

The antecedents for the convention are found in the colonial representative assemblies which spoke on behalf of a larger public and constituted an integral part of the democratic evolution. The specific concept of delegates chosen by party members or clubs to represent them at a central convocation to transact party business and nominate candidates initially gained prominence in the Middle Atlantic States. As early as 1788 and 1792, Pennsylvania convened state-level party assemblies of this nature but had to abandon them due to the then inadequate network of local party clubs required to support the state practice[14]. The decades from 1790 to 1810 saw a mushrooming of the convention idea at local and district levels and, gradually at the beginning, the convention began to supplement and then replace legislative caucuses at the state level. At first, various alternative mixed systems were instituted (basically legislative caucuses with some elected delegates added). The movement received impetus from the collapse of the congressional caucus, and in 1824, New York, Pennsylvania (for the second time), and Rhode Island turned to the "pure" statewide convention system already in use in New Jersey and Delaware. By 1840, the convention had become the principal vehicle for party nominations[15].

CRITICISMS OF THE CONVENTION

The conventions originally were hailed as a significant democratic innovation that helped insure popular control over nominations. The initial euphoria gave way quickly to disillusionment, however, and the institution began to fall into disrepute. The bulk of the early criticism was directed against the local and state meetings. Soon the convention system at every level was under attack.

The cataloguing of convention deficiencies was impressively documented. The general argument was that nominating conventions had become undemocratic exercises in the unrestrained use of power. They denied party supporters control over nominations, the critical stage in the electoral process. Convention operations were particularly susceptible to gross improprieties on the part of the emerging party boss. The tales of high-handed tactics, rowdyism, packed halls, arbitrary parliamentary usages, bought votes, and predetermined candidates and policies are now legendary. Ostrogorski, never a friend to the institution (or for that matter to political parties generally), contended that the conventions

> revealed almost at once the unhealthy politico-social conditions amid which it was introduced. The primary meetings out of which sprang all the successive delegations constituting the hierarchy of the conventions were deserted by the great body of citizens, and the politicians aided by their friends, easily got control of them and bestowed on themselves the nominations to the more or less lucrative posts which they coveted[16].

The conventions, which in truth were susceptible to total control by the party boss, facilitated "the systematic robbery of the public purse" by Tammany Hall and its counterparts throughout the nation, a development to which Ostrogorski and his like-minded colleagues strenuously objected[17].

The attack on convention ills was virtually endless and, in a time (the late 19th century) that provided a receptive market for muckraking newspapers and magazines, their weaknesses became a national fixation. Ostrogorski provides a fair sampling of the criticisms. The party platforms were a "farce"; the machines (through the conventions) nominated weak candidates; the nominees while "more or less respectable" were but "figureheads" for the "dangerous classes" to which the parties catered; honest candidates, if chosen by necessity or mistake, were "stamped with the common hallmark of mediocrity"; convention restrictions such as the "unit rule" (employed by the Democrats until 1968) were decried as undemocratic; the role of the delegate was declared "gratuitous"; and 90 percent of the convention votes were for sale. A delegate vote was treasured because of its "high commercial value" in deciding the fate of prospective governors or presidents and the other kingpins of the political system. And the people, meanwhile, were

> helpless. Imprisoned in the convention system and the dogma of [party] "regularity," they could only ratify unconditionally the selections made for them. . . . "The people have no more control over the selection of the man who is to be the President than the subjects of kings have over the birth of the child who is to be their ruler[18]."

Ostrogorski's final judgment on the convention system was to become famous. "A colossal travesty of popular institutions," he wrote. The "greedy crowd of office-holders . . . disguised as delegates" charged with selecting "the chief magistracy of the greatest Republic of the two hemispheres," as he described the convention members, led him to believe the old saying that "God takes care of drunkards, of little children, and of the United States[19]."

Ostrogorski was an idealist. He expected the very highest level of performance from democratic institutions and what he observed in practice shocked him. He was not atypical for his day. Others echoed his sentiments. The spoils system, patronage, the lack of extensive statutory regulation of convention procedures and the failure to enforce the regulations that did exist, the use of force to gain or restrict entry to conventions or to control their proceedings, the absence of means to challenge convention decisions, the excessive powers concentrated in the presiding officers, the low quality of delegates, and the absence of widespread public participation in the process, all and more were denounced time and again as excesses that challenged the very foundations of democratic government. Two students of nominating processes summed up the views of many on the operation of the system when they wrote that convention abuses "ranged from brutal violence and coarse fraud to the most refined and subtle cunning, and included every method that seemed adapted to the all-important object of securing the desired majority and controlling the convention[20]."

There is no question that the convention system was thoroughly corrupted as an instrument of democratic expression. The quantity of examples of the depth to which the institution had sunk make the point vividly. Perhaps one description of the membership of a Cook County, Illinois, convention in 1896 can serve to illustrate, as one author says, "the appalling degradation that might be observed occasionally in the politics of the period " :

Among the 723 delegates 17 had been tried for homicide, 46 had served terms in the penitentiary for homicide or other felonies, 84 were identified by detectives as having criminal records. Over a third of the delegates were saloon-keepers; two kept houses of ill-fame; several kept gambling resorts. There were eleven former pugilists and fifteen former policemen[21].

Unnecessarily the reporter adds, "The policemen of Chicago at that period were not highly regarded[22]."

Matters had changed drastically since the gentlemanly canvassing for votes among acquaintances of the 1790s. A reaction was building: ". . . though the convention was a good thing in principle and might have been a tolerable thing in practice, a movement to supplant it had begun[23]." The strengths of the convention system would be left for another generation of reformers to redis-cover. Meanwhile, the changes introduced into nominating practices would be radical and, among many other results, the powers and safeguards of the state would intrude themselves irrevocably into the process. Ironically, in time, the new departure for which so much had been predicted would leave its most fervent advocates at least as frustrated as they had been with convention nominations. The defeat of the reformers' hopes this time was crushing. They retired from the field. A long period of gloom and negligence followed, a trance only recently being challenged by the introduction of a series of modest reforms by a new generation of critics with a more realistic appraisal of the promise as well as the weaknesses of political parties.

Their own idealized conceptions as to what democracy *should* be eventually did in the turn-of-the century reformers. The maturation process a mass demo-cratic system undergoes is not necessarily a pleasant sight. It is all the more painful for those whose expectations had advanced little beyond the philosophic assumptions implicit in a Rousseau or a Locke, and who could, with all serious-ness, look to mechanical devices (such as a convention) as a means of instituting a middle-class sense of political morality. The key to the frustration lay in their attempt to divorce politics from the social conditions that supplied its *raison d'être.* The forces being challenged and the corrupt practices which were found disagreeable had their roots deep within a social order in flux. The correlation of one with the other never occurred to the critics. Their constant quest for just one more instrumental change that would secure the order and probity in politics they so badly wanted was doomed to failure.

The convention system, however, gave way begrudgingly. There was none of the element of collapse that marked the quick death of the legislative caucus. Without doubt, politicians had much to gain from a system that so admirably served their needs. There was more, however, to the perseverance and eventual resurrection of the institution than self-interest. The convention performed many useful functions for a political party, the variety and significance of which were not to be appreciated until later. Conventions, in many respects, had become the whipping boy for all the political extravagances of the age[24]. But this realization was to dawn slowly. The immediate goal was to avoid the more flagrant excesses of the convention through the substitution of a new system of popular control. The logical alternative, and seemingly the next step in the extension of democratic controls over the entire nominating process, was (as it was called in those days) the "direct primary," direct because the voters themselves selected the party nominees, rather then delegates acting on their own behalf.

Primaries have had an uneven history. At present, an era of renewed emphasis has begun with primaries increasing in numbers, importance, and variety of use. The questions to be investigated include the manner in which the primary evolved, the nature of the present system (a mix of primaries, conventions, and, to a lesser extent, party committees), and the value of the changes proposed in contemporary nominating procedures. In this last regard, it is well to remember a trade-off between values (direct representation as opposed to a stronger party system) may be significant in deciding what manner of "reform" receives attention. Broader goals can sometimes be achieved through modest procedural changes—the standardization of primary forms from state to state, for example—rather than the complete replacement of troublesome systems.

THE INTRODUCTION
OF THE PRIMARY

By the time dissatisfaction with the nominating conventions had reached fever pitch just after the turn of the century, the "new" primary concept—viewed by many reformers as the ultimate in democratic mechanisms of control—had been around a surprisingly long time. Its ancestry reaches almost as far back as that of the national conventions. The primary was first instituted, most say, in Crawford County, Pennsylvania (and in some quarters, it is still called the Crawford County system) in 1860 by the Republican party. A little more intensive detective work traces the origins to Crawford County, yes, but to the Democrats 18 years earlier. It appears that the use of the primary was suspended by the Democrats in 1850 and then resurrected by the newly created Crawford County Republicans[25]. From that date on, it enjoyed a more or less continuous usage in a scattering of local party contests up until its adoption by a number of states in the early 1900s as the vehicle for selecting presidential delegates.

The primary was considered a bold step in the progressive evolution toward open politics. Control over nominations was correctly believed to be the single most important act within the power of the political parties. The primary by-passed the political boss. The primary took the power of nomination out of their hands and placed it under the control of the party's electorate. The change also introduced another, less noticed, function. In time, the primary also opened internal party selection processes—once left to the discretion of party leaders—to the control of the state. This occurred in two ways. First, since primaries are elections, such factors as as the date, ballot forms, voter qualifications, delegate and presidential nominee filing regulations, and the like were determined by law in virtually every state. Second, as primary elections came to be perceived as the quasi-governmental functions they are, the federal courts in particular, despite an initial (and continuing) reluctance to involve themselves deeply in party affairs, began to rule in a series of tortuously limited decisions over a prolonged period of time against the primaries' most obvious abuses. The main targets were, most significantly, racial discrimination and, to a lesser extent, gross corruptive practices as legislated by the state. The effect was to extend to voters in primary elections (far more so than to those in convention states) the protections implicit in general elections. State intervention was a new and generally welcome development that served to shift the balance of power further in favor of the party's base[26].

PRIMARIES IN
THE EARLY PERIOD

The flirtation with the primary idea began to take serious form during the decade of the 1890s. The state legislatures of Kentucky and Mississippi provided for optional primaries in 1892. Similar authorizations were contained in the Virginia and Massachusetts laws of 1894 and those of Delaware (1897) and Ohio (1898), applicable in all cases (except Massachusetts) to selected counties only. In other states, one or both of the political parties voluntarily turned to primaries for selecting nominees. By 1900, two-thirds of the states had primary laws of some sort, although, curiously, the formal beginning of the system on the national level does not date from these developments. The laws enacted were either far too limited in scope or were discretionary, simply permitting the parties to hold primaries as they chose. But the laws did begin to set the qualifications for participating in primaries and the penalties for certain types of stipulated abuses. Registration qualifications were introduced in some cases and, of at least equal importance, the state began to assume responsibility for the cost of these elections[27]. The direction of the movement was clear.

By 1900, a generation of experimentation gave way to a furious outburst of energy that led to the quick adoption of the primary system of nominations by one state after another. Florida, Oregon, and Minnesota adopted primary laws, all of which were later replaced by tougher standards. The rush was on. By 1917, all but four of the states had some type of primary law covering state or local offices (Table 7.1). The march to adoption was associated with another movement: the tendency to make primaries mandatory, the required method of selecting nominees in 32 of the 44 states. The trend also witnessed the effort to extend to primary elections the regulations against fraud and corrupt practices that characterized general elections. The primary had clearly won the hearts of the

American public[28]. With the backing of such men as Teddy Roosevelt, Woodrow Wilson, Charles Evans Hughes, Robert La Follette, George W. Norris, and Hiram Johnson, the primary was about to enter its most successful era.

THE PRESIDENTIAL PRIMARIES

There was a slight lag in the application of the primary method to the selection of national convention delegates or (this process becomes complex as will be shown) to registering a choice among presidential contenders. Nonetheless, once begun, the process of adoption here, as with other levels of office, spread extraordinarily fast. The turn toward primary control of national convention delegations parallels both the application of the primary to other levels of office (as illustrated) *and* the heyday of the Progressive movement, particularly evident in the Progressive Republicans' strident dissatisfaction with their treatment in national conventions by the Regulars. It is important to recall in this regard that the Republican party was the majority party from approximately 1860 to 1928. The party's control of political offices increased after the Democrats' electorally disastrous shift to the left (and toward the more radical Populists and William Jennings Bryan) in 1896. Factional dissatisfaction leading directly to innovative political forms is likely to occur in the majority party. Such was the case with the presidential primaries in the first two decades of the twentieth century (and such would be the situation in the late 1960s and early 1970s).

What can reasonably be called the first presidential primary—the Wisconsin law of 1905 providing for the direct election of national convention delegates—was instituted because of the schizoid behavior of that state's Republican party in 1904 in selecting two Republican national convention delegations and two completely separate slates of nominees for state office. The division was exacerbated when the Republican National Convention seated the Regulars (or anti-La Follettes) and the State Supreme Court one year later then ruled the Progressive Republicans (or La Follette faction) to be the duly constituted and legally chosen Republican party representatives. Such battles as these, with broadly similar outcomes, would become a familiar staple of Republican politics—with disastrous consequences for the party in the presidential election of 1912—over the next decade[29].

Pennsylvania (1906) and South Dakota (1909) adopted primaries to elect national convention delegates, but the next major departure came with the legislating by Oregon in 1910 of a primary system that was to have lasting impact[30]. The imagination of Oregon voters was apparently sparked by an incident in Alabama when a group of that state's Democrats petitioned its state central committee to place Bryan's name on the primary ballot so that the party voters could legally force (*bind* or *instruct* are the terms usually employed) its convention delegates to vote for their choice. Oregon adopted through the initiative a

TABLE 7.1
THE ADOPTION OF
STATEWIDE PRIMARY LAWS
(FOR STATE OR LOCAL OFFICES) 1901–1915

State	Initial Year of Adoption and/or Extension
Florida	1901 (rev. 1904)
Oregon	1901 (rev. 1904)
Minnesota	1901 (rev. 1904)
Mississippi	1902
Delaware	1903
Wisconsin	1903
Alabama	1904
Texas	1905 (rev. 1908)
Illinois	1905 (rev. 1908)
Michigan	1905 (rev. 1908)
Montana	1905 (rev. 1908)
South Dakota	1905 (rev. 1908)
Louisiana	1906
Pennsylvania	1906
Iowa	1907
Nebraska	1907
Missouri	1907
North Dakota	1907
South Dakota	1907
Washington	1907
Kansas	1908
Oklahoma	1908
Ohio	1908
Arizona	1909
Arkansas	1909
California	1909
Idaho	1909
Michigan	1909
Nevada	1909
New Hampshire	1909
Tennessee	1909
Colorado	1910
Maryland	1910

TABLE 7.1 *(Continued)*

State	Initial Year of Adoption and/or Extension
Maine	1911
Massachusetts	1911
New Jersey	1911
Wyoming	1911
Kentucky	1912
Minnesota	1912
Montana	1912
Virginia	1912
Florida	1913
New York	1913
Ohio	1913
Pennsylvania	1913
Indiana	1915
North Carolina	1915
South Carolina	1915
Vermont	1915
West Virginia	1915

primary law that allowed voters to register their preference for president and vice-president and allow them the opportunity to directly choose the national convention delegates.

The stiffer, more inclusive Oregon contribution immediately became popular. As a newspaper of the day editorialized:

> this popular vote [in the primary] . . . "may readily become the beginning of a great change. It may grow historic, for it may be the inauguration of popular selection by the many of presidential candidates[31]."

Many states agreed. Wisconsin, Nebraska, and California, all states in which the presidential primary was to become of historical importance, as well as three others, followed the Oregon precedent one year later. By 1912, 15 states had provided for presidential primaries in some form and after the bitter delegate battles at the Republican National Convention of that year between the Roosevelt Progressives (later the Bull Moose party) and the Taft Regulars, 9 more states had adopted presidential primary laws by 1916—until recent years the high-water mark in the history of the institution.

The reaction against the primary concept came as abruptly as the movement for its adoption. Alabama legislated a presidential primary in the years after 1916, but it was voided as unconstitutional. Minnesota, Iowa, Vermont, and Montana reverted to convention systems of delegate selection and the primary movement passed into eclipse, the enthusiasm that marked its inception blunted by the realities of its operation.

CRITICISMS OF THE PRIMARY

The objections to the primay were many. The party professionals had long complained of it as an intrusion into their affairs, but their criticism, with its obvious element of self-interest, was discredited. The wave of reexamination of primary nominating practices was led by the same people who had worked so hard to institute it: the academicians, Progressives, writers, newspaper editorialists, civic leaders, and opinion leaders in general who had expected so much from its introduction. The attack from this quarter gave the debate a particular bite.

Voter turnout was low. The proponents had incorrectly assessed the magnitude of the public's indifference to elections. They overestimated the interest of the public in the elections and the number of what were referred to as "intelligent" voters—the highly motivated, well-read mythical democratic person that formed the basis for many of their proposed reforms. The primary was very much a middle-class instrument fashioned by members of this segment of society with the very best of their own qualities in mind. When the broader public failed to share their values, disillusionment followed.

The rates of voter participation clearly were well below what anyone had expected. Turnouts of 57, 31, 34, and 35 percent *as ratios of the total vote cast* in the presidential elections (not measured therefore against the eligible voting age population) as reported by Overacker for the elections of 1912, 1916, 1920, and 1924 are representative[32].

Participation rates of 16, 34, 38, 30, and 20 percent in five primary elections in the state of New York during the period 1912 to 1920 were illustrative of the variation by election and the depths to which these rates could fall[33]. The tendency has persisted. In the 1968 election year, the presidential nominations in both parties were open (after Lyndon Johnson's early withdrawal from consideration). Yet voter turnout measured as a percentage of the party vote in the general election (as against the more demanding criterion of adult population eligible to vote) in the 12 elections for which figures for all parties were readily available ranged from incredible lows of 4 and 8 percent (New Jersey and Illinois) to highs of 68, 72, and 84 percent (Nebraska, Wisconsin, and Oregon). The average turnout in the primary was less than one-half (44 percent) of those voting on election day in November.

Primary elections proved to have an even more deleterious effect on voter turnout for the minority party. In New York during the years 1916 to 1920, the minority Democrats drew only from 13 to 23 percent of their supporters to their primaries while the majority party figures ranged between 31 and 43 percent[34]. In Wisconsin, the drop-off was even more substantial. While the Democrats could attract a vote of from 10 to 46 percent in general elections from 1906 to 1922, their proportion of the total primary vote was an anemic 3 to 14 percent[35]. The average turnout for the second party in the 12 primary states analyzed in the 1968 election year was 33 percent.

Voters gravitated to the majority party contests where the real issues were settled. In the process, they undoubtedly made the majority party primary vote unrepresentative of the party base. If primary outcomes were intended to reflect the views of a party's supporters, their impact was diluted by the influx of members of the opposition party and by independents. Further, the pull of prospective voters to the majority party's primary could further emphasize its dominant position within the state.

This trend led to another controversy. In some states, and Wisconsin is a good example, the primaries were "open"; voters would declare at the polls which party ballot they wanted. Thus, the party exercised no control over its own decisions-making processes. In other states, the pendulum swung 180 degrees in the opposite direction. The primaries were closed to all but party members. In some states, the standard was leniently applied. In other places, it was stringent to the point of excluding some party supporters and recent converts. Illinois, for example, required a person to be formally registered as a party member 23 months prior to the primary election to qualify to vote.

The proprimary advocates never really understood the role of political parties within a democratic society and, more specifically, their unique contribution to the American political experience. They were, of course, fully outraged by the parties' worst features. Party organizations mobilize the electorate and act as representatives, admittedly imperfectly, for their members' views. The people who gain the most from such representation are those normally the least influential in government decisions. Without strong parties, such groups have no effective vehicle through which to put forward their interests. Clearly, the primaries had hurt the political parties. Yet, they had done this without achieving one of their principal objectives: the demolition of the political boss. The primaries invited factionalism; they encouraged party splits and numerous candidates for office; they made coherent policy stands extraordinarily difficult; and they rewarded the colorful and the extremist, anyone in short who could attract (by any means) a political following. Plurality elections meant that the winner in the field did not have to represent even a majority of the obviously unrepresentative primary electorate[36]. And primaries favored, in turn, anyone who could put forward a consistently cohesive vote, as factor that emphasized the advantages of the political boss. The result was a form of political nihilism unwittingly advanced as a means of strengthening political processes.

The reaction to these developments was about as unrealistic as the expectations of the original proponents of the primary concept. Some began to talk of "responsible parties" along the lines of an idealized British system, with a coherence between candidates, party platforms, legislative performance, and the policy wishes of the party's supporters. The chaotic primary system as practiced in the United States posed a threat to such an enlightened party regularity. Consequently, it was also attacked from this perspective. In truth, the American governmental structure and the size and diversity of the nation made any such "responsible party" system as visualized impossible to achieve. But the real debate on this topic (divorced from the primary issue) would not take place until the post–World War II period[37].

There were other criticisms. The quality of candidates had not improved measurably as had been expected with primary nominations. Ballots were too long (a problem in general elections as well) and even the most enlightened voter would have difficulty in selecting intelligently among the array of candidates for municipal judges or state administrative commissions[38]. "Bullet voting" for machine or ethnic candidates arose which some felt should be outlawed. And primaries were expensive, a factor treated in more detail below.

The old-line party leaders had never liked the primary idea. If not fatal to their political aspirations, it had (at the very least) proved an inconvenience. The electorate, while generally apathetic, could be unpredictable. A popular candidate or a particularly intense factional division could attract a relatively large turnout, further threatening the leaders' influence. When given the chance, party leaders were only too happy to turn the clock back to the preprimary nomination practices.

Most vividly, though, the primary in operation had proven to be a disappointment to many of its strongest supporters. The experiment had brought them face-to-face with the realities of democratic performance and it was their disillusionment with what they encountered that brought the movement to a standstill. One critic in the early 1920s quoted Montesquieu to the effect that the "spirit of democracy" fails with the "spirit of extreme equality, . . . when each citizen would fain be upon a level with these whom he has chosen to command him. Then the people, incapable of bearing the very power they have delegated, want to manage everything themselves, to debate for the Senate, to execute for the magistrate, and to decide for the judges. When this is the case, virtue can no longer subsist in the republic[39]." Too much democracy would destroy the nation! It is the bitter irony of this movement, and an indication of how much the mood had changed, that such a despairing statement would have been unthinkable a short generation earlier.

THE PRIMARY IN
PRESIDENTIAL CONTESTS

The primary system rested in a state of suspended animation from roughly the early 1920s to the second half of the 1960s when it excited new interest. It would be incorrect, however, to say that the primary played no role in presidential nominations. It was not the principal road to nomination, but under the right conditions a primary or a set of them could be influential in testing a candidate's appeal and eventually determining (indirectly) the nominee.

When, for example, a nomination was open (there was no president seeking renomination, no obvious "heir apparent," and no single commanding figure in the race), primaries could be especially significant. Theodore Roosevelt and Robert La Follette were able to challenge Taft's renomination through the primaries in 1912, but Roosevelt's commanding vote margin did little to deny Taft's convention victory in one of the most acrimonious of national gatherings. The dour Woodrow Wilson did manage to present himself in the Democratic primaries of the same year as a creditable Progressive alternative to the Regular's favorite, House Speaker Champ Clark. Hiram Johnson and Leonard Wood fought each other tenaciously in the 1920 Republican primaries, but the nomination went to dark horse Ohio senator and his state's favorite-son candidate, Warren Harding. Coolidge proved a formidable vote getter in the 1924 primaries, effectively turning back any challenge the Progressives Johnson and, to a lesser extent, La Follette could mount.

Herbert Hoover and Al Smith won commanding victories in their respective parties' primaries in 1928 and, after previous failures, captured their parties' nominations. Franklin Roosevelt, beat Smith in 1932 in three of the four major primaries in which they faced each other and overall outpolled Smith 3 to 1 in the total primary vote. The victories established his credibility as a campaigner and made it easier for his party's national convention to reject Smith and any commitment to a replay of the 1928 race. The brash Thomas Dewey used the primaries to explode upon the national scene in 1940, and although his victories did not gain him the nomination in that year, his repeat performance four years later—and particularly the humiliating defeat in the Wisconsin primary dealt Wendell Willkie, the party's 1940 candidate who was attempting to reestablish his appeal—insured his choice in 1944.

Eisenhower strategists employed the primaries in 1952 as a successful wedge against the seemingly assured convention nomination of the conservative Robert Taft. Estes Kefauver consistently overwhelmed his Democratic primary opponents in the same year, a feat that established him as a front-runner for the nomination, but no more. Senator John Kennedy needed the primaries in 1960 to prove his vote appeal and, in particular, to demonstrate that despite his Catholicism he could win the presidency. His Wisconsin and, even more significantly, his West Virginia victories moved him into a lead he was able to convert into support from the party bosses in the big states. Richard Nixon beat back any threat New York Governor Nelson Rockefeller might have posed to his presidential nomination by a consistently strong demonstration of his party support in the primaries of the same year. The pattern is clear enough. While primary appeal could not assure a presidential nomination—as Barry Goldwater was to make painfully apparent in 1964—it could be of strategic importance in the fight for the nomination.

The primary system fulfilled some other less noticed functions. It provided national conventions some flexibility. The primary contests spewed forth an endless supply of dark-horse candidates through favorite-son nominations who could claim at least an impressive home-state send-off upon which to base their fledgling candidacies (or barter their delegation's vote). It gave other candidates an opportunity to test their electoral appeal. Henry Cabot Lodge's surprise write-in victory in the New Hampshire primary in 1964 propelled him into the midst of a race he was reluctant to make. Likewise, the legendary General Douglas MacArthur, a man who received lavish press attention, had difficulty translating his public image into a stable voter coalition. His political career underwent an erratic series of tests in three presidential years (1944, 1948, 1952) but for all practical purposes was ended by Harold Stassen's decisive victory in the 1948 Wisconsin primary. Stassen in turn, the onetime "boy wonder" of Minnesota politics, was almost totally a creature of the primary system. A stunning victory in the 1944 Nebraska primary established him as a serious contender and, although he beat Dewey, his principal opponent, in three head-on contests in 1948 and outpolled him decisively in the primary vote overall, his loss to the eventual nominee in Oregon effectively eliminated him from presidential contention. Stassen ran again in the 1952 Republican primaries and as late as 1964 and 1968 was still entering primary contests, well after his political star had been eclipsed. Along the way, scores of other would-be contenders have been eliminated by their failures to impress in strategically critical primary contests.

The "victory" of Senator Eugene McCarthy in the 1968 New Hampshire Democratic primary marks—as does the election year itself—a turning point in presidential nomination politics[40]. McCarthy actually did not win the primary. Rather, he ran a very close second to an incumbent president, Lyndon Johnson, in a race that dramatically showed the incumbent's lack of appeal to his party's electorate. McCarthy had been given little to no chance to unseat Johnson. The challenge, in itself (at least at that point in history), was extraordinary given the control the chief executive exercised over convention nominations. McCarthy followed his New Hampshire success with a victory in the Wisconsin primary. As the dimensions of McCarthy's Wisconsin victory were becoming apparent, Johnson accepted the political realities and announced his withdrawal from the nomination race just prior to the actual vote.

Despite occasional successes, the primaries have served at best as an alternative road to the nomination. There is a difficulty in translating primary votes into convention support. The reasons are many. A majority of the convention are delegates not elected in primaries. Even among those elected, most are not pledged to honor the voters' choice. Often the presidential preference and the actual delegate selection are separate elections and there is no way to ascertain which candidates individual delegates will support. The requirements on these points vary markedly from one state to the next. Any potential presidential contender faces a morass of legislative and administrative requirements within each primary state that make such an indirect manner of appeal for a party's nomination attractive only to those who have no realistic alternative.

The primary route to the nomination is long. No guarantees exist that other major candidates will enter a race (unless the names of all contenders are required to be put on the ballot regardless of their wishes, as in Oregon). Consequently, candidates could do well in a state primary without knowing for sure exactly what they had accomplished. Physically, developing a primary organization and campaigning in a multitude of such states is exhausting. And in some (the winner-take-all variety of which California has been the best example), anything less than victory means the effort has been wasted. A strong candidate could be embarrassed by a poor showing, especially if administered by a relative newcomer or a lucky dark horse. Even when a candidate won, as did Johnson in New Hampshire and Kennedy in Wisconsin in 1960 (the latter with a commanding 56 percent of the vote), the results can be interpreted in such a way that the entire exercise must be repeated before the outcome is accepted as decisive.

Perhaps the most controversial feature of primaries has been their expense. This aspect of primary elections has been well publicized. One example, the 1968 New Hampshire Republican primary, illustrates the magnitude of financing that can be brought to bear in these contests. With the Republican presidential nomination uncommitted, early contenders Romney, Nixon, and Rockefeller (the last employing a less formal write-in campaign) spent, respectively, $280,000, $300,-000, and $15,000 in the nation's first primary. The objective was to win a psychological edge in the presidential preference contest and a claim on the front-runner position that could be defended for the remainder of the prenomination season. Romney withdrew before the final vote count, thus conceivably making Nixon's heavy expenditure ($3.72 per vote) actually a saving. Nixon gained an enormous advantage over his opponents and held it. Romney, of course, still had to make good on his primary costs. He managed to spend in his aborted campaign $160 per vote received on America's most overindulged voters. Win or lose, primaries can demand enormous financing.

Such a level of comparative primary expenditures is not a recent development. Overacker reports per voter expenses in selected presidential primary states for which she would obtain figures at between $0.94 and $1.80 in 1916 and $0.65 and $1.33 in 1920. The association between expense and primary races remains firm for all levels, from presidential contests on down to state primary races[41]. It began to appear to many of its original sponsors that the primary system simply reemphasized the inequities associated with access to great wealth.

Primaries are easily the most fascinating events in the prenomination phase of presidential campaigns. The problems associated with their operation, however, soured many on their value, which in turn further contributed to their deemphasis in presidential contests after 1916. Yet for all their difficulties, primaries contributed a flexibility to presidential nominations not previously enjoyed. And, at least theoretically, they remained the most aggressively democratic mechanism for choosing party candidates ever devised. For these reasons, the primaries played a significant and occasionally decisive role in presidential nominations. More importantly, since 1968 primaries have reemerged as an object of reform attention and their role in nominating contests promises to become increasingly influential. In fact, the fight may be to keep some type of mixed system. A new reform tide has had the possibly unintended consequence of encouraging states to adopt the primary as the easiest way in which to meet performance criteria specified by the political parties (especially the Democrats)[42].

Primaries continue to be among the most complex of political institutions, a fact perhaps fully appreciated only by the candidates who attempt to enter them. To evaluate the proposals for improving primary operations, very much a part of the contemporary dialogue on political reform, it first becomes necessary to gain an appreciation of the types of primaries (and other forms of state nomination practices) that exist and the rules governing their performance.

A DESCRIPTION OF
THE PRESIDENTIAL PRIMARIES

Twenty-two states and the District of Columbia were authorized under state (or District) law to hold primaries in 1972. A description of the common dimensions shared by the primary statutes from this point on invites confusion. Yet an overview is necessary to attain some understanding of why reform in this area seems necessary and the practicality and impact of the proposals under discussion.

Two states, New York and Alabama, confined their primaries solely to delegate selection. The remaining state statutes can be assessed initially according to whether the state held a presidential preference poll in which the primary voters actually chose among the presidential candidates and whether this vote "instructed" the delegates (bound those chosen to vote for the winner). Table 7.2 presents the different types of primary systems.

Primary elections occur in clusters from the opening of the primary season in early March to its close in June (Figure 7.1). Geographically, there is no particular logic to the groupings. The last set of primaries in June, for example, range from the well-covered California contest to races, on the same day, in New Jersey, South Dakota, and New Mexico. The most that can be said is that a rough east-to-west spread exists, beginning symbolically in the snows of New Hampshire and moving through what can be key elections in the Midwest (Wisconsin, Indiana, and Nebraska) to the mists of Oregon and the sun of California.

The Golden State's primary was easily the most significant and decisive of all (until perhaps the Democrats, in their 1972 National Convention, voted not to recognize the winner-take-all formula in the future). The importance of the other races depended on happenstance (the nature of the presidential contest that year, the quality of the primary entrants, vagaries of the media, etc.). A primary victory in this state awarded the winner about one-fifth of the total votes needed for nomination. Historically, candidates who lost California seldom won their party's nomination. In practical terms, Hubert Humphrey's presidential candidacy was doomed in 1972 by his defeat at the hands of George McGovern in this race.

TABLE 7.2
TYPES OF PRIMARY SYSTEMS

Type 1: No direct presidential preference poll; binding delegate selection primary

    California
    Ohio
    South Dakota

Type 2: Advisory presidential preference poll; separate delegate selection primary

    Illinois
    Nebraska
    New Hampshire
    New Jersey
    West Virginia

Type 3: Binding winner-take-all presidential preference poll; separate delegate selection primary

    District of Columbia
    Oregon
    Rhode Island

Type 4: Binding proportionate presidential preference poll; separate delegate selection primary

    Florida
    Maryland
    Massachusetts
    Wisconsin

Type 5: Binding proportionate presidential preference poll; no delegate selection primary

    Indiana
    Michigan
    New Mexico
    North Carolina
    Tennessee

Type 6: Advisory (with option for binding) presidential preference poll; district delegate selection primary

    Pennsylvania

SOURCE: National Municipal League, *Presidential Nominating Procedures* (New York: National Municipal League, 1974), pp. 8–9.

Humphrey's challenge to McGovern's California delegates before the Credentials Committee, had it carried, would have denied the South Dakota senator the margin needed for nomination (although Humphrey, who had relatively few votes, would not have benefited substantially). Barry Goldwater did unusually poorly in the 1964 Republican primaries (his strength lay in states whose nomi-

FIGURE 7.1
THE PRIMARY SEASON
  (BASED ON THE 1972 SCHEDULING OF CONTESTS)

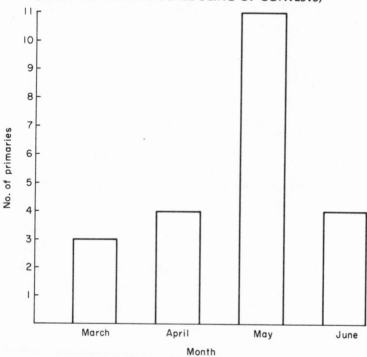

Month

nating procedures were controlled by sympathetic activists). Lodge beat him in New Hampshire (an upset), New Jersey (also on a write-in vote), and, as expected, Massachusetts. William Scranton decisively captured the Pennsylvania primary (with both Lodge and Nixon attracting more support that Goldwater). Nixon, not an active campaigner since his bitter defeat in the California governor's race two years earlier, nonetheless finished second to Goldwater in Nebraska, and even Harold Stassen, certainly not a serious contender but the only alternative on the ballot, ran a respectable race in Indiana. Goldwater finished third in Oregon, well behind the front-runner Rockefeller, one week before the California vote. Yet Goldwater won the critical test with 51.5 percent of the Republican vote over a Rockefeller candidacy plagued by the candidate's personal difficulties. The winning of this key race gave the Arizona senator the legitimacy needed to sustain his candidacy as well as additional delegate votes with which to pad his convention total.

The primaries are grouped heavily in May, which might logically encourage a candidate to hold back and await these and the once-decisive California test. In actuality, this strategy may be acceptable to a dark horse, but it is impractical for a front-runner. Contenders who hope to take the lead and hold it or, conversely, as in the 1972 and 1968 nomination fights, who have such little public support and media attention that they need to demonstrate the appeal of their candidacy, will enter the early primaries. The New Hampshire primary is virtually meaningless in terms of convention votes, but as the nation's first it is heavily covered by the media, and its small electorate must be the most overpatronized in the nation. Florida, a new primary with regional overtones follows, but the next consistently signficant one has been Wisconsin in early April. After this, primaries take their character from the nature of the rival contenders, although Nebraska, another state with a long history of primary operations but a comparatively conservative population, can attract notice. The primary season winds up in late May in Oregon and in early June in California. The Oregon primary is one of the nation's most democratic. It forces all legitimate candidates (as determined by state officials) to appear on the ballot. It is, however, a state with an independent and unpredictable electorate and, consequently, a primary that—after Goldwater's loss in 1964 and Robert Kennedy's in 1968—appears to be losing favor. In part, Oregon's eclipse is due to the overwhelming importance (until 1972) of California's large convention delegation. The California primary takes place immediately after Oregon's, and although it occurs on the same day as three others, it is of *nonpareil* eminence.

Seventeen states as of 1972 had "closed" primaries in which party members only can participate (with membership determined by a wide variety of tests from statements of affiliation to proof of earlier party registration); two (Wisconsin and Michigan) are "open" (that is, any eligible voter can participate); and two others (Indiana and Illinois) are "quasi-open." Indiana considers itself to have a closed primary (restricted to only those who voted for a majority of the candidates of the party), but since the state has no registration by party, the provision is virtually unenforceable. Illinois is open but much against its own wishes. The state had the most stringently controlled primary in the nation—an individual had to register with a party 23 months prior to the election—before the courts threw out the qualification as excessively restrictive.

The 11 states that authorize some form of binding delegate selection provide that the convention votes won be committed to the candidates for one to three ballots (depending on the state) unless released by the candidates or unless their support falls below a certain proportion of the total convention vote (20 to 35 percent). Presidential contenders normally appear on the ballot in a state primary through some type of petition requirement submitted to the proper state official (although, of course, the number of signatures required, the period during which they may be obtained, and the closing date for their submission as well as the standards of validity, if challenged, vary substantially from one state to the next).

To complicate matters further, a small number of states allow the secretary of state's office or a state selection committee or election board to place all eligible candidates on the ballot (a variation of the Oregon practice). The intention is to permit the state's electorate to choose from among all the bona fide contenders rather than be restricted to the few who, of their own volition, choose to enter the contest. The decision to avoid given states is thus taken away from a candidate's strategists. Once declared eligible to appear on the ballot, in order to remove their names from consideration, candidates have to file a public affidavit to the effect that they are not and do not intend to run for their parties' nomination. It takes little imagination to realize that this welter of dates and qualification criteria is open to all forms of political intrigue as potential nominees attempt to capture even the slightest advantage over their rivals.

To compound matters, in at least six states the presidential candidates are *not* given the power to approve or void petitions put forth to place them on the ballot. Although they may prefer not to run in a given state, overzealous supporters (or enemies attempting to embarrass them) may proceed to enter their names, and candidates are powerless to stop them. In another handful of states, delegates can offer themselves on behalf of candidates *without* their approval. This means that individuals who support a presidential contender with little chance of electoral success in the primary can offer themselves as delegates committed to the most popular candidate locally. If they win, and while attending the national convention ostensibly as representatives of their declared candidate, they can work on behalf of the causes or candidates they truly support. A variation of this process results in the party's (as in Michigan) appointing the actual delegates after the presidential contender has won the primary. With potential nominees unable to force selection of their own people, there is no telling who will appear at the national convention ostensibly as their representatives.

Most of the nonmandatory primary states permit candidates to withdraw their names from the ballot should they choose to do so due to resource limitations, a change in the political climate, or the like, but again the variability in dates of notification, from early January and the first week in February to sometime in May, is enormous.

Write-in votes are permitted in some form in 15 states. This allows dissatisfied voters to insert their first choice on the ballot and have it counted. It also encourages some candidates to run modestly financed write-in campaigns to spur voters to put their name on the ballot. Usually, the presidential contender disclaims any connection with the informal campaign. The objective is to demonstrate unexpected strength in a state or to politically hurt (through a good showing) a rival who has gone through the tedious process of officially qualifying for the primary and mounting a personally taxing and costly campaign effort. The "unauthorized" write-in campaign costs less and, in addition, loses its sponsor nothing by a poor showing.

Most states also require qualifying fees from candidates entering its primary and from delegates seeking election. At times, these fees can be prohibitive. In addition, a number of state parties obligate delegates to make an unofficial but nonetheless mandatory contribution to the party coffers[43]. The financial drain on a candidate can be great.

A MULTITIERED PROCESS

To add diversity to a system that does not need it, the presidential contender's campaign is only the most visible aspect of the primary effort. It can also be one of the least important, curiously, in determining the commitment of the national convention delegations in many states. Every state divides its convention votes (the actual number is assigned to the state party by its national committee) among at-large and district (usually congressional) units (Table 7.3). Then the process of delegate certification (who is eligible to seek the position) and choice (who is actually selected to represent the state party at the national convention) is subdivided by state and the type of delegate position being decided (at-large or district).

The operation begins at the lowest level. A precinct, town, city, or county committee (caucus, convention, or primary) selects delegates or nominees for delegate posts, certifies their eligibility, and, when appropriate, places them before the party's electorate. Delegates (or contenders for these positions) selected at one

TABLE 7.3
AT-LARGE AND DISTRICT
METHODS OF DELEGATE SELECTION (1972)

Method of Selecting At-Large Delegates	No. of States Employing Method	
	Democrats	Republicans
Primary	9	12
Convention	29	33
Committee	11	5
National delegate caucus	7	0
Other	2[a]	1[b]
No. at-large delegates	3	0
Method of Selecting District Delegates	Democrats	Republicans
Primary	16[c]	16[d]
District convention	23	20
State convention	5	7
State-level committee	0	1
None	7	7

[a] In Florida and Pennsylvania, the state committee and a national delegate caucus each select a portion of the at-large delegates.

[b] All delegates are selected in district-level delegate selection primaries in Nebraska; some of these delegates are later designated "at-large" by the state convention.

[c] Includes Florida and Wisconsin, where district delegates are selected at preprimary or postprimary open caucuses of a presidential candidate's supporters.

[d] Includes Florida and Wisconsin, where district delegates are selected at a postprimary state-level committee meeting.

SOURCE: National Municipal League, *Presidential Nominating Procedures* (New York: National Municipal League, 1974). pp. 10–11.

level then attend the next highest party gathering where they go through a broadly related series of steps before proceeding to the final selection stage (in a nonprimary state, the state-level convention or committee with the appropriate authority). Table 7.4, to the extent that it is possible, groups the states by type of delegate selection procedures. It serves to reemphasize the individuality of the states in devising procedures attuned to their own political conditions and in response to their historical exigencies.

Finally, and significantly for those desiring change, the methods instituted in each of the states for delegate selection to the national conventions are the by-products of a confusing jumble of governmental and party pressures. State statutes (on occasion, specifications within a state's constitution), and local ordinances, Democratic and Republican state (and lower-level) party rules, and the provisions contained within the "call" issued by the national committees of both parties (usually just prior to or at the beginning of the presidential election year) all influence and help structure the process. The overlapping jurisdictions and the variety of forces that act on these procedures make change all the more difficult.

The number of primaries and the cost of running in them command a major share of the time and budget of presidential candidates inclined to take this increasingly inescapable route to their parties' nomination. The rules governing the operation of primaries are complex. The variety of conditions facing a prospective presidential contender are demanding to the point of deterring participation by major candidates in the majority of these contests. Peculiarly, a front-runner may have the least to gain from entering a large number of primary tests. To the extent that a candidate can win the primary election and still not capture the votes of a state's convention delegation, the outcome represents a perversion of the intentions of the original sponsors as well as of the primary system itself. As long as the individual state and party rules vary to such an exaggerated degree, participation by the number and quality of candiates needed to insure that these constitute a formidable influence in selecting the ultimate presidential nominees is further discouraged. As a consequence, many feel that significant reform of the primary system is urgently needed.

THE NONPRIMARY STATES

Primaries are but one aspect, indisputably the most publicized, however, of the presidential nominating process at the state level. An overview of the *entire* system will provide the broad perspective necessary to evaluate the multitude of reform proposals.

The process is, predictably, ensnarled in local traditions and state practices to the point that generalizations concerning its operations are often difficult to make. As Table 7.4 shows, 21 state parties rely principally on the primary method to choose national convention delegates. This represents but one-third of the 63 state parties (counting the District of Columbia, a total of 102 Republican and

TABLE 7.4
CLASSIFICATION OF
DELEGATE SELECTION PROCEDURES IN 1972

Category I: All Delegates Selected by Primary

Alabama (Republicans)	New Hampshire	Rhode Island
California (Republicans)	New Jersey	South Dakota
District of Columbia (Democrats)	Ohio	West Virginia
Massachusetts	Oregon	Wisconsin (Republicans)[b]
Nebraska (Republicans)[a]		

Category II: All Delegates Selected through Convention System

Alaska	Kansas	North Carolina
Arizona	Kentucky	North Dakota
Arkansas (Democrats)	Louisiana (Republicans)	Oklahoma
Colorado	Maine	South Carolina
Connecticut	Michigan	Tennessee
Delaware	Minnesota	Texas
Georgia (Republicans)	Mississippi	Utah
Hawaii	Missouri	Vermont
Idaho	Montana	Virginia
Indiana	Nevada	Washington
Iowa	New Mexico	Wyoming

Category III: All Delegates Selected by Committee

Arkansas (Republicans)   District of Columbia (Republicans)

Category IV: Delegates Chosen by Combination of Methods

Alabama (Democrats): district, primary; at-large, national delegate caucus
California (Democrats): district, primary; at-large, national delegate caucus
Florida (Democrats): district, primary; at-large, state committee and national delegate caucus
Florida (Republicans): 90% by Committee to Re-Elect the President; 10% by state committee
Georgia (Democrats): district, district convention; at-large, national delegate caucus
Illinois (Democrats): district, primary; at-large, national delegate caucus
Illinois (Republicans): district, primary; at-large, state convention
Louisiana (Democrats): district, district convention; at-large, national delegate caucus
Maryland (Democrats): district, primary; at-large, national delegate caucus
Maryland (Republicans): district, primary; at-large, state committee
Nebraska (Democrats): district, primary; at-large, national committeeman and committee-woman selected at state convention
New York: district, primary; at-large, state committee
Pennsylvania (Democrats): district, primary; at-large, state committee and national delegate caucus
Pennsylvania (Republicans): district, primary; at-large, state committee
Wisconsin (Democrats): district, primary; at-large, national delegate caucus

---

[a] At-large delegates designated from among the district delegates at the state convention.
[b] Delegates selected by state committee in consultation with the Committee to Re-Elect the President at a postprimary meeting.
SOURCE: National Municipal League, *Presidential Nominating Procedures* (New York: National Municipal League, 1974), pp. 11–12.

Democratic parties) that rely exclusively on conventions to choose delegates. Two other Republican state parties (Arkansas and the District of Columbia) employ the committee system to name national convention delegates, possibly the most restricted (to broad-scale influence by party rank and file) of any of the methods available to the parties. Sixteen additional parties at the state level employ varying combinations of possibilities at different stages to nominate delegates directly to the national conference (including, it should be noted, leaving the choice to the presidential candidate's national committee).

Any attempt to regulate the primaries ignores the fact that the changes, even if adopted, would not affect a considerable portion of the state nominating systems and would have only a partial impact on another 16 of them. Such an approach does have the weight of tradition, however. State statutes have been far more aggressive in detailing regulations for the highly visible primary elections than they have been for the operations of party conventions or committees systems. While operating beyond the glare of media exposure, these latter agencies play a far more significant role in selecting the ultimate national convention delegations.

A second point should also be considered. The primaries are often criticized for their unrepresentative voting populations and their low turnouts, reactions in large part (as has been indicated) to the idealized (if unrealistic) expectations of their founders. While it is true that participation in the primaries is often disappointingly low, very little attention has been directed to the other aspect of the problem, the number of people who are involved in delegate selection and presidential nominating politics in the nonprimary states. By any measure of the total number of people involved, participation in presidential nomination processes constitutes an elitist operation. Proportionately few people are directly involved with deciding among the prospective nominees, long considered the most vital step in determining the ultimate caliber and policies of the eventual winner.

Table 7.5 illustrates the contention. It also reveals the different levels of voter involvement for different types of nomination procedures. The table employs turnout estimates for the 35 states and the District of Columbia for which figures were available or for which reasonable approximations could be made. In the table, "caucus" is used as a shorthand notation for nonprimary systems (that is, convention and committee approaches to delegate selection).

The table nicely demonstrates several points. First, and most significantly, the primaries do attract participants in far greater numbers than do the alternative systems. Fifty-nine percent of the eligible Democratic population (*if* this can serve as a base figure) vote in the primaries compared with a meager 6 percent who become involved in the nonprimary states. Crossover voting is a factor in many states and, as a consequence, the exciting and competitive nomination races which the Democrats offered in 1972 swell the totals through the inclusion of independents and Republicans. Wisconsin and Tennessee illustrate the nature of the problem. Both states had more than 100 percent of their estimated Demo-

TABLE 7.5
ESTIMATED DEMOCRATIC VOTER
PARTICIPATION IN THE 1972 PRESIDENTIAL
SELECTION PROCESS, BY STATE

State[a]	No. of Eligible Democratic Voters[b]	Source of Figure for Eligible Democratic Voters	No. of Participants[c]	Type of Delegate Selection Process	Date of Primary or Caucus[d]	Source of Figure for No. of Participants	Participants as % of Eligible Democratic Voters	Comments[e]
Alaska	32,540	Registered Democratic voters 12/70—secretary of state	4,000	Caucus	Spring 1972	DNC	12%	
Arizona	395,656	Average of registered Democratic voters 1970 & 1972—secretary of state	37,000	Caucus	Began January 1972	DNC	9%	
California	5,134,176	Registered Democratic voters 6/72—secretary of state	3,546,518	Primary	June 6, 1972	Secretary of state	69%	Primary of key national importance
District of Columbia	207,537	Registered Democratic voters 5/72—election board	29,658	Primary	May 2, 1972	Election board	14%	
Florida	2,133,310	Registered Democratic voters 2/72—secretary of state	1,264,544	Primary	March 14, 1972	Secretary of state	59%	Busing referendum Wallace candidacy
Georgia	409,321	Average of Democratic presidential vote 1960–72 — CDM	20,000	Caucus	March–May 1972	DNC	5%	

TABLE 7.5 *(Continued)*

State[a]	No. of Eligible Democratic Voters[b]	Source of Figure for Eligible Democratic Voters	No. of Participants[c]	Type of Delegate Selection Process	Date of Primary or Caucus[d]	Source of Figure for No. of Participants	Participants as % of Eligible Democratic Voters	Comments[e]
Illinois	2,220,090	Average of registered Democratic voters 1970 & 1972—secretary of state	1,214,839	Primary	March 21, 1972	Secretary of state	54%	Crossover possibility
Indiana	908,267	Average of Democratic presidential vote 1960–72 — CDM	751,460	Primary	May 2, 1972	Secretary of state	83%	Wallace candidacy Crossover possibility
Iowa	233,702	Average of registered Democratic voters 1970 & 1972 secretary of state	35,000	Caucus	Began January 1972	DNC	15%	
Louisiana	1,624,273	Registered Democratic voters 3/72—secretary of state	15,000	Caucus	Spring 1972	DNC	1%	
Maine	190,831	Registered Democratic voters 6/72—secretary of state	10,000	Caucus	March 19–25, 1972	DNC	5%	
Maryland	1,163,579	Registered Democratic voters 2/72—secretary of state	568,131	Primary	May 16, 1972	Secretary of state	49%	Wallace candidacy
Massachusetts	1,184,623	Registered Democratic voters 4/72—secretary of state	617,756	Primary	April 25, 1972	Secretary of state	52%	

State								
Michigan	1,720,936	Average of Democratic presidential vote 1960–72 — CDM	1,588,072	Primary	May 16, 1972	Secretary of state	92%	Wallace candidacy Crossover possibility
Minnesota	854,430	Average of Democratic presidential vote 1960–72 — CDM	85,000	Caucus	Began February 22, 1972	DNC	10%	
Mississippi	138,403	Average of Democratic presidential vote 1960–72 — CDM	20,000	Caucus	January 7 to February 3, 1972	DNC	14%	
Nebraska	321,612	Registered Democratic voters 4/72—secretary of state	192,137	Primary	May 9, 1972	Secretary of state	60%	
Nevada	120,446	Registered Democratic voters 8/72—secretary of state	4,000	Caucus	February 7–13, 1972	DNC	3%	
New Hampshire	128,229	Registered Democratic voters 3/72—secretary of state	88,855	Primary	March 7, 1972	Secretary of state	69%	
New Jersey	1,384,333	Average of Democratic presidential vote 1960–72 — CDM	76,834	Primary	June 6, 1972	Secretary of state	6%	Crossover possibility
New Mexico	265,491	Registered Democratic voters 4/72—secretary of state	153,293	Primary	June 6, 1972	Secretary of state	58%	
New York	3,666,301	Registered Democratic voters Fall 1971—secretary of state	approx. 732,640	Primary	June 20, 1972	New York Times & others	20%	Candidates not identified by presidential preference

TABLE 7.5 *(Continued)*

State[a]	No. of Eligible Democratic Voters[b]	Source of Figure for Eligible Democratic Voters	No. of Participants[c]	Type of Delegate Selection Process	Date of Primary or Caucus[d]	Source of Figure for No. of Participants	Participants as % of Eligible Democratic Voters	Comments[e]
North Carolina	1,642,603	Registered Democratic voters 4/72—secretary of state	821,410	Primary	May 6, 1972	Secretary of state	50%	Wallace candidacy
Ohio	1,916,720	Average of Democratic presidential vote 1960–72 — CDM	1,212,330	Primary	May 2, 1972	Secretary of state	63%	Crossover possibility
Oregon	656,572	Registered Democratic voters 5/72—secretary of state	408,026	Primary	May 23, 1972	Secretary of state	62%	
Pennsylvania	2,790,627	Registered Democratic voters 4/72—secretary of state	1,374,839	Primary	April 25, 1972	Secretary of state	49%	
Rhode Island	251,966	Average of Democratic presidential vote 1960–72 — CDM	37,864	Primary	May 23, 1972	Secretary of state	15%	Crossover possibility
South Dakota	146,075	Average of Registered Democratic voters 1970 & 1972 — secretary of state	28,017	Primary	June 6, 1972	Secretary of state	19%	
Tennessee	455,894	Average of Democratic presidential vote 1960–72 — CDM	492,721	Primary	May 4, 1972	Secretary of state	100+%	Wallace candidacy Crossover possibility

State	Figure[b]	Basis	Number	Type	Date[d]	Source	%	Notes[e]
Vermont	78,901	Average of Democratic presidential vote 1960–72 — CDM	2,500	Caucus	Began April 1972	DNC	3%	
Virginia	357,597	Average of Democratic presidential vote 1960–72 — CDM	20,000	Caucus	Began April 1972	DNC	6%	
Washington	617,647	Average of Democratic presidential vote 1960–72 — CDM	75,000	Caucus	Began March 1972	DNC	12%	
West Virginia	673,920	Registered Democratic voters 5/72—secretary of state	368,464	Primary	May 9, 1972	Secretary of state	55%	Wallace candidacy
Wyoming	55,552	Registered Democratic voters 3/72— secretary of state	1,200	Caucus	Began March 1972	DNC	2%	
Wisconsin	858,937	Average of Democratic presidential vote 1960–72 — CDM	1,128,584	Primary	April 4, 1972	Secretary of state	100+%	Crossover possibility Wallace candidacy

[a] Figures for 16 states are unavailable either because there were no voter registration requirements, there was no party enrollment, or inadequate records were kept.

[b] This figure is based on either the number of Democrats registered at the time of the delegate selection process or on the average number of Democratic voters compiled by CDM from the 1960, 1964, 1968, and 1972 official presidential election results.

[c] For the sake of simplification, the many complicated delegate selection processes have been divided into two basic categories, primary and caucus systems.

[d] This date marks either the date of the primary or caucus which began the delegate selection process.

[e] This column reflects specific situations that may have influenced voter turnout or caucus participation.

SOURCE: Compiled by the Coalition for a Democratic Majority from the sources cited in the table.

cratic strength participating (a reasonable but not necessarily accurate measure)[44]. The lesson seems to be that when people are offered the opportunity to become involved in something meaningful, they will participate.

It also would seem that primaries recognized as important, such as California's, attract large numbers of voters—a contention long made by the party leaders of that state in their efforts (within the Democratic party) to retain the winner-take-all principle. Candidates who speak to and excite a specific constituency can also stimulate turnout. The rates of participation for primaries in which Governor George Wallace ran appear to bear this out. Michigan Indiana, Florida, North Carolina, and West Virginia, as well as Wisconsin and Tennessee, could boast of representative to extraordinarily high levels of participation (allowing for the crudeness of the measure). Finally in this regard, crossover voting does permit people not associated with the party to become involved in determining its presidential candidates. The indicators are oblique but the pattern is clear. The Republican primaries offered no attraction. An incumbent president, firmly in control of his party, was seeking renomination and, with the exception of the weak and unpopular campaigns of Congressmen Paul McCloskey on the left and John Ashbrook on the right, he faced no opposition. The Democratic field was open to all comers and the nomination was there to be captured. Given the opportunity, independents and Republicans appear to have turned out for the Democratic primaries.

Overall, rates of participation varied from lows in the teens (the District of Columbia, Rhode Island, and South Dakota) to turnouts of one-half to two-thirds (comparable to general election results) to abnormally high representations. For all their faults, the primaries do immeasurably better than the convention and committee systems in allowing people a direct influence in deciding the presidential nominee. Almost 17 million people (16,715,000) voted in the Democratic primaries. A fraction of the primary total (328,700) participated in delegate selection in the 13 nonprimary states[45]. Only five caucus states involved 10 percent or more of their Democratic base figures (no matter how calculated or lenient the regulations ascertaining party membership) and none exceeded 20 percent. The average level of voter turnout was 6 percent, about one-tenth that of the primaries. If popular involvement is the objective of reformers, and to a large extent it is, then primaries quite clearly appear to be the best mechanism available.

REFORM OF PRESIDENTIAL
NOMINATING PROCEDURES

There are essentially two categories of reform advocated for presidential nominating procedures. The first, a national primary, would effectively scrap in toto the systems now in effect. The second is a combination of proposals to standardize especially primary and, to a far lesser degree, nonprimary nominations.

THE NATIONAL PRIMARY   The national primary concept is not new. It began with the Progressives, especially Teddy Roosevelt, and is as old as the idea of state presidential primary elections. It has been repeatedly dusted off and reintroduced. The idea finds new friends as frustration with the operations of the system in effect grows. Bills to enact a national primary have been introduced into each of the recent Congresses[46]. And public support for a national primary, measured by the periodic questions included in the Gallup and other polls, appears to be high[47].

While well intentioned, the national primary concept represents a radical alternative that could destroy what is left of the party system. The elections would resemble nonpartisan contests and southern primaries with all their attendant ills: low turnout, a confused voting public, little policy coherence, a tendency toward emphasizing demagogic and personal excesses, a lack of accountability by office-holders to organized party electorates, an undue emphasis on media influence, high personal expenses, and disorganized public relations-type campaigns. Party supporters would probably have less direct say in deciding their parties' nominee in a national primary system designed to award them such power than they do at present. Most proposals contain the proviso that if the primary winner does not attain a certain proportion of the vote (40 to 50 percent), a runoff election would follow within a month.

For some curious reason (actually a desire to reduce the campaign period), the national primary would be scheduled (in those bills that specified the date) during the last week in August or at the end of the first week in September, presumably just after the Labor Day holiday. The timing could not be worse for political interest would be at its lowest at the end of the summer and voter turnout, more than likely, would be extremely low. Also, given the greater number of entries in the field, voters would be less likely to understand their relative merits and policy positions.

The probability is high also that this lottery form of party nomination would result in one or two candidates with the *least* appeal qualifying for the runoff. To illustrate, the party center and, for the Democrats, moderate left and, for the Republicans, moderate right are likely to be represented by the majority of presidential contenders, making it difficult for the electors to choose among them. Thus, the center's vote—that representing the balance of party members—would be split. Candidates who could assure themselves of a strong individual identity, compared with the party image of the centrist candidates, and with a fair degree of electoral support could do well. This means that a regional candidate or the representative of a factional or ideological extreme within the party could perform relatively well. A vehicle intended to further democratize nominations then would have the adverse effect. It could attract a small and unrepresentative turnout and it could narrow the choice of contenders to those representing the extremes of the party coalition. The eventual nominee would then, conceivably, have an unfortunately narrow base of electoral support.

The bills on this subject presently pending before the Congress have the effect of institutionalizing the present party system at the very time the two major parties are being called upon to legitimize their existence. For example, the proposals would limit competition for the nomination to only bona fide party loyalists and several would prohibit any party that did not receive a minimum of 10 percent of the vote in the *previous* presidential election from holding a national primary[48]. The effect could be to introduce an element of rigidity into the system that is not now present. At least one proposal would establish a national commission to set standards for primary contenders. The commission would have the power to rule individuals off the national ballot. Such an unfortunate precedent could open party nominations to gross official misconduct and, similar to many other well-intended ideas, could actually work to weaken the operations of the democratic system.

And finally, the argument that a national primary would decrease campaigning is difficult to sustain. All of the contenders would still have to make the financial and physical effort necessary to reach voters in all of the states prior to the national primary. What order there is now in the combination of systems, insufficient as it may be, would be lost. Also, a successful candidate for the presidency would actually have to run *three* national races (assuming a runoff) within a period of approximately 10 weeks.

The contemporary mix of primary, state convention, and committee systems with their various hybrids permits a flexibility in seeking the nomination that has enormous advantages. Winning candidates must perform well in a variety of political environments. They must demonstrate an appeal to the party's electorate as well as an ability to work with state and local elective officials and party officeholders. Their abilities and personal skills are constantly being tested. Yet the mixed system allows for organized dissent to develop and for insurgent and minor candidates to test their strength. If the dissatisfaction proves to be widespread or if a dark horse demonstrates personal appeal and political acumen, the results can directly influence the final nomination.

The present system is not perfect. Yet it does provide a set of political hurdles similar to the problems a president eventually must master in building a coalition to support his policies. The system is flexible and it is sensitive to new influences. It does give the parties at the state level a role in the nominating process and it can be used as a vehicle through which these can be strengthened and reformed rather than liquidated. Anything that serves to destroy what could be considered the nation's largest and most representative public interest groups should be avoided. The mixed system, for all its faults, is far superior to the proposed alternative of a national primary. Reform efforts would be better spent, first, on insuring that the number of statewide primaries do not exceed roughly one-half of the total state systems. Anything approaching a total reliance on primaries would seriously compromise the advantages claimed for the hybrid nominating operations now in favor. Secondly, reform energy would be better expended on opening to rank-and-file control more of the nonprimary nominating procedures and, more broadly, coordinating and simplifying the complex regulations that now so thoroughly confuse operations at the state level. It is to this last area that attention now shifts.

STANDARDIZING NOMINATING PROCESSES There are a number of proposals that attempt to rationalize present nominating procedures through some form of federal intervention. A broad view of the problems as seen from Washington was given by Congressman Morris Udall, the author of one of the more reasonable legislative proposals and, not coincidentally, an aspirant for his party's nomination in 1976. Udall's succinct illustration of the problems faced in the primaries allows a view of these devices from the perspective of the would-be candidate.

> Lacking uniform rules and procedures, the primaries are not a reasonable yardstick of a candidate's potential support in a general election.
>
> Depending on where he or she chooses to run, the candidate may be a contestant in a beauty contest meeting all others head-on; in an election in which delegates pledged to a candidate are selected; or in a primary that blends both approaches. If the rules vary, so do the prizes. A victory in Illinois does not guarantee the candidate one delegate; 51 per cent in Florida could theoretically yield little convention support if the candidate does not win a majority in each of the State's congressional districts; a plurality in Indiana will assure him of the backing of that State's delegates for one ballot; a similar showing in Oregon will lock in delegates until victory or the bitter end. A candidate who can do well in New Hampshire or Wisconsin, but is unknown elsewhere, may want to dodge primaries on the west coast. Yet he may be listed on the Oregon ballot anyway, particularly if he is a promising Democrat and the controlling State official a Republican, or vice versa. . . .
>
> A candidate's future is in the hands of a hodgepodge of laws, regulations, and faceless officials over whom he has no control or recourse[49].

The argument is well put. Udall concluded, as have so many others, that "the primary trail is too long, too expensive, too unrewarding[50]."

The congressman suggested three criteria against which to measure objectives for incipient reforms:

> One, establish reasonable perimeters within which a meaningful battle can take place (i.e., limit the primary season but not to a "sudden death" national primary). Second, assume that contests will be held between the major candidates and held in a way that rules out [a] major distortion of the results. And
>
> Third, equalize the risks, and insure that a successful effort will be rewarded with an appropriate prize (e.g., committed delegate votes)[51].

The presentation is thoughtful as is the congressman's proposed National Primary Act. It provides a standard against which a number of the legislative proposals can be assessed.

The Udall bill recommends, in perhaps its most distinctive feature, a limitation of primaries to three dates: one set during the first week of April, a second in the third week in May, and the last occurring in the final week of June. Others have advocated similar restrictions. Some propose primary elections only during July or in the 30 days prior to the party's national convention. Yet another bill that has received national attention would prohibit any congressional primaries (presumably thus mounting pressure for others to be held at the same date) before the first week in August and it would force the national parties to hold their conventions during the third week in August.

The objective, of course, is clear. The potential effect of these proposals, however, should be carefully weighed. Who benefits from late primaries? Who gains if, in any way, the primary season can be delimited, regardless of the specific device proposed? Who has the most to lose in prenomination and general election campaigns that are restricted to a certain number of weeks or months? Quite clearly, the incumbent (regardless of office) profits the most from such seemingly harmless proposals. The advantages of incumbents, which are enormous, would be further accentuated Competition would be decreased and the results could be quite harmful. A president has four years of public exposure, a U.S. senator six. Potential opponents need all the time they can command to attract attention to themselves, their views, and their candidacies.

Most of the congressional bills also contain provisions for a type of election or primary committee to certify candidates to compete in these elections and to enforce common standards of procedural operation. Most would require delegates to attend the national conventions committed to whomever won their vote in the primary. The bills also confine participation to the major parties through qualification rules of varying degrees of severity (for example., candidates of parties that received 10 percent of the vote or 10 million votes in the previous presidential election). There are also measures to reimburse the *states* for their expenditures in primary elections, a provision that would undoubtedly encourage states to adopt this method of delegate selection.

Each of these plans, in varying degrees, is open to the type of objections directed against the national primary. Regardless of intention, they would insinuate the federal government into a process that despite its serious faults is best left to the states. The tone of the bills indicates that eventually little of consequence would be left to the discretion of the states or the national parties. The sorry record of the nonpartisan regulatory commission, with which the operation of the national primary committee can be fairly compared, would indicate that avoiding devices of this nature would in itself be enlightening. These preliminary congressional programs which begin to deal with the difficulties in presidential nominations, tend to introduce more problems of a serious nature than now exist. The present system is preferable to what is likely to evolve from a national specification of rules for nominating operations no matter how benevolent the goal of its creators.

The most interesting of the contemporary projections, and the one that has received the most favorable attention, is the plan for a series of step-wise *regional primaries.* The idea, as originally introduced by Senator Bob Packwood (R., Ore.), would allow five regional primaries to be held between the first week in March and the first week in July[52]. The states would be grouped in clusters roughly corresponding to the following geographical areas: the Northeast (10 states, though no state would be forced to hold a primary); the Midwest (6 states); the South (9 states, the District of Columbia and 3 territories); the Plains states (a group of 12 stretching from Canada to the Gulf); and the Far West (13 states and 1 territory). The order of primaries would be determined by lot by a national primary committee and all eligible candidates (as determined by the committee) would be placed on the ballot and, as in Oregon and other states, would have to file an affidavit of noncandidacy to be excused from the election. There is a bias toward the status quo in the qualifying provisions, but candidates other than those of the major parties with a small amount of funding or a good degree of organization could qualify—although, of course, the arbiter of the rules in this case would be the national commission.

The regional primary plan appears to have a sense of order and precision when first considered. When weighed more carefully against the present arrangement, it may not be as radical *nor* as simplifying a proposal as it appears. The primary season would still be long and expensive and there is no particular economic or poltical logic to the regional groupings beyond a degree of convenience that also may be illusionary. The major departures in the program are the now familiar effort to centralize real power in a presidentially appointed, congressionally approved national body. The introduction of such a powerful governmental agency acting as a certification body and administrative vehicle is an enormous and unprecedented departure in American nominating politics.

If the welter of broadly similar proposals pending before the Congress is unacceptable, what then can be done to improve presidential nominating procedures? First, the entire system should be left, as it is now, in the hands of the states and the national parties. With this as an operating principle, a number of suggestions can be offered:

1. Primaries should be closed, but regulations concerning party membership should be lenient (for example, 15 to 30 days prior to registration) to encourage a high voter turnout and to nullify crossover voting.

2. Presidential preference votes and the selection of national convention delegates should be combined (in effect, a discarding of the irrelevent "beauty contest" primaries).

3. Presidential contenders above a certain base (10 percent of the primary vote) should receive their proportionate share of the state's national convention delegation unless they win a majority (which allows for a bit of drama and corresponds to the criterion of success for most elections), in which case they would receive all of the state convention's vote (a displacement—to an extent—of the already embattled winner-take-all primary)[53].

4. Delegates should be committed to supporting the candidate who wins their votes in the primary (the precise specifications, as they are now, can be left to the states).

5. Delegates could not offer themselves on behalf of presidential contenders without their written approval.

6. A prospective delegate or slate of delegates should have their candidate affiliation or their "uncommitted" status printed on the ballot.

7. Presidential candidate and delegate qualification fees and petition requirements should be uniform (identical standards applied to both the representatives of the major parties and those not so affiliated) and they should be reasonably lenient.

8. The federal government should pay the primary costs of the presidential contenders after they demonstrate a certain basis of support (as now provided in federal law) but should *not* reimburse the states for their primary or nonprimary election expenditures.

CONCLUSION

Hubert Humphrey, who is emminently qualified to speak on the issue, has called the primary road to presidential nominations "politically, financially, spiritually and physically debilitating." Undoubtedly, it is. The orchestration of requirements, political demands, publicity, resources, and the like severely challenges even the most adept of campaigners (as Humphrey's experience in this regard would indicate). There is a movement for reform and undoubtedly change of some nature is coming. Much remains to be done to rationalize and simplify the procedures *without fundamentally changing their basic character.* The reform pressure should be brought to bear on the states, as the national parties (see Chapter 8) have begun to do. Such a strategy for reform is bound to be slow, piecemeal, and, without doubt, unsatisfactory to some. The disillusionment it may foster should be balanced by the knowledge that the present difficulties are tolerable. The greatest concern in this area, quite unlike the others discussed in this book, is to protect against the introduction of a federal presence in a system traditionally left to the states. The potential harm that could be done in the name of reform is enormous. Inviting federal regulation of state nominating procedures could initiate a regimentation in approach and control over state procedures that eventually could have the most unfortunate of consequences.

NOTES

1. George D. Luetscher, *Early Political Machinery in the United States* (New York: De Capo Press, 1903, reprinted 1971), p. 71.

2. See Willis D. Hawley, *Nonpartisan Elections and the Case for Party Politics* (New York: John Wiley & Sons, 1973), Eugene Lee, *The Politics of Nonpartisanship* (Berkeley: University of California Press, 1960), and Charles Adrian, "Some General Characteristics of Nonpartisan Elections," *American Political Science Review* 46 (September, 1952): 766–76.

3. Edward McChesney Sait, *American Parties and Elections* (New York: Century, 1927), p. 238

4. Luetscher, *Early Political Machinery* p. 65.

5. Ibid., pp. 63–64.

6. Ibid., p. 65.

7. Ibid., p. 69.

8. Joseph Charles, *The Origins of the American Party System* (New York: Harper & Row Torchbooks, 1961), p. 6. This book is a particularly good discussion of the differences that set the stage for the development of the two-party system and the men who played a principal role in this creative exercise. For an incisive analysis of the same period, see also Richard Hofstadter, *The Idea of a Party System* (Berkeley: University of California Press, 1969).

9. See Section VI (Selections 53 to 61) on "The National Nominating Caucus" in Noble E. Cunningham, Jr., ed., *The Making of the American Party System 1789 to 1809* (Englewood Cliffs, N.J.: Prentice-Hall, 1965), pp. 123–32.

10. Sait, *Parties and Elections* pp. 241–42.

11. M. Ostrogorski, *Democracy and the Organization of Political Parties,* vol. 2, *The United States,* ed. and abrdg. by S. M. Lipset (Garden City, N.Y.: Doubleday Anchor, 1964), p. 22.

12. Luetscher, *Early Political Machinery* p. 151.

13. See Richard C. Bain and Judith H. Parris, *Convention Decisions and Voting Records,* 2d ed. (Washington: The Brookings Institution, 1973) and Paul T. David, Ralph M. Goldman, and Richard C. Bain, *The Politics of National Party Conventions* (Washington: The Brookings Institution, 1960).

14. Luetscher, *Early Political Machinery* p. 75.

15. Sait, *Parties and Elections* pp. 242–60, Luetscher, *Early Political Machinery* p. 117, and Charles E. Merriam and Louise Overacker, *Primary Elections* (Chicago: University of Chicago Press, 1928), pp. 1–2.

16. Ostrogorski, *Democracy and Political Parties* p. 40.

17. Ibid., p. 89.

18. Ibid., p. 53.

19. Ibid., p. 143.

20. Merriam and Overacker, *Primary Elections* p. 5.

21. From R. M. Easley, "The Sine-qua-non of Caucus Reform," *American Political Science Review* 16 (1897): 322–24 and reported in E. M. Sait, *American Parties and Elections,* 3d ed. (New York: Century, 1942), p. 243.

22. Easley, "The Sine-qua-non of Caucus Reform."

23. Sait, *Parties and Elections,* 3d ed., p. 341.

24. For an assessment of the strengths of the convention system, see Herbert McClosky, "National Conventions versus a National Presidential Primary—Fact, Fiction, and Realities," *New York Times Magazine* (July-August, 1968).

25. Theodore W. Cousens, *Politics and Political Organization in America* (New York: Praeger, 1942), pp. 364–65. A good bibliography of the early works on the subject can be found in this book. For a view different from that found in Cousens from an official of the country (Crawford) concerned, see Ernest Hempstead, "Forty Years of Direct Primaries," *Primary Reform* (Ann Arbor: Publications of the Michigan Political Science Association, February 9, 10, 1905), pp. 31–54.

26. Merriam and Overacker, *Primary Elections* pp. 23–39.

27. Ibid., pp. 37–39.

28. Ibid., pp. 60–107.

29. The Republican candidate, William Howard Taft, the incumbent, finished third in the 1912 presidential race with only 23.2 percent of the vote. Woodrow Wilson, the Democrat, won with 41.8 percent and Theodore Roosevelt's Bull Moose Progressives finished second with 27.4 percent of the presidential vote.

30. Many date the Oregon primary as the beginning of presidential primaries.

31. Quoted in Louise Overacker, *The Presidential Primary* (New York: Macmillan, 1926), p. 12. This book is the most complete source for the developments of the presidential primary in its early phases. The quotation is from an Oregon newspaper that in turn quoted with obvious approval the original commentary from an Alabama newspaper on the merits of the practice when developed earlier in that state. The Oregon primary represented the first effort to institutionalize the system.

32. Ibid., p. 143.

33. Louise Overacker, "The Operation of the State-Wide Direct Primary in New York State," in *The Direct Primary*, ed. J. T. Salter, (Philadelphia: The Annals of the American Academy of Political and Social Science, 1923), p. 145.

34. Ibid., p. 146.

35. Arnold Bennett Hall, "The Direct Primary and Party Responsibility in Wisconsin," in Salter, *Direct Primary* p. 51.

36. The most influential statement of this point of view can be found in V. O. Key, Jr., *American State Politics: An Introduction* (New York: Knopf, 1956). Key's *Southern Politics* (New York: Random House Vintage Edition, 1949) represents the most penetrating analysis of primaries in one-party states. A more recent analysis of related problems is available in Austin Ranney, "Turnout and Representation in Presidential Electorates," *American Political Science Review* 66 (March, 1972): 21–37, Ranney and Leon Epstein, "The Two Electorates: Voters and Nonvoters in a Wisconsin Primary," *Journal of Politics* 28 (August, 1966): 598–616, and Ranney "The Representativeness of Primary Electorates," *Midwest Journal of Political Science* 12 (May, 1968): 224–38.

37. See Committee on Political Parties, American Political Science Association, *Toward a More Responsible Two-Party System* (New York: Rinehart, 1950). The report appeared originally as a supplement to the *American Political Science Review* 44 (September, 1950).

38. For a more recent example of the same type of criticism, see Roy Reed, "New Voter Form Stirs Mississippi," *New York Times,* August 7, 1972, p. 21.

39. Karl F. Geiser, "Defects in the Direct Primary," in Salter, *Direct Primary,* p. 39. Two more recent overviews of primary nominating systems are James W. Davis, *Presidential Primaries: Road to the White House* (New York: Crowell, 1967), and Gerald

Pomper, *Nominating the President* (Evanston, Ill.: Northwestern University Press, 1963).

40. Consult the discussion in Chapter 8.
41. Overacker, *The Presidential Primary,* pp. 137–62.
42. These developments are treated in Chapter 8.
43. See Commission on Party Structure and Delegate Selection, *Mandate for Reform* (Washington, D.C.: Democratic National Committee, 1970).
44. In both cases, the average vote for Democratic presidential nominees during the period 1960 to 1972 was used as a base rather than any the total number of registered Democratic party members.
45. The figures presumably are representative for all nonprimary states. If so, then a total of between 700,000 and 750,000 participated in delegate section in the nonprimary states, far below the estimated 16.7 million in the 22 states holding primaries.
46. Senator Mike Mansfield (D., Mont.), along with various cosponsors, introduced a bill for a national nominating primary into successive Congresses over the last three decades. For one such introduction by Mansfield and then Senator George Aikin (R., Ver.), consult the *Congressional Record–Senate,* March 13, 1972, pp. 53828–53830. See also House Joint Resolution 3, "Proposing an Amendment to the Constitution of the United States Regarding the Election of the President and Vice President and the Nomination of Candidates for the Presidency" and House Resolution 18, "To Provide for the Selection of Candidates for President of the United States in a National Presidential Primary Election, and for the Election of a President and a Vice President by Direct Vote of the People, and for Other Purposes," both introduced on January 3, 1973, by Congressman Al Ullman (Dem., Oregon).
47. For the results of one such poll, see Jack Dennis, "Trends in Public Support for the American Political Party System" (Paper delivered at the Annual Meeting of the American Political Science Association, Chicago, Ill., August 29-September 2, 1974), pp. 15–16.
48. One bill before the Congress goes so far as to limit participation in the national primaries to the two parties with a majority of members in the Congress.
49. Congressman Morris Udall, "Campaign 1972—The Year of the Rat," *Congressional Record–House,* March 20, 1972, p. H2248.
50. Ibid.
51. Ibid., p. H2249.
52. See, for an explanation, "Statements on Introduced Bills and Joint Resolutions," by Mr. Packwood (for himself and Mr. Stevens), *Congressional Record,* Proceedings of the 92d Cong., 2d sess. vol. 118, May 2, 1972, no. 70, 12 pp. (supplied by Senator Packwood's office).
53. The idea was introduced by Congressman Udall and it makes a good deal of sense. The Democratic party has come out in favor of proportional representation (see Chapter 8). Yet a majority would win any other election in the United States. Such a provision would stimulate a good deal of interest in a number of the primaries (California's, for example).

8

National
Party Structure
and Political
Representation

Emphasis on political reform predates the events of Watergate. There is no better example than the area of party structure. Reform of political operations within the Democratic party—where most of the discontent has resided and where virtually all substantial change has taken place—dates back to the National Convention that nominated Lyndon Johnson in 1964. The convention's outcome was preordained—Johnson, who had assumed the presidency less than a year earlier after the assassination of John Kennedy, would be renominated without difficulty. To stimulate interest in an otherwise predictable affair, the president attempted to create suspense over his eventual choice of a running mate. To an extent, he succeeded. Yet, there did turn out to be more to the convention than either Johnson or the media anticipated.

A totally unexpected series of challenges were initiated by problack political groups from the South directed against the closed selection processes employed in choosing several national convention delegations. The most newsworthy of these unanticipated (and from the national party's point of view, unwelcome) challenges involved the Mississippi Freedom Democratic party, in particular. The recitation of racial abuses at the midpoint in an era of a newfound civil rights awareness stimulated a good deal of publicity. Anxious to resolve the controversy as quickly as possible, the Democrats gave the blacks token representation at the convention and formally agreed to establish a committee to investigate their grievances in the convention's aftermath.

The effects of the compromise were underestimated at the time. The token representation served to acknowledge that blacks were indeed discriminated against in delegate selection. It meant that the party could, in the face of immense embarrassment to a significant element of its coalition (blacks), no longer tolerate the hands-off attitude that had so long characterized its credentials policy. Things would be different in 1968, 1972, and thereafter for segregationist white regulars from the South who did not keep their delegate selection processes open to blacks.

The committee established by the 1964 convention provided the greatest surprise of all. Approaching its work quietly and with little media attention, the Special Equal Rights Committee, as it was called, first under Governor David Lawrence of Pennsylvania and, upon his death, and for its most active period, under Governor Richard Hughes of New Jersey, set a pattern the far better known McGovern-Fraser Commission was to follow later. First, it drafted a policy statement which it awkwardly called the "six basic elements."

1. All public meetings at all levels of the Democratic Party in each State should be open to all members of the Democratic Party regardless of race, color, creed, or national origin.

2. No test for membership in, nor any oaths of loyalty to, the Democratic Party in any State should be required or used which has the effect of requiring prospective or current members of the Democratic Party to acquiesce in, condone, or support discrimination on the grounds of race, color, creed, or national origin.

3. The time and place for all public meetings of the Democratic Party on all levels should be publicized fully and in such a manner as to assure timely notice to all interested persons. Such meetings must be held in places accessible to all Party members and large enough to accommodate all interested persons.

4. The Democratic Party, on all levels, should support the broadest possible registration without discrimination on grounds of race, color, creed, or national origin.

5. The Democratic Party in each State should publicize fully and in such manner as to assure notice to all interested parties a full description of the legal and practical procedures for selection of Democratic Party Officers and representatives on all levels. Publication of these procedures should be done in such fashion that all prospective and current members of each State Democratic Party will be fully and adequately informed of the pertinent procedures in time to participate in each selection procedure at all levels of the Democratic Party organization.

6. The Democratic Party in each State should publicize fully and in such manner as to assure notice to all interested parties a complete description of the legal and practical qualifications for all officers and representatives of the State Democratic Party. Such publication should be done in timely fashion so that all prospective candidates or applicants for any elected or appointed position within each State Democratic Party will have full and adequate opportunity to compete for office[1].

Secondly, it interpreted its mandate from the 1964 convention as giving it the power to enforce its policies on all state parties. The penalty for lack of compliance would presumably be the unseating of the state's delegation to the next national convention (1968) by that convention's Credentials Committee and, if appealed to the floor, the convention's membership. Acting upon this conception of its authority, the Special Committee circulated its six basic elements to the state parties during the summer of 1967 and informed them that they *must* enforce the rules or face disbarment from the next national gathering.

The move was an extraordinarily bold one. There is some question whether a select committee can act in the name of the national party or whether it can require a state party to conform to its will. Many wondered if the convention's mandate had indeed conferred on the group this kind of authority or if it had been anticipated by the convention that gave birth to the reform committee. It was problematical, too, whether a credentials committee yet to be chosen for an upcoming national convention would feel any obligation to abide by standards promulgated by an interim committee to which it had no relationship. And finally, while there was no question of the authority of a national convention to establish and enforce criteria for its own membership, nothing as ambitious as what the (Richard) Hughes Committee proposed had ever been attempted before. Within a national party system notorious for its chaotic decentralization and lack of central direction, the seeds of revolution were being quietly sown. The problems were then legal, historical, institutional, and, most dreaded of all, highly political.

The Special Equal Rights Committee did have a number of things in its favor. There was little sympathy for an unreconstructed southern point of view on the racial question and many felt change was long overdue. Secondly, the balance of sentiment in 1964 and, as events were to show, in 1968 clearly supported the actions of the convention's unheralded reform committee. The party center from organized labor to the big-city bosses supported a set of strict ground rules in a quarrel over representation that had flared intermittently, but intensively, since at least 1948, and some would say 1936[2]. Such a consensus was not to greet the changes to be initiated after 1968, however. Thirdly, the national party signified its support of the six elements by officially incorporating them into the call for the 1968 convention issued in January of 1968. And finally, Governor Hughes was appointed chairman of the 1968 convention's Credentials Committee. No doubt existed about the party's stand or its dedication to enforcing its fair play rules.

There were, of course, some costs. On a personal level, it was rumored that Hughes's role in leading the Special Committee and later in chairing the Credentials Committee sessions that applied the guidelines cost an able and popular man whatever chance he might have had as one of several finalists for the vice-presidential nomination. The institutionalization of the new mood alienated many white southerners who traditionally cast a Democratic vote. It contributed to the changes underway in the region and helped expand within the South the appeal of third-party candidacies such as that of George Wallace in 1968. Most significantly for present purposes, and least understood at the time, it created a precedent that a far more powerful and ambitious reform group could apply later on.

THE 1968 DEMOCRATIC CONVENTION

By the time the Democrats had assembled in Chicago during a humid week in late August, the problems of southern antiblack white regulars ranked somewhere near the bottom of the convention's concerns. The preliminaries to the convention had been unusually nasty. An incumbent president, personally unpopular and in difficulty with his own party over his war policies in Viet Nam, withdrew his bid for renomination after a weak showing in the New Hampshire primary and an expected defeat in Wisconsin. An insurgent movement led at first by the seemingly quixotic senator from Minnesota, Eugene McCarthy, and then about the time Johnson was to withdraw, the more politically feared senator from New York, Robert Kennedy, made remarkable gains as the primary season wore on. As the insurgents grew in strength, many party regulars and federated labor —both of whom bitterly opposed the new movement—did all in their power to assure a convention membership that would be sympathetic to the administration's heir apparent, Vice-President Hubert Humphrey. Since the regulars controlled most of the procedures in the states for selecting the national convention delegates, their impact was substantial. It was also bitterly resented by the insurgents who, appealing mostly to political newcomers—professional people, young persons, and housewives—came to find the political selection processes arbitrarily closed to their influence.

But what was turning out to be a disastrous year for the Democrats only became worse, culminating with the frantic Chicago convention. Robert Kennedy, the insurgent candidate with the broadest party appeal and the one given a fair chance for the party's nomination, was assassinated in early June on the night of his biggest political victory in the California primary. McCarthy, effectively foreclosed from any significant role in the upcoming convention, did not appear to be a threat for the nomination. Humphrey, in turn, seemed incapable of demonstrating any independence from the Johnson foreign policies or of appealing to the considerable segment of disaffected Democrats. The vice-president was unenthusiastically supported by Johnson and his most important political representative at the convention, Governor John Connally of Texas, who, along with organized labor, took turns embarrassing Humphrey and not so subtly threatening to withdraw their support at the first sign of Humphrey's responsiveness to the growing discontent. Both sides—the party regulars and the insurgents/would-be reformers—were angry, defiant, and, for different reasons (one in power, the other wishing it), threatened. Both were determined to be heard and the party seemed hell-bent on self-destruction.

The 1968 Chicago convention was undoubtedly the ugliest and most violent either party had experienced. The chaos inside the convention hall was matched and even exceeded by the struggles outside between the demonstrators and the Chicago police, joined later by the National Guard. The brutality, the clubbings, the filthy language, the Yippie "love-ins," and the rash charges of city officials, police, insurgent leaders, and delegates, all dedicated to insuring that their point of view would prevail, were vividly carried to millions of homes through on-the-spot television coverage. All of this occurred as the troubled delegates were attempting to nominate a presidential contender supposedly to win a national election[3]. That Humphrey came so close in the final popular vote—totally unexpected until the last week to 10 days of the campaign, too late to capitalize on the tide—is probably a tribute to the lack of wide support for his opponent, Richard M. Nixon.

The convention could not be forgotten. The split within the party was deep and it lasted well past Nixon's inauguration; in fact, the recriminations from the event were to surface repeatedly during the reform movement to follow and up through the 1972 National Convention and campaign and even to the 1974 midterm convention. Before it had run its course, the Democratic coalition was to be restructured, reform was to work its will, America's participation in the Viet Nam War (the event some contend triggered the entire fight) was to become history, the Watergate scandal was to be uncovered (and, in its fashion, resolved), and Richard Nixon was to be again a private citizen (pressured to relinquish the presidency by an impeachment process well along in its deliberations) living in San Clemente, California.

But all of these events were in the future in August of 1968. The most immediate consequence of an indelible convention was the mandating, little noticed at the time, of two reform commissions; one to study and improve upon delegate selection and the other to recommend ways to codify the convention's laws and modernize its procedures. The two reform committees were, respectively, the Commission on Party Structure and Delegate Selection (the McGovern-Fraser Commission) and the Commission on Rules (the O'Hara Commission). Both were appointed in early February of 1969. From this point on, they bore little relationship to each other.

The Commission on Rules approached its duties slowly and quietly. It did become ultimately embroiled in some unnecessary party bickering, but for the most part its work was unglamorous and received little public attention. It did update and improve convention procedures, in the process spreading power a little more evenly among delegations and limiting the potentially arbitrary exercise of authority by national party leaders, the convention chairman, and whoever might control the national party bureaucracy at a given time. Perhaps its most notable contribution lay in applying formal arbitration procedures to the process of credentials ajudication, a reform again little appreciated when first installed[4]. Along with the McGovern-Fraser guidelines, it was to become a point of controversy in the preliminaries to the 1972 convention, leading most notably to the bitter fight over the "Daley delegation.[5]" The O'Hara Commission reforms were accepted by the National Committee (with several modifications) and by the 1972 convention. Its work, however, was not the subject of widespread party debate or the cause of sweeping party change. These results were achieved by its reform cousin, the McGovern-Fraser Commission.

The Delegate Selection Commission began quickly and never stopped running. George McGovern was chosen chairman and he gave the 28-member commission aggressive leadership. McGovern had been a reluctant candidate for the position. He had made a bid to run for the presidential nomination after Robert Kennedy's death and McCarthy's clear inability to expand his support. He was acceptable to the liberal-insurgent wing of the party, he was a close personal friend and former neighbor of Humphrey's, and, more importantly, he had endorsed Humphrey as soon as he won the nomination (which McCarthy had not). Former governor and then U.S. Senator Harold E. Hughes of Iowa (no relation to New Jersey's Hughes), a tough populist, was named vice-chairman. Hughes had led a successful ad hoc committee drive to found the new reform committees prior to and during the Chicago convention.

Within a month of his appointment, McGovern had named Robert W. Nelson, a party professional with an extensive background in campaign management and government work, as staff director. Nelson, in turn, recruited a small core of able staff associates and a large reserve of volunteers that performed remarkably well. The commission's first meeting was held on March 1 and by April they were organized well enough to begin 17 public hearings in all regions of the country. The field hearings tapped all shades of party opinion and invited a variety of proposed solutions for the party's ills. Their most notable contribution was the public record made of abuse of party procedures in state after state. In most states, delegate selection processes were vague and left considerable discretion to party officials. Under pressure, these party officeholders could employ their authority to good advantage. The hearings were well covered by the media and contributed directly to the building momentum for change.

By September, the commission members entertained consideration of the first proposals for structuring a set of broad guidelines against which to measure each state's national convention delegate selection methods. The tentative standards were circulated to state parties, national party leaders, the media, academicians, and anyone else who had a stake in or something to contribute to the resolution of the problems uncovered. By late November, the commission had met again to adopt its final 18 regulations and transmit these to the states.

The 18 "guidelines" as the McGovern-Fraser Commission called them were intended to be general rules of procedural fair play that would guarantee open access to and fair representation of all shades of party opinion and presidential candidate support. The guidelines[6]:

1. required that state parties must take "affirmative steps" to include minority groups on their convention delegations "in reasonable relationship to the group's presence in the population of the State."

2. required state parties to do the same for young people (defined as those 18 to 30 years old) and women. These two items comprised the "quotas" so much discussed, although the commission formally indicated that these were not their intent.

3. "urged" reform of registration procedures, a proposal ignored since it was not required.

4. required state parties to prohibit all excessive costs and fees (over $10) on delegate selection processes and to forbid any petition requirements in excess of 1 percent of the standard used to judge Democratic party strength.

5. required state parties to have written rules covering delegate selection and guaranteeing uniform times and dates for different stages of the procedures and easy accessibility of places to participate.

6. prohibited proxy voting.

7. required state parties to make clear to party members how they would participate in delegate selection and to separate these events from other party affairs.

8. set a quorum for meetings concerned with delegate selection at 40 percent.

9. required state parties to choose alternates in a manner similar to that for selecting the original delegates and to fill vacancies through a "timely and representative" party committee, the original body that named the delegate or the convention delegation acting as a committee.

10. banned the unit rule.

11. "urged" proportional representation of each presidential contender's strength at each level of delegation, a proposal that was not required and therefore was not enforced.

12. required state parties to select 75 percent of their delegates from units no larger than congressional districts and to allocate their delegate positions within the state through a formula giving equal weight to population and some measure of Democratic strength (for example, registered Democrats in the state or the Democratic vote in one or a combination of presidential elections).

13. required state parties to give public notice of the time, location, and rules for all meetings concerned with delegate selection; and to provide prospective delegates (or slates of delegates) the opportunity to declare on the ballot the presidential candidate they supported or to state that they were uncommitted.

14. prohibited ex officio delegates.

15. "urged" the adoption of means to allow only Democrats to participate in the party's delegate selection while still keeping enrolling procedures flexible enough to allow new supporters to join the party; since it was not required, it did not receive attention.

16. required state parties to select all delegates in the calendar year of the national convention and all party committees with a direct role in the process to be chosen in the same year.

17. limited the proportion of a state's national convention delegation that could be appointed by a party committee to 10 percent.

18. required state parties to provide all the previous safeguards and protections to insure the openness of the procedures for framing slates of candidates;

to insure that any slate running on behalf of a presidential contender be assembled in cooperation with the candidate; and to be careful that no slate be given preferential treatment.

The guidelines sent to the states were accompanied by two notices. One assessed the individual state's regulations against the standards set forth by the commission and indicated where and in what manner the state party was required to alter its methods to comply with the national guidelines. The other notified the state parties (in a message to be repeated constantly) that the changes were *mandatory*. A state delegation risked not being seated at the upcoming 1972 National Convention if it did not meet or could not prove it had made a full faith effort (the exact wording was "all feasible efforts," a proviso that was strictly interpreted) to institute the new rules.

The period from early 1970 until the convention in July of 1972 was devoted to implementing the guidelines. First under McGovern and then, when he resigned at the beginning of 1971 to seek the presidency, under Congressman Donald M. Fraser of Minnesota, the commission worked with the state parties to achieve the desired reforms. It did unusually well. By its count, 40 state parties and the District of Columbia were in "full compliance" and 10 states were in "substantial compliance" (one guideline or a portion thereof, usually involving statutory modification, had not been met)[7]. The achievement is remarkable. For the first time to any significant degree, a national party had promulgated and each state had adapted to federal criteria determining how a party should behave to insure due process procedural guarantees and standards of fair representation to all who participated in its presidential delegate selection deliberations. It could mark a turning point for a rather loose association of state parties whose organization and decision making had changed little during the history of its confederation.

There was, of course, controversy. The "quotas" were repeatedly attacked. Individual states and state party leaders rebelled, although not in concert, thus denying them the effectiveness of a coordinated full-scale revolt. And the Credentials Committee was to face more challenges than ever in its history: 82 from 31 different states, involving at one time over 40 percent of the convention's membership. The committee, and the convention, proved supportive of the new rules, thus reaffirming their status as party law[8].

THE REFORM CONTROVERSY
CONTINUES: A REAPPRAISAL OF THE
MCGOVERN-FRASER COMMISSION'S ACTIONS

The controversy leading up to and including the convention coupled with the disastrous McGovern campaign led to a strong reaction against the guidelines, culminating in the post–1972 period in an attempt to scrap the reforms or, should that fail (as it did), to modify their more disputed aspects. The 1972 convention capitulated to the intense discontent of the time by mandating a new reform commission to reevaluate the delegate selection regulations. The New Delegate Selection or Mikulski Commission, the latter name in deference to its chairwoman, City Councilwoman Barbara Mikulski of Baltimore, inherited an unwelcome job[9].

Nonetheless, within two years it had met its obligations and gone out of existence, replaced by a Compliance Review Commission intended to monitor the states' application of the revised guidelines (a duplication, under less disputed conditions, of the second phase of the McGovern-Fraser Commission's efforts). The Mikulski Commission made numerous alterations in the guidelines, rendering them more palatable to the states without, it is fair to say, compromising their integrity. With the help of the 1972 convention's decision on several issues (winner-take-all primaries, closed [to non-Democrats] party processes), it actually extended a number of provisions, effectively clarifying ambiguities in the original rules while defusing their most controversial aspects. The quotas were eliminated. A statement was substituted in their place that outlawed discrimination and recommitted the party to the six basic elements of the Special Equal Rights Committee, both items basically a reaffirmation of past stands. It did require "affirmative action programs" (to become the new watchwords of the struggle) to expand participation in party affairs to essentially minority groups (women are included under this term despite their being a majority of population) in proportion to their numbers in the state Democratic party's electorate— actually a tougher standard than that of the original McGovern-Fraser Commission. A failure to reach a proportionate level of categorical representation was not to constitute a prima facie case of discrimination. The burden of proof in such cases, in a significant change, would switch from the state party to the litigant.

Convention "privileges," although not voting rights, were extended to national committee members, Democratic governors, U.S. senators, and congressmen. This action corrected situations in which the National Convention had been denied the experience of these professionals because they had failed to be elected as delegates, although it did avoid the distrusted "ex officio" delegate status. Closed slatemaking (the crux of the argument against the "Daley 59," as they were called) was legalized as long as no one slate in the primary received preferential treatment either in state law or through the use of party resources. All slates were to be treated equally. Presidential candidates would have to give their permission for an individual to seek a delegate position in their name (instead of allowing potential delegates to declare for the person most likely to win rather than their true choice as happened on occasion in 1972).

Proxy voting which had been prohibited was permitted if individuals established their credentials at meetings and then chose to leave. No one person could hold more than 3 proxy votes. The 40 percent quota was eliminated at the first stage of delegate selection since usually no one is quite sure at that point what size the group should be. The formula for apportioning delegates within a state was loosened to allow the individual state parties more discretion in the matter. Party bodies were allowed to appoint up to 25 percent of a state's delegation, which helped return a large degree of control to the party regulars who felt discriminated against by the earlier rules. And so on. Most of the remaining changes were clarifications of existing rules that eliminated a good deal of confusion while, less noticeably, standardizing the application of the rules.

The most significant innovation of the Mikulski Commission was the institutionalization of a measure providing for proportional representation for every presidential candidate who received at first 10 and later 15 percent of the vote at successive levels of the delegate selection process. The commission reaffirmed the 1972 convention's action in both voiding winner-take-all primaries (the basis of the California challenge to McGovern's delegates and an issue on which the original Delegate Selection Committee had not committed itself) and in restricting participation in party selection to party members only.

Finally, the Compliance Review Commission was established in a compromise between regulars and reformers under the leadership of party centrist Robert Wagner, former mayor of New York, to supervise the states in meeting the revised guidelines. It was hoped that a skillful monitoring process would eliminate the disruptions that characterized the numerous credentials flare-ups in the two previous conventions. Its work completed, the Mikulski Commission passed into history.

THE CHARTER (SANFORD) COMMISSION

One major item of business had been left over from the early reform period. The 1968 convention had authorized its reform offspring to investigate and recommend improvements for party structures. Both of the early reform committees—the O'Hara and McGovern-Fraser Commissions—claimed jurisdiction in the area, resulting in a stalemate. With the bulk of their principal obligations completed, the two reform committees decided in the fall of 1971 to pursue the matter jointly. Under the prodding primarily of Fraser, they drafted and presented to the 1972 convention a "party charter" intended to restructure and stabilize the episodic national party organization[10]. Unfortunately, for the charter (or party constitution), it was presented to the party, the public, and the media too late (May of 1972) in the preconvention period to command much attention. It became lost at the convention itself—deliberation on its contents being continually postponed to allow for the resolution of more pressing matters and it finally fell victim to the effort to reconcile centrists and McGovernites. Few wished to give any further attention to proposals that revived the debate over reforms which had so severely divided the party. On the convention's last night, the membership did authorize a new group (the Charter Commission, to be chaired by former Governor Terry Sanford of North Carolina) and it enlarged the National Committee from a base of 110 to what was expected to be a more representative 303.

The format of the new Charter Commission's deliberations resembled those of the McGovern-Fraser and O'Hara Commissions. Unlike the Mikulski Commission, it had to create something anew (rather than accommodate itself to procedures already in effect). It began early with an auspicious public meeting in May of 1973 in which McGovern, the symbol of the old reforms, called for accommodation, and he and virtually every other party leader of consequence (and especially Humphrey) preached party unity and compromise. The Sanford Commission, more so than the original reform committees, attempted to represent party centrists. With a national chairman, Robert Strauss, in office who wished most of all to draw the party together and focus its energies on winning office; encountering strident opposition from George Meany and Al Barkan of the AFL-CIO (both on ideological grounds and because these labor officials sensed their influence within party councils threatened); chaired by a moderate not previously associated with reform (Sanford); almost universally disparaged by party regulars; and, finally, former supporters (O'Hara for example) now aligned with the antireform regulars, the commission's success and its eventual contribution to a stable national party institution appeared in serious doubt.

The Charter Commission appeared to flounder initially. It did not have a clear idea of what was expected of it; it was buffeted by the antireform forces (led, in particular, by the AFL-CIO leadership) infuriated by the events of the 1972 campaign year; and it was too large (164 members) to acquire easily the consensus on goals and the working harmony of either of its two predecessors. The group did, however, have some things in its favor. It had, if it chose, a blueprint from which to work (the original party constitution drafted by the McGovern-Fraser and O'Hara Commissions). Among its members was Congressman Donald Fraser, a quiet but thorough worker who eventually would organize the nucleus of a liberal bloc that provided a coherent set of proposals opposing those of the party's right. And its chairman was a skilled professional, a calm and experienced party centrist, and a personally likable and fair individual respected by all elements within the party. Under his gentle prodding, the commission would eventually find its bearing and proceed with its work. In the end, its almost totally unexpected contributions would amaze even the most ardent of the early prore- form advocates[11].

The commission proceeded steadily but unspectacularly with its efforts. The critics, while still wary, found little to upset them and the technical details of the deliberations were such that few found them of interest. Its principal accomplishment during the first year and a half of its existence seemed to be its willingness to proceed with a midterm convention, authorized by the 1972 convention but opposed by many. The party's leaders appeared annoyed by this historic first and its conservatives, having failed to prevent it from being held at all, did manage, in a series of hotly contested votes, to force its rescheduling from midsummer of 1974 to a month *after* the November congressional elections so as not to embarrass the party's candidates and to confine its deliberations to *only* the provisions of the charter itself. Unexpectedly, the course of political events, and especially the administration's inability to deal forcefully with the deepening recession and inflationary price spiral, had these same conservatives and party regulars loudly attacking the restrictions as the convention drew near, a move that eventually succeeded in opening the convocation to at least the discussion of relevant contemporary issues.

The commission membership assigned to the regular party organizations in the states the principal responsibility for establishing the methods of delegate selection and (if they so chose, as some did) the control over who would be chosen[12]. A weak review process was instituted at the national level, faintly resembling the credentials procedures of a presidential convention. Party leaders did all in their power to understate the midterm convention's significance and to divert attention from its (and the Charter Commission's) deliberations. Overall, little was expected of the December convention, and the major hope of most in the party was that it would pass virtually unnoticed. Its major contribution to the party, most seemed to believe, would be negative; if it did not further exacerbate party tensions, it could be judged a success.

In the shadow of the upcoming meeting, the Charter Commission quietly proceeded with its duties, watched closely only by a few interested bystanders[13]. Outside of the continuing fight over the scope of deliberations and the timing of the convention, nothing of great public consequence occurred, particularly in relation to the substance of their recommendations, until the August preceding the November elections. In March of 1974, the commission membership adopted an unofficial draft of its proposed charter. The mid-August meeting was intended to settle the issues outstanding and to mold the final instrument to be presented to the December convention. Little controversy was expected and neither side included many absolutists committed to positions likely to seriously divide the gathering. The three questions carried over from the March meeting included *requiring* midterm conferences (and, a step further, the time, composition, and agenda for these gatherings) rather than making them optional; establishing a judicial council modeled along the lines of the Supreme Court to codify and apply party law in such a manner as to avoid devisive intraparty fights and prolonged court battles, occurrences repeatedly experienced as a consequence of the 1972 controversies and a development (especially the federal court suits) the national party feared[14]; and a provision on the tenure of the national chairman. On the last item, some favored a chairman elected for four years at or immediately after the National Convention (and therefore the presidential nominee's choice) and others desired an additional election early in the year following the presidential election to insure an impartial chairman responsive to all elements within the party. In truth, as both sides were quick to admit, these were not the type of issues to stir passions or, for that matter, to predetermine the party's (or the charter's) destiny.

The AFL-CIO leadership, however, was bent on making its will dominant. Without having to make any additional effort, the federation appeared to have all the votes needed to carry its proposals. Nonetheless, and with the blessing and support of the national chairman and his staff, the AFL-CIO went through an intricate series of motions in the interim between committee meetings that involved replacing commission members who resigned or could not attend the August session with substitutes more loyal to the right-wing position. This feat accomplished, they prepared for the meeting. First, and with little effort, the conservative forces quickly voted down the liberal alternatives on the charter issues before the commission. Then the right wing indulged in a bad case of overkill. They attempted to void the fragile compromise on affirmative action that had been adopted by the Mikulski Commission and, in turn, the Democratic National Committee and the Sanford Commission as a substitute for the quota concept. The conservatives did not want affirmative action to apply to all party affairs (only to delegate selection) and they wanted to replace the words *insure representation* (of minorities) with *encourage participation*. The black delegates felt they had already given up too much in the Mikulski Commission's weakening of the original McGovern-Fraser rules and they were angered by the new assault. The commission members, attempting to compromise, then included four alternatives in the proposed constitution and left the issue for the December convention to resolve.

Then the party conservatives initiated another attack. They proposed that prohibitions on the unit rule and winner-take-all primaries (mandated by the 1968 and 1972 National Conventions respectively) be stripped from the charter and left to party bylaws, presumably where the party's right could more easily modify or eliminate them entirely. The conservatives, led by the Meany-Barkan forces, then wanted to void the ban requiring national convention delegates to be elected during the year of the presidential contest.

The opening of these issues to debate proved a strategic mistake and caused a backlash that would eventually cost the conservatives dearly. The most immediate response was a walkout of the moderate to liberal forces led by the blacks, sufficient to force Sanford to adjourn the meeting for lack of a quorum and to carry the problems over to the midterm conference[15]. The media predicted a "titanic battle" in Kansas City, host to the convention, and few disagreed[16].

A series of meetings took place between liberals and National Chairman Strauss and among various members of the Charter Commission membership leading up to the expected showdown. All sides were tense. The regulars had not wanted the session, fearing it would exacerbate party differences. Their doubts appeared justified. Reformers now believed that not only a meaningful party constitution hung in the balance but also the essence of the reforms that dated back to the Special Equal Rights Committee. Their expectations seemed realistic.

No one stood to gain much and the biggest loser of all, of course, would be the party itself.

The important breakthrough came from the Democratic governors. Gathering in mid-November, shortly after the Democratic landslides in the off-year election and only weeks before the midterm convention was to open, the governors endorsed the original language and intent of the Mikulski proposals. In reality, they symbolized a turn in party affairs that gained momentum through their actions and would sweep the basically centrist gathering at Kansas City. In turn, they rejected—potentially at some political cost—the AFL-CIO position (for which they had been actively lobbied by officials of federated labor) and they emphasized the need for a party coherence that could lead to victory two years hence[17]. The delegates to the December convention responded to the same pressures influencing the governors and endorsed the initiatives they had taken. For many Democrats, the November victories had brought home the electorate's distaste for a Republican party badly scarred by Watergate, the Nixon pardon, and the mounting economic woes. Future political success depended on party unity. All factions believed that the experiences of 1972 and 1968 had to be avoided at all cost. More remarkably, consensus was to be achieved through the adoption of a progressive party constitution more reformist than any would have dared to predict.

Strauss was to play a key role in the events. Responding to the dominant party mood and recognizing that the base of the party's constituency had shifted, pushing the party's center into a more reformist stance, Strauss, reluctantly at first, but with increasing determination during the months between the August meeting and the opening of the Kansas City convention and most noticeably during the sessions themselves moved increasingly away from the hard-core AFL-CIO position. The national chairman saw himself as a unifier, not an ideologue. He wished to lead in the direction that the party base wanted to go. He had been elected national chairman with the strong backing of the Meany and Barkan faction. At first, he tried, on repeated occasions, to accommodate federated labor's views and those of the party regulars in general, sharing their belief that the reformers were a divisive, one-shot (1972) phenomenon that did not reflect true party sentiment. Although his relationship with the AFL-CIO and Barkan, its political director, had been stormy, Strauss basically acted on these beliefs from the period of his election in December of 1972 through the August blowup. Apparently, his thinking began to change during the fall months as one group after another questioned his position. His actions during the convention indicated a newfound awareness of where the party's best interest lay.

Unquestionably, Strauss distrusted the whole idea of a midterm convention. He would have liked to abolish or ignore it. His hope was that the Kansas City convocation would be the first and last of its kind. His approach to the entire matter was to exert as much direct control over the proceedings as he could. This he did most effectively. The Charter Commission met in Kansas City a few days before the convention opened to shape its final proposals. These it passed on to a 52-member rules committee of the convention, also chaired by Strauss (an unusual occurrence), which was designed to moderate any excesses in the charter and to shape a final proposal as close as possible to what the party majority could be expected to accept. This completed, Strauss then presided over the convention itself, reliquishing his post only to Sanford, who adeptly chaired the debate over the substance of the new constitutions's provisions. Perhaps Strauss's greatest accomplishment was, through personal intervention and bargaining, to achieve the public blessing of Mayor Daley, now welcomed back as a party member in good standing after his acrimonious ouster from the 1972 convention ("I'd do almost anything to go out of here unified and beat those water-walking Republicans"[18]), on a document Strauss and others realized was going to represent a new departure for the national party organization.

In the course of events, the AFL-CIO leadership was destined to suffer a defeat of major consequence and one for which it promised retribution. In the convention's most emotional moment, the secretary-treasurer of California's AFL-CIO took the floor to shout at Strauss, "You stand with us . . . or this party will go down to ruin in the presidential election of 1976[19]." The AFL-CIO's official nonsupport for the 1972 presidential ticket eliminated any chance McGovern might have had to run a respectably competitive race. The AFL-CIO had been the principal funder (dispensing about $3 million, mostly to Democrats[20]) and the best organized supporter of Democratic candidacies (not an unfamiliar role) in the 1974 off-year election. Its efforts and the resources it invested exceeded those put forth on behalf of Democrats by any party committee or any other interest group. If one considers these factors, the significance of federated labor's opposition becomes apparent. The Democratic party had indeed set itself on a new course. How successful it would be in winning office and to what extent it had in actuality opened its procedures to better represent its basic constituencies would be left for the future to tell.

THE DEMOCRATIC CHARTER

The party constitution adopted at Kansas City is an unusual document, the first of its kind for any major American national party in history. Its intent was to revitalize and modernize structures that had evolved with little change since the late 1840s. The party, it was hoped, could be made relevant to the closing decades of the twentieth century. In the process, a subtle shift of power would occur: more authority would gravitate to the national party while at the same time the procedures of both the state and, more specifically, the federal party would be democratized. To the extent that an essentially lifeless and unresponsive organization could be made both more accountable to and representative of its grassroots membership, the reforms would be a success. The experiment was a worthy one.

As adopted on December 7, 1974, the Democratic Charter[21]:

    importuned the national party to take responsible positions on matters of policy that reflected the concerns of its supporters, a role it had attempted to fulfill through such agencies as the Democratic Advisory Council (1956–60) and the more recent Democratic Policy Council (1970) but one which some congressional and other party leaders felt it had no business playing;

    required the national party to assist local and state organization, raise and disburse funds, and help its nominee campaign for president, all traditional duties of the national party;

    continued to recognize the National Convention as the supreme governing body of the party and required state parties to adapt their practices and rules to the national party standards and "to take provable positive steps" to change their state laws to conform to the charter and the National Convention directives should they conflict, an explicit and novel recognition of the national party's dominance;

    enforced the principles underlying the McGovern-Fraser and Mikulski Commissions' guidelines for delegate selection to national conventions (including affirmative action proposals; a ban on the unit rule; proportional representation of a presidential contender's strength; party processes restricted to Democrats only; delegate selection confined to the presidential election year, although permitting committees selected openly as much as two years earlier to be involved) —a reaffirmation of the regulations promulgated by both delegate selection committees and indisputable evidence that these were permanent changes;

    allocated national convention delegates through a choice of formulas giving equal weight to either population or electoral vote and to the Democratic vote for president;

    bound the National Committee as it did the rest of the party to operate under the charter;

    enlarged the National Committee to 350 members;

    extended to elections of National Committee personnel guarantees of "full, timely, and equal' opportunities for all Democrats to participate, watchwords of the McGovern-Fraser reform era;

    provided incentive for the National Committee membership to elect and, more importantly, hold accountable its Executive Committee. Until the changes introduced at the 1972 National Convention, the Executive Committee served as little more than a lethargic extension of the national chairman's authority;

    allowed (the optional alternative) for midterm party conferences to be held, with the time, place, agenda, and final decision of their being convened left in the hands of the National Committee;

    established a Judicial Council to be appointed by the National Committee whose function ". . . shall be to review and approve state plans for the selection of delegates to the National Conventions and to decide challenges to such state plans, provided, however, that the right of the Democratic National Convention and [the] Democratic National Committee to settle credentials disputes concerning their respective bodies shall not be abridged"; an innovative but somewhat more modest proposal than originally anticipated;

created a national finance council to fund party affairs, the institutionalization of a vehicle that had been used in a more ad hoc fashion for several years (an approach the Republican party had employed with notable success);

established a National Education and Training Council to implement "education and training programs for the Democratic Party in furtherance of its objectives," a broad and unclear grant of authority to a new agency (responsible to the Executive Committee) roughly analogous to programs sponsored by the more centralized European democratic parties and one of the proposals for which the entire charter had been attacked for attempting to "Europeanize" the party. Funds would be budgeted for the council by the National Committee one year in advance (a most unusual occurrence for the normally penurious Democrats) to allow it to plan systematically its efforts "to reach every young citizen as they enter the electorate" in order "to encourage a lifetime of meaningful political participation," an effort that Fraser in particular supported;

banned discriminatory practices and endorsed affirmative action programs "... to encourage full participation by all Democrats, with particular concern for minority groups, native Americans, women and youth" in both delegate selection processes *and in all party affairs.* The charter further prohibited the "imposition of mandatory quotas" in any party activity, but the language was not strong enough to pacify the AFL-CIO leaders. The affirmative action guarantees sought by blacks and liberals offended federated labor, who viewed them as implied quotas among other things, more than any other action taken by the midterm conference;

denied the right to challenge a convention delegation on the basis of its ultimate composition (presuming, for example, an imbalance between the representation of the groups specified and their proportionate presence in the Democratic electorate "... if the state party has adopted and implemented an approved and monitored affirmative action program." This provision was intended to avoid confrontations over delegations that while openly chosen did not meet certain levels of (principally) minority group representation, as happened at the 1972 Miami Beach convention. This was another explicit denial of any effort to implement the quota idea but again one not satisfactory to the AFL-CIO;

permitted the National Committee to authorize national convention representation (as was done in Kansas City) for groupings of Democrats "in areas not entitled to vote in Presidential elections," for example, the overseas citizens whose disfranchisement is discussed in Part I of this book;

allowed for the establishment or continuation of regional party organizations (for the East, Midwest, South, Far West, etc.);

authorized the National Committee to "adopt and publish a code of fair campaign practices, ... *recommended* for observance by all candidates campaigning as Democrats." (Italics added.) A product of the post-Watergate era, the fair campaign code was not made mandatory because of the practical difficulty and potential embarrassment of having Republicans and other Democrats requesting the National Committee (or some other Democratic agency) to censure their Democratic opponents. The publicity generated could prove harmful to the party and the Democrats, of course, had no way of imposing their code on Republican, third-party, or independent candidates for elective office. The politics if not the ethics of the situation make sense;

required that all meetings of the National Committee, its Executive Committee, and all official party commissions be open to the public and that no secret votes be allowed. This was a relatively new development that, surprisingly, grew out of the McGovern-Fraser and O'Hara Commissions' emphasis on open deliberations;

forced the National Committee to prepare and make available to the public an annual report to include, among other items, an accounting of their financial status, a type of public exposure and accountability both political parties, traditionally secretive on such matters, attempted with remarkable success to avoid;

made all state parties adopt and file with the National Committee within 30 days of their ratification *written* rules for the conduct of all party business. This was seemingly a small point but malleable and unspecified rules had long proven a source of great power to party leaders. The McGovern-Fraser Commission had found a similar provision relating to delegate selection procedures one of the most difficult to enforce on the state parties;

provided that the charter could be amended by a majority vote of the National Convention or a two-thirds vote of a national conference called for that explicit purpose, or of the less authoritative National Committee *if* (in the last case) written notice of the proposed changes had been distributed to members and to the media at least 30 days in advance of the meeting; a proposal intended to avoid any potential abuse of the amendatory powers.

For the organizationally chaotic, decentralized, and unstructured American political parties, conditions especially true for the less organizationally astute Democratic party, the newly instituted party constitution signaled the beginning of a concerted drive to revivify the party. The intent was to make the party relevant to the demands of a technologically advanced society and an increasingly more sophisticated electorate. All of this was taking place at a time when political parties themselves stood in disrepute and their future contributions to democratic society were suspect.

REPUBLICAN REFORM
AND THE RULE 29 COMMITTEE

The Republican party had not ignored the stirrings evident in their competitors. If anything, the Republicans had a longer history of reform, reaching back in an unbroken pattern to the early to mid-1960s. But the Republican reform effort was considerably different from that of their Democratic colleagues. In the first place, the Republican party was markedly better organized and funded—especially, although not exclusively, at the national level. Their national headquarters staff was larger, more professional, and suffered less turnover and abrupt dislocations than did that of the Democrats. The rules for their national conventions had been codified early and they had a continuity in the administration of conventions (through a specific division of the national staff that supervised these operations) that was foreign to the ad hoc approach of the Democrats.

Secondly and of more consequence, the Republican reform efforts focused on problems the Democrats would find narrow in scope and possibly even of less tangible value than their own concerns. Not having experienced anything similar to the Democratic trauma over their 1968 convention or an equivalent broad-based insurgent-reform movement within their own ranks, the Republican party had confined its perspective to questions of convention orderliness and the better presentation and publicizing of the party's positions on issues. Such difficulties might have appeared a luxury to the more deeply troubled Democratic party.

Thirdly, the Republican party emphasized the exclusively federal nature of the party system, as had the Democrats prior to the Special Equal Rights Committee, the McGovern-Fraser Commission, and the new party constitution. The Republicans, however, during the post-World War II period, and as the Democrats were forced into a more activist role nationally in supervising local and state parties particularly in relation to racial excesses, had become perhaps more politically committed to the ideological implications of a highly decentralized party system. *Authority* over state matters such as delegate selection standards resided at the lower levels. This emphasis did not prohibit a strong national headquarters staff from emerging, but it did require that the national party assure a basically supportive and supplemental posture to state party actions. Noninterference was emphasized. Power, if not always political resources, remained at the state level. Within this framework, any reform recommendations that impinged on what were considered state processes, even if adopted by the national convention, were accepted only as suggestions. The differences between the two national parties in approaching this issue were fundamentally and diametrically opposed.

The foregoing should not imply that the Republican party did not have difficulties or, if it did, that it failed to recognize them. The Republicans—despite their capture of the presidency in both 1968 and 1972—found themselves and their policies appealing to an increasingly diminishing segment of the electorate. Upon examination, their delegate selection procedures were at least as restrictive and arbitrary as those employed by the Democrats in 1968 and earlier. Although no general mood of discontent existed within party ranks, more progressive party leaders began to wrestle with the problem of what to do.

The 1968 National Convention did authorize the creation of a reform commission, the DO (Delegates and Organization) Committee. Its membership, unlike the Democrats, was confined to National Committee personnel—generally the more successful and established party representatives—and it did not experience the sense of urgency or enjoy the staff resources available to its Democratic counterpart. The committee did attempt to move toward the goal set by Present Richard Nixon to become the "party of the open door" and it did issue two reports[22].

The 1972 Republican National Convention, in turn, did act on such recommendations as a ban on proxy voting, open delegate selection meetings, the prohibition of automatic (ex officio) delegates, the election rather than selection of congressional district and at-large delegates (unless state law specified otherwise), the rejection of fees in excess of statutory requirements, appeals for the National Committee to help prospective candidates familiarize themselves with delegate selection processes, a move for broader representation on the party's executive committee, the rejection of secret voting by committees of the Republican Convention, and the enactment of a new delegate allocation formula (a move which began as an effort to make the convention membership more representative of the populous areas and ended with a complex proposal that ratified, in a circular manner, the status quo). Each of these items, with the exception of the apportionment plan, is an improvement. The DO Committee and the 1972 convention went well beyond its predecessors in these regards.

The committee did not meet all the issues to come before it, however. It floundered most dramatically on possibly the most significant one, the attempt to open the party to new groups. The reformers could never statisfactorily resolve the question of how to approach or insure increased minority group representation, a benign version of the quota issue that had bedeviled the Democrats. The National Convention did, in an extension of its Rule 32, prohibit discriminatory practices. It also adopted a provision that "*The Republican National Committee* and the Republican State Committee or governing committee of each State shall take positive action to achieve the broadest possible participation *by everyone* in party affairs, *including such participation by women, young people, minority and heritage* [ethnic] *groups and senior citizens in the delegate selection process*[23]." (The italics in orginal denote the new language adopted in 1972.)

Rule 29 of the new bylaws provided that a committee "broadly representative of the Republican Party" be appointed to "work with" the state parties "relating to the Rules adopted by the 1972 Republican National Convention[24]." The language is intentionally broad and vague and it contains none of the wording that allowed the McGovern-Fraser Commission to institute the reforms it did in the interim between national conventions. It was implicitly understood, however, that the primary mission of the new reform committee would be to struggle with the issues raised by the language of the expanded Rule 32, the question of participation by minorities.

The Rule 29 Committee (named after the bylaw that created it) was to present a final report to the Republican National Committee no later than January 1,

1975. In practice, and ironically, this meant that the Rule 29 Committee was meeting at the exact same time in December of 1974 that the Democrats were holding their uneasy midterm convention in Kansas City. In another coincidence, Governor Christopher S. Bond of Missouri used an address before the Republican Governor's Conference, meeting only days before the reform commission gathered, to warn that the party could not bind itself "to some narrow ideology that denies the constructive role of government in our society." The reference could be interpreted as a cautious acceptance of an assertive national party (as well as governmental) role, something on the order of the McGovern-Fraser tack. Bond went on to say that the ideological approach he had attacked "would surely point us [the Republican party] toward extinction—and we would deserve nothing better[25]." The message is blunt. It is reinforced by two facts of political life the Republicans had to face, one of recent occurrence and the other, and more serious, of longer duration. First, the party had lost over 40 congressional seats to the Democrats in the previous month's elections. And secondly, the number of people in the electorate identifying with the Republican party was consistently declining, standing at about one-fifth of the eligible electorate. These concerns, plus the ominous shadow of Watergate, would haunt the Rule 29 Committee's December deliberations.

The persistent question was still what to do about fulfilling the objective of being the "party of the open door," a term still in vogue. The liberals at the gathering, led by Congresswoman Margaret M. Hechler (Mass.), Senator Peter V. Domenici (New Mexico), Congressman William A. Steiger (Wisc.), the committee's chairman, and Bond, won the first round. The Hechler-sponsored proposal, which won initial approval from one of the subcommittees that preceded the business of the full committee, required state parties to establish positive action plans to attract women, minorities, youth, and the poor into the party. These state proposals would be reviewed by the National Committee and by the National Convention's rules committee, tactics suspiciously close to the type of sanctions threatened in earlier years by Democratic reformers. Bonus votes would be given to states that complied with the suggestions for improved outreach programs. Approval for each state's plan would be required before its delegation could be seated at the National Convention.

This measure proved too harsh for the full committee membership. The reaction, led by Governor James E. Holshouser, Jr., of North Carolina and Clarke Reed, the Mississippi party chairman, diluted the requirement to read that a state party was urged (not required) to submit "examples" of proposals (not the plan itself) "designed to create the opportunity for participating in all party activities for all people regardless of race, creed, national origin, religion, sex or age[26]." Also, the state parties were called on to "take positive action and endeavor to assure greater and more equitable participation" of the groups in question and "to increase their representation at the 1976 national convention[27]." These proposals were ratified by voice vote.

There is an implicit understanding that a credentials committee might possibly sanction a state delegation's membership (a motion to exclude this eventuality, thus rendering the new reforms totally impotent, was beaten back by a 29 to 14 vote). The wording is indirect and the requirements for compliance loose enough, however, that a credentials committee rebuff would be highly unlikely. The Rule 29 Committee stressed that enforcement remained voluntary and, in fact, inserted in its recommendations wording to the effect that the rule was not "binding upon any state or state organization." The idea of a quota was specifically disavowed[28]. Still, when all is considered, the adoption of the proposals must be viewed as a reform victory and one, as both pro and con advocates believed, that went about as far as the party's majority was likely to go.

The second major concern of the committee was to institute safeguards against a repetition of Watergate-type campaign excesses. The reformers adopted a rule, opposed by the National Chairwoman Mrs. Mary Louise Smith, whereby the National Committee's chairperson—actually the group had debated what to call the party's presiding officer: "chairman" (sexist), "chairperson" (awkward), "chair" (accepted)—would have to approve all expenditures in a presidential campaign over $1,000. And, in an effort to give the National Committee a full measure of control over presidential campaigns, it was recommended that a seven-member committee headed by the national chairperson be created to receive "periodic reports" from the presidential candidate's campaign committee and that a member of the National Committee sit on the board of the committee. Steiger admitted this action represented "only part of what needs to be done to overcome the effects of Watergate" and he added that it would be "terribly, terribly disheartening" if the National Committee failed to exercise the control over presidential campaigns he and others felt was necessary[29].

In actuality, it is extraordinarily difficult for a national committee with no particular ties to a grassroots constituency and with its chairperson usually appointed by or at least acceptable to the president (or presidential candidate) to stand up to and, with no real power, correct abuses in a campaign with which he could be expected to be in sympathy. The burden placed on the National Committee and its leadership may be both too great and, worse, unrealistic.

Its work completed, the Rule 29 Committee disbanded. Its recommendations would have to be approved by both the Republican National Committee and the 1976 Republican National Convention. If adopted by both bodies, the anti-Watergate measures would go into operation the day after the 1976 convention adjourned. The positive action program would not take effect until the 1980 presidential election year.

Undoubtedly, there is discontent within Republican ranks over such questions as its shrinking proportion of the electorate and unethical campaign tactics. It remains to be seen if the party can do anything of consequence to correct these difficulties. Meanwhile, and to the consternation of some party members, Mrs. Smith announced, at the time the Rule 29 Committee's proposals were being presented, that the Republican party was initiating a $2 million public relations campaign to bring the party's message home to the voters. In reply to critics within the party, she later denied, in her own words, that the media campaign was "some artificial, phony, public relations hustle[30]."

CONCLUSION

The opening lines to the preface of this book spoke perhaps lightly of cycles, inertia, life, and death. The American party system may be entering a period of fundamental political change—or its recent signs of reform may simply be the death throes of old, and no longer very relevant, political institutions. "We have brought the national Democratic party back to life," Robert Strauss proclaimed in his closing remarks to the 1974 miniconvention. Allowing for hyperbole, one can only hope that the party is on its way to establishing itself as a meaningful agency representing the best interests of its large constituency. At best, only a beginning has been made in the tumultuous but highly productive years since the 1968 Chicago disaster.

The problems facing the Republican party are, by any accounting, even more severe. By its own admission, and based on a survey conducted for the national party headquarters, only 19 percent of the voting age population considers itself Republican, a 2-point difference from the most recent Gallup poll estimates and a 10 percent drop since the Eisenhower era. Among those entering the electorate since 1960, only 15 percent call themselves Republican. As to qualities associated with the party, only 6 percent of the electorate referred to it as "honest," 7 percent as "trustworthy" and, in contrast, 25 percent saw it as "corrupt." As Mrs. Smith, the national chairwoman remarked, the Republican party was at an "all-time low[31]."

The conclusion reached by the Republican national chairwoman may apply more broadly to the entire party system than anyone would care to believe. A multidimensional study of public support for political parties reported on in 1974 and using as indicators such variables as the decline in party identification, feelings of trust, confidence, and significance, the perceived need for reform, respondents' estimates of the adequacy of the parties' performance and their ability to represent the individual's needs, and the extent to which people believe they have a say in party affairs revealed some disquieting results. Professor Jack Dennis of the University of Wisconsin, author of the report, concluded that "the political party system has undergone a marked erosion of its legitimacy among members of the American mass public in the past ten to fifteen years. In several respects such support has moved to dangerously low levels[32]." Parties, it said, may be seen as "a vital, if perhaps diseased, organ of the body politic[33]." The trend had set in well before Watergate (most noticeably in the 1960 to 1964 period) and has accelerated from 1968 onward. Watergate, however, could only serve to reinforce the widespread negativism already apparent. As for reformers, and their task will not be easy, the author cautions that they

> should take account of the harsh fact of low public legitimacy of the institution. . . . The mass base of institution support is especially weak at this time; and this condition is worsening with each passing year. A mighty effort will . . . be required to reestablish the parties at the modicum of confidence and commitment that they enjoyed even a decade ago. Without such an effort, we may be called upon in the not so distant future to witness the demise of a once prominent institution of American government and politics[34].

The conclusions are harsh but justified by the data that preceded them. It is likely that neither party recognizes the extent of its difficulty. Should they, and the party system itself, decline further, the consequences could be most unfortunate. Political parties make unique and vital contribution to democratic government. The parties organize and articulate the views of the mass electorate. Without them, atomistic individuals—unless possessing great wealth or influence —are likely to be little more than the passive recipients of whatever a government chooses to do. Yet the public support for parties—with little wonder—has faded and continues to decline. The burden would appear to be on the parties themselves to prove their relevance to a changing society and to execute with some degree of effectiveness the responsibilities to which they have fallen heir.

NOTES

1. Commission on Party Structure and Delegate Selection, *Mandate for Reform* (Washington, D.C.: Democratic National Committee, 1970), p. 39, note 1.
2. See Allan P. Sindler, "The Unsolid South: A Challenge to the Democratic National Party," in *The Uses of Power,* ed. Alan F. Westin, (New York: Harcourt, Brace & World, 1962), pp. 229–83, Abraham Holtzman, "The Loyalty Pledge Controversy in the Democratic Party," in *Cases on Party Organization,* ed. Paul Tillett, (New York: McGraw-Hill, 1963), pp. 124–54, and Richard C. Bain and Judith H. Parris, *Convention Decisions and Voting Records,* 2d ed. (Washington, D.C.: The Brookings Institution, 1973).
3. For a specific review of the events outside of the convention hall and, as the report was to describe it, the "police riot" that ensued, see A Report Submitted by the Chicago Study Team, Daniel Walker, Director, to the National Commission on the Causes and Prevention of Violence, *Rights in Conflict* (Washington, D.C.: National Commission on the Causes and Prevention of Violence, 1968).
4. See the final report of the committee, Commission on Rules, *Call to Order* (Washington, D.C.: Democratic National Committee, 1972), and its two preliminary reports, *Issues and Alternatives* (Washington, D.C.: Democratic National Committee, 1969) and *Supplement to Issues and Alternatives* (Washington, D.C.: Democratic National Committee, 1970). Both of the preliminary reports can be found in *Call to Order,* appendix C, pp. 100–31.

5. For an account of this episode, see William J. Crotty, "Anatomy of a Challenge: The Chicago Delegation to the Democratic National Convention," in *Cases in American Politics,* ed. Robert Peabody, (New York: Praeger, 1976).

6. These can be found in the Commission's *Mandate for Reform,* which also provides the rationale for each guideline.

7. See Commission on Party Structure and Delegate Selection, *The Party Reformed* (Washington, D.C.: Democratic National Committee, July 7, 1972).

8. Through Credentials Committee and convention actions 67 delegates were unseated and 162 were added for a net gain of 95. The additions included 102 women, 39 youths, 27 blacks, 6 Latin-Americans, and 2 Indians.

9. Actually the formal name of the Mikulski Commission was identical to that of the original McGovern-Fraser Commission, the Commission on Party Structure and Delegate Selection. New Delegate Selection Commission or Mikulski Commission were popularly used for clarity and to distinguish it from its predecessor.

10. See Commission on Rules and Commission on Party Structure and Delegate Selection, *"We Reform That We May Preserve": A Proposed Charter of the Democratic Party of the United States* (Washington, D. C.: Democratic National Committee, June, 1972). The charter was originally presented on May 19, 1972. A copy of the party charter can also be found in the Commission's *Call to Order,* appendix D, pp. 133–43.

11. The charter eventually adopted by the 1974 midterm convention bears a striking resemblance to the proposal put before the 1972 National Convention by the combined Rules and Party Structure and Delegate Selection Commissions.

12. The bulk of these decisions were made at the meeting of the commission in Fort Collins, Colorado in July of 1973. See Sanford's memo to "The Chairman and Members, Democratic National Committee," dated July 23, 1973 (Washington, D.C.: Democratic Charter Commission, 9 pp.) which presents the decisions as to the midterm convention's size, apportionment of delegates among the states, manner of electing delegates, time, challenge procedures, agenda, groundrules, and the like.

13. The depiction may be too passive. The AFL-CIO had actively (some of its supporters felt even too actively) involved itself in the Charter Commission's deliberations (as well as, for that matter, those of the Mikulski Commission). A group of more liberal unions led by representatives of the United Auto Workers, the American Federation of State, County, and Municipal Employees, the Communications Workers of America, the International Association of Machinists, the Graphic Arts International Union, the Chemical and Atomic Workers, and the International Union of Electrical, Radio, and Machine Workers found themselves increasingly opposed to the Meany-Barkan actions and more aligned with the reform elements. Two ideological party groups, the Coalition for a Democratic Majority, formed by regular to conservative party members and led by Congressman O'Hara and a group of political scientists, and the smaller and less affluent proreform Democratic Planning Group, led by Alan Baron, monitored the commission's deliberations and kept their respective memberships informed of developments. Each group, of course, attempted to influence the commission to accept positions it favored.

14. The anxiety of the national party over the federal court cases centered on the fear that the courts would begin to set the rules for national party operations, a develop-

ment that could destroy whatever authority remained at the national party level. Traditionally, the courts had taken a hands-off attitude in party squabbles. The federal courts became involved usually only in flagrant abuses of civil rights involving blacks (see Chapter 1). The host of court cases arising out of 1972 expanded the types of questions to be brought before the courts and two (one immediately prior to the opening of the convention in 1972 and the other in 1975) actually reached the Supreme Court. It was the type of potentially destructive litigation that many in the national party hoped to avoid.

15. See Christopher Lydon, "Divided Democrats Face Major Fight at Charter Convention in Kansas City," *New York Times,* October 16, 1974, p. 71, and David S. Broder, "Rift Ends Charter Session," *Washington Post,* August 19, 1974.
16. Lydon, "Divided Democrats."
17. On the Democratic Governors' Conference, see Christopher Lydon, "Democratic Governors Uphold Compromise on the Make-up of Conventions," *New York Times,* November 11, 1974, p. 24, and David S. Broder, "Democratic Governors Agree on Anti-Bias Rules," *Chicago Sun-Times,* November 19, 1974, p. 28.
18. Quoted in the Democratic Planning Group's Newsletter, Alan Baron, ed. (Washington, D.C.: Democratic Planning Group, January, 1975), p. 4.
19. Tom Littlewood, "Democrats Scrap Delegate Quotas," *Chicago Sun-Times,* December 8, 1974, p. 3. For other commentaries on the dispute with the AFL-CIO (specifically the Meany-Barkan wing), see Christopher Lydon, "Labor's Power Broker Frustrated by Democrats," *New York Times,* December 6, 1974, p. 26, Charles Bartlett, "Meany vs. Democrats," *Chicago Sun-Times,* December 4, 1974, p. 74, and Lydon, "Meany Is Reported Ready to Declare Labor's Formal Break with the National Democratic Party," *New York Times,* December 13, 1974, p. 24. Lydon, in the last article, reports that Strauss personally had been threatened with "defeat and ruin" if he did not stand with federated labor on the party disputes. Meany and Barkan had also soured on one of Strauss's predecessors, Lawrence O'Brien, for his role in the reform effort prior to 1972 and for his role in chairing the 1972 National Convention.
20. Lydon, *New York Times,* December 6, 1974.
21. The following is taken from: Democratic Charter Commission, *Charter of the Democratic Party of the United States* (Adopted December 7, 1974) (Washington D.C.: Democratic National Committee, 1974), 10 pp.
22. The DO Committee, *Programming for the Party Future, Part I* (Washington, D.C.: Republican National Committee, January 15–16, 1971) and *The Delegate Selection Procedures for the Republican Party, Part II* (Washington, D.C.: Republican National Committee, July 23, 1971).
23. Republican National Convention, *Rules* (adopted by the Republican National Convention at Miami Beach, Florida, August 21, 1974) (Washington, D.C.: Republican National Committee, 1972), p. 14.
24. Ibid., p. 9.
25. "Wide Appeal Urged by G.O.P. Governor," *New York Times,* December 5, 1974, p. 10.
26. David E. Rosenbaum, "G.O.P. Unit Moves to Reform Rules," *New York Times,* December 9, 1974, p. 1.

27. Lou Cannon, "G.O.P. Votes to Broaden Party," *Chicago Sun-Times,* December 9, 1974, p. 2.

28. Ibid.

29. "G.O.P. Control in Presidential Drives Sought," *Chicago Sun-Times,* December 8, 1974, p. 28, and Rosenbaum, "G.O.P. Unit Moves to Reform Rules."

30. Christopher Lydon, "Republicans Plan To Combat Decline; 'Public Relations Hustle' Is Rejected," *New York Times,* December 14, 1974, p. 14.

31. Ibid.

32. Jack Dennis, "Trends in Public Support for the American Political Party System" (a Paper Delivered to the Annual Meeting of the American Political Science Association, Chicago, Ill., August 29-September 2, 1974), p. 22. For the author's earlier assessment of related problems, see Dennis, "Support for the Party System by the Mass Public," *American Political Science Review* 60 (September, 1966): 600–615.

33. Dennis, "Trends in Public Support."

34. Ibid.

IV
CONCLUSION

The Reform
Cycle

Americans have demonstrated a remarkable willingness to experiment with political forms throughout history. They have shown an ingenuity in experimenting with political structures in attempts to devise procedures that better serve the needs of a democratic nation. There is a line of progression to the process—and this is its most encouraging feature—toward an ever increasing democratization of political power. The reforms themselves tend to cluster in highly concentrated and usually quite brief periods of time. These reform periods run in cycles. They usually follow a long and clearly demonstrated need for change. Often the need is generalized and encompasses several different areas of political life. The efforts to improve political life are characteristically highly concentrated in time, and emotionally intense and exhausting. They are followed by long spells of inertia and general disinterest. This state of apathy continues until new abuses arise that demand attention, or until the old ones have become too obvious to ignore. The pressure for remedial action mounts and a new reform cycle evolves.

The reform cycle follows a general pattern which can be divided into four stages: the problem, the crisis, the reform, and the reaction.

A REFORM MODEL

THE PROBLEM A political problem of general consequence to a democratic society begins the reform cycle. It exists, independent of other concerns, and usually progressively worsens. It does, of course, receive attention on a sporadic basis from the media, some politicians, and an occasional citizen group. But the attention is seldom sustained and never intensive enough to mobilize broad support among the public and its elected representatives sufficient to engender meaningful change.

The problem stage of the process is easily illustrated. The question of who should be eligible to vote and what preconditions should be met is perhaps the longest running controversy in this regard. The debate continues. It is no longer very dramatic and consequently it is difficult to muster intelligent public support for change. To make matters worse, the controversy, despite its broad implications—the immediate concern is over the large number of nonvoters and how they may affect the viability of the political system—turns into a debate over highly technical, sophisticated, and, worst of all, dull proposals that compete for public attention. Under these conditions, the problem is likely to continue indefinitely, or until a crisis occurs.

Two other topics covered in this book—the political party system and the influence of wealth on political processes—demonstrate classic problems of political reform. Virtually everyone appears dissatisfied with the way political parties operate, the service or lack of service they provide, the difficulty they have in providing meaningful policy alternatives, and then their inability to act upon these once in office, the seemingly helter-skelter manner in which they select, in particular, their presidential nominees, and their generally poor performance as agencies representative of the public's best interests.

The proposals advanced to reform (some would say destroy) the parties are legion. The history of party reform in this sense is long, paralleling the life of the parties themselves. Yet profound change is most unlikely; it occurs only under extraordinary conditions.

The invidious influence of wealth on politics, particularly the financial corrupting (or biasing) of electoral institutions and the people's elected representatives has long worried interested citizens. Reform efforts began in the post-Civil War period, but *effective* regulation of finances and the policies intended to redistribute and equalize monetary resources had to wait until the 1970s. Even then, the impact of the new laws remained in doubt. In the period between the Civil War and Watergate, the incessant scandals over funding led to stopgap measures, sufficient to calm a momentarily alarmed electorate but not consequential enough to seriously inconvenience the politicians and corporate leaders who benefited most from the status quo. Quite intentionally, the modifications introduced lacked the teeth to effect formidable, systematic, and permanent change. More often than not, the new laws were simply ignored.

THE CRISIS What then does it take to elevate a smoldering and long-term problem to the level at which it demands and receives serious attention? It takes a single (or a series of) highly dramatic, eminently visible event(s) to demonstrate to even the most ill-informed and unconcerned of citizens the serious nature of the difficulty. The more dramatic and upsetting the act, the more likely profound change is to occur.

The civil rights revolution of the 1960s led to permanent changes in many aspects of American life. Among these were the voting laws. Not only did blacks begin to gain an effective franchise in the South, but the movement led to a questioning of all the outmoded restrictions on the franchise, some of which date back centuries and many of which reflect the pettiest of impulses. As a consequence, the Voting Rights Acts (specifically the 1965 act and its successors) began to enroll blacks in the South. This led, in turn, to a more general questioning of voting restrictions, a renewed interest in who votes and who does not and whom elected officials actually speak for, an easing of enrollment standards throughout the nation, a concern with (and improvements in) the complex system of absentee voting, a 30-day residency period recommended in a historic Supreme Court decision (a truly memorable improvement), and so on. The process moves on, and it turns to areas not originally considered as targets for change.

More recently, the movement has lost much of its dynamism, but it still manages to push along. The legislation before the Congress has been examined in detail and, by any accounting, is the most significant on the agenda. Still, less noticeable changes of consequence are occurring at the state level. By the mid-seventies, mail registration was adopted by 14 states and the District of Columbia. In all, an estimated 41 percent of the voting population appeared to be the beneficiaries of this modest improvement. The state laws, of course, differed and their ultimate impact could only be guessed. Indicative of the pitfalls of this piecemeal approach to improved voter registration is the New York State Supreme Court's decision to invalidate that state's mail registration statute on the grounds that it was incompatible with New York's constitution. Meanwhile, the old arguments about who benefits politically and who gets hurt—the state's Republican party was involved in the suit—gained momentum. Coincidentally, and as a direct result of this one ruling, the number of citizens affected in the nation by the eased registration procedure declined (temporarily, as it turned out) from 4 out of 10 to approximately 3 out of 10. The state legislation then introduced and passed a constitutionally acceptable mail registration proposal. At best, the state-by-state approach is uncertain. It can take decades and reversals of gains once achieved, as in New York, can be expected.

The simplification of federal and state procedures and the efforts to equalize access to the ballot were not achieved easily. They were preceded by 100 years of litigation in the federal courts. Those who witnessed the sit-ins, the fire bombings of churches, the lynchings and assassinations, the beatings and cattle prods that marked the height of the civil rights protest would like to erase the painful memories of an unsettling era. It was an ugly business and some paid dearly for the gains that accrued later. And yet, the litigation, the demonstrations, and even the violence may all have been necessary to accomplish the reforms needed.

The 1968 campaign year was devastating. Two major assassinations (Robert Kennedy and Martin Luther King), the abdication of an embittered president, the charges over unfair and closed delegate selection procedures, all marked a tense and unpleasant period. The year may have been best dramatized by the Democratic National Convention in Chicago. The clubbings and vulgarities, the "police riot" (as one commission report termed it), Mayor Daley and his delegates shouting obscenities at a platform speaker, the unnerving disorder within the convention hall itself, all of this was brought home to Americans, visually and emphatically (primarily through television), along with the nomination of the Democratic standard-bearer, then Vice-President Hubert Humphrey. Yet it took the events of this unfortunate year to provide the stimulus for the most profound changes in delegate selection, presidential nominations, convention operations, and, more generally, party management techniques to occur since the Progressive era.

Watergate is the event most directly associated with the profound revolution in the rules governing campaign financing ever to be instituted in the United States. These proposals had been discussed and written about by academicians and reformers at least since the time of Teddy Roosevelt and Woodrow Wilson. The climate, it should be noted, was receptive and the Congress in unusually bold moves in the early seventies had begun to institute effective, if limited, regulations of expenditures. But it took Watergate and its revelations about the 1972 presidential campaign, in particular, to institute the most radical departure, the public financing of federal elections. The battle, of course (as shall be shown), was far from over with the passage of legislation, but the precedent had been set.

THE REFORMS   The third stage in the process is the enactment of the reforms themselves. In many cases, this is curiously anticlimactic. Most of the proposals have been around for generations, often introduced into successive Congresses or debated in periodicals or among intellectuals. The events leading to the specific reforms claim the headlines. Many times the reforms, once the need is unmistakably shown and the public aroused, can be enacted expeditiously and with relatively little fanfare. Debates that occupied experts for decades (for example, how to *insure* that blacks are in fact being registered, that the viability and constitutionality of a federal presence in local enrollment practices is safeguarded, or that the means for enacting a fair formula to distribute funds among contenders for federal office are provided) have a way of being quickly resolved, disappearing in the general wish to enact changes designed to placate an angry public.

Attention then turns to the actual operation of the reforms and the modifications they can introduce into the system. This stage can be truly fascinating, making up in excitement and controversy for what the actual reform often lacks.

THE REACTION   The implementation phase of the reform cycle is crucial. Often it receives relatively little public scrutiny. The general electorate, satisfied that something has been done, redirect their concern to events that affect their lives more directly. The brief coalition that massed to demand the change dissolves. Worse possibly, many of the vanguard that had led the fight for the reforms also fade away. Some are satisfied and, similar to the public more generally, turn their energy to other pursuits. Others, and this may be more typical, become disillusioned with the new reforms, which never quite accomplish—and usually fall far short of—what was expected of them. In many cases, the reforms have been oversold, sometimes grossly so, in the effort to mobilize support for their enactment. They contain loopholes. They do not, for example, truly equalize campaign resources. Implementation of the legislation is not always equitable. The political parties in the postreform phase quietly sink back into patterns indistinguishable from their earlier ways. The reforms, in turn, can, and most often do, lead to totally unanticipated consequences.

If former leaders in the fight for change become angered and disillusioned and retreat to other concerns, the field may be left to antireformers. These individuals, the most antagonistic to the new ways and the most hurt by them, never seem to lose their motivation. They are quite happy, as the coalition supporting the reforms begins to crack, to revoke the new procedures or, if this is not feasible, to mold them to their own interests. Whatever is left after this final stage will remain as the accepted way of conducting affairs until dissatisfaction again begins to mount and a new reform cycle begins.

The fourth stage can actually be broken down into four substages. First, the reforms never accomplish all of their goals and sometimes not even their principal ones. Dissatisfaction sets in, compounded by the general indifference of many of the original proponents of change. Second, the reforms never work as intended. Unanticipated and unintended consequences result. Some of these can be as disturbing as the abuses that originally led to the cry of reform.

Third, a strong reaction arises. Opponents sense that the time is appropriate for a massive counteract. This can lead to repeal or, more likely, an effort to modify the reforms, supposedly to improve them to satisfy the criticisms raised. The real intention of the opponents is to render the reforms as impotent as possible and to reinstitute, as much as is feasible, the status quo ante.

Fourth, and finally, whatever manages to survive this last effort at emasculation will serve as the standard of operation for the foreseeable future.

The process that characterizes the postreform stage can be briefly illustrated. There was little that anticivil righters could do at the height of reform fever to effectively scuttle the 1965 Voting Rights Act. They did manage to limit the act's duration to five years, however, insuring for themselves another opportunity, in a possibly more receptive environment, to curtail the original legislation or at least nullify its most stringent provisions. In 1970 they tried again. They expanded the act to include the entire country (not just the South), hoping this would anger and embarrass northern representatives, leading to a quiet death for the obnoxious legislation at some unspecified point in the legislative mill. The Nixon Administration (unlike the Johnson Administration) obviously did not favor reenactment.

The strategy backfired. The act was passed in 1970 and again in 1975 and, in fact, became a vehicle through which election codes and enrollment practices throughout the country were modernized and democratized. Although the critics did weaken sections of the bill, they were reduced primarily to relying on an administration sympathetic to the South and a more restricted franchise, indulging the states by refusing to challenge or void obviously discriminatory practices.

Such a strategy can be only of short-term consequence, changing when an administration more aggressive in insuring black voting rights takes office.

The strong negative reaction to the primaries (as discussed in Chapter 7) did not nullify the movement to establish a primary system. It did bring the rash of adoptions to a standstill, however, and it introduced a long period of basically no change or improvement in the individual states' practices that lasted well into the 1970s.

The stimulus for a new period of experimentation with the primary emerged from the Democratic party's difficulties in nominating a representative presidential candidate in 1968. The McGovern-Fraser Commission, in particular, attempted to liberalize arbitrary and outdated state rules governing participation in delegate selection for national conventions. To many state parties, the easiest method of meeting fair participation guidelines was to opt for a presidential primary to replace caucus and convention systems at the state level.

By 1976, 30 states had presidential primaries and the mixed system was in potential jeopardy. At this point, the old cries against primaries resurfaced: they were too expensive, they were exhausting; the strain placed on candidates was inhuman; they occurred in no logical order and electorally irrelevant states (New Hampshire, for example) gained undue importance; and so on. What was the next step to take? Some argued for a national presidential primary, again not a new proposal. Others, inhospitable to the new reforms, harped on their difficulties with the intention of relaxing the more stringent guidelines and returning as much as possible to the pre-'72 practices. To a degree, the latter group enjoyed some success.

The corpus of the reform guidelines—the true target of the critics and not the primaries or the much-discussed and later abandoned quotas—nonetheless did manage to survive a spirited counteract. Virtually unnoticed by the critics or the media (with the proponents having quietly left the field), the guidelines had worked a revolution of sorts. Spurred on by the example of what at the time seemed McGovern's hopeless pursuit of his party's presidential nomination in 1972, *and* the promise of some federal funding to underwrite their nomination fights, over a dozen candidates tried for the nomination: Senators Bentsen, Jackson, Robert Byrd, Church, Bayh, Mondale (briefly) and, less formally (receiving attention as a periodic write-in and poll favorite), Hubert Humphrey; Congressman Morris Udall; former Senator Fred R. Harris; Governors Milton J. Shapp of Pennsylvania and Jerry Brown of California; former Governors Carter, Wallace, and Sanford (all southerners, in itself a sign of the new party tolerance); and former vice-presidential nominee (under McGovern) Sargent Shriver. In addition, several other incumbent governors (Carey of New York and Walker of Illinois) managed to convey their interest in the ultimate nomination. With the exception of Jackson and the perennial Humphrey, who appealed to the regulars and conservatives within the party that had dominated the national conventions through 1968, the rest would have had to be considered long shots at best, with little chance even to receive meaningful attention in the prereform period. The nomination of a Jimmy Carter would have been unthinkable.

The most dramatic, and potentially the most consequential, of the events discussed in this book is the public funding of elections coupled with the forceful regulation of spending. The events leading up to the new reforms and the provisions included in these were presented in Part II (Chapters 4 through 6) of this book. The reaction to these revolutionary changes provides an appropriate illustration of the uncertainty, recriminations, and eventual reformulations that mark the postreform stage. In this case, all three branches of the federal government and both major political parties were involved in the resolution of a profoundly significant issue. The grounds for the compromise that resulted may not do justice to the original motivations of the reform advocates, but they serve to rescue a series of reforms badly in need of help. Pragmatism and a realistic evaluation of who benefits (and what the public will and will not tolerate) has as much to do with what emerges in the final stage of reform as other, potentially loftier, considerations.

THE FEDERAL FUNDING AND REGULATION OF ELECTIONS: A CASE STUDY OF POSTREFORM ADJUSTMENT

The new campaign regulations introduced by the Congress at the height of the reaction to Watergate came under attack quickly. Few legislators strongly favored the laws they had fathered. Many felt uneasy with the potential regulatory monster they had created, the Federal Election Commission (FEC). The reforms were enacted out of fear of public retribution—particularly in the off-year election of 1974—and out of the vague but not unrealistic hope that they might further advance the edge held by incumbents. The House, especially, had been reluctant to approve the new laws. The opposition was symbolized by Chairman Wayne Hays of the House Administration Committee, the body with jurisdiction over the new laws. Hays was to be the principal actor in the drama to unfold.

Hays led the House forces in Senate-House conference committee, intended to resolve the differences between the House measure and its more liberal Senate counterpart. The congressman managed to obtain notable concessions. The price to be paid if Hays's demands had not been met was no legislation at all. As a consequence, federal funding for House and Senate elections, as contained in the Senate-passed bill, was abandoned. Four of the six members of the new election commission were to be appointed by the congressional leadership, rather than all six by the president. The limit on campaign expenditures was kept low, reinforcing the advantages in name recognition and resources held by officeholders. And either house of the Congress was given a 30-day grace period to reject any regulations drafted by the new commission (as required under the 1974 law for implementation) before they could go into effect. These last three provisions were to cause difficulties.

The opponents of the FEC and the federal role in campaign regulation more generally had a number of options available to them. They could, for example, attempt to limit the independence of the FEC, the critical point in the enforcement chain, by having the Congress scrutinize closely all commission's actions and regulations and, in the latter case, reject those they found unsatisfactory. Secondly, they could cut the FECs appropriations and, consequently, its staff size, thus reducing its effectiveness. Third, they could modify the laws governing the FEC and federal campaign regulation more broadly, eliminating their more controversial points and rendering them more congenial to the critics. Fourth, they could simply abolish the FEC. And fifth, they could attempt to accomplish the same end by testing the constitutionality of the new laws in the federal courts.

Options one and two involved relatively little risk since they emphasized few publicized legislative stratagems that had proven effective in the past. The FEC would continue, seemingly little changed, but rendered impotent and, most importantly, subservient to the Congress. The third and fourth alternatives would have to follow a public denouncement of the FEC and its actions. The need for change would have to be established. The final hurdle, a court test, would most assuredly follow any legislation as politically innovative as the 1974 law. All five possibilities were to be pursued.

The initial battle came early. The Congress disputed the first two regulations passed by the commission. The FECs first move was a bold one. It attempted to regulate congressional slush funds—a politically sensitive issue dating back in public memory, at least, to Nixon's vice-presidential campaign in 1952 and the famous Checkers speech. Congressmen and senators accepted unlimited private contributions from outside sources and then used these (in addition to their annual budgets) for transportation, newsletters, Christmas cards, flowers, and anything they so desired. The FEC proposed to hold congressmen, in the year preceding their election, and senators, in the two years before again facing the voters, accountable for many money thus spent for directly political purposes. Further, money so used would be counted against the incumbents' campaign ceiling.

The Congress was enraged. The Senate defeated the proposal 48 to 47, thus assuring it would never take effect. The vote was deceptive in its closeness. Only one senator (Clark of Iowa) spoke in favor of the regulation. Hatfield (R., Ore.) charged that the commission was incompetent. Pell (D., R.I.), an independently wealthy man, argued that it was "ridiculous" for the FEC to oversee the manner in which he spent his personal funds in seeking public office[1]. Watergate seemed to be quickly forgotten. Other senators, exercising an Alice-in-Wonderland type of logic, found the regulation discriminatory. The ban was twice as long for senators (who, of course, served three times longer in office) and it was not applied to challengers (who had no such slush funds or any other advantages of incumbency—estimated by the Americans for Democratic Action to amount, for House members, in direct monetary terms alone, to half a million dollars[2]—and whose political expenditures would count against their permissible campaign budgets).

The commission attempted to recoup its loss with a more modest change, seemingly nothing more than a bookkeeping alteration. Henceforth, all congressional and senate candidates would be required to file all spending and contribution reports *first* with the commission (not with the clerk of the House or the secretary of the Senate), requiring the FEC, in turn, to send microfilm copies of all such information to the respective congressional agents within two working days.

It would appear a great congressional principle—perhaps comparable to the "national security" invoked by the executive branch or the "executive privilege" arguments of the Nixon years—had been infringed upon. Wayne Hays and his committee were determined that no such change would occur. Said the congressman, "Since the clerk [of the House] is charged under the law with being the custodian of the reports, he ought not to have a whole bunch of people handling these papers before they get to him[3]." Since the law would be modified by the regulation, Hays's argument is hardly persuasive; in fact, it can not even be considered a serious defense of the congressional action. Yet, as later debate on the House floor was to demonstrate, the chairman's position—if not his logic— was strongly supported by leaders in both political parties.

Hays's committee voted the regulation down 18 to 1. After reconsideration, the group changed the vote to 19 to 0. It then reported the measure, with a negative recommendation, to the floor. The House voted 275 to 148 against the proposal. The FEC was not allowed to appear before the House Administration Committee to explain or defend its resolution. The committee's report to the House did not contain any information of the FECs position or its reasoning, a most unusual legislative action and one that helped deprive proponents of the measure with grounds for supporting it. Hays placed the measure on the suspension calendar, another short-circuiting of the legislative process that denied the House Rules Committee its normal role in transmitting bills to the floor (and one that would have perhaps provided the bill with another hearing).

Hays could not have accomplished these actions without the full support of the House leadership on both sides of the aisle. While remaining the most visible figure in the battle, he clearly spoke for the majority sentiment in the Congress. Hays went on to use any form at his disposal to indicate the congressional anger over the early commission actions. He threatened to cut its budget severely and began talking of the bloated size of the FEC staff.

The Federal Election Commission, quite clearly this time, got the message. It "required," reluctantly and despite what it said would be "added cost and confusion," that candidates for Congress file their reports with the appropriate House and Senate officials. Effective control over these documents remained, as it had in the past, with the people being regulated.

The commission had interpreted its role aggressively. In September and October, in addition to the slush fund regulation and the filing provision, it had required a candidate's legal and accounting fees for political services to be charged against his campaign ceiling. It argued that such services were "at least indirectly made to influence the election of Federal candidates since one's election is jeopardized by conduct that may violate the law[4]." By November, the FEC had accepted the realities of its political existence and was looking for ways to please Wayne Hays and the power-brokers in both political parties.

The commission's change in demeanor can be illustrated by one other case. Senator Lloyd Bentsen, a candidate for the Democratic party nomination, requested an early FEC clarification on what constituted political expenditures covered by the campaign ceiling. The commission ruled that for a declared candidate "all speeches made before substantial numbers of people were presumed [to be] for the purpose of enhancing his candidacy[5]." By November, the FEC saw the matter differently. At that point, they ruled that Gerald Ford, who was seeking the Republican nomination, did *not* have to charge the costs of his 1975 travels (although he would his 1976 expenditures) to make political speeches among Republicans at party gatherings against his campaign budget. The Republican National Committee had budgeted one-half million dollars to subsidize Ford appearances at party functions. If counted against Ford's total allowable prenomination limit of $10 million, it would have constituted a considerable expenditure of a scarce resource.

Ronald Reagan, also a candidate for the Republican nomination, did not believe the ruling fair. The commission then, informally, suggested the national committees pay for all such outlays by presidential candidates, an unlikely prospect for the Republicans and a ludicrous proposition for a Democratic party just the other side of bankruptcy. The commissioners were not pleased by what they had been forced to do, but they were politicians enough to realize that by late fall they were not in the independent or dominant position they once assumed.

Predictably, Wayne Hays and other critics were not assuaged. If anything, the ranks of the opponents appeared to be growing and they were becoming bolder. "The law is absurd," bellowed feisty John Pastore to his Senate colleagues. "We created a monster. . . . All we needed was to set a limit on spending, [and] to have full disclosure. That would have been a two-page law that everyone would have understood. We have a law now that even the people who wrote it do not understand[6]." Pastore had led the Senate sponsors in the conference committee attempt to resolve Senate and House differences in the original bill. It is little wonder that Hays managed to extract such a high price for its passage.

Meanwhile, Hays himself was busy. The chairman proposed an amendment to the 1974 act that would permit FEC regulations to become law *only if passed by both houses of the Congress within 30 days.* Since nothing (excepting perhaps resolutions negating FEC actions) proceeded through the legislative mill within such a brief period, the power of the commission would be significantly reduced.

One anonymous FEC official commented, "The practical effect of this is that Hays could draft regulations that were acceptable to him and not let anything else out of his committee, eventually forcing us to send up his version[7]." Undoubtedly, the assessment was correct. No more messy debates or, should the proposal carry, legislators forced to go on public record opposing rulings intended to open campaign procedures and regulate their abuses. In an ironic sidelight, the Hays amendment was appended to the postcard registration bill (see Chapter 3), which reformers wanted enacted and which had already passed committee and was awaiting a floor vote.

The critics of the FEC had made significant gains within the very first months of the new group's life. They had placed it on the defensive, limited its jurisdiction, and convincingly illustrated who had final authority. The future could only promise more of the same.

Options one through three had been used and they successfully achieved their goal, the intimidation and subordination of the new commission. No lawmaker was quite ready to call publicly for the infant commission's abolition quite so early. Even the voluble Hays, beginning to feel the pressure of being the bogeyman in the whole affair, while implying the 1974 act was unneeded and a product of the "hysteria of Watergate," felt that "we should give it one election to see how it works[8]."

A broad attack on the assumptions underlying federal regulation was to come from another direction. A case pending before the Supreme Court questiondd the FECs constitutionality as well as the legitimacy of other aspects of the controversial campaign law. Before turning to this debate, and the mad scramble that ensued after the Court's decision, the unforeseen effects that can emerge when reforms become operational should be illustrated.

ONE STEP FORWARD, TWO BACK: THE UNANTICIPATED CONSEQUENCES OF REFORM

Organized labor had traditionally been allowed to maintain its power to extract "voluntary" contributions from its membership and then to disperse these through " educational" committees such as COPE (Committee on Political Education). The contributions were as voluntary as a withholding tax, yet the power to collect them had withstood both legislative and judicial challenge. The ability to continue collecting and dispersing political funds was the price labor extracted for support of the campaign reform legislation.

Again, there was nothing new about the arrangement. The Republican party had ample financial sources. The Democratic party did not. Organized labor was its biggest contributor and labor's financial support, technical expertise, and campaign services were of inestimable value to the Democrats. Still, labor support was a mixed blessing. It could provide the muscle behind the upset victory of a Durkin in New Hamsphire (discussed earlier) and it could provide most of the organizational and campaign resources for a Humphrey in the 1968 presidential campaign. But organized labor, under the octogenarian George Meany, interested itself in issues—anti-Communism and the Viet Nam War—and became embroiled in personality clashes that went well beyond economic concerns. It actively entered Democratic primary races to defeat candidates that took the "wrong" side on the war question (Ohio's John Gilligan in his effort to win the Democratic party's Senate nomination) and its neutrality in 1972 which decidedly favored Nixon deprived McGovern of whatever slim chance he might have had to win the presidency.

Labor's power was both envied and resented by corporate business. Having failed to limit organized labor's influence, business leaders tried a new tack. In August of 1975, the Sun Oil Company (Sunoco), a conservative political force, petitioned the FEC for an advisory ruling on whether it could raise voluntary funds to channel to candidates in return for support of "the private enterprise system and . . . other types of businesses in which petroleum-oriented industries may be engaged from time to time[9]." The only restriction on dispersing funds presumably would be those contained within the campaign regulatory acts ($5000 per candidate, for example). But if corporations generally—the United States Chamber of Commerce actively supported the move while the National Association of Manufacturers prepared to help individual businesses create COPE-like units—took advantage of the opening, the amount of funding channeled to Republicans and business-oriented and conservative candidates generally would be awesome. In a sense, many of the abuses discussed in Chapter 5 would no longer be necessary; massive campaign funding from private corporations would be quite legal. This aspect of the new law had not been anticipated.

The FEC was asked to rule on whether such a fund would, in fact, be legal; whether the corporation could collect money from employees, stockholders, or the public, none of whom would influence the distribution of the funds; whether the corporation could spend directly in elections to promote candidates it favored, rather than going through the candidate's treasury; and what, if any, limits could be placed on the amounts of money used in such endeavors.

While an anxious business community waited, the commission debated the merits of the proposal. By a 4 to 2 vote, and while admitting "the potential for coercion which is inherent in the employment relationship," the commissioners permitted corporations to solicit both their employees and their stockholders for political funds. Corporations could use company funds both to collect the money and to maintain committees to disperse it. Left unsaid in the rush of events and in the hectic months to follow was whether each corporation (and union) was limited to one political action committee that could contribute a maximum of $5000 to a candidate. Given the number of corporations (and trade unions), the effect would be bad enough. If corporations could allow subsidiaries and branch offices (and unions, every state and local affiliate) to sponsor its own political agency, then the limit on contributions, and hence influence, would be as meaningless as it was in the 100 years preceding Watergate.

The effect of the commission's ruling, undoubtedly, could be enormous. Earlier, the commission decided to allow the political action committee of the Associated Milk Producers (a group that should be familiar from Chapter 5) to put its funds directly into voter registration and get-out-the-vote campaigns. Another longtime labor ploy, these supposedly nonpartisan activities would be used selectively to register and vote those friendly to the association's views. The FEC was preventing Watergate-type abuses by legalizing them—not exactly the remedy the commission's sponsors favored.

Some indication of the new ruling's effect can be gauged by the number of corporations—in anticipation of a favorable judgment—that moved early to create such political agencies. Spurred by a series of seminars throughout the country given by the Chamber of Commerce to acquaint corporate leaders and trade associations with the ways such committees were created and how they operated, 75 corporations; 37 banks, insurance companies, and brokerage houses; 102 business associations; and 19 brokerage houses, savings and loan associations, and the like had political funding units by the time of the FEC decision. In addition to Sun Oil and the Milk Producers, other corporate names establishing committees should be recognizable: Lockheed, General Telephone, Anaconda, American Cyanamid, General Electric, U. S. Steel, Pacific Gas and Electric, and Manufacturers Hanover Trust. By early 1976, an estimated $16 million had been amassed by political action committees within corporations for investment in that year's political campaigns.

Ideally, the political and financial muscle of organized labor would have been curbed under the new laws. Instead, the FEC rearranged the political landscape by extending to all corporations privileges long exercised by the trade unions. The "quiet revolution" the National Association of Manufacturers had foreseen in the ruling had indeed come to pass. The buying of candidates was not quite as illegal as it had been before[10].

THE SUPREME COURT
AND CAMPAIGN REFORMS

One source of opposition to the 1974 campaign law was entirely predictable. Eugene McCarthy and James Buckley constituted the most visible figures in a strange coalition (see Chapter 6) that challenged the law in the federal courts. The group spoke for a broader constituency. They claimed that the statute discriminated against third and minor parties and independent candidacies and that its limitations on contributions represented a constraint on freedom of expression. The objections to the law were complex and the case quickly made its way to the Supreme Court.

"Speech is money, and money is speech," said Justice Potter Stewart when the four and one-half hours of oral arguments were made before the Court[11]. Justice Harry A. Blackman found his colleague's argument persuasive and took the opportunity to say so. A one-to-one relationship between money and free expression would occur most readily to men of substance sensitive to the needs of the classes from which they were drawn. Taken to its extreme, the scheme the late ultraconservative Texas oil man, H. L. Hunt, proposed makes some sense: the rich should be given voting power in direct correspondence to their financial means (say 50,000 votes for a millionaire, 100,000 for a billionaire). If Justice Stewart's view had merit, then the problem of inequality of opportunity for political expression might best be resolved by helping the less well off to become richer[12]. A Rockefeller could spend, as Nelson has attempted, virtually any sum ($1 million? $500 million?) of his or his family's considerable fortune to elect himself to public office. The argument hardly seems credible.

But this is not the point. Stewart's response did indicate that the Supreme Court had serious reservations about certain aspects of the law and that it was in a mood to strike at least parts of it down. Matters did not improve when the justices began to quote lwayers for the opponents in questioning the arguments raised by those defending the law. The defense itself was somewhat disarrayed. The Justice Department, charged with the responsibility of defending the commission, after pondering its role decided it could not in good conscience totally fulfill its obligation. Rather, while submitting a brief in favor of the 1974 law and the FEC, the department also entered one on the other side agreeing that potential First Amendment abuses did exist in the act. Nonetheless, in the final analysis, both sides were represented by independently able legal talent.

Judging by their questions and comments, the justices seemed most concerned with the issues of identifying contributors, restrictions on the amounts private individuals could spend on political activity, and the provisions affecting smaller political parties. The reservations expressed were generally indicative of the final decision. On January 30 of the election year, the Court handed down its decision which, as to be expected on such an inclusive piece of legislation, was mixed and confusing. Parts of the act were validated and others were struck down. Upheld were the provisions[13]:

restricting contributions to $1000 in primaries and general elections;
requiring full disclosure of campaign donations and expenditures and detailed recordkeeping;
permitting the federal funding of elections;
relating to the treatment of third, minor, and new parties and independent candidacies (these were not held to be unnecessarily arbitrary or unreasonable).

The Court found that these aspects of the law served the public interest by guarding against "the reality or appearance" of fraud in elections stemming from a dependence on large contributions and by "informing the electorate and preventing the corruption of the political process." The legislation, on these issues, was not "overbroad"; it represented "a reasonable and minimally restrictive method of furthering First Amendment values"; and it safeguarded the integrity of the electoral process "without directly impinging upon the rights of individual citizens and candidates to engage in political debate and discussion." The federal funding of elections, rather than restricting free speech, constituted a constitutionally valid attempt "to use public money to facilitate and enlarge public discussion and participation in the electoral process."

These rulings represent significant gains for campaign reform. Basically, the heart of the law had been reaffirmed and the new departure of supplying public monies for federal campaigns was found to be an admirably legal exercise of legislative discretion. To this point, the decision—and the reasoning supporting it—would appear enlightened. Of greater immediate consequence were the provisions the Court invalidated. The Court ruled that:

the limitations on campaign spending in House and Senate contests were voided (these varied with the size of the constituency), a move that many welcomed, feeling low expenditures favored incumbents;

presidential candidates who did not accept federal funds did not have to observe the $10 million prenomination ceiling (or any limit for that matter) on expenditures;

House, Senate, and the presidential candidates who did not accept federal funds could spend as much of their own money or that of their immediate families as they desired (rather than being restricted to $25,000, $35,000, and $50,000 respectively);

a private citizen could spend any amount of money he desired (rather than being limited to $1000 per candidate in an election) to elect or defeat any candidate or in behalf of any issue through any media outlet or in any manner he chose;

The Federal Election Commission was exercising basically executive functions and its manner of selection violated the "appointment clause" of the Constitution. The commission retained only its investigatory and informative powers. In addition to the way specified for selecting commissioners, the FEC's power to bring civil actions against violators, to make rules interpreting and executing the 1974 act, to disqualify federal candidates who failed to file reports, and to authorize convention expenditures in excess of those specified were negated. Past FEC actions were accorded de facto legitimacy, but the Congress was given only 30 days to reconstitute the commission along the lines decreed by the Court or it would be stripped of the powers granted to it.

Generally, the reasoning behind the provisions struck down (excluding the commission itself) was that they constituted unacceptable restrictions on First Amendment freedoms of expression. The Court interpreted the main significance of the law to be in preventing corruption and preserving the integrity of the electoral process. The provisions struck down did not substantially advance such a goal, they reasoned, and they introduced restrictions of a severe constitutional nature. The Court gave little weight to arguments on behalf of the regulations that attempted to equalize candidate and campaign resources.

The complexity of the decision dulled initial reactions (in fact, at first it was believed that the rulings would have little effect on the campaign). Then the implications began to become clear. The rules of the game had been rewritten at the beginning of a presidential election year and with the primary and caucus delegate selection mechanisms already in progress. The Congress was given 30 days to restructure the FEC and, coincidentially, decide if it or some other agency should disburse federal funds.

The Court had not been overgenerous in the time it gave the legislators, but it had at least provided some leeway. Given the commission's rocky history, its rulings on slush funds and corporate political action groups, the striking of House and Senate federal funding from the final act by the conference committee, and its generally poor relationship with the Congress, it could be expected that remedial action would be difficult to initiate. Critics would be given another opportunity—simply by not acting—to disable the commission. In actuality, the Congress would only have to change the method for selecting four of the six commissioners to meet the Court's objections. But proposing legislation would give opponents the opportunity to gut not only the FEC but also other aspects of the campaign regulations they found objectionable. At the same time, however, proponents of stricter regulation and more inclusive financing were presented with another chance to close loopholes in the 1974 act and to extend its provisions. In short, the whole question was reopened.

The Supreme Court's decision also raised questions, in turn, about the 44 state statutes that regulated campaign contributions and expenditures, the 37 states with laws restricting campaign spending, and the 10 that authorized public funding of state elections. All would have to be reevaluated.

Some found solace in the Court's actions. Nelson Rockefeller could joke that the decision has "got to be a disappointment to my family." In a more serious vein, he assured the American people that they wanted wealthy people in public office. Those "of inherited means," said Rockefeller, are less likely to be involved in ethic conflicts than someone who "has had to fight his way up." Wealthy public officials "won't have strings on them" and "won't be looking for opportunities to make money in office[14]." Millionaire Charles Percy agreed. The good senator asked, "Do you want to be represented by a failure—someone who never showed he could manage? Making a profit in business is one proof of success[15]." At times, it is difficult to remember that this is the final quarter of the twentieth century. Maybe Rockefeller and Percy were simply reflecting the facts of political life, at least as found in the U.S. Senate. A majority of the membership of this august body held assests in 1975 of $250,000 or more and 22 were millionaires either in their own right or in partnership with their wives[16].

THE CONGRESS RESPONDS

Wayne Hays had not exactly been quiet while the Supreme Court deliberated the constitutionality of the campaign reform legislation. He had called the FEC's chairman, Thomas Curtis, to the Administration Committee after a congressman reported to the Ohio Democrat that the commission was investigating him for allegedly giving a Cadillac to an Indian for his support in an election. Hays was outraged. "You've got some bums down there," he roared at Curtis. "You'll fire them or you'll be financially out of business. We're going to cut the guts out of your appropriation. Take it from me it's going to happen[17]."

Nonetheless, with the Court's decision, Hays again emerged as the most important individual in the struggle just beginning. Senate action was expected without great difficulty. The House would again be the battleground and, at first glance, prospects for meeting the Court's deadline did not appear promising. In fact, according to Hays, a 30-day time limit was impossible. "Did you ever know Congress to act in 30 days on anything? I've got some other priorities. I'm a realist. I'm going to run as fast as I can, but I'm not going to run blindly into something." The congressman then revealed he would introduce a bill within days to abolish the FEC and replace it with a "strict and constitutional system to monitor full disclosure of election campaign contributions and expenditures[18]." Another congressman, speaking anonymously, said, "A majority of my peers in the House don't want an election law. They want to be free to wheel and deal and spend as they bloody well please." As Congressman Frank Thompson explained it, the only hope was that if Congress did not act responsibly, the "incumbents will look like crooks and be driven from office. In an election year, Congress has to respond with a law[19]."

Unquestionably though, Hays was in the catbird seat and he was going to have his fun. He enjoyed the attention, at least initially. Concerning the federal subsidies to presidential contenders, the chairman was unkind but on target. Speaking on the candidates, Hays remarked, "I'm not going to see them deprived of their feeding at the trough." This "trough" was to become the principal concern in preserving the system in operation. As for the FEC, he was less sympathetic. "I don't think anyone on my committee," said the chairman smiling, "would want the commission to survive in disemboweled form[20]."

After the initial shock, various proposals began to be submitted for congressional approval. Senators Hugh Scott and Edward Kennedy introduced a bill authorizing federal funding for Senate and House campaigns. Similar proposals had passed the Senate, but never the House, in three of the previous five years. A related bill was introduced in the House by influential party figures, Philip Burton and John Anderson, the Democratic and Republican leaders of their respective caucuses. Reportedly, the plan had been endorsed by a majority of the House members, although not by Wayne Hays.

Congressmen John Brademas and Frank Thompson, arguing that the Congress should not ignore "the opportunity to refine and improve the law," proposed reconstructing the FEC to meet the Court's objections (the president, subject to Senate confirmation, would appoint all six commissioners)[21]. Brademas and Thompson also would permit the FEC to retain its powers to require reports from candidates, to pass on regulations, to give advisory opinions, and to administer the federal subsidies. The congressmen then added a new element: a special federal prosecutor within the FEC with criminal enforcement powers. The new prosecutor and his deputy would be appointed by the president with Senate approval from opposing political parties and would serve five-year terms.

Congressmen Abner Mikva and Bill Frezel believed a simpler plan more appropriate, fearing "it could be too late" if Congress attempted to thread its way through all the plans before it. They would continue the FEC through the election year, making the corrections needed to satisfy the Supreme Court. President Ford favored the last approach and, in the bargain, promised to reappoint the sitting commissioners, although he did stress the commission should expire at the end of the election year and the entire matter should be reconsidered. Funds for the election under way would thus be assured. At the other extreme, a freshman Republican from Illinois introduced a bill to repeal the matching funds given presidential contenders. The congressman was appalled that public money was being handed over to "10 self-appointed apostles of the Democratic Party running all over the country with their separate road shows telling the American people how the country can be saved from the devil Republican administration[22]."

Wayne Hays had a better idea. The congressman still wanted the FEC abolished and indicated that its fund-dispensing duties should be temporarily turned over to the comptroller general, head of the General Accounting Office. Democratic National Chairman Robert Strauss found the plan attractive and endorsed it in a press conference. "I get along with Bob Strauss," said Hays. "We're on the same side. I'm going to get his $2 million for him[23]."

Less impressed was Common Cause. A spokesman called the measure a "backroom deal" and hinted ominously of "a Democratic Party scandal in the making[24]." FEC Chairman Thomas Curtis put the matter in perspective. "An independent commission is vital. It's the key. It's the bedrock[25]."

Time passed. The Court extended the grace period three weeks. Meanwhile, both political parties and their candidates meticulously followed FEC regulations, now without any controversy. Serious action on a new bill began to materialize. Again, Hays, perhaps undergoing a modest change of heart under the prodding of organized labor, introduced a 54-page bill to his committee that would have overhauled the FEC. Contained within the bill was a proposal to limit corporations to soliciting only its stockholders and executives for political funds. Labor unions faced no such restrictions.

One way or another, it was clear that the two political parties (whose national committees at this point had received $1.6 million) and their presidential candidates (who had been certified to receive $9 million, with more to come) very much liked the idea of federal money. Insuring the continued flow of these funds was paramount. Less significant, it would seem, was the future of the FEC.

Several days after the final Supreme Court deadline, the legislative logjam broke. The Senate passed (55 to 28) its version of the new bill and the House (241 to 155) followed with its own on April 1. A House-Senate conference committee then met to resolve the differences between the bills. The conference committee, sandwiching its deliberations around the Congress's Easter recess, did not report a compromise bill until April 28. On May 3, the House ratified the amended bill 291 to 81 and the Senate followed suit, 62 to 29, three days later. After heated and prolonged negotiations and the very real prospect that no bill would emerge from the congressional labyrinth, it appeared that the federal funding of presidential elections had overcome its most serious obstacle.

The new legislation was different in several important respects from the old. Most significantly, no limits were placed on corporations or unions in spending funds to solicit from or politically influence, respectively, corporation executives and stockholders or union members. Both corporations and unions were permitted to solicit by mail (in order to minimize any threat, implicit or otherwise, of economic coercion) each other's constituencies (for example, a corporation's political action committee could canvass all of the firm's employees, union members as well as management personnel) twice a year. The political action committees of the corporations (or broader trade groups) and the unions could also spend without limits on behalf of any candidate, party, or issue they championed. The only restriction in all of these cases was that, for the first time, they would have to file public reports detailing their expenditures.

In line with the Supreme Court's decision, a private individual not connected to a presidential campaign and not coordinating his activities with that of a candidate's could spend as much money for political purposes as he chose. The national committees of the respective parties were allowed to invest, if they wished to, an additional $3.3 million in the campaigns of their presidential nominees; and the presidential and vice-presidential candidates could spend a combined total of no more than $50,000 of their own money to advance their cause. And finally, bookkeeping provisions were required only for donations of $50 or more.

In one of the innumerable sidelights that mark the passage of any significant piece of legislation, Senators Barry Goldwater and George McGovern led the fight to increase the honorariums a legislator could receive from $15,000 to $25,000 a year. Their colleagues were understandably sympathetic. Both Goldwater and McGovern claimed to gain no personal advantage from the relaxation of the provision, arguing that the $25,000 they had contracted to receive as television commentators at the upcoming national conventions was not specifically prohibited in either the new or old law. To convince the representatives of a more reluctant House (few of whose members could ever expect such honorariums), the Senate conferees agreed to drop a proposal, opposed by the House delegation, that would have required all federal employees who earned $25,000 or more to submit annual financial statements on their economic condition.

The battle for the new funding law was not quite over. President Ford proved reluctant to sign the new bill, and no one was certain that a presidential veto could be overturned. Ford harbored deep reservations about the entire concept of governmental funding of campaigns. Furthermore, he distrusted organized labor's power and objected on constitutional grounds to other aspects of the legislation. During the negotiations, he had informally indicated that if something close to what had finally emerged from the conference committee was passed by the Congress he would be reluctant to veto it. Still, the president needed to be persuaded. Among others, the chairwoman of the Republican National Committee and the leaders of the Republican campaign committees in the House and Senate journeyed to the White House to appeal for support of the legislation.

On May 11, the president signed the bill. At the same time, he directed his attorney general to contest its most debatable provisions in the courts. As passed by the Congress, the legislation allowed for a 30-day period in which either house could veto any FEC ruling. Further, the Congress had severely narrowed the substance and applicability of the technical rulings the FEC could issue. Since the latter did not require congressional approval, this action insured that relatively little would escape legislative review. These provisions appeared to be a gross violation of the whole concept of an independent regulatory commission, of far more gravity than the appointment procedures that formed the heart of the Supreme Court's initial objections.

Despite the president's signature, a revitalized FEC still was not in operation. New commissioners had to be appointed and then approved by the Senate before the agency could grant any funds. The easiest course would be to reappoint the original six FEC members, and Ford would have preferred this approach. It was no longer possible. In early May, the former chairman of the FEC, Thomas Curtis, had resigned from the commission. He cited two reasons: the leash placed on the FEC by the Congress; and a provision of the new law specifically written to embarrass and provoke Curtis. The "Curtis clause" asserted that to prevent conflicts of interest, it was expected that commissioners "would not participate in full-time law practices while serving on the commission." Curtis had a lucrative practice in Missouri, which he felt he could not afford to give up. Embittered, he returned to his home state to surface later as a vocal supporter of Ronald Reagan, Ford's opponent for the Republican presidential nomination.

On May 17, Ford renamed five of the original commissioners as well as a replacement for Curtis. With the approval of the presidential appointments by the Senate on May 21, the 59-day hiatus was over and the FEC was back in business. By late summer, the Democratic and Republican nominees were authorized to spend $21.8 million each in government funds—a sum substantially below what either McGovern or Nixon had spent four years earlier—to advance their candidacies for the presidency. With this action, a long-sought reform and the first step in the government assumption of campaign costs at all levels had become a reality.

POLITICS AS USUAL
(OR "THE BEAT GOES ON")
DEPARTMENT

Meanwhile, these activities were not taking place in a vacuum, although the comments of several of the Supreme Court justices in hearing the suit and the failure of any legislators to draw attention to the events unfolding might suggest that it was. A reaction to the post-Watergate sentiment had set in and public interest was moving rapidly back towards a weary antireform stance. Nonetheless, a flood of revelations began to descend on a puzzled and tired public from the rash of criminal and civil court cases, regulatory and legislative investigations, and foreign inquiries that snowballed out of the Watergate mess.

The revelations were unnerving. American corporations admitted giving more than $300 million in bribes, political contributions, and payoffs to domestic and foreign political candidates, officeholders, and political parties and in agents fees, some legal and some not. Exxon paid $46 to $50 million to Italian politicians. Northrop transmitted $450,000 in bribes to two Saudi Arabian generals. It also admitted illegal political contributions within the United States that amounted to $1.1 million, with another $30 million in "questionable" payments (bribes and "consultant fees") to foreigners. Lockheed told the Securities and Exchange Commission that since 1970 alone it forwarded $2.2 million, although a later government report put the figure at over $200 million[26], to foreign officials and political groups (and this at a time when the U.S. government had authorized federal backing for a $250 million loan in 1971 to help the financially troubled aircraft builder). Gulf put $10.3 million into political funds. Five million dollars was given to government officers in Lebanon, Italy, Bolivia, and South Korea. An equal sum was illegally invested in American campaigns. Ashland Oil made $15.1 million in questionable overseas payoffs and allocated another $1.1 million for illegal American political donations. United Brands endowed Honduras officials with $2 million in return for an easing of the export tax on bananas. Mobil Oil totaled political contributions of $2.1 million distributed among politicians in Canada and Italy. Occidental Oil invested $3 million in Venezuelan politicians. Other corporations begrudgingly admitted questionable funds distributed as contributions. These included such names as: Tenneco, American Home Products, NCR, Goodyear, Carnation, Johnson & Johnson, Citgo, Del Monte, FMC Corporation, General Motors, ITT, IBM, Merck, General Tire, Westinghouse, McDonnell Douglas, Raytheon, Phillips Petroleum, Ashland Oil, Honeywell and Carrier Corporation. Even smaller businesses managed to draw attention: for example, a bank in Albuquerque contributed $35,000 illegally to political campaigns. The practice was widespread, and every time new figures were announced, the allegedly illegal violations increased in scope and in the amount of funds involved.

Meanwhile, the government was busy. The Internal Revenue Service announced, roughly every six months, that it was aggressively investigating possible tax violations. The congressional committees filed their reports and held out the promise of future remedial legislation of some sort. But a paralysis of will appeared to mark the entire effort. Indicative of the mood, albeit a rare example, was a congressional committee that emerged from inactivity (it had been created in 1950 to investigate defense contracts but had done little) to review charges that Northrop had illegally entertained Defense Department representatives at a hunting lodge in Maryland. The 22 military officials involved were reproved by their superiors for a "severe error of judgment" and nothing more. Of more substance, a Pentagon audit indicated that $21 million in lobbying costs and another $94,000 charged to the government by the corporation for a plane to transport its guests were questionable. (The questionable cost figure later escalated to $9.9 million, which included all forms of political wrongdoing.)

Northrop returned $564,013 to the Air Force, money it had improperly obtained from government contracts and used for political entertaining and political contributions. It received no other penalty. An alert Defense Department then initiated investigations into federally paid "entertainment" costs included in contracts awarded to (and again the names are familiar) Raytheon, Rockwell, Hughes Aircraft, Martin Marietta, Boeing, General Dynamics, Lockheed, Sperry Rand, Gruman, LTV Corporation, and 43 other defense contractors. These actions were a direct consequence of the committee's work. For its pains, the House voted to terminate it.

The corporations themselves moved, of course, to police their own improprieties. Northrop, for example, under the pressure of continuing public disclosures and from a class action suit resulting from illegal contributions to the 1972 Nixon campaign, was forced to act. The company's directors forced Thomas V. Jones, Northrop's president, chairman, and chief executive officer, to relinquish the title of chairman. Jones had pleaded guilty in federal court in 1974 to contributing $150,000 in corporate funds to the Nixon effort. The crime was a felony and he could have received five years in a federal prison. Instead he was fined $5000 and Northrop was fined an additional $5000.

In settling the stockholder court action, the company agreed to install a new president, which it did. At the same time, the controversy having died down and with profits increasing, the board of directors reinstated Jones, the man most clearly identified with the company's fortunes, as chairman. He had kept his title as chief executive officer. "Jones has been, is and will be No. 1 in this company," said a Northrop representative[27].

Exxon was equally diligent. Again, action of some kind was necessitated by a shareholders' suit. The corporation authorized $27 million in secret political payments to Italian officials between 1964 and 1971 and an additional $29 to $32 million, in the company's words, was "siphoned out" of corporate funds without authorization during the same period for political purposes. The world's largest corporation admitted to "errors of business judgment," but it could find no grounds for acting against any company officials. Its chairman earlier had announced that other such payments in Australia and Japan, in amounts he could not recall, had been halted[28].

Oil money has always managed to find its way into politics. The results for the industry have been gratifying. There are many examples from which to choose. Congress passed the Tax Reduction Act of 1975 which contained a brief clause defining dividends as oil-related, foreign-source income. This wording saved Aramco $35 million in taxes. Aramco was a Saudi Arabian–American oil consortium that included four giants of the oil industry, Exxon, Mobil, Texaco, and Standard Oil of California. No one is exactly sure how and by whom the wording was inserted in the bill. The legislation went into the House-Senate conference committee without the mysterious definition and emerged with it. When opponents realized the significance of the change, they managed to force a vote on it in Wilbur Mills's Ways and Means Committee, the group that would pass it on to the House for final consideration. The clause was upheld 19 to 17. Many of the congressmen voting for the provision received campaign donations, directly or indirectly (that is, through law firms representing the oil industry) from oil companies. The frustrated opponents of the uncontemplated change in tax status for the oil grants were reduced to advocating legislation that stenographic records be kept of conference committee negotiating sessions (none are).

A majority of the senators who voted for natural gas deregulation received political contributions from oil companies, including Gulf, Phillips, and Ashland Oil. Many oil corporations own solely or in partnership natural gas companies as well as natural gas fields and reserves.

Gulf is a particularly interesting case. It is the nation's seventh-ranking corporation in size, with $16 billion in sales and over 50,000 employees. It was founded by and has been long identified with the Mellon family of Pittsburgh, who still control one-fifth of Gulf's stock. The family has been active over the years in promoting conservative candidates and causes. Under pressure from the Securities and Exchange Commission and with a renewed interest in the case indicated by the Watergate Special Prosecutor's office, Gulf authorized a committee of its directors, under an outside lawyer, John J. McCloy, to investigate its secret political activities. The almost 300-page report that emerged shocked many.

Gulf was the largest corporation to admit such illegal political donations. The total overall came to a reported $12.3 million for a 14-year period (1960 to 1973). Gulf gave almost $5 million to foreign politicians, governments, and political parties, including roughly $4 million alone to the dominant Democratic Republican party of Korea prior to the 1971 election in that country and almost one-half million dollars to public officials in Bolivia.

Since the corporation's illegal domestic payments far exceeded any known similar activities of other American companies, they received the greatest attention. The tale was a juicy one. Senate Minority Leader Hugh Scott had received approximately $10,000 a year over a 10-year period. Payments may have been made to every member of the Senate Watergate Committee, excepting its chairman, Sam Ervin. Russell Long, the principal force in writing tax legislation in the Senate, had been given $40,000. President Ford, while a member of the House, had been the beneficiary of illegal monies. Among other politicians allocated illegal corporate funds were Senators Howard Baker, William Brock, Mark Hatfield, Ted Stevens, J. Glenn Beall, Daniel Inouye, John Sparkman, Harry Byrd, Jr., Robert Byrd, Hubert Humphrey, and Lloyd Bentsen; former Senator Fred Harris; Governor Milton Shapp; and a number of House members. Among the vignettes to emerge was the report that $50,000 in illegal monies was delivered to Lyndon Johnson after his election to the vice-presidency in 1960 and, under pressure from Charles Colson and the Nixon Administration, Gulf agreed to pay for a nationwide television rerun of the Tricia Nixon–Edward Cox White House wedding.

Gulf had also been busy in the state of Texas. Its chief lobbyist, Claude C. Wild, Jr., had $50,000 to $60,000 a year to distribute. Illegal corporate funds had been delivered to, among others, a former governor, state legislators, state supreme court justices, and members of the Texas Railroad Commission, the body that regulated oil and gas within the state.

The report did have an impact. The Justice Department and the Internal Revenue Service took the opportunity to announce they were working on in-depth investigations of the allegations. The Senate Ethics Committee was placed in something of an awkward position since its chairman, Howard Cannon, had been identified as receiving cash in a sealed envelope during the 1960s. The attorney general of Texas filed damage suits against both Gulf and Phillips amounting to $1.4 million for illegal corporate payments to Texas politicians. Of greater interest perhaps, Gulf's board of directors met for 16 hours 15 days after the report's release and, with the Mellon family pushing for a change, replaced the company's chairman, Bob R. Dorsey and two lesser officials. Gulf had already pleaded guilty to charges brought by the Special Prosecutor's Office of making illegal corporate contributions to presidential candidates Nixon ($100,000), Mills, and Jackson in 1972. The company had been fined $5000 and its chief lobbyist (Wild) $1000. Concerning Dorsey's role in the broader scandal, the report said that "he perhaps chose to shut his eyes to what was going on[29]." The business community found the disciplinary actions significant.

The most intriguing aspect of the controversy emerged when Gulf, feeling, it said, a responsibility to its stockholders, attempted to recoup some of its $12 million in illegal donations. It asked the politicians who had accepted the illegal funds to return them. Howard Baker agreed to return the half of his contribution that had been taken from company funds. Most of the other beneficiaries either had no reaction or professed an inability to recall any Gulf contributions, including Hugh Scott, the recipient of over $100,000 from the corporation. John McCloy, the lawyer heading the committee that wrote the report, was indignant. He was ill-mannered enough to suggest that the government was hypocritical in its failure to prosecute or even condemn politicians accepting illegal funds. In the government's defense, it was not only politicians that it proved lax in prosecuting.

Boeing admitted making $70 million in foreign payoffs since 1970 alone. The company said the payments were commissions not bribes, but it did admit that the money might have made its way to government officials. But despite the travails of Boeing and Northrop, the granddaddy of problem organizations in this area has to be Lockheed.

Lockheed had invested a reported $12.6 million in Japanese politicians alone. The facts surrounding the payoffs were intriguing. A priest had been used in Japan as a bagman and a former Lockheed official was serving as ambassador to Japan when the scandal broke. The Japanese parliament was outraged and began formal hearings into charges that some of the money had been funneled through prominent Japanese intermediaries to public officials. One rightist publicly advised a principal dishonored by the scandal to commit suicide. In the United States, in another development, a former company officer charged that Lockheed promised Air Force colonels postretirement jobs for steering foreign military contracts to the aircraft manufacturer.

Lockheed's illegal funds also apparently found their way into the Netherlands, a charge that upset the Dutch parliament enough to initiate an inquiry into the proceedings. There was good reason to be alarmed. The money allegedly penetrated to the highest levels of the Dutch government. Prince Bernhard, the husband of Queen Juliana, who also served as inspector general of the Dutch military forces, reportedly accepted $1.1 million from Lockheed. The queen, "a terribly moral person" according to one Dutch commentator, gave indications that she might abdicate if the charges proved true. Why would Bernhard, a member of the wealthy Dutch ruling family, ever accept questionable funds from a plane manufacturer? "He has never been regarded as enormously bright," said one Dutch official, "but if he actually took money . . . he must have been much stupider than anyone believed[30]."

Lockheed, following Gulf's lead, did direct a four-man group of outside directors to investigate the scandal. Within a month, Lockheed's two top executives and three other senior officers, including the director of its Far Eastern operations, resigned. The officials would receive their pensions and full company benefits and Lockheed reserved the right to hire them back as paid consultants as needed.

Lockheed had very little to say about the entire affair. In fact, Lockheed appeared most reluctant to reveal anything to anyone. The General Accounting Office, under the agreement by which Lockheed had received its government-backed loan, was required by law to "make a detailed audit of all accounts" of the corporation, including, if the GAO chose, its records on foreign payments. Further, the contract with the government for the loan gave the GAO "sole discretion to determine the documents . . . needed[31]." Lockheed refused to let the agency see its records, while at the same time announcing it could not meet the schedule for repaying its loans nor could it offer a new timetable.

The Securities and Exchange Commission is another federal agency that periodically announced it was investigating firms concerning illegal political funds. While not quite up to the IRS's announced inquiry into 110 corporations for similar abuses, the SEC's examination of a reported 84 firms (55 from *Fortune* magazine's top 500) was formidable enough. Senator William Proxmire, chairman of the Senate Banking Committee, thought it might be a good idea to have the chairman of the SEC go on record as saying he would settle for nothing less than full disclosure concerning the foreign bribes by American companies. The chairman refused to do it. He would not even reveal what types of disclosure should be or were being required.

Several senators backed the SEC's position. Texas's John Tower argued, "There comes a point where the people's right to know must be subordinated to the people's right to be secure." National security? "It's beyond me," countered Proxmire, "to understand how disclosure is the threat to our country. It's the criminal acts, the bribes that are the threat[32]." The focus did seem to have become blurred.

It should not be inferred from all of these accounts that the government was not meeting the problem head-on. The administration had turned to the United Nations for help. It thought it might be useful if that organization developed a policy on international corporation bribery and it promoted the efforts of the Organization for Economic Cooperation and Development to draw up a voluntary code to control political payoffs by multinational businesses. The code would depend, of course, on moral persuasion. It would have no enforcement powers.

The 10 corporations with the largest proportion of defense contracts for the fiscal year 1975 were (in order): Lockheed ($2.1 billion), Boeing ($1.5 billion), United Technologies ($1.4 billion), McDonnell Douglas ($1.4 billion), Grumman ($1.3 billion), General Dynamics ($1.3 billion), General Electric ($1.2 billion), Litton ($1 billion), Hughes Aircraft ($1 billion), and Rockwell International ($723 million).

Lockheed paid no taxes on its $29.8 million income for the 1974 tax year. LTV corporation, Occidental Petroleum, Texaco, Mobil, and McDonnell Douglas, as well as a number of other oil companies, banks, and utilities paid their taxes for the same year at an effective rate of 10 percent or less.

CONCLUSION

The broad themes of this book can be quickly summarized. Money is power, a doctrine unnecessarily reaffirmed by the Supreme Court. Its effects on politics can be devastating (Chapters 5 and 9). Its influence is extraordinarily difficult to control (Chapters 4, 6, and 9). This much should be clear. Yet the battle to enforce financial responsibility in politics and eventually equalize campaign resources and hence access to public office is, at last, in the early stages.

Roughly one-half of the adult population does not even bother to vote, much less take part in any more meaningful form of political activity (Part I). But the problem is not insoluble. The administrative changes outlined in Chapter 3, especially the Universal Voter Enrollment Plan, would do much to insure everyone the opportunity to vote. After minimizing the procedural hurdles, then one could in truth argue that it is the responsibility of citizens themselves to exercise their franchise. Technical discussions on the mechanics for implementing a voter enrollment system or the merits of postcard registration do not excite public interest and it is quite likely that broad support for such proposals will be hard to elicit. Is it possible that enlightened political leaders, goaded by a small cadre of representative citizen groups, will, nonetheless, act?

The national party organizations and party procedures for determining presidential nominees are obvious targets for reformers (Part III). The problems in each of the areas are somewhat different. The organizational structures of the political parties (Chapter 8) remain badly in need of modernization and democratization (defined as power emanating from the bottom up). Party organizations are antiquated institutions. In a fast-changing social and political order, they are under pressure to legitimize their operations and better perform their representative functions—a view the political parties themselves would probably not share. Maybe the party charter adopted by the Democrats in their 1974 midterm convention represents a beginning.

Presidential nominating procedures are indeed chaotic, expensive, and exhaustive (Chapter 7). The problem in this regard is to insure that if any reforms are instituted, they do not overcentralize power in a national agency and that they do not lead to any overly rigid set of procedures. The latter might admirably serve a political candidate's needs but not adequately meet the individual citizen's desire for a meaningful input into the nomination decision. A healthy decentralization may well be desirable in this area.

Reform comes gradually and, at times, painfully slowly. The need for reform often has to be demonstrated over and over again, and most frequently it takes a crisis situation to arouse broad public concern and responsible official action. Even then, reforms once made are never secure. Often, the changes do not accomplish the desired end. Always, they introduce new problems. And the effort to repeal and render them impotent continues unabated by their critics, comfortable *and* powerful within a system that has rewarded them generously.

Nonetheless, reform is in the American tradition. The trend and direction is clear and persistent. The emphasis is, and has been, on increasing the individual citizen's power over and responsibility for the collective political destiny. The war is never over. This is, in truth, a campaign that never ends. Much remains to be done to solidify reforms already begun that truly serve broader social purposes and to begin to attack those areas still sorely in need of enlightened concern.

NOTES

1. Warren Weaver, Jr., "Senate Rejects 'Slush Fund' Curb," *New York Times,* October 9, 1975, p. 25.
2. "Vast Cash Advantage Held by U.S. House Incumbents," *Chicago Sun-Times,* August 8, 1975, p. 11.
3. Warren Weaver, Jr., "Wayne Hays Will Again Table Election Board on Rule," *New York Times,* October 20, 1975, p. 28.
4. Warren Weaver, Jr., "Campaign Costs Cover Legal Fees," *New York Times,* October 17, 1975, p. 5.
5. Warren Weaver, Jr., "Ford Travel Costs in '75 Exempted from Ceiling," *New York Times,* November 21, 1975, p. 1.
6. Warren Weaver, Jr., "Election Commission Stirs Worry and Confusion in Congress," *New York Times,* October 27, 1975, p. 18.
7. "Hays Drafts Curb on Election Unit," *New York Times,* November 16, 1975, p. 57.
8. Warren Weaver, Jr., "Critic Wants '76 Test of Campaign Law," *New York Times,* November 3, 1975, p. 24.
9. Warren Weaver, Jr., "Ruling Is Sought on Election Fund," *New York Times,* August 24, 1975, p. 25.
10. Bruce F. Freed, "PAC: Businessmen's Answer to COPE," *(Congressional Quarterly)* as reported in *Chicago Daily News,* January 8, 1976, p. 37, "Employees' Political Fund OKd by Board," *Chicago Tribune,* November 19, 1975, p. 15, and Warren Weaver, Jr., "Elections Panel to Allow Companies to Raise Funds," *New York Times,* November 19, 1975, p. 1.
11. "High Court Hears 4 Hours of Campaign Law Argument," *Chicago Sun-Times,* November 11, 1975, p. 28.
12. Lesley Delsner, "High Court's Queries Hint Doubt on Parts of New Election Law," *New York Times,* November 11, 1975, p. 1.
13. The following is taken from the published opinion of the Supreme Court in *Buckley* et al. v. *Valeo, Secretary of the Senate* et al., nos. 75–436, 75–437 (January 30, 1976).
14. Tom Littlewood, "Public Likes Wealthy in Office: Rocky," *Chicago Sun-Times,* February 5, 1976, p. 11.
15. *U.S. News & World Report,* March 1, 1976, p. 60.
16. Richard D. Lyons, "Most Senators Get Political Advantage from Their Own Wealth," *New York Times,* December 12, 1976, p. 26.
17. "Vows Slash of Election Unit's Funds," *Chicago Sun-Times,* January 28, 1976, p. 28.
18. David E. Rosenbaum, "Hard Congress Fight Seen on Saving Agency," *New York Times,* January 31, 1976, p. 12.
19. Ibid.
20. William J. Eaton, "Rep. Hays Holds Ace in Fight over Campaign Finance Act," *Chicago Daily News,* February 3, 1976, p. 7.
21. Tom Littlewood, "Campaign Law Enforces Urged by Democrats," *Chicago Sun-Times.* February 7, 1976, p. 38.

22. Ibid.
23. "Key House Member Joins Move for G.A.O. to Pay Vote Subsidy," *New York Times,* February 6, 1976, p. 24.
24. "Strauss Calls for Fast Reprieve of Election Law," *Chicago Sun-Times,* February 4, 1976, p. 45.
25. William J. Eaton, "Strauss 'Deal' to Scuttle Campaign Bd.," *Chicago Daily News,* February 4, 1976, p. 52.
26. "List 20 Firms' Foreign Bribes," *Chicago Daily News,* November 11, 1975, p. 36.
27. Soma Golden, "Northrop's Board Reappoints Jones to Its 2 Top Positions," *New York Times,* February 19, 1976, p. 51.
28. William D. Smith, "Exxon's Study of Payoffs in Italy Finds No Basis in Action against Its Officers," *New York Times,* January 31, 1976, p. 33, and "List 20 Firms' Foreign Bribes."
29. Michael C. Jensen, "On Ouster, Gulf Found No Choice," *New York Times,* January 15, 1976, p. 47.
30. David Murray, "Juliana May Quit over Lockheed Flap," *Chicago Sun-Times,* February 12, 1976, p. 12.
31. Robert M. Smith, "Lockheed Keeps Data from G.A.O.," *New York Times,* March 5, 1976, p. 39.
32. Robert M. Smith, "S.E.C. Chief Refuses to Take a Position on Public Disclosure at Bribe Hearings," *New York Times,* March 4, 1976, p. 43.

Author Index

Numbers in parentheses indicate note numbers. Italic numbers indicate pages on which complete references occur.

Subject Index

A

absentee voting, 94–96
Adams, John, 13
Adams, John Quincy, 46–47, 199
age, voter participation and, 55, 56
age qualifications, 5, 11, 14
Agnew, Spiro, 139
Alabama
  congressional election (1966), 112
  congressional election (1972), 117, 118
  gubernatorial election (1970), 112
  nomination process, 206, 207, 214, 221
  poll tax, 24
  voting, 23, 24, 40–41, 62, 63, 65–67, 78, 84, 86
Alaska
  nomination process, 221, 223
  voting, 84, 86
Alexander, Herbert E., 113, 132
ambassadorships, sale of, 158–163
Amerada Hess Corporation, 147
American Airlines Inc., 145, 151–153, 175
American Civil Liberties Union, 96
American Cyanamid Company, 279
American Federation of Labor-Congress of
  Industrial Organizations (AFL-CIO), 83,
  248, 250–252
American Iron and Steel Institute, 132
American Motors Corporation, 146
American Petroleum Institute, 132
American Revolution, 6–9
American Ship Building Company, 145
Anaconda Company, 279
Anderson, John, 283
Annenberg, Walter, 158, 160
Anthony, Susan B., 21
Anti-Masonic party, 199
Aramco, 289

Arizona
nomination process, 221, 223
voting, 21, 82, 84, 86
Arkansas
  nomination process, 206, 221
  poll tax, 24–25
  voting, 23, 24–25, 40–41, 62, 78, 85, 86
Arthur, Chester A., 170
Ash, Roy, 134
Ashbrook, John, 228
Ashland Oil Corporation, 146, 147, 150–151,
  289
Aspin, Les, 147
Associated Milk Producers, 140–143, 279
Atomic Energy Commission (AEC), 134, 135
Austria, registration in, 74

B

Baker, Howard, 115, 117, 118, 290
Barkan, Al, 248, 151
Barnes, Wallace, 128
Bartlett, Dewey, 118
Bayh, Birch, 272
Beall, J. Glenn, 290
Beare v. *Smith* (1971), 38
Belgium, registration in, 76
Bendix Corporation, 146
Bentsen, Lloyd, 126, 128, 129, 272, 276, 290
Bernhard, Prince of the Netherlands, 291
Bipartisan Committee on Absentee Voting, 95,
  96
Blackman, Harry A., 280
blacks
  Democratic National Convention (1968),
    238–239
  voting, 13, 17, 18, 22–34, 53, 56, 60–68
Blackstone, Sir William, 7
Blanton, Ray, 118